The Sacred Harp

1991 Edition

THE SACRED HARP

1991 Revision

The Best Collection of Sacred Songs, Hymns, Odes, and
Anthems Ever Offered the Singing Public for General Use

MUSIC COMMITTEE:

Hugh McGraw, General Chairman

Richard L. DeLong   Toney Smith
Raymond C. Hamrick   Jeff Sheppard
David Ivey   Terry L. Wootten

Copyright © 1991 by Sacred Harp Publishing Company, Inc.
All Rights Reserved. International Copyright Secured.

ISBN 0-9727398-0-7

DEDICATED TO

All lovers of Sacred Harp Music, and to the memory of the illustrious and venerable partriarchs who established the Traditional Style of Sacred Harp singing and admonished their followers to "seek the old paths and walk therein."

PREFACE

Since the Sacred Harp was first compiled in 1844 by Benjamin Franklin White, it has been revised only four times: 1869, 1911, 1936 and 1991. However, an appendix was added in 1850, 1859, 1960, 1967, and 1971. So, you see, the Sacred Harp has been left alone for most of its life.

Each revision and each appendix was done to put new life in the books, each time adding new or present-day authors. This is the main reason it has lasted so long and will continue to survive.

We bless and revere the memory of those venerable patriarchs who dedicated their lives to the support of Sacred Harp music and through whose efforts and leadership the book was improved at various times. Today the book is more popular and is used throughout the United States of America.

In conclusion, we the music committee appointed by the President of the Sacred Harp Publishing Company, Inc., in 1985 thank all who have spoken words of encouragement or helped us in any way. We respectfully submit the work performed by us, and we hope and pray that it will satisfy the great demand of the music people throughout this country.

Respectfully submitted,

The Music Committee

MUSIC

Since the history of the Original Sacred Harp and a sketch of the authors and composers of its tune, odes, and anthems have been included in this *1991* Revision, perhaps it will not be out of place for this writer to make a few observations on the subject of music, the greatest art and science to attract the attention of mankind since the advent of the human family into the world. God himself, in the beginning, set all things to music, even before man was made, and it has continued from that time up to the present and will continue throughout eternity.

Back as far as Jubal, "the father of all such as handle the harp, pipe, and organ" (Genesis 4:21), music is mentioned 3,875 years before Christ. Vocal Choruses of men are mentioned in the Bible 556 years before Christ. Two of the oldest books in the Bible, Genesis and Job, refer to the musical elements which entered into the religious services of the Jews from their earliest history. By music, the deliverance of the Jews from Egyptian bondage was perfected (see Exodus 15:1). Its sweetness made the banks of the Red Sea ring with joy at the Jews' deliverance.

For a long time, great events were celebrated with gatherings of musicians who came together from all over the land of Judea. Oftentimes martial music—musical instruments together with vocal choruses— was used to direct the movements of the Israelites in peace or war. David was greeted with music after his battle with, and slaughter of, the Philistines. David, the sweet singer of Israel, organized his musicians into choruses of four thousand men divided into twenty-four groups. Each group had its own president, musical leader, and director (I Chronicles 6:31-32). David, a man after God's own heart, with his musical talent charmed and astonished the entire world. Truly he was the greatest musician that had lived in the world up to his time.

In hundreds of places in the Old Testament, song and music are mentioned as being crowning events of life. God spoke to Job out of the whirlwind and said of the creation, "The morning stars sang together, and all the sons of God shouted for joy" (Job 38:7).

Wherever we look in nature we are confronted with the sweetness and charms of music. Even in inanimate life we see, feel, and hear evidences of it: the whistling wind as it moves through the trees and rings out its melodies; the musical rhythm of the oceans, rivers, and streams as they perform their proper functions; the pleasant sound of the rain as it falls upon the roof, soothing and comforting with its melodious sweetness. In animal life we also find evidence of music: the steady hum of the busy little bee as he toils among the flowers; the songs of the birds as they skip from branch to branch in the trees and warble their little melodious notes of cheer.

The effect of music upon the human family has been the most wonderful of any gift with which human nature is endowed. In many places in the Old and New Testament, we have evidences of its effect on man. Even the prison doors at Philippi, at the dead hour of midnight, refused to hold their fastenings, and their locks sprang from their sockets; and the shackles fell from the prisoners' feet when Paul and Silas raised their voices in songs of praise to God. Witnessing that miracle, the prison keeper cried, "Men and brethren, what shall I do to be saved?" (Acts 16:30).

Music is a God-given faculty that by sounding its melody and harmony opens the doors to human hearts and souls and brings man back to his first relationship with God. It is the sweet union which keeps men in close relation with the hearts of men while they live in the world and which will strike the sweet chords in that spirit land where mortality does not enter and where spiritual songs are sung throughout Eternal Ages.

Ruth Denson Edwards

ACKNOWLEDGMENTS

Elder Marshall Avery	Scripture reading for songs
Elder Homer Benefield	Scripture reading for songs
Dr. John Garst	Rewriting Rudiments and writing *Organization and Conduct of Singings and Conventions*
Don Bowen	For continuously searching and finding numerous typographical errors in the 1991 revision
Dr. William J. Reynolds	History of hymn writers
Mary Lou Reynolds	Proofreader of words
Dr. Warren Steel	History of songwriters and verification of dates and proofreader of book in general
Charles L. Towler, Senior Music Editor, Pathway Music	Music Engravings
Church Pension Fund	Permission to use three scriptures from *The Book of Common Prayer*, pages 313, 353, 481
Mary Rose O'Leary	Book cover design
Carolyn Deacy	Book cover design

RUDIMENTS OF MUSIC

Revised by John Garst

Author's Note. The *Sacred Harp* tradition is separate and distinct from other musical traditions. Accordingly, these rudiments are based on those of previous editions of the *Sacred Harp* by Paine Denson (*Original Sacred Harp, Denson Revision*, 1936), Joe S. James (*Original Sacred Harp*, 1911), and B. F. White and E. J. King (*Sacred Harp*, 1844), except where these are incomplete or where they conflict with actual practice.

CHAPTER I
INTRODUCTION

1. **Sounds** are our perceptions of vibrations in the air, which are caused by vibrating objects. A **musical tone** is a continuous sound of pleasing quality and definite pitch, high or low. **Noise** is a harsh, irregular, and confused sound that lacks a definite pitch.

Musical tones are produced by vibrations of strings, wires, reeds, and diaphragms of musical instruments; of the lips in playing certain wind instruments; and of the vocal cords in singing. Vibrations of shorter or tighter strings produce tones of higher pitch, while those of longer or looser strings produce tones of lower pitch.

2. **Absolute pitch** is measured by the **frequency** of vibration, which is given in cycles (vibrations) per second. High pitch corresponds to high frequency. A person with good hearing can perceive tones with frequencies from approximately sixteen to nearly forty thousand cycles per second.

Relative pitch is used in the *Sacred Harp*. The relative pitches of two tones make an **interval**, which is defined technically as the *ratio* of the higher frequency to the lower one.

We can recognize intervals by ear, that is, by listening, and we recognize the same interval whether the absolute pitch is high or low. Whether "Happy birthday to you" is sung by a low voice or a high one, we recognize the tune by recognizing the same intervals between successive tones.

3. In addition to pitch, a musical tone has **accent** (degree of emphasis), **length** (duration in time), and **volume** (loudness).

4. In **music**, tones of various pitches, accents, lengths, and volumes are sounded successively (**melody**) or simultaneously (**harmony**). Accordingly, the description of music is divided into **rhythmics** (timing, length, and accent), **melodics** (pitch), **dynamics** (volume), and **harmony** (blending of tones).

5. The *Sacred Harp* uses **four-part harmony**. The parts, in order of increasing pitch, are **bass** (sung by men), **tenor** (men and women), **alto** (usually women), and **treble** (men and women). The doubling of the tenor and treble (and sometimes the alto) in the vocal ranges of men and women creates an effect of six-(or seven-)part harmony.

6. In **musical notation**, all aspects of melodics, rhythmics, dynamics, and harmony are represented by printed characters. To "note" a piece of music is to write it in musical notation. Hereinafter, following common usage, "music" refers to the notation, the sounds that it represents, or both.

7. **Notes** (♩ ♪ ♫) represent musical tones, including pitch, accent, length, volume, and sequence in time. Hereinafter, following common usage, "note" refers to either the printed character or the tone it represents, or to both.

The **head** of each note is one of **four shapes**. Each shape denotes a particular **syllable**. A **triangle** (◁) is **Fa** (pronounced "faw"), an **oval** (○) **Sol** ("sole"), a **square** (□) **La** ("law"), and a **diamond** (◇) **Mi** ("mee"). The shapes and syllables are related to pitch.

In conversation, syllables are sometimes called "notes" or "shapes." Thus, in **"singing the notes,"** one sings the syllables, as given by the shapes of the notes.

Rests are periods of silence or the characters that represent them. See Chapter II, Section 8.

8. Notes are placed on a **staff**, a series of five parallel, horizontal lines with spaces between them. The **lines** and **spaces** are counted upward, **1-2-3-4-5** (lines) and **1-2-3-4** (spaces). The **space below the staff** is immediately below line 1, and the **space above the staff** is immediately above line 5.

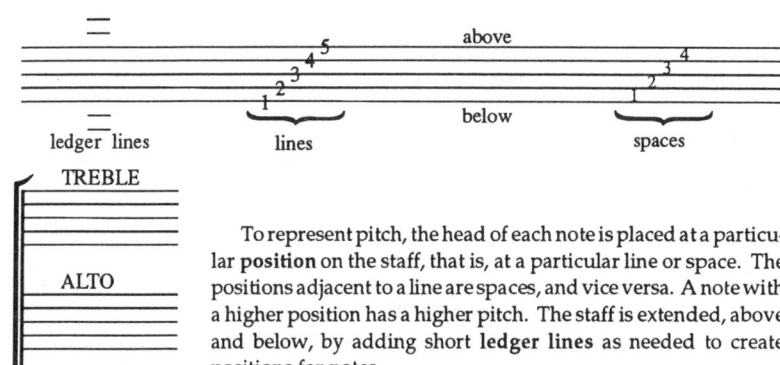

To represent pitch, the head of each note is placed at a particular **position** on the staff, that is, at a particular line or space. The positions adjacent to a line are spaces, and vice versa. A note with a higher position has a higher pitch. The staff is extended, above and below, by adding short **ledger lines** as needed to create positions for notes.

9. Each part has a separate staff. The staffs (or staves) for the parts are placed one above the other and joined at their left ends by a pair of vertical lines to make a **brace**. The figure shows the order of the parts. When there are only three parts, the alto is omitted.

A segment of a staff or brace extends across the page from left to right, then the staff or brace is continued (if necessary) as another segment below the first. Each part is continued on the appropriate staff of the brace.

10. Music is read from the first page on which it is printed to the last; on a given page, it is read from top to bottom; and on a given segment of the staff, notes and rests are read from left to right. This is the same order as words in printed text. Each syllable of the words is printed below (or sometimes above) its note.

11. The music for the first line of the familiar Handel tune for "Joy to the world! the Lord is come," shows how notes follow one another across the staff. It also illustrates other aspects of notation and provides a starting point for understanding scales and intervals. These details are discussed later, where this illustration will be cited briefly as JOY.

12. Modern **standard notation** is written in **round notes** (the head of every note is oval) instead of the **shaped notes** used in the *Sacred Harp*. With certain accomodations, *Sacred Harp* notation can be read by a round-note reader by ignoring the shapes of the notes. The necessary accomodations concern time signatures, method of marking time, and tempo (Chapter II, Sections 10-15); misbarred notation (Chapter II, Section 21); and key signatures and scales for minor keys (Chapter III, Section 15; Chapter IV, Section 4; and Chapter VIII, Sections 13 and 14).

CHAPTER II
RHYTHMICS

1. **Rhythmics** treats the arrangements of notes and rests in time. Thus, it is concerned with patterns in time and accent.

2. Time is measured in **beats**, short periods of equal length, usually less than a second, that follow one another and fill time without leaving any "holes."

3. Beats are grouped into larger units of time called **measures**, which are separated in notation by **measure bars**, light vertical lines across the staff. Measures are counted successively from the beginning of the piece of music, as printed.

In a brace, corresponding measures of the various parts are aligned vertically and are performed simultaneously. A broad bar, or **phrase bar**, is often used as a measure bar, but its main purpose is to mark the end of one line or phrase of poetry and the beginning of another.

A broad bar followed closely by a narrow one marks the beginning of a segment of a staff. A **double bar** (two broad bars) marks the end of the notation of a piece of music.

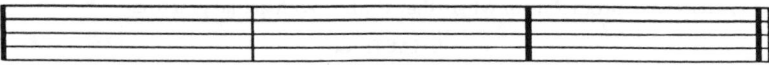

4. **Form** may require that certain musical passages be repeated, sometimes to the same words, sometimes to different ones. A **repeat mark** consists of a row of dots, usually one in each space (or sometimes two dots, one above and the other below the third line). If placed to the left of a measure bar, a repeat mark shows that the preceding passage is to be sung twice. In this case, the passage to be repeated extends to the previous repeat mark, or, if there is none, to the beginning. If the repeat mark is to the right of a measure bar, it shows that the following passage is to be repeated. The passage to be repeated extends to the next repeat mark, or, if none follows, to the end.

5. The figures 1 and 2, or **double ending**, at the close of a composition (or a phrase within it) indicate that the preceding passage is to be sung twice, using the notes under the 1 the first time and those under the 2, instead, the second time. If the notes under the 1 and 2 are tied together, then one sings both the second time.

6. **D.C.** or **Da Capo**, usually placed above the staff, is a directive to return to the beginning and to finish at the end of the first strain or phrase. **D.S.**, or **Dal Segno**, directs a return to the sign (𝄋). The label **Fine** (Italian for "end") may mark the end, following a D.C. or D.S. Repeats are not observed after a D.C. or D.S., and if there is a double ending, the second is used.

7. Notes have **relative lengths** as follows.

length: 1   1/2   1/4   1/8   1/16
note: o   𝅗𝅥   ♩   ♪   𝅘𝅥𝅯
relative length: whole   half   quarter   eighth   sixteenth

For any shape, the same system of **stems** (short vertical lines), **color** [**white** (open) or **black** (filled) head], and **flags** (hanging from the stem at the end opposite the head) is used to denote relative lengths.

A whole note   o   is equal in length to
Two halves   or
Four quarters   or
Eight eighths   or
Sixteen sixteenths

The duration of a note (in time) of a given relative length may vary from one piece to another, or even from one performance of the same piece to another, but the durations for the various relative lengths are always proportional as shown above.

8. **Rests** denote silence. **Whole, half, quarter, eighth,** and **sixteenth** rests have the same lengths as the corresponding notes. This figure shows the values of rests and their positions on the staff.

whole   half   quarter   eighth   sixteenth

9. A **dot** placed immediately to the right of a rest or the head of a note increases its length by half, so that a **dotted** note or rest is 1-1/2 times as long as it would have been without the dot.

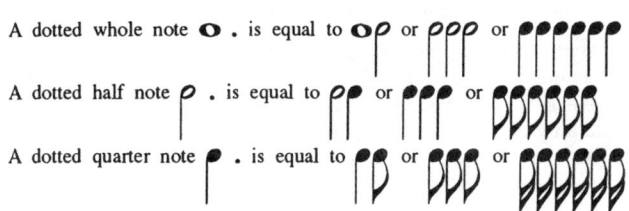

10. A **time signature** denoting the **mode of time** precedes the first note or rest of a piece of music. One whole number is placed over another. Each change in the mode of time is indicated by a time signature at the point of change. In JOY the time signature is 2/4.

The lower number specifies a note (by length) and the upper one specifies the number of these notes that will fill a measure completely and exactly. Thus, 2/4 indicates that two (2) quarter notes (1/4) will fill a measure. Any combination of notes and rests with the same total length will also fill a measure.

The lengths of notes and rests in beats follow from the number of beats in a measure. In previous editions of the Sacred Harp, the Rudiments state that 2/2, 4/4, 2/4, 6/4 and 6/8 measures contain two beats, while 3/2 and 3/4 measures contain three. However, the upper figure of a time signature is often interpreted as the number of beats in a measure, so that 4/4 has four beats per measure and 6/4 and 6/8 have six.

11. The modes of time fall into three types: common time, triple time, and compound time.

(a) There are three modes of common time. In each, a measure contains two or four beats. Most notes fall on even divisions of a beat, that is, on the beat, half beat, quarter beat, etc.

In the first mode 2/2 of common time, two half notes fill a measure. A half note receives one beat.

In the second mode 4/4 of common time, four quarter notes fill a measure. A half note receives one beat if a measure contains two beats, and a quarter note receives one beat if a measure contains four beats.

In the third mode 2/4 of common time, two quarter notes fill a measure. A quarter note receives one beat.

b) Two modes of triple time are used in the Sacred Harp. In each, a measure contains three beats. Most notes fall on even divisions of a beat.

In the first mode 3/2 of triple time, three half notes fill a measure. A half note receives one beat.

In the second mode 3/4 of triple time,

three quarter notes fill a measure. A quarter note receives one beat.

(c) Two modes of **compound time** are used in the *Sacred Harp*. In each, a measure contains two or six beats. Most notes fall on divisions of the two beats by three or on one of the six beats.

In the first mode $\frac{6}{4}$ of compound time, six quarter notes fill a measure. A dotted half note receives one beat if a measure contains two beats, and a quarter note receives one beat if a measure contains six beats.

In the second mode $\frac{6}{8}$ of compound time, six eighth notes fill a measure. A dotted quarter note receives one beat if a measure contains two beats, and an eighth note receives one beat if a measure contains six beats.

12. In performance, the **leader marks** (or **beats**) **time** with hand and arm motions. Singers may also mark time, provided that they follow the leader precisely.

The first beat of each measure is marked with a downward stroke of the hand, a **downbeat** (symbol **d**). The beat begins at the end of the stroke. For two-beat measures, the second beat is marked with an upward stroke, an **upbeat** (symbol **u**). Thus, time is marked by the series |d u|d u|. In JOY, down- and upbeats are denoted
                                        1-2- 1-2-
by down and up arrows over the notes.

Three-beat measures are marked |d d u|d d u|. The first down stroke should end with
                              1-2-3 1-2-3
the forearm near a horizontal position, so that there is room for the second down stroke.

Four- and six-beat measures can be marked with these same hand strokes. Thus, the $\frac{4}{4}$ mode of time can be marked and |d u|d u| and $\frac{6}{4}$ and $\frac{6}{8}$ |d   u |d   u |.
                                                                    1-2-3-4 1-2-3-4   1-2-3-4-5-6 1-2-3-4-5-6

Although leaders may assume considerable discretion in the manner of marking time, modest downward and upward strokes are much to be preferred to "winding", "grabbing" and "snatching" methods.

13. Every measure must contain notes and rests whose lengths (in beats) add up to that of a measure, exactly, in the given mode of time. The student should verify that this is true of each measure of JOY. Sometimes a partial measure at the beginning is complemented by another at the end, so that the two together make a whole measure.

14. A note or rest that begins at the beginning of a beat is said to fall **on the beat**. Other notes are **off the beat**.

The first note or rest in each measure falls on the first beat of that measure. A note that falls on the first beat of a measure is given a **primary accent** by enunciating it a little more emphatically and making it a little louder than others.

A note falling on the second beat of a two-beat measure of common or compound time is given a **secondary** (less pronounced) **accent**. In triple time, the secondary accent is on the third beat. In a four-beat or six-beat measure, the secondary accent is on the third ($\frac{4}{4}$) or fourth ($\frac{6}{4}$ or $\frac{6}{8}$) beat.

The student can get a good feel for the inherent rhythms of the various modes of time by reciting the counts of the beats with the proper accents, as follows, where boldface represents a primary accent and italics a secondary one:

12|**1**2|**1**2|**1**2| --------------------------- ($\frac{2}{2}$ $\frac{2}{4}$ $\frac{2}{8}$ $\frac{6}{4}$ $\frac{6}{8}$)

12*3*|**1**2*3*|**1**2*3*|**1**2*3*| ----------------------- ($\frac{3}{2}$ $\frac{3}{4}$)

In four- and six-beat measures, the accents are:

12*3*4|**1**2*3*4|**1**2*3*4|**1**2*3*4| ---------------- ($\frac{4}{4}$)

123*4*56|**1**23*4*56|**1**23*4*56|**1**23*4*56| ---- ($\frac{6}{4}$ $\frac{6}{8}$)

Accents should be distinct, but if overdone the performance will sound "choppy."

Under special circumstances, where there is syncopation or misbarring (Sections 20 and 21), accents are displaced from their normal beats.

15. **Tempo** is the frequency (speed) of beats. In the *Sacred Harp*, the mode of time is a guide to tempo. In common time, $\frac{2}{2}$ is slower than $\frac{2}{4}$, which is slower than $\frac{2}{8}$. In triple time, $\frac{3}{2}$ is slower than $\frac{3}{4}$, and in compound time, $\frac{6}{4}$ is slower than $\frac{6}{8}$. In associating tempo with the time signature, the *Sacred Harp* tradition follows a practice dating back to the mensural notation of the 13th century.

Evenso, tempo is at the discretion of the leader. It should be appropriate to the music and poetry, and it should be neither so slow as to drag intolerably nor so fast as to give the impression of racing or to inhibit the clear pronunciation of the words.

In standard notation, a measure of $\frac{2}{2}$ is usually shorter (in seconds) than one of $\frac{4}{4}$, the opposite of the *Sacred Harp* tradition.

An accurate tempo can be set with a **metronome**, a mechanical or electrical device for marking the beginnings of successive beats with sounds or flashes of light. The notation **mm = 120** means that there are 120 equal beats per minute.

16. The student should practice singing both the **notes** (syllables, corresponding to shapes) and **words** (text, **poetry**) of JOY while marking time. Time should be marked smoothly and evenly. Due attention should be given to accents. The student should also practice randomly chosen selections from the *Sacred Harp*. It is not necessary to sing these passages. To practice timing and accent, one can recite the notes, words, or any

nonsense syllables. To divide beats evenly in giving notes their proper lengths, it may be helpful to think "1-and-2-and..." or "1-a-and-a-2-a-and-a...." To divide beats into thirds, think "1-and-a-2-and-a...."

17. A **slur** is a curved line spanning notes of successively differing pitches (different positions on the staff), and a **tie** is a similar line spanning notes of the same pitch (same position on the staff). In either case, one syllable of the poetry is applied to all of the notes of the group. In singing, enunciate the syllable at the first note and continue it smoothly through the other notes. Notes with joined flags (**beams**) are treated as slurred.

18. A **triplet** is a group of three notes of equal length to be sung in the time of two. It is denoted by a figure 3 above or below the group of three notes: ♪♪♪. To help execute a triplet in one beat, think "1-and-a" or "2-and-a". The length of the beat for the triplet must be the same as that of a typical beat. To help execute a triplet in two beats, divide each beat into thirds and let each note of the triplet occupy two successive thirds: "(1and)(a-2)(and-a)," where the parentheses enclose the fractions of beats that correspond to a single note of the triplet.

19. A **hold (pause)** ⌒ placed over a note or rest shows that it may be held beyond its normal length, at the *reasonable* discretion of the leader.

20. **Syncopation** occurs when a short note at a naturally accented beat in a measure is followed immediately by a longer note, which is usually held through the beginning of the next beat. In such a case, the accent shifts to the longer note.

21. Poetry, like music, has natural accents (see Chapter VII). When the natural accents of the poetry do not correspond to those of the printed music, the notation is said to be **misbarred**.

In performing a misbarred piece, one follows the notation in marking time but not in singing accents. Where there is a conflict between the poetry and the music, the poetry overrules the music and determines the accents.

CHAPTER III
MELODICS

1. **Melodics** concerns pitch and patterns of successive pitches.

2. Letters **A, B, C, D, E, F,** and **G** are assigned to notes. Each letter corresponds to a particular position on the staff and relative pitch. For successive ascending positions on the staff, the letters fall in alphabetical order, starting over with A after G. However, the letters don't have the same positions on every staff.

3. The **clef** assigns a particular letter to a particular position on the staff. Two clefs are used in this edition of the Sacred Harp. The **treble clef**, 𝄞, which appears at the beginning of JOY, assigns G to the second line. It is used for the tenor, alto, and treble parts. The **bass clef**, 𝄢, assigns F to the fourth line and is used for the bass part. The **alto clef**, 𝄡, was used in early editions of the *Sacred Harp* to place C on the third line of the staff.

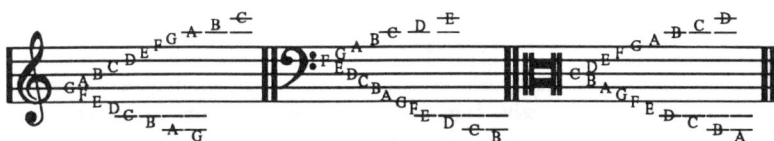

4. *Sacred Harp* music should be pitched so that all singers can reach their parts comfortably. Thus, the notation does not adhere to the international standard **concert pitch**, in which the frequency of A above "middle C" is **440 cycles per second**.

5. The **unison** consists of two notes with the same pitch. The **octave** is an interval in which the frequency of the higher note is exactly twice that of the lower. The octave relationship is so strong that notes one or more octaves apart are sometimes treated as if they were unisons. Further, notes that are exactly one or more octaves apart have the same letter, shape, and syllable. In JOY the interval between "Joy" and "come" is one octave. The corresponding notes are both F, both triangles, and both Fa.

6. A **half step** (or **half tone**) (symbol h) is the smallest interval recognized in Western music. Twelve successive half steps span one octave exactly. In JOY, the intervals "Joy to" and "the Lord" are half steps. In the letter system, the intervals B-C and E-F are half steps.

7. The **flat** (♭) and **sharp** (♯) symbols are related to half steps. The flat lowers, and the sharp raises, the pitch of the affected note by a half step. Thus, B♭ (pronounced "B-flat") is a half step lower than B. To emphasize that B is not flat or sharp, the **natural** symbol (♮) can be used: B♮ (pronounced "B-natural").

8. Two successive ascending half steps span one **whole step** (or **whole tone**) (symbol **w**). In JOY, the intervals "to the," "the world," "world! the", "Lord is," and "is come" are all whole steps. The intervals A-B, C-D, D-E, F-G, and G-A, are whole steps.

9. A **scale** is the set of different pitches used in a piece of music. In the standard representation of a scale, the notes are arranged in order of ascending pitch, beginning with the fundamental note, which is called the tonic, and spanning one octave. Notes outside that octave are exactly one or more octaves lower or higher than those in it. The

upper tonic is included in order to show the interval leading to it, even though it is related to the tonic by an octave. The scale for JOY is illustrated.

10. The scales used in the *Sacred Harp* are **heptatonic** (seven-tone), meaning that they consist of seven pitches in a span of one octave, not counting the upper tonic. **Hexatonic** (six-tone) and **pentatonic** (five-tone) scales are regarded as heptatonic scales with gaps in them.

11. The **degrees** of a scale are its successively ascending pitches. The eight degrees spanning one octave are numbered beginning with the tonic as 1, as shown in JOY. Degree 8 is also degree 1 of the next higher octave of the scale. Degree 8 may also be labeled degree 1a ("1 above"). Similarly, degree 1b is one octave below degree 1 and degree 5aa is two octaves above degree 5.

Adjacent degrees of a heptatonic scale are represented by notes at adjacent positions on the staff. Thus, the successive degrees of an ascending scale are represented by notes at successive positions. No position is skipped or repeated. The student should verify this for the scale shown in JOY.

12. Two **scales** (or **modes**) are recognized in *Sacred Harp* notation, **major** and **minor**. Either scale can be in any **key**, that is, its tonic can be any letter (natural, flat, or sharp) or pitch. The tonic lends its letter to the name of the key. Thus, "key of E♭ major" denotes the major scale with tonic E♭, while "key of C♯ minor" denotes the minor scale with tonic C♯.

13. From degree 1 to degree 8, the major scale (Ionian mode) has the syllable sequence Fa-Sol-La-Fa-Sol-La-Mi-Fa and the interval sequence w-w-h-w-w-w-h, with half steps at degrees 3-4 (La-Fa) and 7-8 (Mi-Fa).

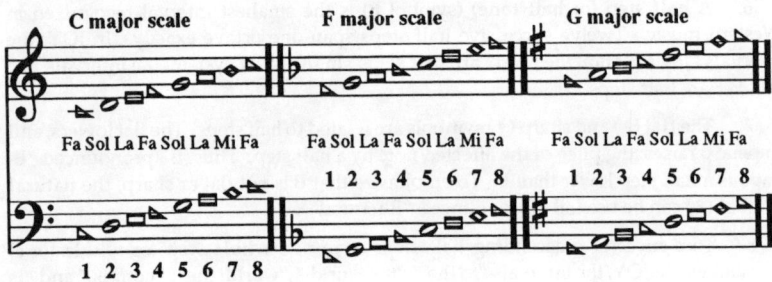

The figure illustrates the following principle for the keys of C, F, and G major: *The degrees of a scale have the same shapes, syllables, and relative positions on the staff in every key and under every clef.* The student should study the figure carefully and verify this statement. This is the principle that allows shaped notes to be read by their shapes and relative positions.

The eight notes of JOY are those of a descending major scale. The student can use the pitches of JOY to establish those of the degrees of the major scale. The major scale should be practiced, with the syllables given by the shapes of the notes, until it becomes second nature. With practice, one can learn to sing the correct pitches when presented with the notes of the scale in any order.

14. A **key signature** is a set of flats or sharps at particular positions on the staff. It is placed near the left side of each segment of the staff and at other points if necessary. Each flat or sharp in the key signature affects every note that follows it on the same line or space (until another key signature appears). In JOY, the key signature consists of one flat at B.

The key signature, or its absence, denotes the key by assigning a letter to the syllable Mi. If there is no key signature, Mi is B. When there is one flat, as in JOY, Mi is E. (See Chapter IV.)

Any piece of major music can be noted in any major key. If the key is changed, the notes may move, as a group, up or down on the staff. If one note moves up three positions, then every note moves up three positions, and so do the half- and whole-step intervals between notes at adjacent positions on the staff.

Some pieces would require excessive use of ledger lines if written without a key signature. This is avoided by a proper selection of a key signature.

15. The minor scale printed in the *Sacred Harp* is the natural minor (Aeolian mode). Its syllable and interval sequences are La-Mi-Fa-Sol-La-Fa-Sol-La and w-h-w-w-h-w-w, with half steps at degrees 2-3 and 5-6.

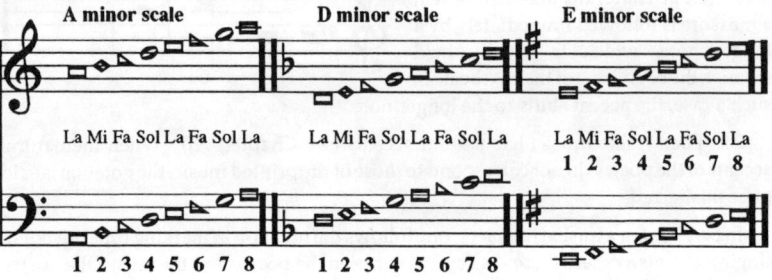

The natural minor scale can be constructed from the major scale by moving the tonic from Fa down to La (Section 19).

Traditionally, minor music is sung in the Dorian mode, with the sixth degree a half step higher than the natural minor notation indicates. The interval sequence is w-h-w-w-w-h-w, with half steps at degrees 2-3 and 6-7 (see Chapter IV, Section 4; and Chapter

RUDIMENTS OF MUSIC

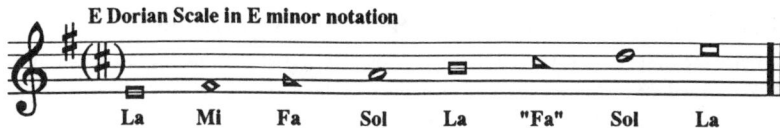

E Dorian Scale in E minor notation

La Mi Fa Sol La "Fa" Sol La

VIII, Sections 13 and 14).

It is traditional to sing "Fa" at the sixth degree, even though the pitch actually corresponds to "Fi" (Section 20). The C♯ in parentheses in the key signature of the figure is understood but not printed in Sacred Harp notation.

16. The sounds of major and minor music are different. To some, minor music seems to be dark, somber, sad, or mournful, while major music seems to be bright and joyous. However, these are not natural responses to the music, they are learned. In the Sacred Harp, settings of texts to music do not conform to naive notions of sad minor and joyful major music; minor music can be joyful.

A feeling for the difference in sound between major and minor can be gained from the following exercise. At the left is the notation for the familiar major-key jingle "Come, little children! Sing this!" (brief citation: SING). At the right is another jingle, in a minor key, set with the same words and using the same pitches. The student should sing both tunes, obtaining the pitches for the notes of the minor tune from the corresponding notes of the major one. A difference in the flavor of the sound will be clear.

C major   A minor

Come, lit-tle chil-dren! Sing this! Come, lit-tle chil-dren! Sing this!

SING is in the **natural** keys, that is, keys without a signature, so that all notes are natural, not flat or sharp. The natural keys are C major and A minor.

17. **Intervals** are named after degrees of the scale. If an interval is the same as that between the first (tonic) and the fifth degree of the scale, the interval is called a fifth. In a major key, the following intervals between degrees of the scale are all fifths: Fa(1)-Sol(5), Sol(2)-La(6), La(3)-Mi(7), Fa(4)-Fa(8), etc.

Intervals of an octave or less include **unison, minor second** (half step), **major second** (whole step), **minor third, major third, perfect fourth, perfect fifth, minor sixth, major sixth, minor seventh, major seventh,** and **octave**. The fourth and fifth are **perfect** because they are the same intervals in both major and minor scales. **Thirds, sixths,** and **sevenths** differ in major and natural minor scales, with the minor interval being a half step less than the major interval in each case. Thus, the minor third spans one-and-a-half steps, while the major third spans two whole steps.

Augmented means increased, and **diminished** means decreased, by a half step. Thus, an **augmented fourth** is the same as a **diminished fifth**, an interval of three whole steps.

18. Shaped notes facilitate reading music. The shapes carry the same information as the clef and key signature. Thus, a shaped-note reader can ignore both the clef and key signature and use only the shapes of the notes and their relative positions on the staff. However, one who reads by the methods of standard musical notation must determine pitch by staff position only and must pay careful attention to the clef and key signature.

19. **Relative** major and minor keys have the same signature. Examples include C major/A minor, F major/D minor, and G major/E minor.

The major tonic is Fa above Mi, and the natural minor tonic is La below Mi. Thus, the tonic of a natural minor scale is a minor third below that of its relative major scale.

Relative major and minor scales

20. An **accidental** is a flat, sharp, or natural used within a measure. It affects all subsequent occurrences of the degree on which it is placed until the measure ends or another accidental appears at the same degree. An accidental natural at a particular degree can cancel the effect of a flat or sharp in the key signature. The *Sacred Harp* contains very few accidentals.

The syllables for notes with accidental sharps are Fi ("fee"), Si ("see"), and Li ("lee"). Those for flats are Say, Lay, and May. Accidentals can be used to represent the **chromatic scale**, in which each successive interval is a half step.

Fa Fi Sol Si La Fa Fi Sol Si La Li Mi Fa

Fa Mi May La Lay Sol Say Fa La Lay Sol Say Fa

CHAPTER IV
KEYS

1. To find the tonic from note shapes, locate Mi. The major tonic is Fa above Mi, and the natural minor tonic is La below Mi. If Mi is absent, it would lie between the La and Fa that are a third apart.

The last note sounded in the bass part is always the tonic. If the syllable is Fa, then the key is major, and if it is La it is minor. Under the treble clef, it lies two positions higher on the staff than under the bass clef.

2. Under the natural key signature, the positions on the staff represent the pitches of the C major and A minor scales. If the fourth degree of the C major scale, C-w-D-w-E-h-F-w-G-w-A-w-B-h-C, is raised by a half step, the resulting order of intervals is that of the G major scale, G-w-A-w-B-h-C-w-D-w-E-w-F#-h-G. The fourth degree of the original C major scale, when raised a half step, becomes the seventh degree of the the G major scale, in which the tonic (G) is a fifth higher than the original tonic (C). Conversely, lowering the seventh degree of the G major scale lowers the tonic by a fifth, converting the scale to C major. The relative minor scales are affected in a parallel fashion. These changes apply, with analogous results, to any key.

3. By starting with C major/A minor and repeatedly adding sharps (one at a time) to raise the fourth degree, a series of new keys and key signatures is generated. If flats are added instead, to lower the seventh degree repeatedly, another series is generated.

All possible keys are reached in these **transpositions of the key by fifths**.

Once the first sharp is placed (at F), the position of each succeeding sharp is a fifth above the last: F#, C#, G#, etc., and once the first flat is placed (at B), each succeeding flat is a fifth below the last: B♭, E♭, A♭, etc.

Mi is always at the position of the last sharp (already present) or the next flat (that could be added) to the signature. For example, two sharps are at F and C, Mi is C#, and the key is D major/B minor. Similarly, three flats are at B, E, and A; Mi is D, and the key is E♭ major/C minor.

4. Round-note readers can obtain the proper key signature for the Dorian mode (Chapter III, Section 15) by dropping the last flat or adding another sharp to the natural minor key signature.

CHAPTER V
DYNAMICS

1. **Dynamics** concerns volume (loud or soft).

2. *Sacred Harp* dynamics are mostly discretionary. The singing is usually strong, with a natural tendency for higher notes to be louder. This tendency must not be overdone. Singers should pay careful attention to the leader, who will use smaller motions for softer passages and larger motions for louder ones.

3. Italian words and abbreviations used as directives for volume include **pianissimo, pp** (very soft); **piano, p** (soft); **mezzo piano, mp** (moderately soft); **mezzo, m** (moderate); **mezzo forte, mf** (moderately loud); **forte, f** (loud); and **fortissimo, ff** (very loud). Those for varying volume are **crescendo, cres** or ──◁ (growing louder) and **diminuendo, dim** or ▷── (growing softer). The swell ──◁▷── is a combination in which a crescendo is followed by a diminuendo. An **organ tone** has the same volume thoughout.

CHAPTER VI
MECHANICS OF SINGING

1. Tones are produced only while exhaling, under the control of the **diaphragm**, a muscular partition between the chest and abdominal cavity. Whether standing or sitting, the body should be erect and completely free of unnatural motions, allowing the diaphragm to function properly.

2. Inhale as needed to maintain a firm voice, but never so as to interrupt the flow of the music. The best places are at punctuation marks in the text, at the ends of phrases, and after emphatic words. Inhale with the lips partly closed in order to protect the sides of the throat, which should be kept open at all times while singing.

3. The voice should be pure, full, firm, and certain. Good delivery depends on a correct position of the body, complete control of the breath, proper positions of the throat and mouth, and firm action of the vocal cords. Unnatural contractions or distentions of

the mouth or throat should be avoided. One should open the mouth enough to avoid obstruction of the tone by the lips or teeth.

4. The voice should be natural and unpretentious. The ideals of popular, art, concert, and opera singing do not apply to the *Sacred Harp*. In particular, few traditional **Sacred Harp** singers produce a conscious **vibrato**, or pulsation of the voice. In group singing, vibrato can create undesired harmonic effects.

5. Every word should be pronounced correctly and distinctly. Words are divided into syllables as they are vocalized naturally, not necessarily as the dictionary may divide them. Thus, one sings "mu-sic" (not "mus-ic") and "sto-ry" (not "stor-y").

6. "The" is pronounced "thee" when it precedes a word beginning with a vowel (a, e, i, o, u, sometimes w or y) or vowel sound. Otherwise, especially if unaccented, it can be pronounced "thuh."

THEE angel of the the Lord came down.

THEE iron fetters yield.

THEE honor of thy name.

Were THEE whole realm of nature mine?

THEE yearning of the heart.

CHAPTER VII
METER

1. Poetic **meter** is the pattern of accented (symbol /) and unaccented (symbol —) syllables. The fundamental unit is the **foot**. The common feet are the **iamb**, **trochee**, **anapest**, and **dactyl**.

iamb = — /   trochee = / —   anapest = — — /   dactyl = / — —

2. The titles in the Sacred Harp are for tunes or pieces of music. Each tune is suited to a particular poetic meter. A metrical designation, printed next to the title, gives the meter of the appropriate poetry. Any poetry with this meter can be sung as a tune is not restricted to the poetry printed with it.

3. One type of **metrical designation** gives the number of syllables in each line and number of lines in a stanza (verse). Thus, 9898 denotes a four-line stanza with nine and eight syllables per line, alternating. In addition, some standard meters are named.

common meter, C.M.:	iambic 8,6,8,6
common meter double, C.M.D.:	iambic 8,6,8,6,8,6,8,6
long meter, L.M.:	iambic 8,8,8,8
long meter double, L.M.D.:	iambic 8,8,8,8,8,8,8,8
short meter, S.M.:	iambic 6,6,8,6
short meter double, S.M.D.:	iambic 6,6,8,6,6,6,8,6
common particular meter, C.P.M.:	iambic 8,8,6,8,8,6
long particular meter, L.P.M.:	iambic 8,8,8,8,8,8
meter hallellujah, H.M.:	iambic 6,6,6,6,8,8
common meter hallelujah, C.H.M.:	iambic 8,8,6,8,8,6
meter 12s, M.T. or 12,12,12,12:	anapestic 12,12,12,12
meter 8s and 7s:	trochaic 8,7,8,7
meter 11s:	anapestic 11,11,11,11
meter 7s:	trochaic 7,7,7,7

4. **Particular meter, P.M.**, denotes poetry with its own peculiar meter, that is, not one of the standard meters. A hymn in a particular meter requires a special tune for that meter.

CHAPTER VIII
HARMONY AND COMPOSITION

1. Harmony consists of tones sounded simultaneously. Composition involves the art of binding tones together in a pleasing and interesting way.

2. Harmony is the most distinctive feature of *Sacred Harp* music. It sets it apart from most other music.

3. Late 18th-century New England composers (represented in the Sacred Harp by Billings, Read, Swan, Morgan, and others) used harmony that is basically **tertian**, that is, based on intervals of thirds. In contrast, the harmony used by the early 19th-century compilers of singing-school manuals (such as the *Sacred Harp*) is basically **quartal**, that is, based on intervals of fourths and their close relatives, fifths. In the early 20th century, alto parts were added to the three-part pieces in the *Sacred Harp*, resulting in a hybrid harmony, part quartal and part tertian.

4. *Sacred Harp* harmony does not follow the rules of **conventional harmony**, which were well established by the late 18th century. Billings fiercely declared his independence ("I don't think myself confined to any rules of composition laid down by any who went before me") and he practiced what he preached. Later compilers of singing-school manuals copied their rudiments from one another and, ultimately, from works describing conventional harmony, but they paid little attention to these rudiments when composing or arranging.

5. In **polyphony**, no one part stands out. *Sacred Harp* music is polyphonic. The tune (melody, air) is carried by the tenor part, but the other parts, ideally, are good melodies on their own, making all parts interesting.

Conventional harmony is **homophonic**. The tune is assigned to high voices, usually the soprano, so that it will stand out. The other parts provide unobtrusive harmonic support.

6. A **dyad** is a combination of two notes not related as unisons or octaves. A **triad** is a similar combination of three notes. For the present purposes, both are considered to be **chords**. The fundamental note of a chord is called its **root**, and a chord is in its **root position** when the root is the note of lowest pitch.

Triads are used in tertian harmony, including conventional harmony. A conventional triad consists of the root plus the third and fifth scale degrees above it. The name of the triad is the same as the **harmonic name** of its root.

Tonic   Supertonic   Mediant   Subdominant   Dominant   Submediant   Subtonic

Triads of minor scales are named analogously.

Dyads, especially fourths and fifths, are the fundamental chords of quartal harmony.

7. In *Sacred Harp* (polyphonic) harmony, quartal or tertian, the chord changes frequently, often with every successive note. Thus, the harmony is **dispersed** or **freely moving**. In conventional harmony, the same chord is often used for several successive notes, or even measures.

8. Harmony is based on ideas of **concord (consonance)** and **discord (dissonance)**, of **tension** and **resolution**, and of **progression**. Some intervals are classified as concords and others as discords. A concord is a pleasing, stable-sounding harmonic interval. A discord is a displeasing, unstable-sounding one. A discord provides tension (you wish it would go away), and the progression from a discord to a concord resolves that tension. Harmony consists of an interesting progression through a series of discords and concords.

9. In the quartal harmony of the *Sacred Harp*, the concords are unison, perfect fourth, perfect fifth, and octave. All other intervals are discords. Sometimes the third is treated as if it were a concord.

A fifth is the **inversion** of a fourth, and *vice versa*. For example, Fa(1)-Fa(4) is a perfect fourth in root position. If Fa(4) is transposed an octave lower, the resulting **inverted fourth** is a perfect fifth, Fa(4b)-Fa(1). Root-position and inverted chords use the same degrees of the scale, some in different octaves.

10. In conventional tertian harmony, the concords are unison, major and minor thirds, perfect fifth, major and minor sixths, and octave. All other intervals, including the perfect fourth, are discords. Triads are built of successive concords, although some interesting effects can be achieved by blending a concord with a mild discord.

Triads can be used in the root position, the **first inversion**, where the root is transposed an octave higher, leaving the middle note of the root position as the lowest of the inverted chord, or the **second inversion**, where the root and middle notes are transposed octaves higher, leaving the highest note of the root position as the lowest of the inverted chord.

11. The discrepancies between the lists of concords and discords for quartal and tertian harmony show that the sense of consonance and dissonance is conditioned (learned). In composing, one should explore the harmonic possibilities and evaluate each case by its sound in its own context. It is best not to be a slave to a preconceived list of concords and discords.

12. One rule of conventional harmony that is frequently violated in the *Sacred Harp* states that chords should be complete triads (or triads augmented with another note). In fact, most of the chords in 19th-century compositions are dyads. Even when alto parts were supplied in the 20th century, many of the chords were left as dyads by having the alto double a note in the existing harmony. This is especially true of minor pieces.

13. Another rule of conventional harmony prohibits the motion of parts in parallel (or consecutive) fifths and octaves, where two voices maintain a constant interval over several notes. Parallel octaves are built into Sacred Harp singing when men and women sing the same part. In addition, parallel fifths between parts are a natural part of quartal harmony, and they abound in the Sacred Harp.

The parallel fifths between the bass and tenor parts in measures 6-7 of WONDROUS LOVE (159) are especially interesting because they suggest that the composer intended the Dorian mode (which is sung in practice), not the natural minor (which is written).

In this passage, all of the printed intervals are perfect fifths except the one marked with an "x", which is a diminished fifth. When WONDROUS LOVE is sung in Dorian mode, all of the intervals in question are perfect fifths.

14. Parallel fifths result when two parts have the same sequence of intervals in the upper and lower **tetrachords** of the major or Dorian scale. The lower tetrachord consists of degrees 1-4 and the upper tetrachord of degrees 5-8. For the major scale, the interval sequence within each tetrachord is w-w-h, and for the Dorian mode, it is w-h-w. For the natural minor scale, however, the interval sequences differ in the lower (w-h-w) and upper (h-w-w) tetrachords.

RUDIMENTS OF MUSIC

15. A **mutual tone** belongs to each of two successive chords. If a part has a mutual tone in the first chord, it can retain that note in the second chord, thereby binding the two together.

16. A **passing tone** is a discord that is introduced, usually as part of a slur and always at an unaccented part of the measure, to help the melody pass from one principal note to another. An **accessory tone** is similar tone that lies between two notes of the same pitch.

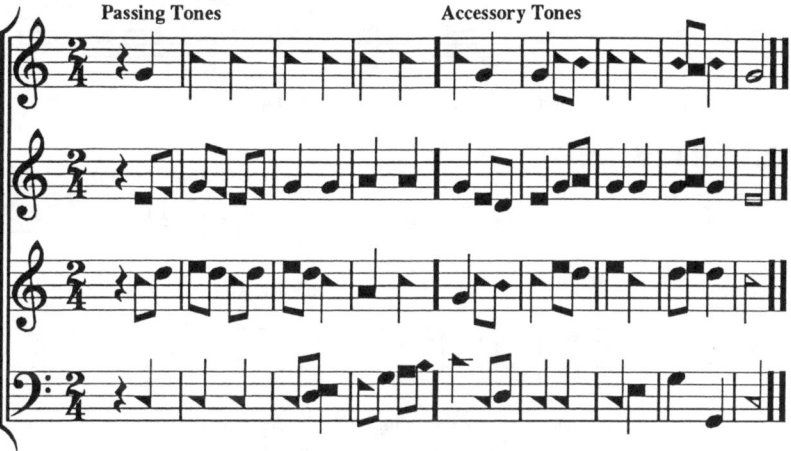

17. Like chords, the notes of the tune itself wander through unstable pitches on the way to the final resting pitch, which is almost always the tonic. A tune that ends on another note sounds unfinished.

The last chord of a piece is almost always rooted in the tonic. In three-part harmony, it is usually the tonic-fifth dyad, while in four-part major pieces, it tends to be the tonic triad. Even in four parts, however, minor pieces tend to end with the tonic-fifth dyad.

18. Given a tenor part (tune), many composers write the other parts in the order bass, treble, alto. Whatever order is used, each part should be an interesting melody on its own. While writing a part, the other parts should be kept in mind, so that interesting possibilities are not excluded.

The best teacher is example. The student composer should study the harmonies in the *Sacred Harp*, especially those of pieces that he or she particularly admires. The possibilities of both quartal and tertian harmony, and their mixtures, should be considered.

Certain keyboard instruments and almost all desktop computers allow musical composition with recording, playback, and easy editing, providing promising possibilities for the *Sacred Harp* composer.

CHAPTER IX
MUSICAL FORMS

1. A **song**, in a general sense, is any utterance with a musical modulation, whether by the human voice or those of birds or other animals. "Song" is often used to refer a piece in the *Sacred Harp*.

2. An **anthem** is a composition set with words that are taken from the Bible, prayer book, or other sacred writing.

3. An **ode** is a musical setting of a poem of noble sentiment and dignity of style, especially one commemorating or honoring a particular subject, such as a person or special occasion.

4. A **prelude** is an introductory portion of a piece of music.

5. There are many types of **chants**. In general, a chant is recited in a musical tone, mostly on one pitch (or a few), sometimes without evident rhythmic form.

6. A **hymn** is a song of thanksgiving to, praise to, or love of God.

7. A **psalm** is a song based on a text from the Book of Psalms of the Old Testament of the Bible. Psalms may be paraphrased or rewritten in a metrical fashion. The Biblical psalms were originally Hebrew songs.

8. A **spiritual song** is a song with sacred content, usually not a psalm or hymn, as in the Biblical phrase, "psalms, hymns, and spiritual songs."

9. A **set piece** is a piece of music set with particular words and designed to be used with those words only.

10. A **fuguing tune** has at least one section in which the parts fall in one after the other, with the same or similar rhythm and with related melodic lines, at different pitches. At the end of the section, the parts come together. LENOX (40), NORTHFIELD (155), and ALABAMA (196) are excellent examples.

RUDIMENTS OF MUSIC
Chapter X - Singing Exercises

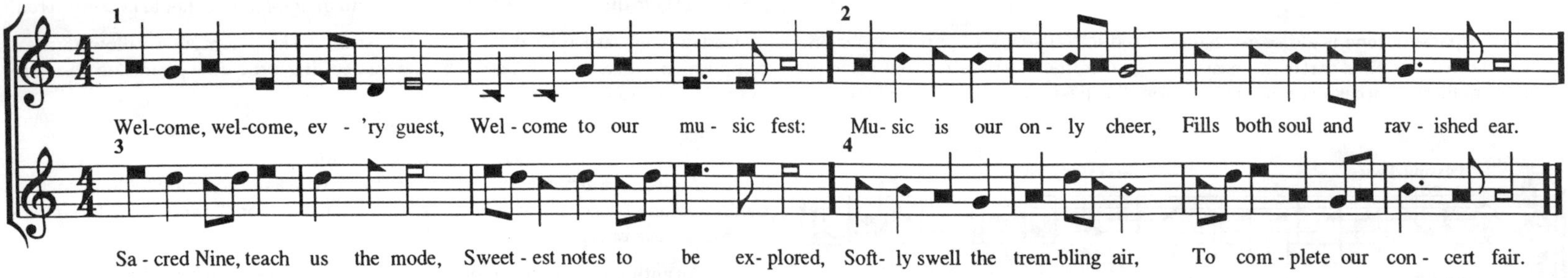

1. Wel-come, wel-come, ev-'ry guest, Wel-come to our mu-sic fest: Mu-sic is our on-ly cheer, Fills both soul and rav-ished ear.

3. Sa-cred Nine, teach us the mode, Sweet-est notes to be ex-plored, Soft-ly swell the trem-bling air, To com-plete our con-cert fair.

THE YOUNG CONVERT. L.M.

Christian Harmony, 1805.

Won-der, won-der won-der; Won-der, won-der, won-der; Their

When con-verts first be-gin to sing, Won-der, won-der won-der, Their hap-py souls are on the wing, Won-der, won-der, won-der; Their

theme is all re-deem-ing love, Won-der, won-der, won-der; Fain would they be with Christ a-bove, Won-der, won-der, won-der.

theme is all re-deem-ing love, Won-der, won-der, won-der; Fain would they be with Christ a-bove, Won-der, won-der, won-der.

RUDIMENTS OF MUSIC

FIRE ALARM. In Four Parts.

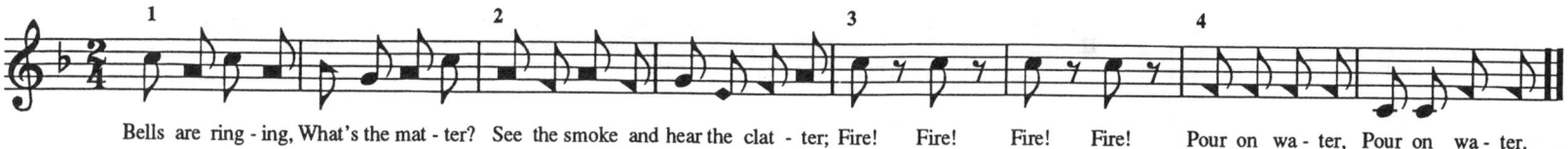

Bells are ring-ing, What's the mat-ter? See the smoke and hear the clat-ter; Fire! Fire! Fire! Fire! Pour on wa-ter, Pour on wa-ter.

CHAPTER XI
ORGANIZATION AND CONDUCT OF SINGINGS AND CONVENTIONS

1. An **annual singing** lasts one day and a **convention** two days or more. In another sense, a convention is an organization that sponsors singings. A **special singing** occurs only once, has a frequency other than annual, or occurs irregularly. Most **all-day singings** last from 9 or 10 a.m. to 3 or 4 p.m. Conventions, churches, or other groups sponsor **singing schools**, where one can learn to read music and sing from the *Sacred Harp*.

2. Although the proceedings at singings tend to be informal, there is a formal structure of officers and committees, and the minutes of singings are usually published.

3. The singers sit in rows of pews or chairs that face to the center of a hollow square. To the immediate left and right of the tenors are the basses and trebles, respectively. The altos face the tenors.

4. A session begins with a call to order by the chairman, who leads a selection, calls upon the chaplain (or another) for an opening prayer, makes welcoming remarks, and presides over the election of new officers. Typically, officers include chairman, vice chairman, secretary, treasurer, and chaplain. Arranging and memorial committees, and sometimes others, such as finance, hospitality, and resolutions committees, are appointed by the chairman.

5. The chairman calls the group to order after each recess and generally presides. The vice chairman may replace the chairman, at the discretion of the chairman or if the chairman is absent. The secretary keeps the minutes, which include a brief description of the proceedings, a list of leaders and the page numbers of the pieces led, and reports of committees. The treasurer collects donations, the main purpose of which, usually, is to cover the expense of having the minutes printed. The offices of secretary and treasurer are sometimes combined. The chaplain may be called on to lead in prayer at opening, dinner, and closing. The arranging committee identifies leaders and calls on them to lead, often giving notice to the next leader as well. The memorial committee identifies those who have died since the last meeting (and sometimes others) and formulates a memorial lesson and report. The locating committee determines the location of the next session of the body. The resolutions committee drafts resolutions.

6. When called, the leader steps into the hollow square, faces the tenor section, and announces the page number of his or her selection ("159," or "number 45 top," or "EASTER ANTHEM, page 236"). Others may repeat the page number so that all may hear it correctly. After everyone has a chance to find the page, the leader or other designated person sounds the pitches of the tonic and others, possibly the dyad or triad built on the tonic or the opening notes of all of the parts. The leader commences after the singers have had time to find their pitches. The notes (syllables Fa, Sol, La, and Mi) are sung first, then the words of one or more verses. At many singings, a leader is allotted two songs, but this depends on the time available and the number of leaders present. After finishing ("teaching a lesson"), the leader retires to his or her regular seat, making way for a new leader.

7. A recess of five minutes or more is taken every hour or so. After a recess, the chairman or vice chairman calls the singers ("class") back by standing in the hollow square, calling a number, and leading it. Those who are not in their seats hear the singing and soon take their places.

8. At the memorial lesson, usually just before lunch, the chairman of the memorial committee may make remarks, read the names of the deceased, and lead songs in their memory. These duties may be shared with others.

9. Where circumstances permit, dinner on the grounds is from 12 noon to 1 p.m. There is a blessing by the chaplain or another, after which all help themselves from a long table. Usually, the food is provided by local people, often by members of the host church or community.

10. HOLY MANNA (59) and PARTING HAND (62) are often, but by no means always, used as opening and closing songs.

BETHEL. C.M.

"And Enoch walked with God, and he was not, for God took him." -- Gen. 6:24.

F Minor William Cowper, 1772.

AYLESBURY. S.M.

"According to thy name, O God, so is thy praise unto the ends of the earth: thy right hand is full of righteousness." -- Ps. 48:10.

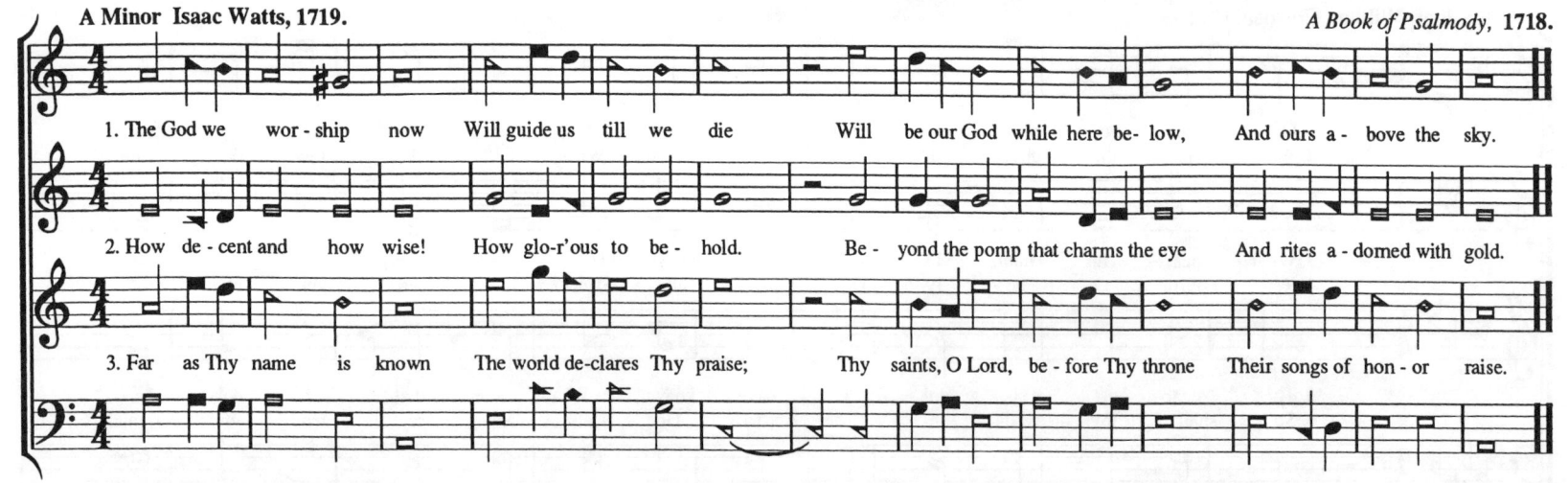

1. The God we worship now Will guide us till we die Will be our God while here be-low, And ours a-bove the sky.
2. How de-cent and how wise! How glo-r'ous to be-hold. Be-yond the pomp that charms the eye And rites a-domed with gold.
3. Far as Thy name is known The world de-clares Thy praise; Thy saints, O Lord, be-fore Thy throne Their songs of hon-or raise.

WELLS. L.M.

"But the day of the Lord will come as a thief in the night..." -- 2 Peter 3:10.

1. Life is the time to serve the Lord, The time t'in-sure the great re-ward; And while the lamp holds out to burn, The vil-est sin-ner may re-turn.
2. Life is the hour that God has giv'n To es-cape hell and fly to heav'n; The day of grace, and mor-tals may Se-cure the bless-ing of the day.
3. The liv-ing know that they must die, But all the dead for-got-ten lie; Their mem'ry and their sense is gone, A-like un-know-ing and un-known.

FAIRFIELD. C.M.

"And so I will go in unto the king . . . and if I perish, I perish." -- Esther 4:16.

A Minor Edmund Jones, 1787.   Hitchcock.

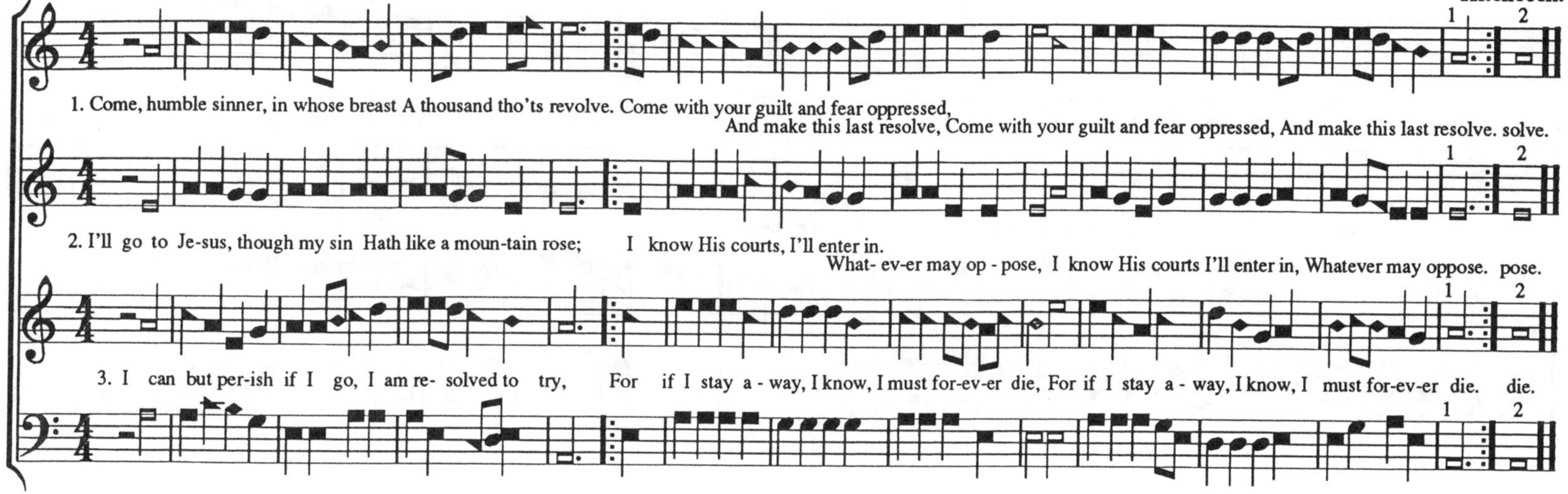

1. Come, humble sinner, in whose breast A thousand tho'ts revolve. Come with your guilt and fear oppressed, And make this last resolve, Come with your guilt and fear oppressed, And make this last resolve. solve.

2. I'll go to Je-sus, though my sin Hath like a moun-tain rose; I know His courts, I'll enter in. What-ev-er may op-pose, I know His courts I'll enter in, Whatever may oppose. pose.

3. I can but per-ish if I go, I am re-solved to try, For if I stay a-way, I know, I must for-ev-er die, For if I stay a-way, I know, I must for-ev-er die. die.

TRIBULATION. C.M.

"O magnify the Lord with me, and let us exalt his name together." -- Ps. 34:3.

D Minor Isaac Watts, 1709.   *Patterson's Church Music,* **1813.**

1. Death, 'tis a mel-an-chol-y day To those who have no God, When the poor soul is forced a-way To seek her last a-bode.

2. In vain to heav'n she lifts her eyes, For guilt, a heav-y chain, Still drags her down-ward from the skies To dark-ness, fire, and pain.

29

LOVE DIVINE. 8 & 7.

"God is love; and he that dwelleth in love dwelleth in God, and God in him." -- 1 John 4:16.

C Major Charles Wesley, 1747.
Thomas Waller, 1869.
D.C.

Love divine, all love excelling, Joy of heav'n to earth come down; Jesus, Thou art all compassion, Pure, unbounded love Thou art;
Fix in us Thy humble dwelling, All Thy faithful mercies crown!
Visit us with Thy salvation; Enter ev'ry trembling heart.

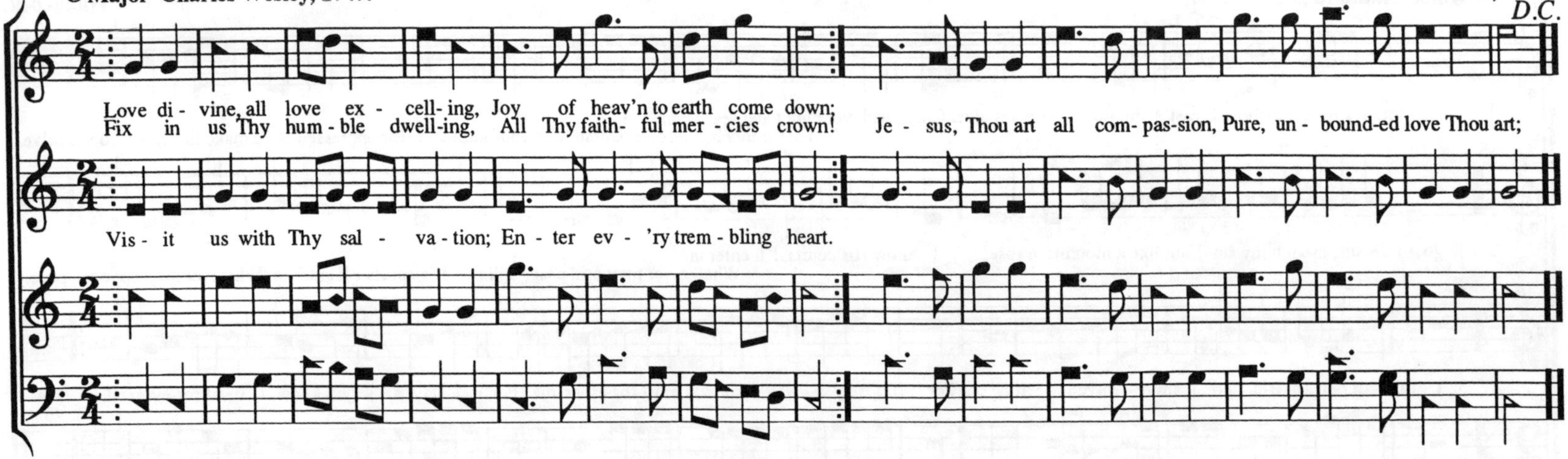

PROSPECT. L.M.

"Blessed are the dead who die in the Lord." -- Rev. 14:13.

C Major Isaac Watts, 1707.
Graham, 1835.

1. Why should we start and fear to die? What tim-'rous worms we mortals are! Death is the gate to endless joy, And yet we dread to enter there.

2. The pains, the groans, the dying strife, Fright our approaching souls away; And we shrink back again to life, Fond of our prison and our clay.

3. O if my Lord would come and meet, My soul would stretch her wings in haste, Fly fearless through death's iron gate, Nor feel the terrors as she passed.

4. Jesus can make a dying bed Feel soft as downy pillows are; While on His breast I lean my head, And breathe my life out sweetly there.

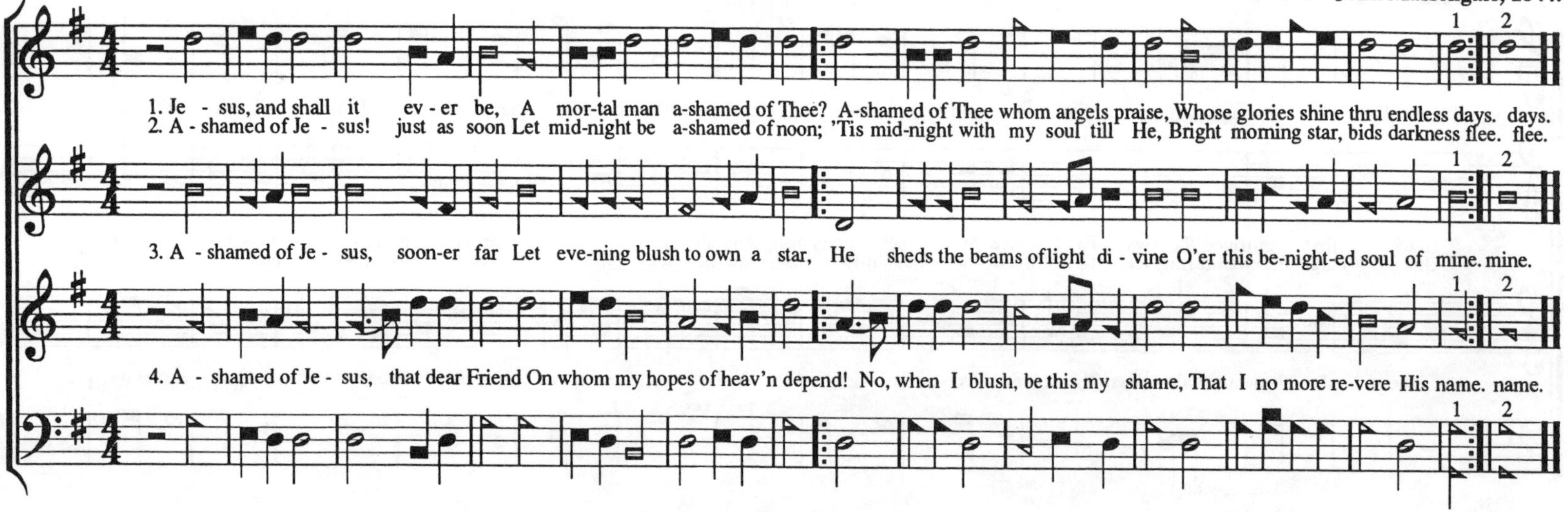

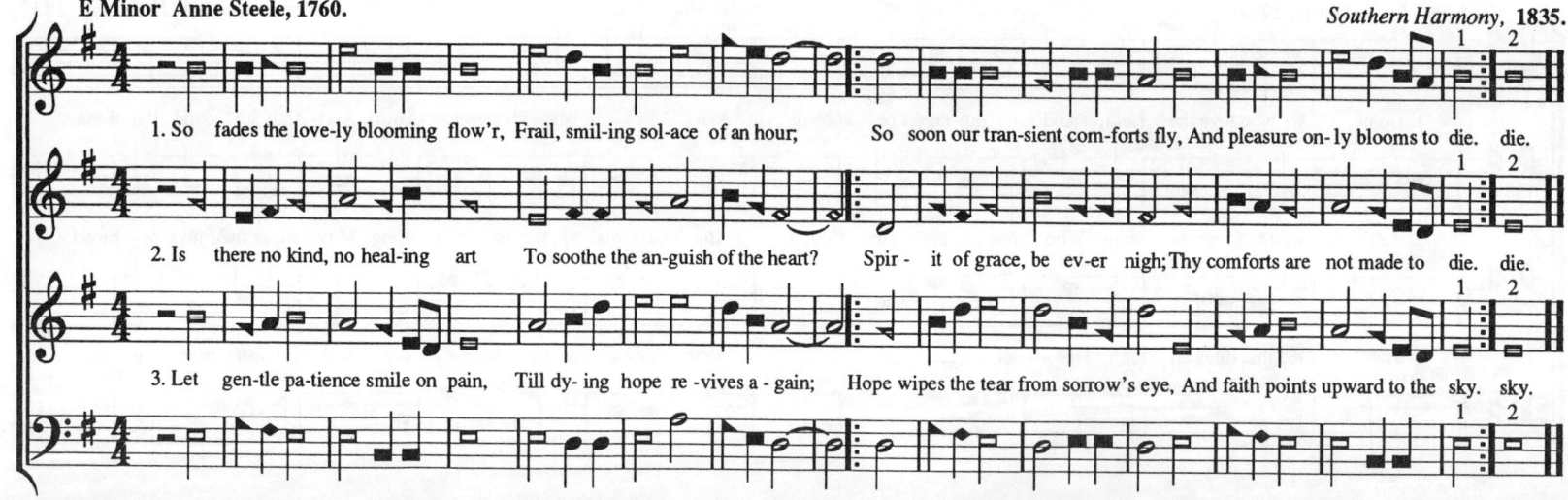

WEEPING SAVIOR (First). S.M.

"And when he was come near, he beheld the city and wept over it." -- Luke 19:41.

F# Minor Benjamin Beddome, 1787.
Arr. - E. J. King, 1844.

1. Did Christ o'er sin-ners weep? And shall our cheeks be dry? Let floods of pen-i-ten-tial grief Burst forth from ev-'ry eye. eye.
2. The Son of God in tears The won-d'ring an-gels see; Be thou as-ton-ished, O my soul, He shed those tears for thee. thee.
3. He wept that we might weep; Each sin de-mands a tear; In heav'n a-lone no sin is found, And there's no weep-ing there. there.

ABBEVILLE. S.M.

"They were all filled with the Holy Ghost, and they spake the word of God with boldness." -- Acts 4:31.

G Major Benjamin Beddome, 1800.
Arr. - E. J. King, 1844.

1. Come, Ho-ly Spir-it, come With en-er-gy di-vine, And on this poor, be-night-ed soul With beams of mer-cy shine. shine.
2. Melt, melt this fro-zen heart; This stub-born will sub-due; Each e-vil pas-sion o-ver-come, And form me all a-new. new.
3. Mine will the prof-it be, But Thine shall be the praise; And un-to Thee will I de-vote The rem-nant of my days. days.

THE GOSPEL POOL. S.M.
"Expectation of the poor shall not perish for ever." -- Ps. 9:18.

F Major John Newton, 1779.
Edmund Dumas, 1869.

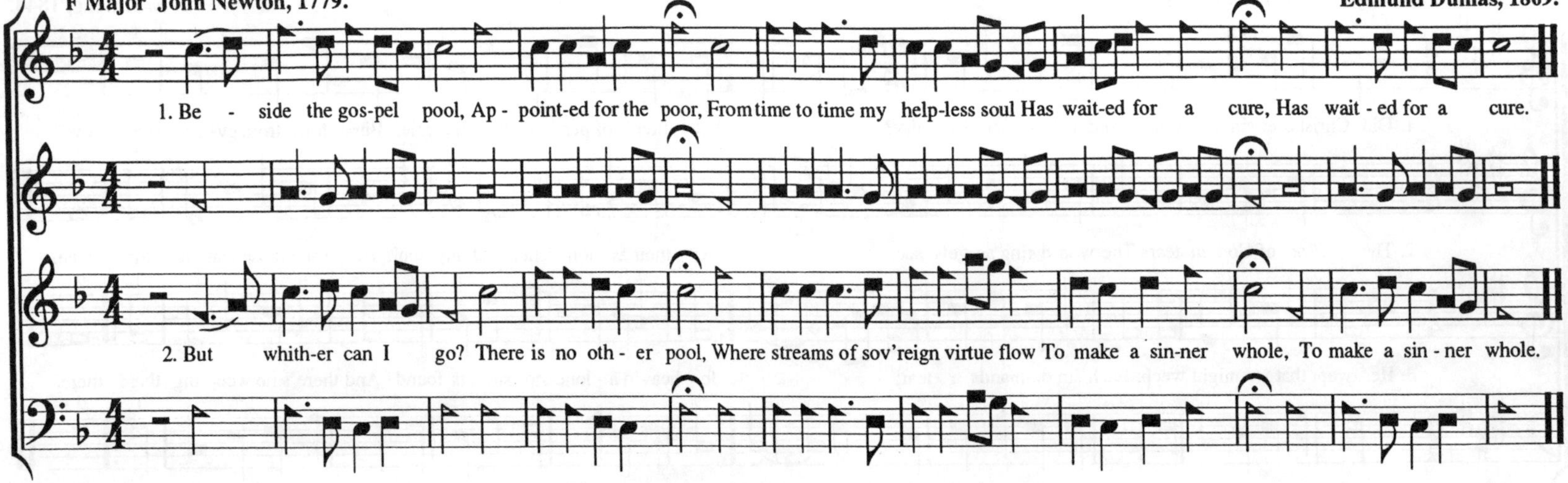

1. Be - side the gos - pel pool, Ap - point - ed for the poor, From time to time my help - less soul Has wait - ed for a cure, Has wait - ed for a cure.

2. But whith - er can I go? There is no oth - er pool, Where streams of sov - 'reign virtue flow To make a sin - ner whole, To make a sin - ner whole.

ST. THOMAS. S.M.
"Sing unto the Lord, bless his name." -- Ps. 96:2.

A Major Isaac Watts, 1719.
Aaron Williams, 1770.

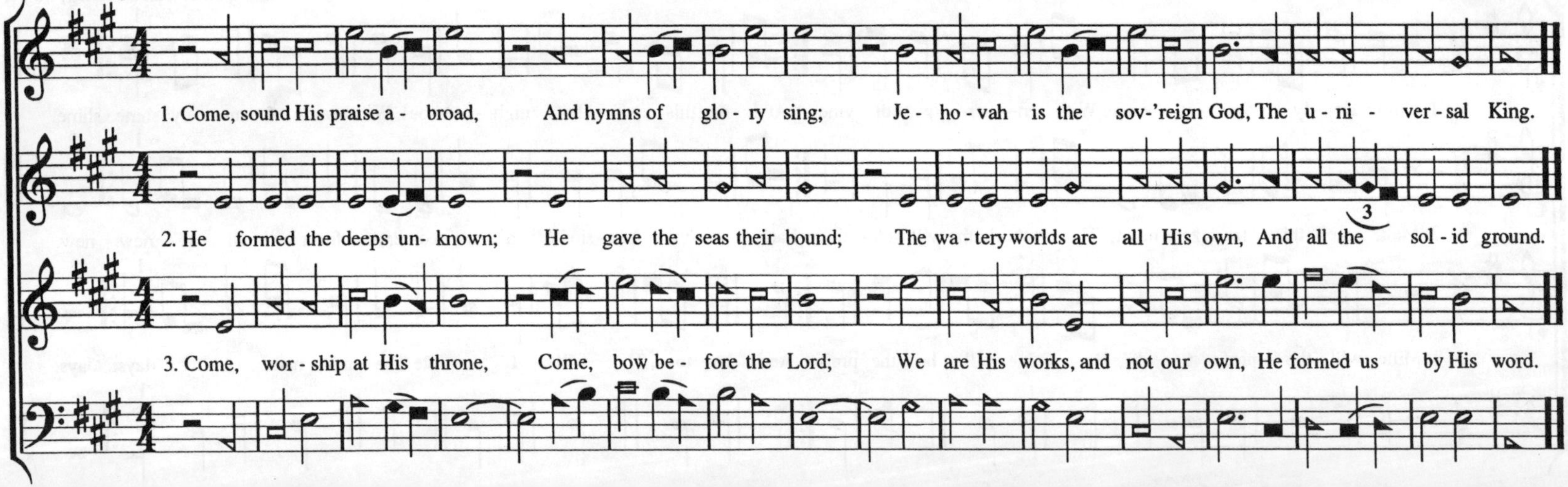

1. Come, sound His praise a - broad, And hymns of glo - ry sing; Je - ho - vah is the sov - 'reign God, The u - ni - ver - sal King.

2. He formed the deeps un - known; He gave the seas their bound; The wa - tery worlds are all His own, And all the sol - id ground.

3. Come, wor - ship at His throne, Come, bow be - fore the Lord; We are His works, and not our own, He formed us by His word.

AMERICA. S.M.

A Minor Isaac Watts, 1719.

"The Lord is merciful and gracious, slow to anger, and plenteous in mercy." -- Ps. 103:8.

Truman S. Wetmore, 1798.

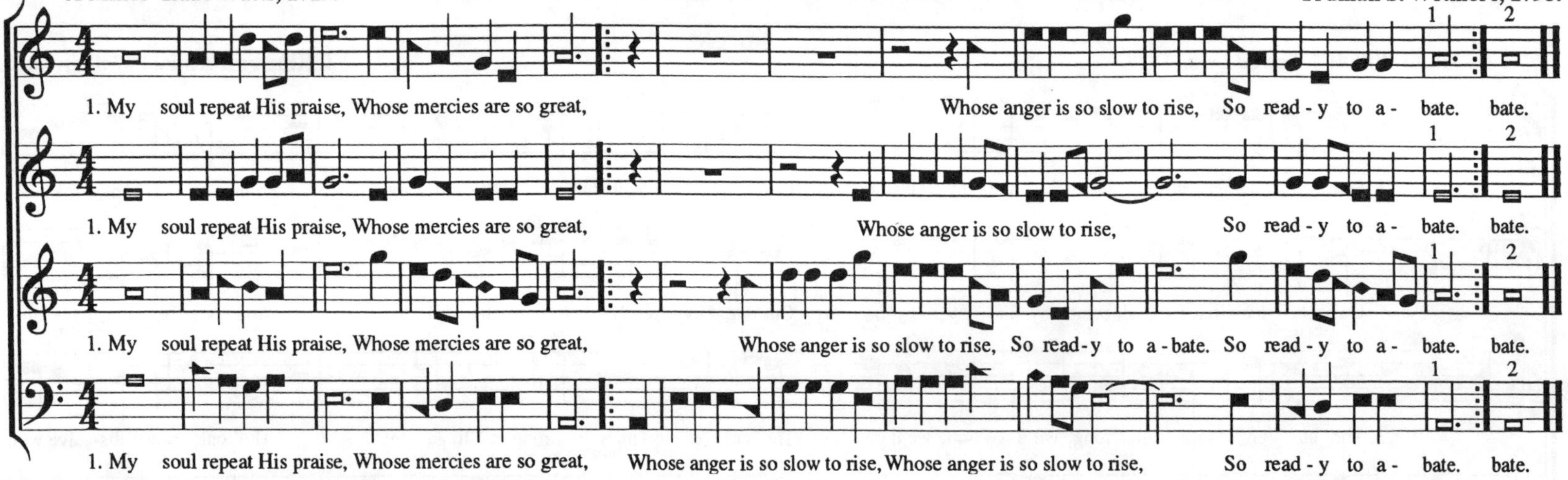
1 2
1. My soul repeat His praise, Whose mercies are so great, Whose anger is so slow to rise, So read - y to a - bate. bate.
1 2
1. My soul repeat His praise, Whose mercies are so great, Whose anger is so slow to rise, So read - y to a - bate. bate.
1 2
1. My soul repeat His praise, Whose mercies are so great, Whose anger is so slow to rise, So read-y to a-bate. So read - y to a - bate. bate.
1 2
1. My soul repeat His praise, Whose mercies are so great, Whose anger is so slow to rise, Whose anger is so slow to rise, So read - y to a - bate. bate.

2. High as the heav'ns are raised, Above the ground we tread,
So far the riches of His grace, Our highest tho'ts exceed.

3. His pow'r subdues our sins, And His forgiving love,
Far as the east is from the west, Doth all our guilt remove.

NINETY-FIFTH. C.M.

"Give dilligence to make your calling and election sure: for if ye do these things, ye shall never fall." -- 2 Pet. 1:10.

A Major Isaac Watts, 1707.

Patterson's Church Music, 1813.

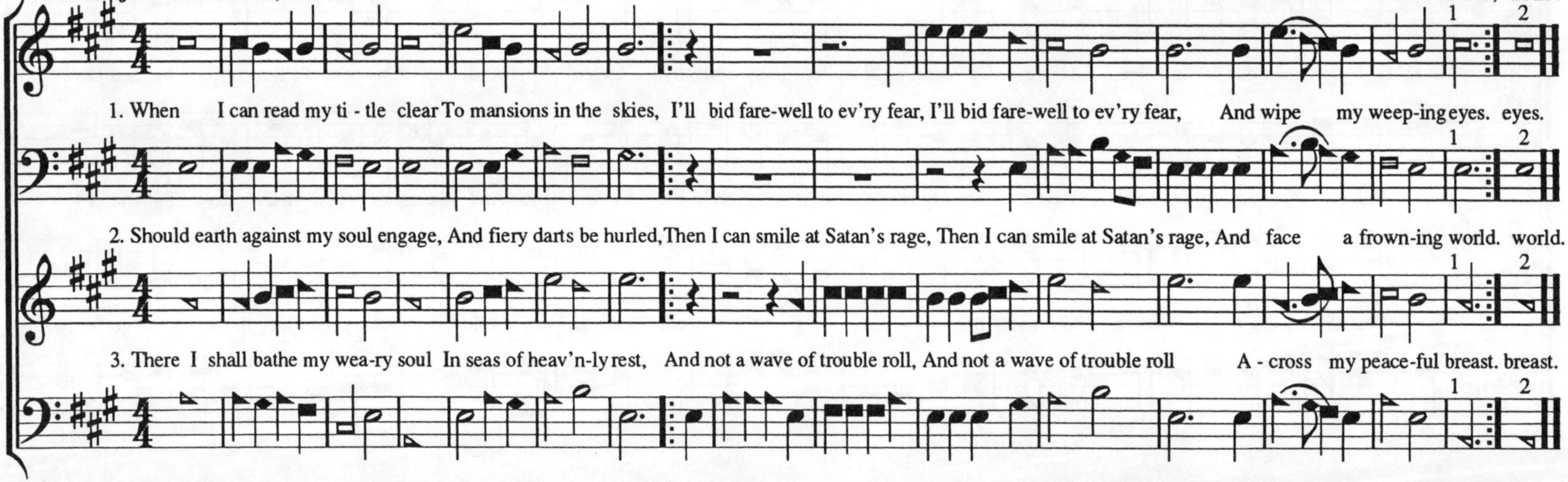
1 2
1. When I can read my ti - tle clear To mansions in the skies, I'll bid fare-well to ev'ry fear, I'll bid fare-well to ev'ry fear, And wipe my weep-ing eyes. eyes.
1 2
2. Should earth against my soul engage, And fiery darts be hurled, Then I can smile at Satan's rage, Then I can smile at Satan's rage, And face a frown-ing world. world.
1 2
3. There I shall bathe my wea-ry soul In seas of heav'n-ly rest, And not a wave of trouble roll, And not a wave of trouble roll A - cross my peace-ful breast. breast.
1 2

ESTER. L.M.

"Flee also youthful lusts... call on the Lord out of a pure heart." -- 2 Tim. 2:22.

F Major *Hall's New Collection, 1804.* John S. Terry, 1869.

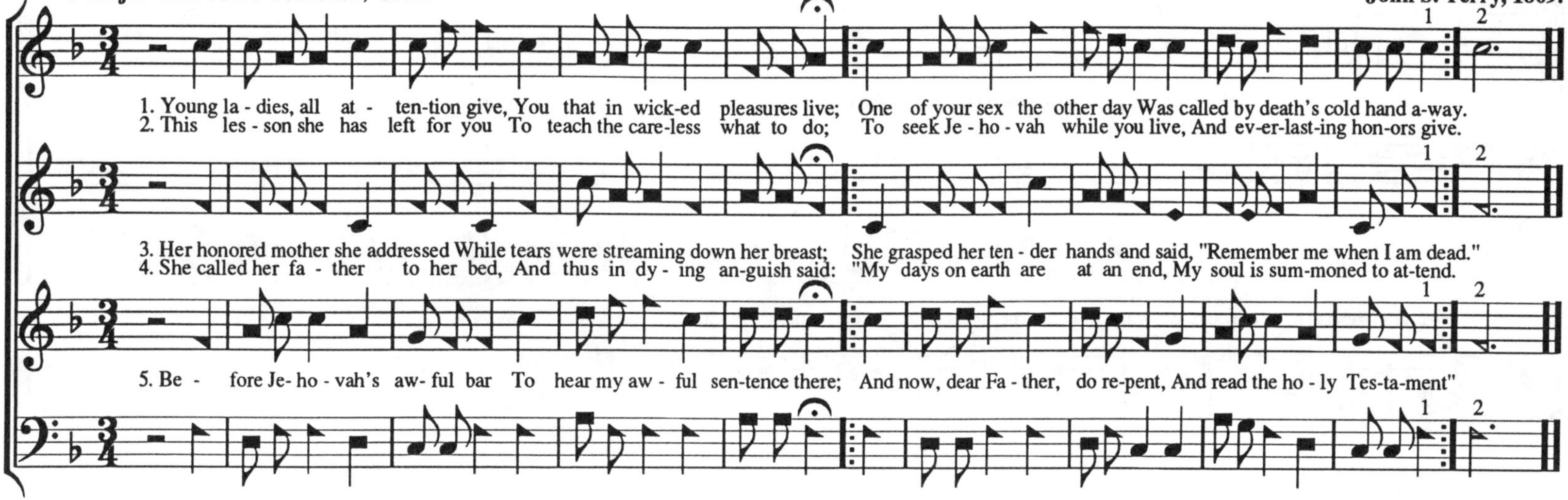

1. Young la-dies, all at-ten-tion give, You that in wick-ed pleasures live; One of your sex the other day Was called by death's cold hand a-way.
2. This les-son she has left for you To teach the care-less what to do; To seek Je-ho-vah while you live, And ev-er-last-ing hon-ors give.
3. Her honored mother she addressed While tears were streaming down her breast; She grasped her ten-der hands and said, "Remember me when I am dead."
4. She called her fa-ther to her bed, And thus in dy-ing an-guish said: "My days on earth are at an end, My soul is sum-moned to at-tend.
5. Be-fore Je-ho-vah's aw-ful bar To hear my aw-ful sen-tence there; And now, dear Fa-ther, do re-pent, And read the ho-ly Tes-ta-ment"

LIVERPOOL. C.M.

"Remember now thy Creator in the days of thy youth." -- Ecc. 12:1.

F Major *Hall's New Collection, 1804.* Arr. - M. C. H. Davis, 1835.

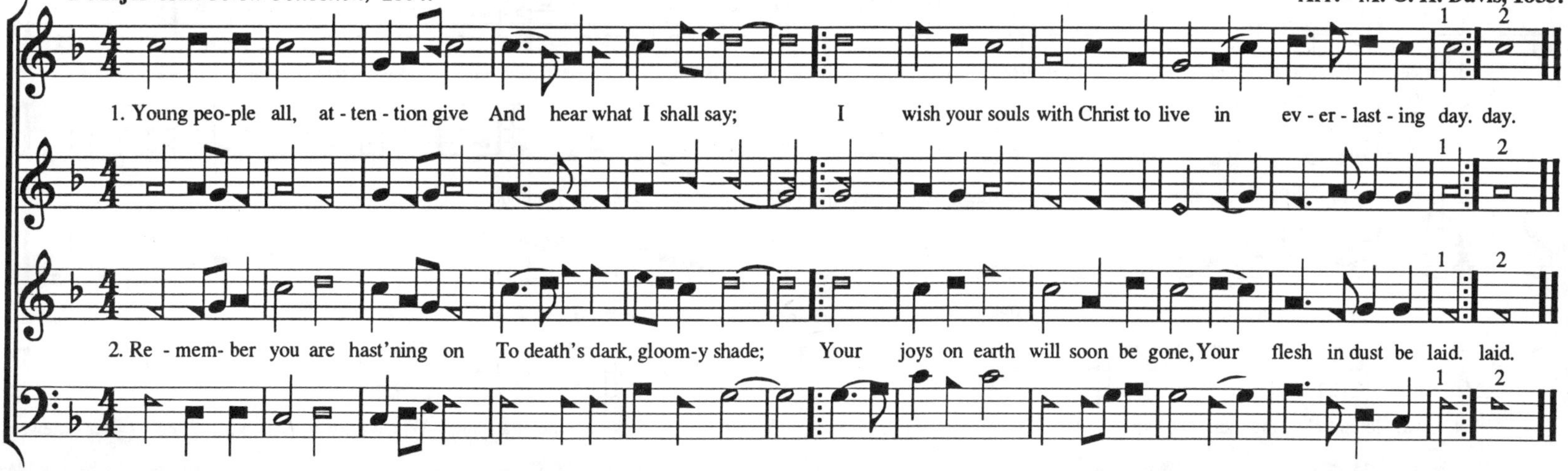

1. Young peo-ple all, at-ten-tion give And hear what I shall say; I wish your souls with Christ to live in ev-er-last-ing day. day.
2. Re-mem-ber you are hast'ning on To death's dark, gloom-y shade; Your joys on earth will soon be gone, Your flesh in dust be laid. laid.

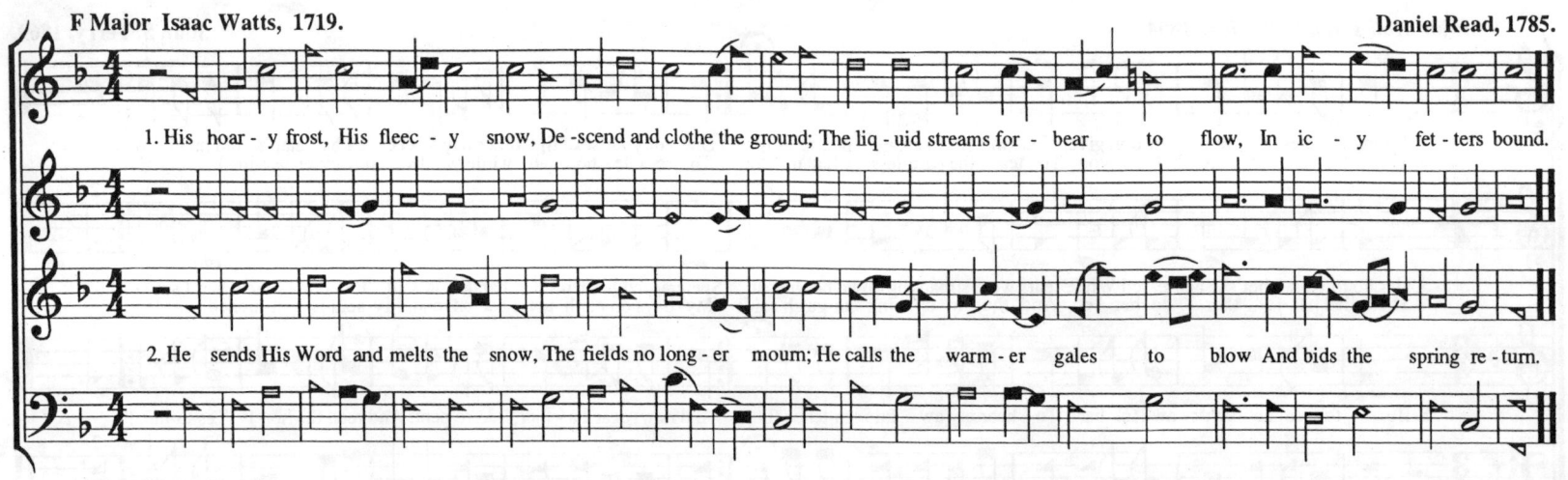

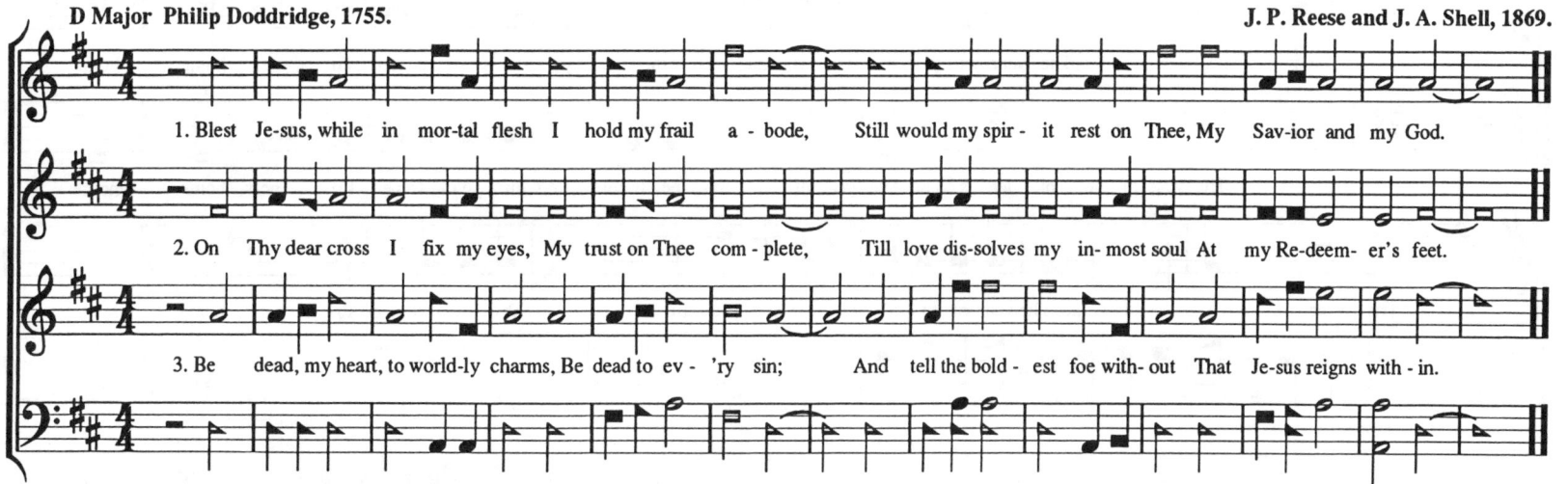

CLAMANDA. L.M.D.

"If the Lord delight in us, then he will bring us into his land, and give it to us." -- Num. 14:8.

E Minor *Collection of Hymns and Spiritual Songs,* **1814.**

Say, now ye love-ly so-cial band Who walk the way to Ca-naan's land;
Ye who have fled from Sod-om's plain, Say, do you wish to turn a-gain? O have you ven-tured to the field, Well-armed with hel-met, sword and shield? And shall the world, with dread a-larms, Com-pel you now to ground your arms?

PRIMROSE HILL. C.M.

"Give dilligence to make your calling and election sure: for if ye do these things, ye shall never fall." -- 2 Pet. 1:10.

G Major Isaac Watts, 1707.

NEW BRITAIN. C.M.

"And David the king came and sat before the Lord, and said, Who am I, O Lord?" -- 1 Chron. 17:16.

C Major John Newton, 1779. *Columbian Harmony*, 1829.

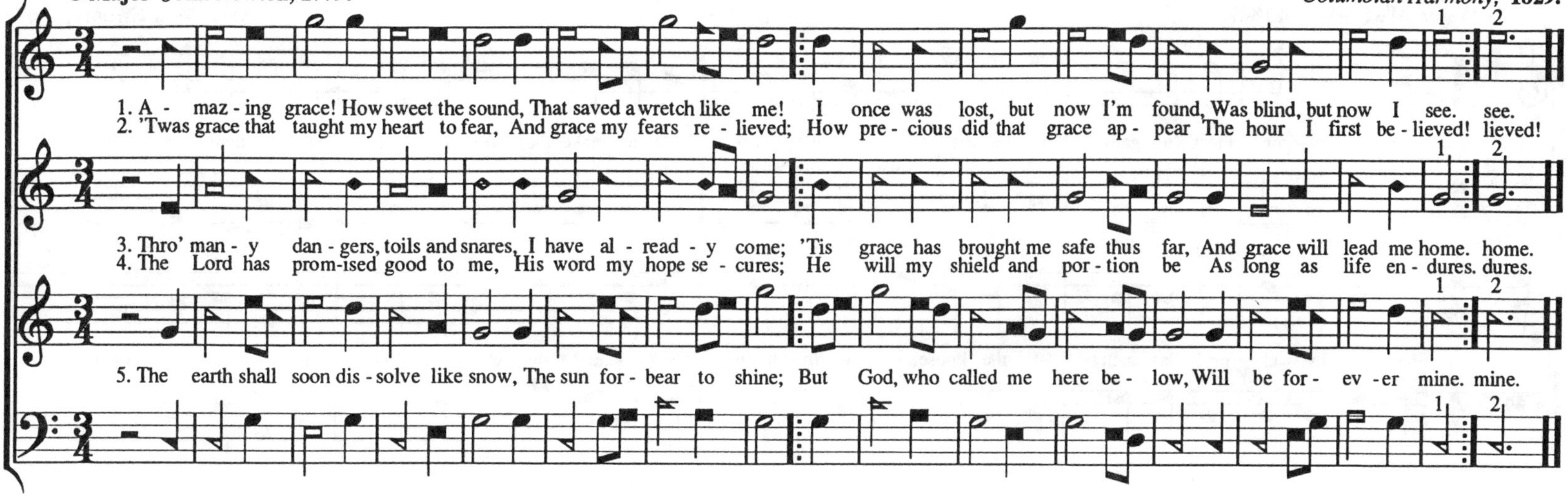
1. A - maz - ing grace! How sweet the sound, That saved a wretch like me! I once was lost, but now I'm found, Was blind, but now I see. see.
2. 'Twas grace that taught my heart to fear, And grace my fears re - lieved; How pre - cious did that grace ap - pear The hour I first be - lieved! lieved!
3. Thro' man - y dan - gers, toils and snares, I have al - read - y come; 'Tis grace has brought me safe thus far, And grace will lead me home. home.
4. The Lord has prom-ised good to me, His word my hope se - cures; He will my shield and por - tion be As long as life en - dures. dures.
5. The earth shall soon dis - solve like snow, The sun for - bear to shine; But God, who called me here be - low, Will be for - ev - er mine. mine.

IMANDRA NEW. 11s.

"He that loveth not his brother abideth in death." -- 1 John 3:14.

F Major Thomas Cleland, 1807. *Southern Harmony*, 1835.

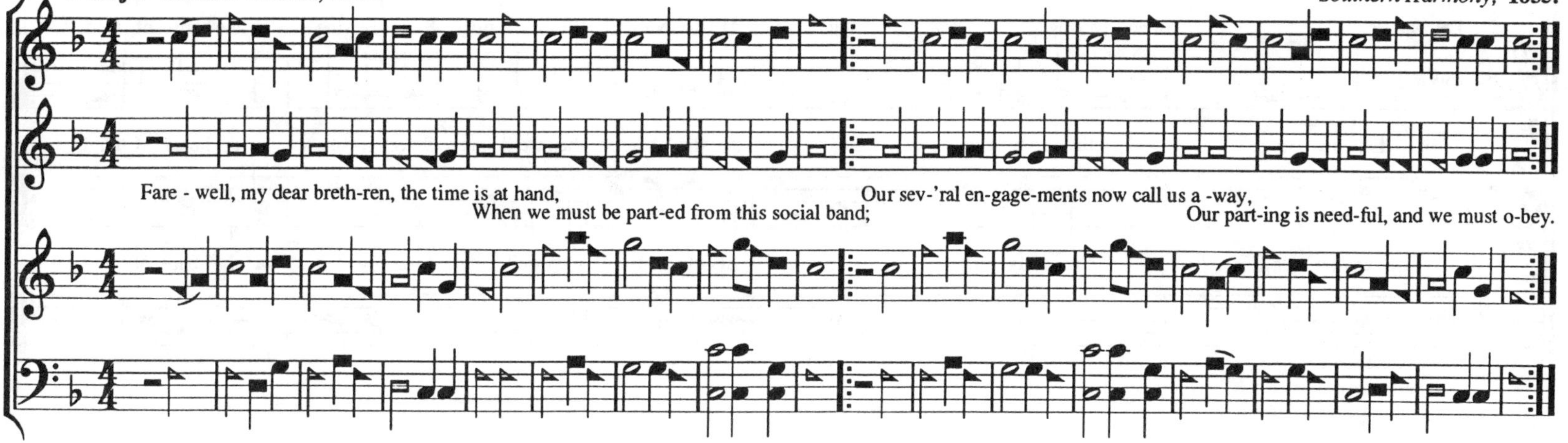
Fare - well, my dear breth-ren, the time is at hand,
When we must be part-ed from this social band;
Our sev-'ral en-gage-ments now call us a -way,
Our part-ing is need-ful, and we must o-bey.

LET US SING.

Meet in "a house not made with hands, eternal in the heavens." -- 2 Cor. 5:1.

G Major W. F. Moore, 1867.   Arr. - W. F. Moore, 1867.

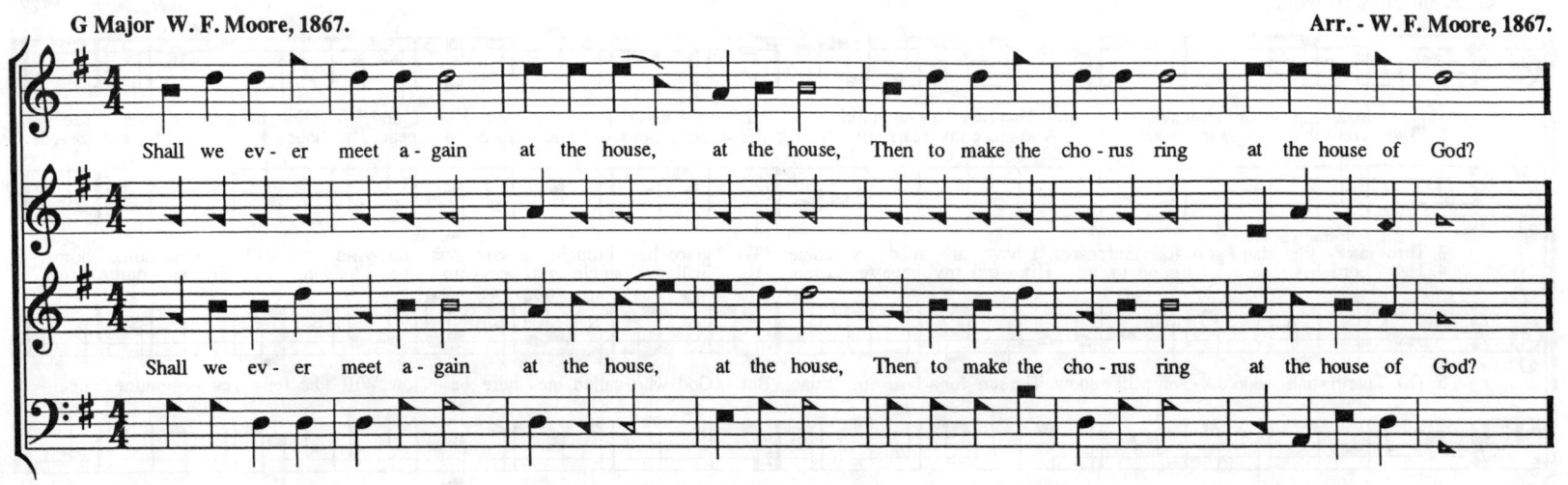

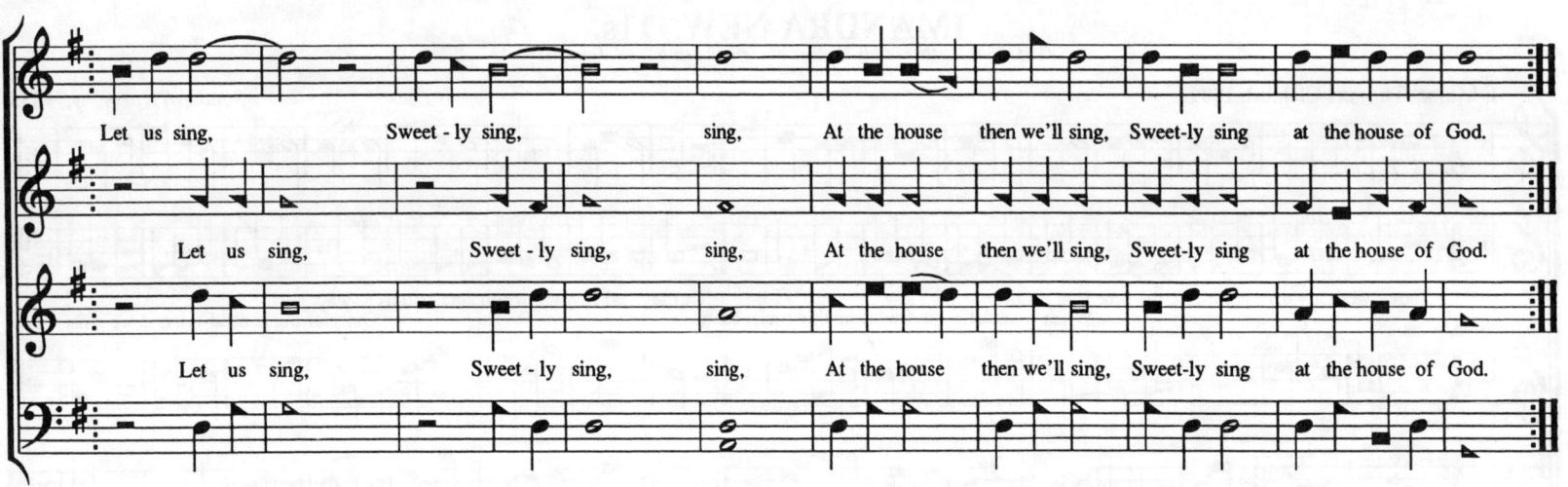

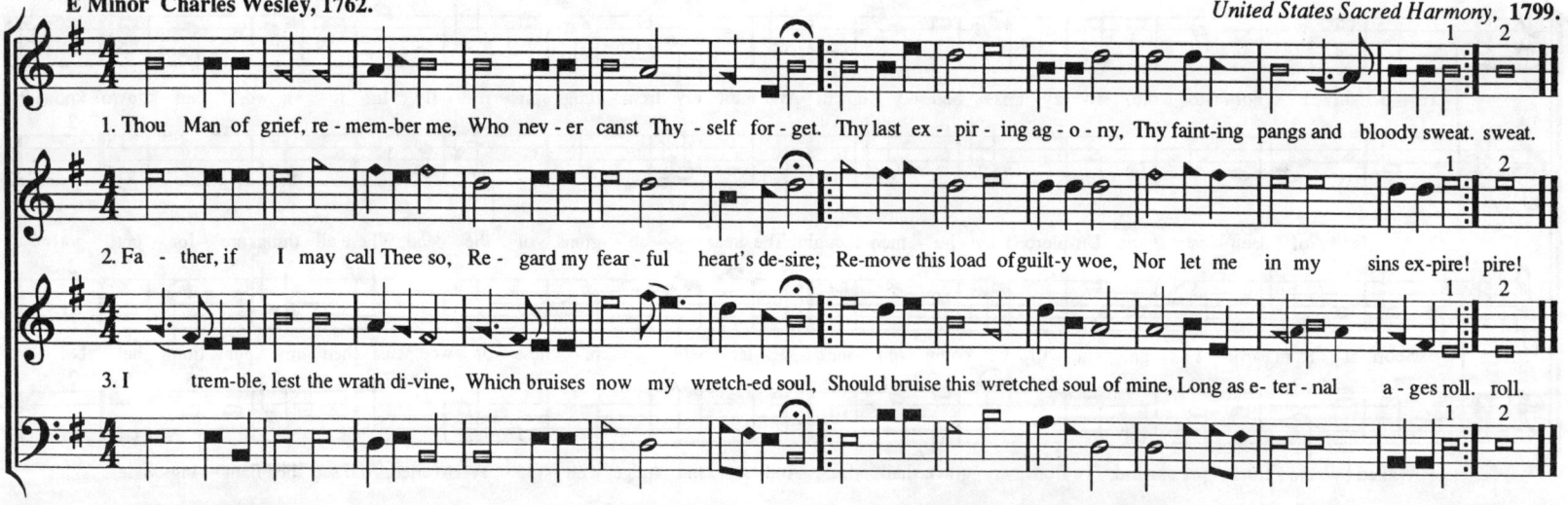

OLD HUNDRED. L.M.

"Sing, O ye heavens... shout, ye lower parts of the earth: break forth into singing, ye mountains, O forest and every tree therein." -- Isa. 44:23.

A Major *New Version*, 1696.   *Psaumes de David,* 1551.

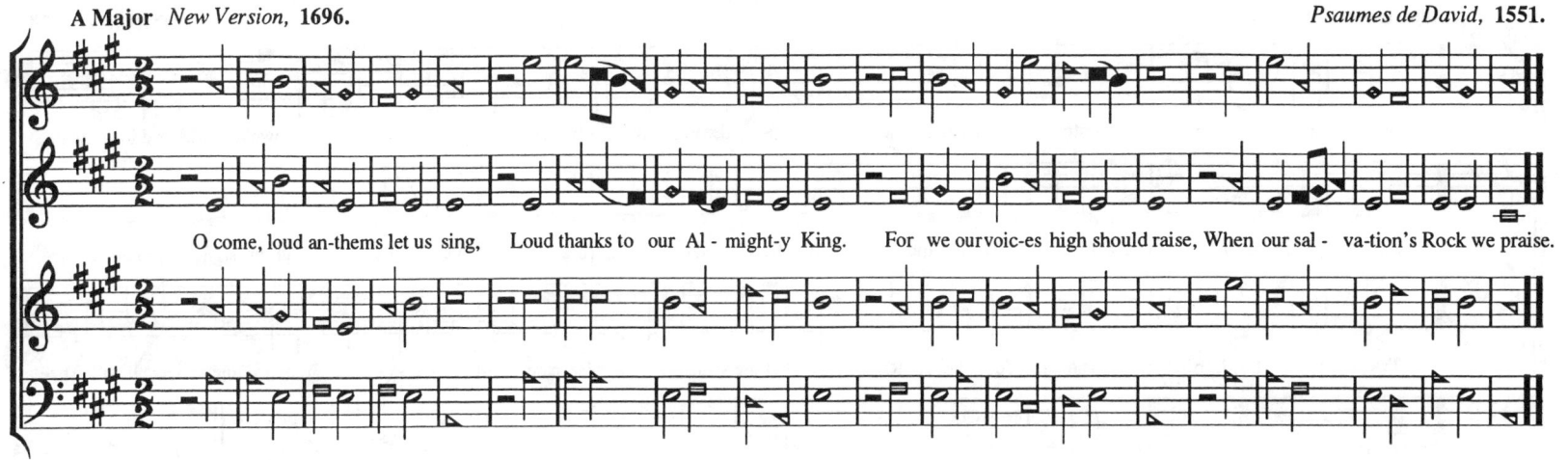

O come, loud an-thems let us sing, Loud thanks to our Al - might-y King. For we our voic-es high should raise, When our sal - va-tion's Rock we praise.

MEAR. C.M.

"What if God, willing to show his wrath, and to make his power known, endured with much long-suffering? -- Rom. 9:22.

G Major *Isaac Watts,* 1719.   *A Sett Of Tunes,* 1720.

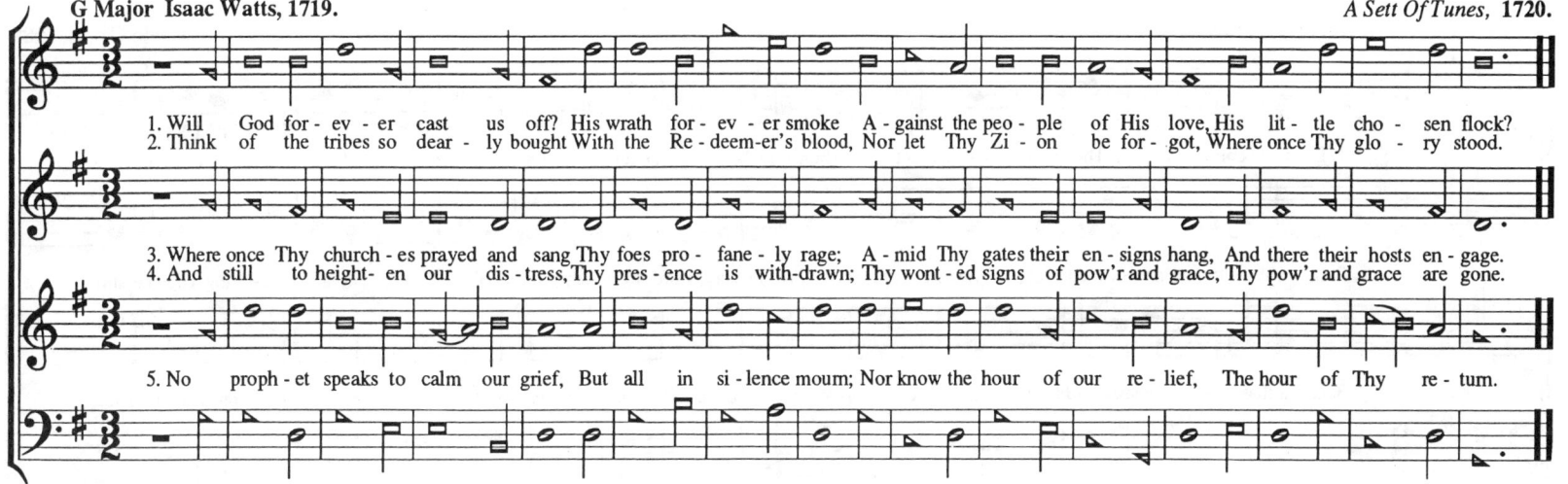

1. Will God for - ev - er cast us off? His wrath for - ev - er smoke A - gainst the peo - ple of His love, His lit - tle cho - sen flock?
2. Think of the tribes so dear - ly bought With the Re - deem-er's blood, Nor let Thy Zi - on be for - got, Where once Thy glo - ry stood.
3. Where once Thy church - es prayed and sang Thy foes pro - fane - ly rage; A - mid Thy gates their en - signs hang, And there their hosts en - gage.
4. And still to height - en our dis - tress, Thy pres - ence is with-drawn; Thy wont - ed signs of pow'r and grace, Thy pow'r and grace are gone.
5. No proph - et speaks to calm our grief, But all in si - lence mourn; Nor know the hour of our re - lief, The hour of Thy re - turn.

MY HOME (First). C.M.
"Thine eyes shall behold the land." -- Isa. 33:17.

ALBION. S.M.

"Where two or three are gathered together in my name, there am I in the midst of them." -- Matt. 18:20.

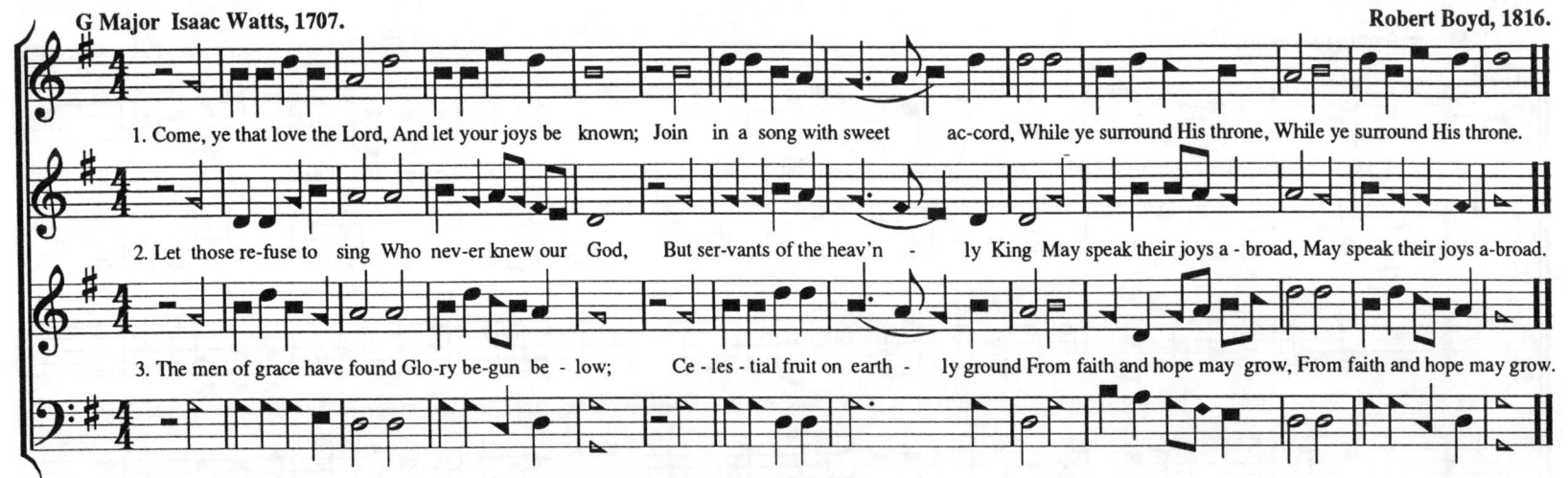

1. Come, ye that love the Lord, And let your joys be known; Join in a song with sweet ac-cord, While ye surround His throne, While ye surround His throne.
2. Let those re-fuse to sing Who nev-er knew our God, But ser-vants of the heav'n-ly King May speak their joys a-broad, May speak their joys a-broad.
3. The men of grace have found Glo-ry be-gun be-low; Ce-les-tial fruit on earth-ly ground From faith and hope may grow, From faith and hope may grow.

CHARLESTOWN. 8s, 7s.

"Jesus, thou Son of David, have mercy on me. And many charged him that he should hold his peace." -- Mark 10:47, 48.

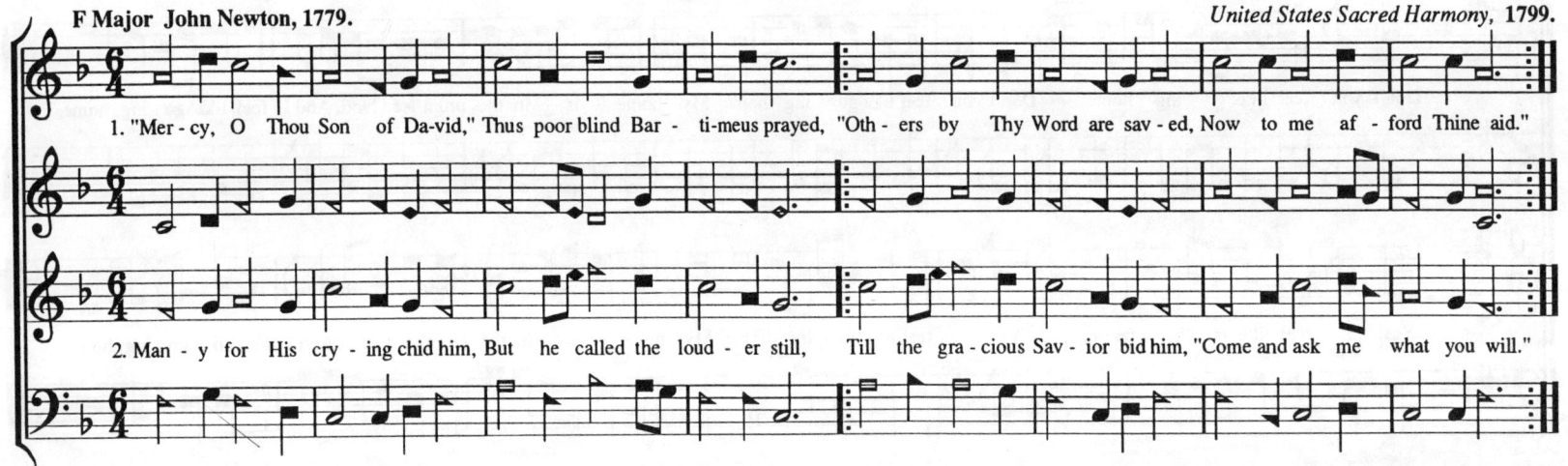

1. "Mer-cy, O Thou Son of Da-vid," Thus poor blind Bar-ti-meus prayed, "Oth-ers by Thy Word are sav-ed, Now to me af-ford Thine aid."
2. Man-y for His cry-ing chid him, But he called the loud-er still, Till the gra-cious Sav-ior bid him, "Come and ask me what you will."

THE BLESSED LAMB. 8s & 7s.

"Make sweet melody, sing many songs, that thou mayest be remembered." -- Isa. 23:16.

See the hap-py fac-es wait-ing, On the banks be-yond the stream; Je-sus, Je-sus is their theme. See, they whis-per; Hark! they call me, Sis-ter spir-it, come a-way;
Sweet re-spons-es still re-peat-ing,

Lo, I come, earth can't con-tain me; Hail, ye realms of endless day! Hail, hail, hail, hail, hail the bless-ed Lamb; Glo-ry, glo-ry, glo-ry to His name.

COLUMBIANA. 8,7.

"And God is able to make all grace abound toward you." -- 2 Cor. 9:8.

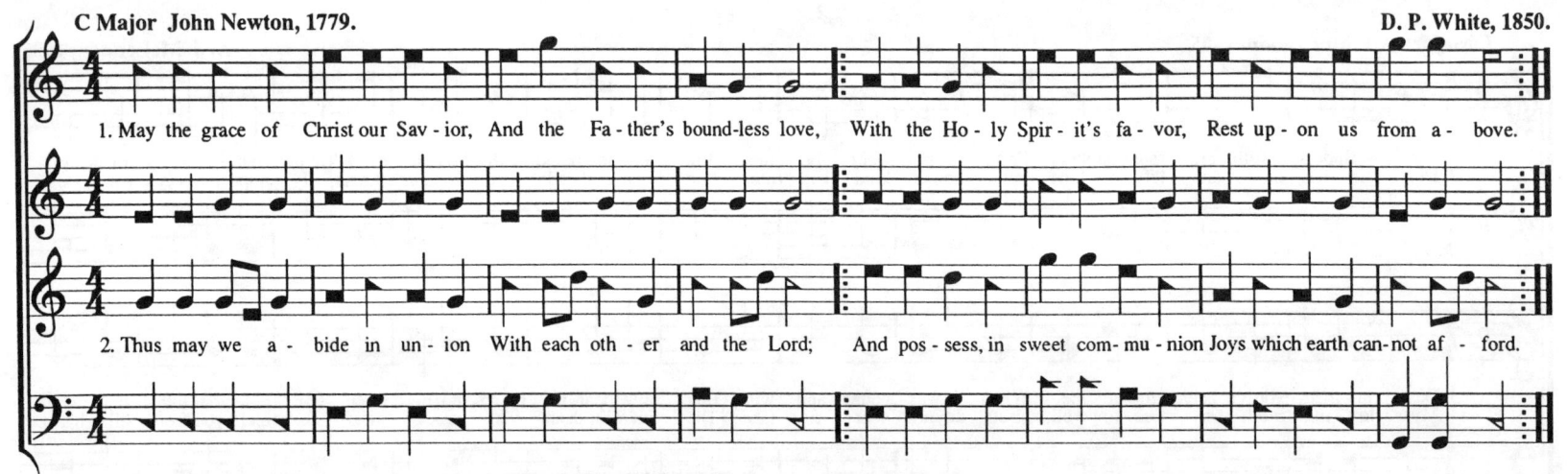

1. May the grace of Christ our Savior, And the Father's boundless love, With the Holy Spirit's favor, Rest upon us from above.
2. Thus may we abide in union With each other and the Lord; And possess, in sweet communion Joys which earth cannot afford.

VILLULIA. 8,7.

"Because of the blindness of their heart." -- Eph. 4:18.

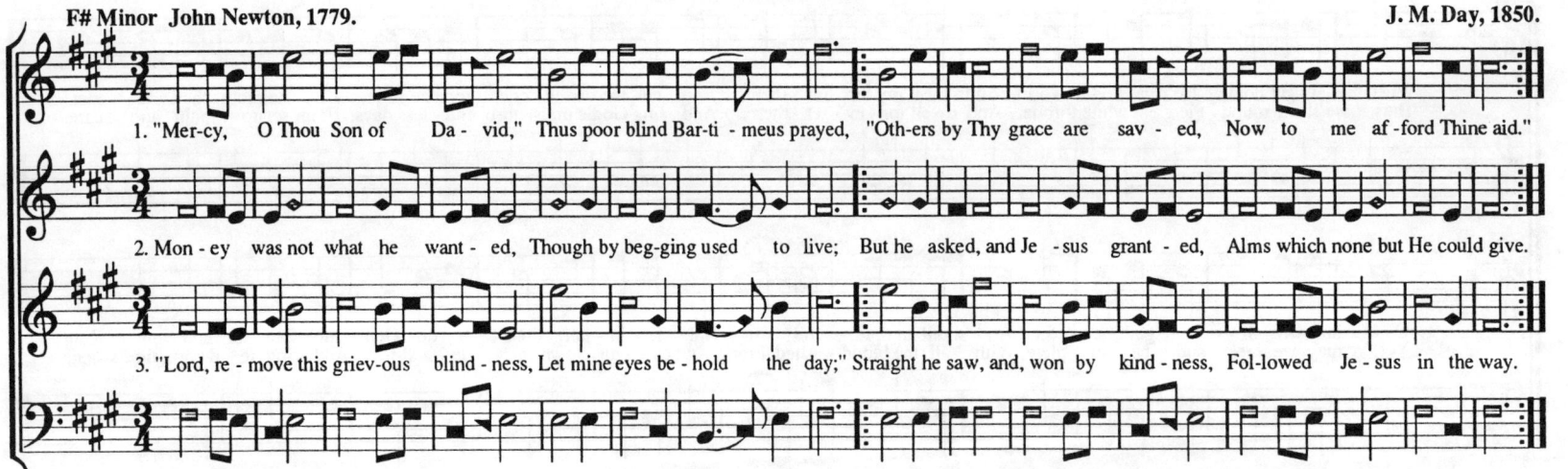

1. "Mercy, O Thou Son of David," Thus poor blind Bartimeus prayed, "Others by Thy grace are saved, Now to me afford Thine aid."
2. Money was not what he wanted, Though by begging used to live; But he asked, and Jesus granted, Alms which none but He could give.
3. "Lord, remove this grievous blindness, Let mine eyes behold the day;" Straight he saw, and, won by kindness, Followed Jesus in the way.

CHRISTIAN SOLDIER. C.M.

"Watch ye, stand fast in the faith, quit you like men, be strong." -- 1 Cor. 16:13.

G Major Isaac Watts, 1724.

F. Price, 1835.

HOLY MANNA. 8s & 7s.

"Worship the Lord in the beauty of holiness." -- Ps. 29:2.

C Major George Atkin, 1819.
William Moore, 1825.

1. Breth-ren, we have met to wor-ship, And a-dore the Lord our God;
All is vain un-less the Spir-it of the Ho-ly One comes down; Breth-ren, pray and holy man-na Will be show-ered all a-round.
Will you pray with all your pow-er, While we try to preach the word?

2. Brethren, see poor sinners round you,
    Trembling on the brink of woe;
Death is coming, hell is moving,
    Can you bear to let them go?
See our fathers, see our mothers,
    And our children sinking down;
Brethren, pray and holy manna
    Will be showered all around.

3. Sisters, will you join and help us?
    Moses' sisters aided him;
Will you help the trembling mourners,
    Who are struggling hard with sin?
Tell them all about the Saviour,
    Tell them that He will be found;
Sisters, pray, and holy manna
    Will be showered all around.

4. Is there here a trembling jailer,
    Seeking grace, and filled with fears?
Is there here a weeping Mary,
    Pouring forth a flood of tears?
Brethren, join your cries to help them;
    Sisters, let your prayers abound;
Pray, O pray that holy manna
    May be scattered all around.

5. Let us love our God supremely,
    Let us love each other, too;
Let us love and pray for sinners,
    Till our God makes all things new.
Then He'll call us home to heaven,
    At His table we'll sit down;
Christ will gird Himself, and serve us
    With sweet manna all around.

DAY OF WORSHIP. L.M.D.

"When ye come together, every one of you hath a psalm, hath a doctrine, hath a tongue, hath a revelation, hath an interpretation." -- 1 Cor. 14:26.

G Major Anonymous. R. F. & E. K. Davis, 1848

1. Dear peo-ple, we have met to-day To sing, to hear, to preach and pray;
It is our Fa-ther's great com-mand, The road that leads to His right hand; But oh, the sad and aw-ful state, Of those who stand and come too late, The fool-ish vir-gins did be-gin To knock, but could not en-ter in.

PARTING HAND. L.M.

"But as touching brotherly love ye need not that I write unto you: for ye yourselves are taught of God to love one another." -- 1 Thes. 4:9.

G Major John Blain, 1818.
Arr. - William Walker, 1835.

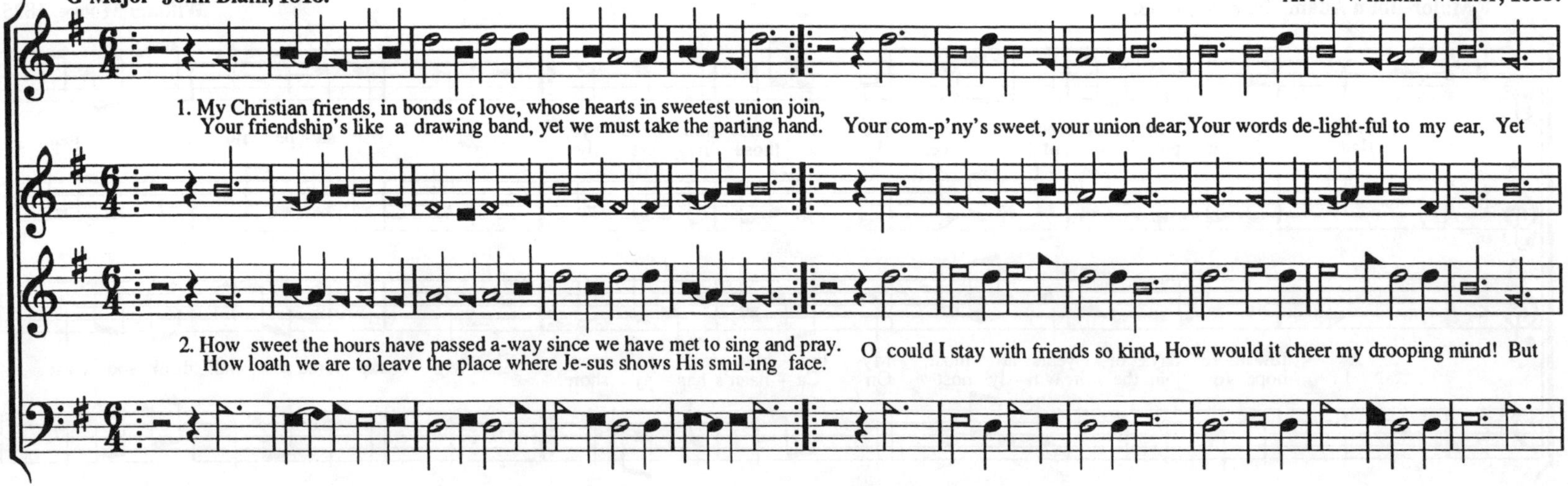

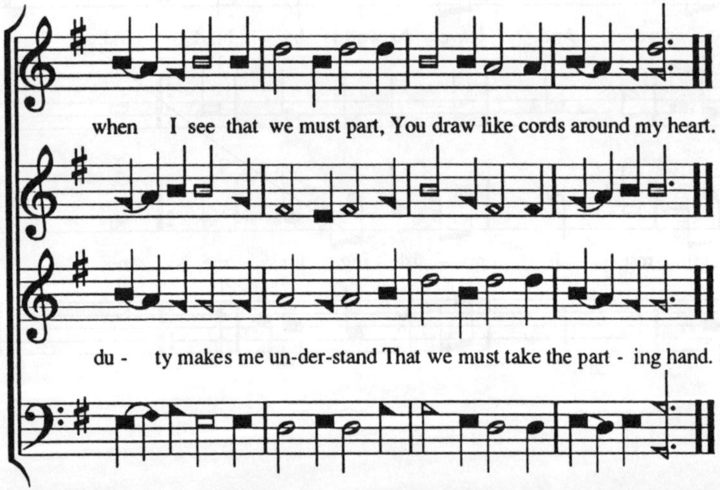

1. My Christian friends, in bonds of love, whose hearts in sweetest union join,
Your friendship's like a drawing band, yet we must take the parting hand.
Your com-p'ny's sweet, your union dear; Your words de-light-ful to my ear, Yet when I see that we must part, You draw like cords around my heart.

2. How sweet the hours have passed a-way since we have met to sing and pray.
How loath we are to leave the place where Je-sus shows His smil-ing face.
O could I stay with friends so kind, How would it cheer my drooping mind! But du-ty makes me un-der-stand That we must take the part-ing hand.

3. And since it is God's holy will,
We must be parted for a while,
In sweet submission, all as one,
We'll say, our Father's will be done.

My youthful friends, in Christian ties,
Who seek for mansions in the skies,
Fight on, we'll gain that happy shore,
Where parting will be known no more.

4. How oft I've seen your flowing tears,
And heard you tell your hopes and fears!
Your hearts with love were seen to flame,
Which makes me hope we'll meet again.

Ye mourning souls, lift up your eyes
To glorious mansions in the skies;
O trust His grace -- in Canaan's land
We'll no more take the parting hand.

5. And now my friends, both old and young.
I hope in Christ you'll still go on;
And if on earth we meet no more,
O may we meet on Canaan's shore.

I hope you'll all remember me
If on earth no more I see;
An interest in your prayers I crave,
That we meet beyond the grave.

6. O glorious day! O blessed hope!
My soul leaps forward at the thought
When, on that happy, happy land,
We'll no more take the parting hand.

But with our blessed holy Lord
We'll shout and sing with one accord,
And there we'll all with Jesus dwell,
So, loving Christians, fare you well.

COLUMBUS. C.M.D.

"Now the just shall live by faith: but if any man draw back, my soul shall have no pleasure in him." -- Heb. 10:38.

F# Minor *Mercer's Cluster,* **1823.** *Columbian Harmony,* **1829.**

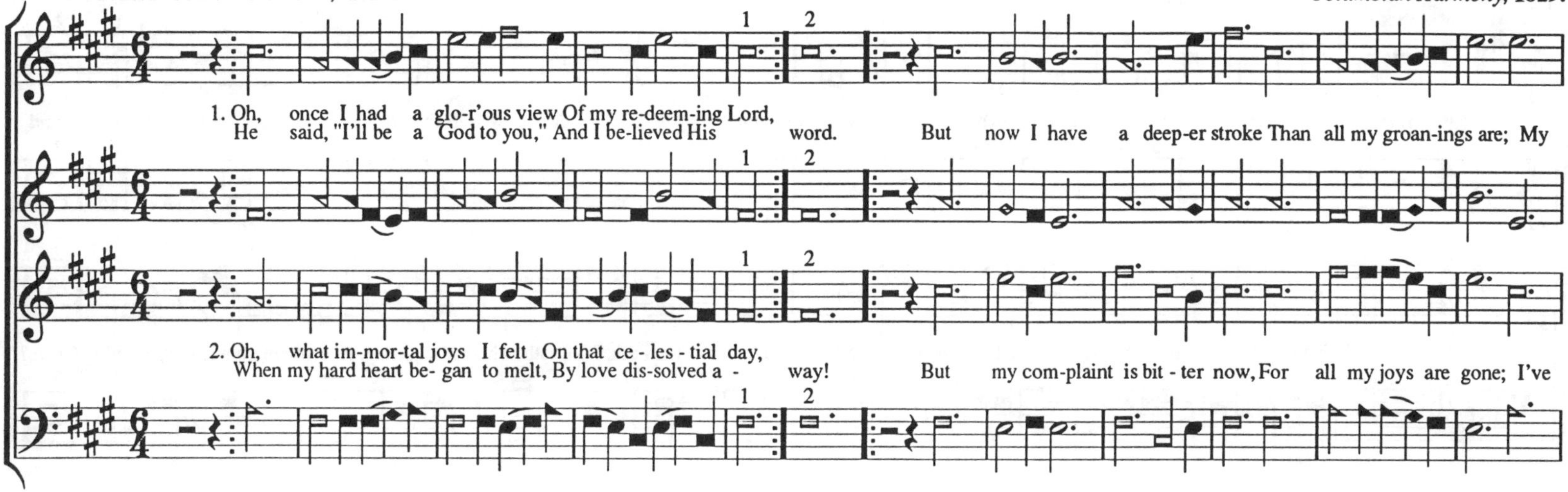

1. Oh, once I had a glor'ous view Of my redeeming Lord,
He said, "I'll be a God to you," And I believed His word.
But now I have a deeper stroke Than all my groanings are;
My God has me of late forsook; He's gone, I know not where.

2. Oh, what immortal joys I felt On that celestial day,
When my hard heart began to melt, By love dissolved away!
But my complaint is bitter now, For all my joys are gone;
I've strayed! I'm left! I know not how; The light's from me withdrawn.

3. Once I could joy the saints to meet,
To me they were most dear;
I then could stoop to wash their feet,
And shed a joyful tear;
But now I meet them as the rest,
And with them joyless stay;
My conversation's spiritless,
Or else I've naught to say.

4. I once could mourn o'er dying men,
And longed their souls to win;
I travailed for their poor children,
And warned them of their sin;
But now my heart's so careless grown,
Although they're drowned in vice,
My bowels o'er them cease to yearn--
My tears have left mine eyes.

5. I forward go in duty's way,
But can't perceive Him there;
Then backward on the road I stray,
But cannot find Him there;
On the left hand, where He doth work,
Among the wicked crew,
And on the right I find Him not
Among the favored few.

6. What shall I do? Shall I lie down
And sink in deep despair?
Will He forever wear a frown,
Nor hear my feeble prayer?
No; He will put His strength in me,
He knows the way I've strolled,
And when I'm tried sufficiently
I shall come forth as gold.

SALEM. L.M.
"Christ died for our sins." -- 1 Cor. 15:3.

1. He dies, the Friend of sinners dies! Lo Salem's daughters weep around: A solemn darkness veils the skies, A sudden trembling shakes the ground.
2. Say, "Live for-ev-er, glorious King, Born to redeem and strong to save!" Then ask, "O Death, where is thy sting, And where thy vic-t'ry, boasting Grave?"

ORTONVILLE. C.M.
"Thy name is as ointment poured forth." -- Song of Sol. 1:3.

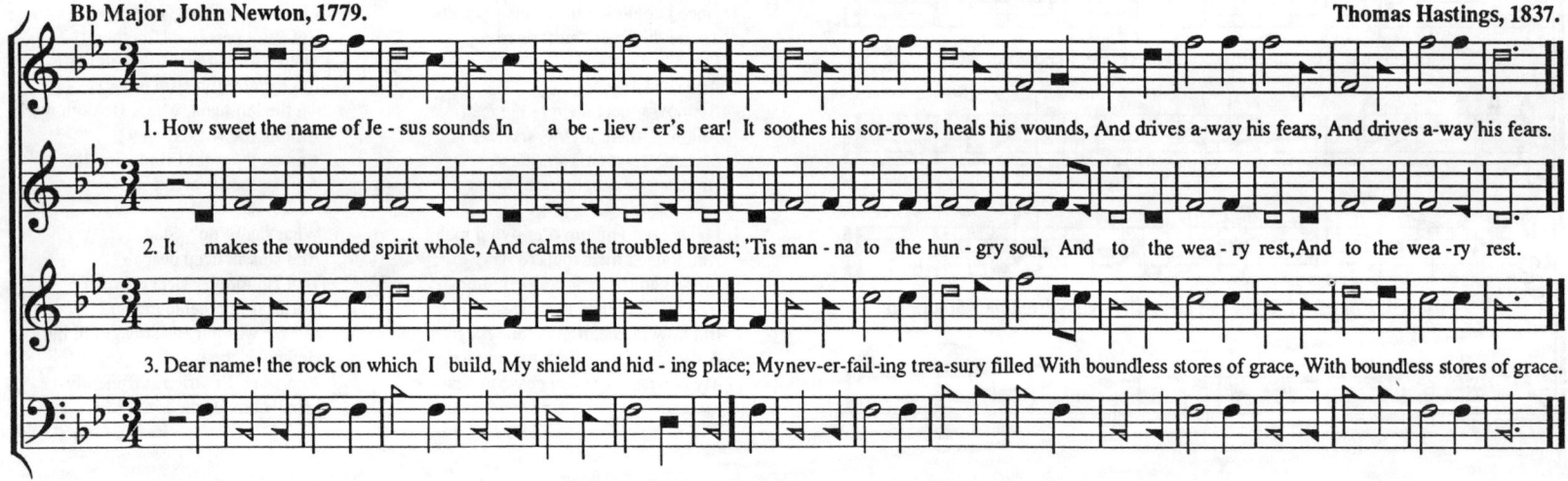

1. How sweet the name of Jesus sounds In a believer's ear! It soothes his sorrows, heals his wounds, And drives away his fears, And drives away his fears.
2. It makes the wounded spirit whole, And calms the troubled breast; 'Tis manna to the hungry soul, And to the weary rest, And to the weary rest.
3. Dear name! the rock on which I build, My shield and hiding place; My never-failing treasury filled With boundless stores of grace, With boundless stores of grace.

MINISTER'S FAREWELL. C.M.D.

"A friend loveth at all times." -- Prov. 17:17.

G Major Baltimore Collection, **1803.**
Wyeth's Repository, Part Second, **1813.**

1. Dear friends, fare-well! I do you tell, Since you and I must part; Your love to me has been most free, Your conversation sweet;
How can I bear to jour-ney where With you I can-not meet?
I go a-way, and here you stay, But still we're joined at heart.

2. I trust you'll pray both night and day, And keep your gar-ments white; If you die first, a-non you must, The will of God be done;
I hope the Lord will you re-ward With an im-mor-tal crown.
For you and me that we may be The Chil-dren of the light.

FAREWELL TO ALL (First). L.M.D.

"Prepare to meet thy God." -- Amos 4:12.

G Minor John Blain, **1818.**
J. P. Reese, **1859.**

And now, my friends, both old and young, I hope in Christ you will go on;
I hope you'll all re-mem-ber me, If you on earth no more I see.
And if on earth we meet no more, Oh, may we meet on Canaan's shore.

D. C. - An in-t'rest in your prayers I crave, That we may meet beyond the grave.

GAINSVILLE. 7s.
"Humble yourselves therefore under the mighty hand of God, that he may exalt you in due time." -- 1 Pet. 5:6.

A Major William Hammond, 1745.
W. D. Jones, 1869.

1. Lord, we come be-fore Thee now, At Thy feet we hum-bly bow; O do not our suit dis-dain; Shall we seek Thee, Lord, in vain?
2. Lord, on Thee our souls de-pend; In com-pas-sion now de-scend; Fill our hearts with Thy rich grace, Tune our lips to sing Thy praise.
3. In Thine own ap-point-ed way Now we seek Thee, here we stay; Lord, we know not how to go, Till a bless-ing Thou be-stow.
4. Send some mes-sage from Thy word That may joy and peace af-ford; Let Thy Spir-it now im-part Full sal-va-tion to each heart.
5. Com-fort those who weep and mourn; Let the time of joy re-turn; Those who are cast down lift up, Strong in faith, in love, and hope.
6. Grant that all may seek and find Thee a God su-preme-ly kind; Heal the sick, the cap-tive free, Let us all re-joice in Thee.

SAVE, MIGHTY LORD. L.M.
"The Lord . . . was received up into heaven, and sat on the right hand of God." -- Mark 16:19.

F Minor John Cennick, 1743.
J. A. and J. F. Wade, 1854.

1. Je - sus, my all, to heav'n is gone, Save, mighty Lord, O, save, save, might-y Lord, And send converting power down, Save, might-y Lord.
   He whom I fix my hope up-on, Save, mighty Lord.
2. The way the ho-ly proph-et went, Save, mighty Lord, O, save, save, might-y Lord, And send converting power down, Save, might-y Lord.
   The road that leads from banishment, Save, mighty Lord.
3. The King's high-way of ho-li-ness, Save, might-y Lord, O, save, save, might-y Lord, And send converting power down, Save, might-y Lord.
   I'll go, for all His paths are peace, Save, might-y Lord.

LEANDER. C.M.D.

"Then answered Peter and said unto him, Behold, we have forsaken all, and followed thee." -- Matt. 19:27.

A Minor Isaac Watts, 1707.
Tennessee Harmony, 1818.

1. My soul for-sakes her vain de-light And bids the world fare-well; Base as the dirt be-neath the feet And mis-chie-vous as hell.

2. There's noth-ing round this spa-cious earth That suits my soul's de-sire; To bound-less joy and sol-id mirth My no-bler thoughts as-pire.

No long-er will I ask your love, Nor seek your friend-ship more; The hap-pi-ness that I ap-prove Is not with-in your pow'r. pow'r.

Oh, for the pin-ions of a dove To mount the heav'n-ly road; There shall I share my Sav-ior's love, There shall I dwell with God. God.

72 THE WEARY SOUL. C.M.D.

"Come unto me, all ye that labor and are heavy laden, and I will give you rest." -- Matt. 11:28.

F Major John A. Granade, 1803. J. T. White, 1844.

1. Ye weary, heavy-laden souls Who are oppressed and sore, Tho' chilling winds and beating rains, And enemies surrounding us, Take courage and be bold.
Ye trav'lers thro' the wilderness To Canaan's peaceful shore, And waters deep and cold,

2. Farewell, my brethren in the Lord, Who are for Canaan bound, I hope that I shall meet you there In man-sions of e-ter-nal bliss,
And should we never meet again Till Gabriel's trump shall sound, On that delightful shore, Where parting is no more.

BELLEVUE. 11s.

"He hath said, I will never leave thee, nor forsake thee." -- Heb. 13:5.

Bb Major Rippon's Selection, 1787. Arr. - Z. Chambless, 1844.

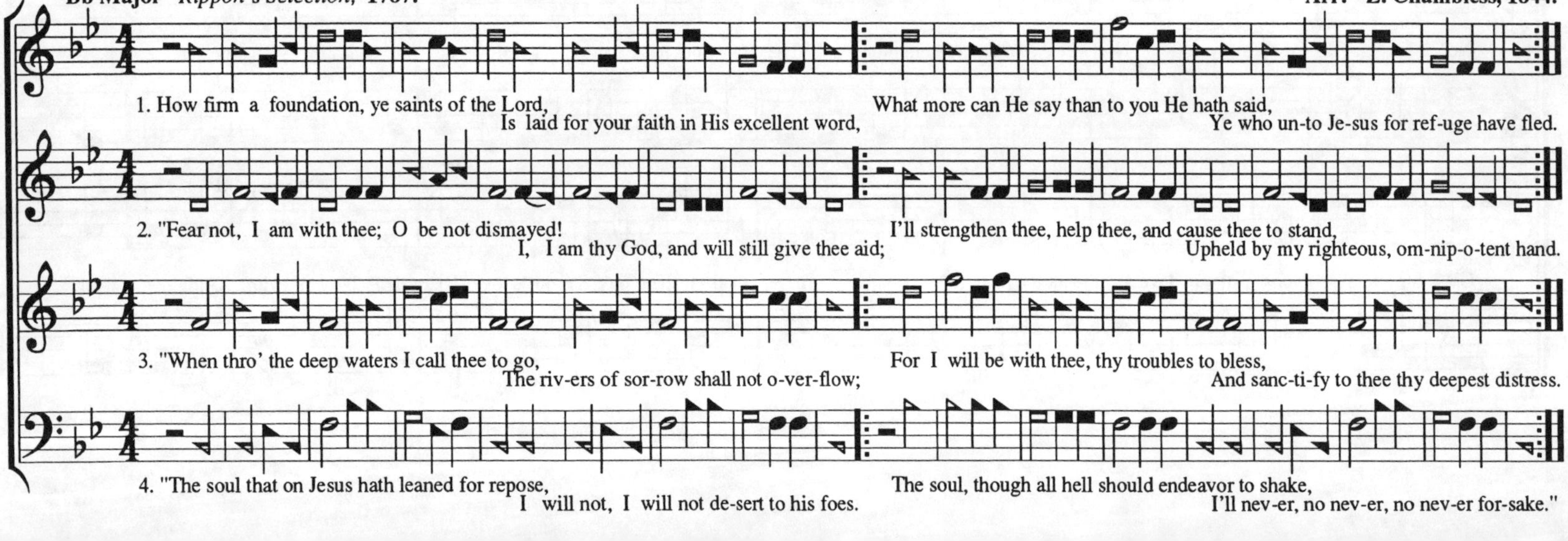

1. How firm a foundation, ye saints of the Lord, What more can He say than to you He hath said,
Is laid for your faith in His excellent word, Ye who un-to Je-sus for ref-uge have fled.

2. "Fear not, I am with thee; O be not dismayed! I'll strengthen thee, help thee, and cause thee to stand,
I, I am thy God, and will still give thee aid; Upheld by my righteous, om-nip-o-tent hand.

3. "When thro' the deep waters I call thee to go, For I will be with thee, thy troubles to bless,
The riv-ers of sor-row shall not o-ver-flow; And sanc-ti-fy to thee thy deepest distress.

4. "The soul that on Jesus hath leaned for repose, The soul, though all hell should endeavor to shake,
I will not, I will not de-sert to his foes. I'll nev-er, no nev-er, no nev-er for-sake."

CUSSETA. L.M.

"Create in me a clean heart, O God; and renew a right spirit within me." -- Ps. 51:10.

Bb Major Erhart Hegenwalt, 1524; J. C. Jacabi, 1722. John Massengale, 1844.

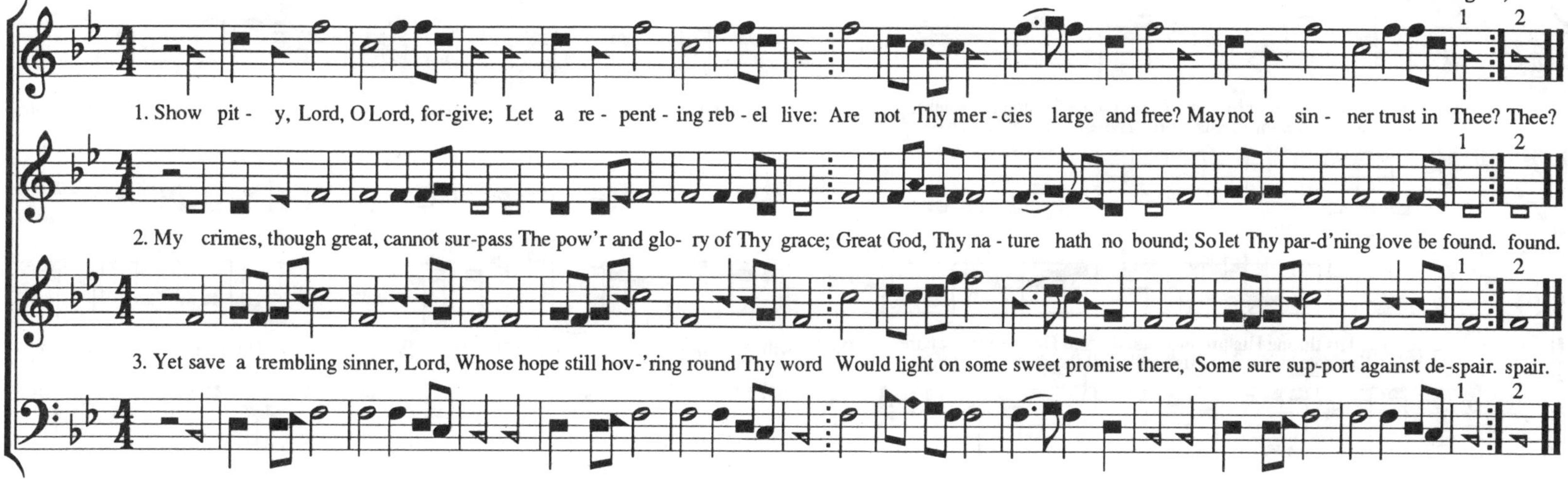

1. Show pit-y, Lord, O Lord, for-give; Let a re-pent-ing reb-el live: Are not Thy mer-cies large and free? May not a sin-ner trust in Thee? Thee?

2. My crimes, though great, cannot sur-pass The pow'r and glo-ry of Thy grace; Great God, Thy na-ture hath no bound; So let Thy par-d'ning love be found. found.

3. Yet save a trembling sinner, Lord, Whose hope still hov-'ring round Thy word Would light on some sweet promise there, Some sure sup-port against de-spair. spair.

ARLINGTON. C.M.

"Whosoever therefore shall be ashamed of me and of my words . . ." -- Mark 8:38.

G Major Isaac Watts, 1707. Thomas A. Arne, 1762.

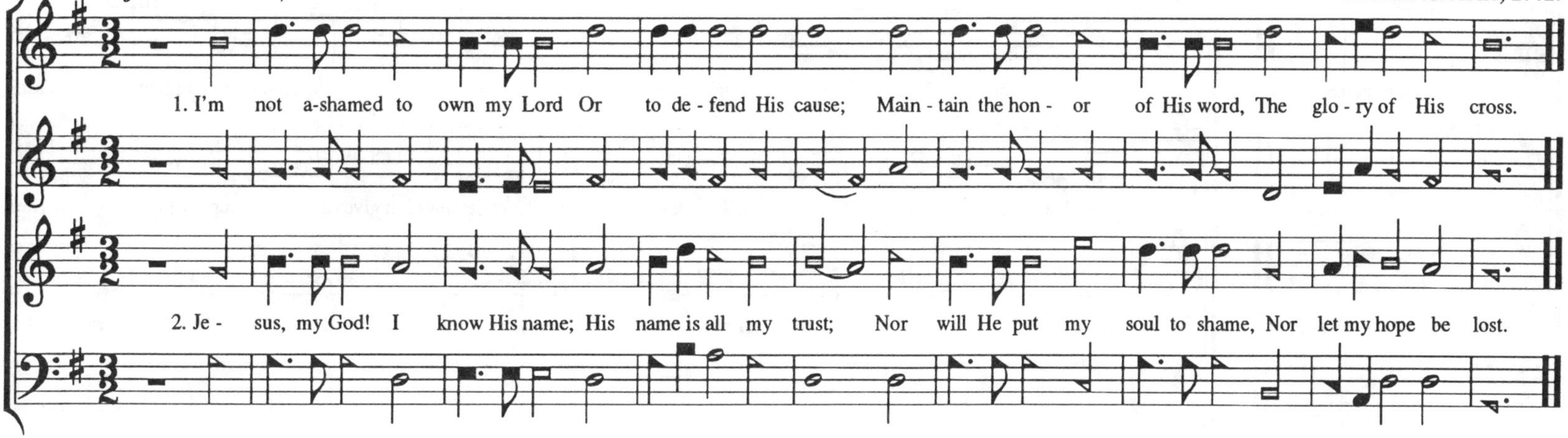

1. I'm not a-shamed to own my Lord Or to de-fend His cause; Main-tain the hon-or of His word, The glo-ry of His cross.

2. Je-sus, my God! I know His name; His name is all my trust; Nor will He put my soul to shame, Nor let my hope be lost.

74 THE ENQUIRER. C.M.

"Whereby, when ye read, ye may understand my knowledge in the mystery of Christ." -- Eph. 3:4.

G Minor Isaac Watts, 1707. B. F. White, 1844.

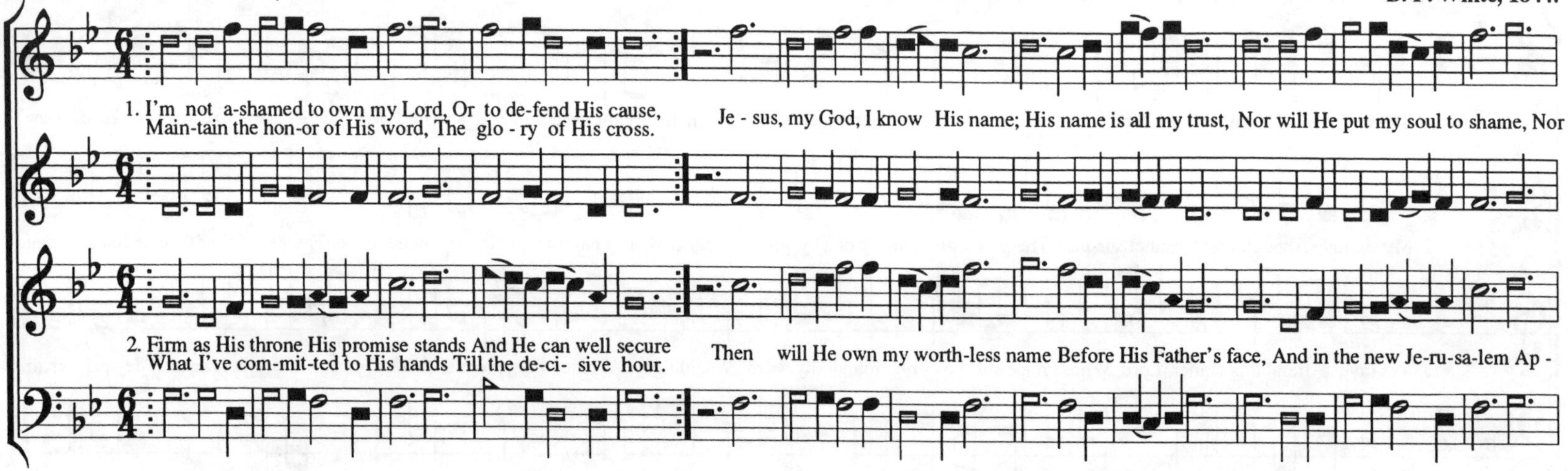

1. I'm not a-shamed to own my Lord, Or to de-fend His cause, Je - sus, my God, I know His name; His name is all my trust, Nor will He put my soul to shame, Nor
Main-tain the hon-or of His word, The glo - ry of His cross.

2. Firm as His throne His promise stands And He can well secure Then will He own my worth-less name Before His Father's face, And in the new Je-ru-sa-lem Ap -
What I've com-mit-ted to His hands Till the de-ci- sive hour.

let my hope be lost.

point my soul a place.

KING OF PEACE. 7s.

"No good thing will he withhold from them that walk uprightly." -- Ps. 84:11.

A Minor John Newton, 1779. Arr. - F. Price, 1835.

1. Lord, I can-not let Thee go, Till a bless-ing Thou be-stow: Do not turn a - way Thy face, Mine's an urgent, pressing case.

2. Dost Thou ask me who I am? Ah! my Lord, Thou know'st my name: Yet the question gives a plea To sup-port my suit with Thee.

3. Thou didst once a wretch behold, In re - bel-lion blindly bold, Scorn Thy grace, Thy pow'r de-fy; That poor reb-el, Lord, was I.

I WOULD SEE JESUS. C.M.D.

"And they shall see his face; and his name shall be in their foreheads." -- Rev. 22:4.

L. P. Breedlove, 1867.

HOLINESS. 6 lines, 7s.

"If any of you lack wisdom, let him ask of God." -- Jas. 1:5.

G Major *Providence Selection of Hymns, 1820.* Arr. - E. J. King, 1844.

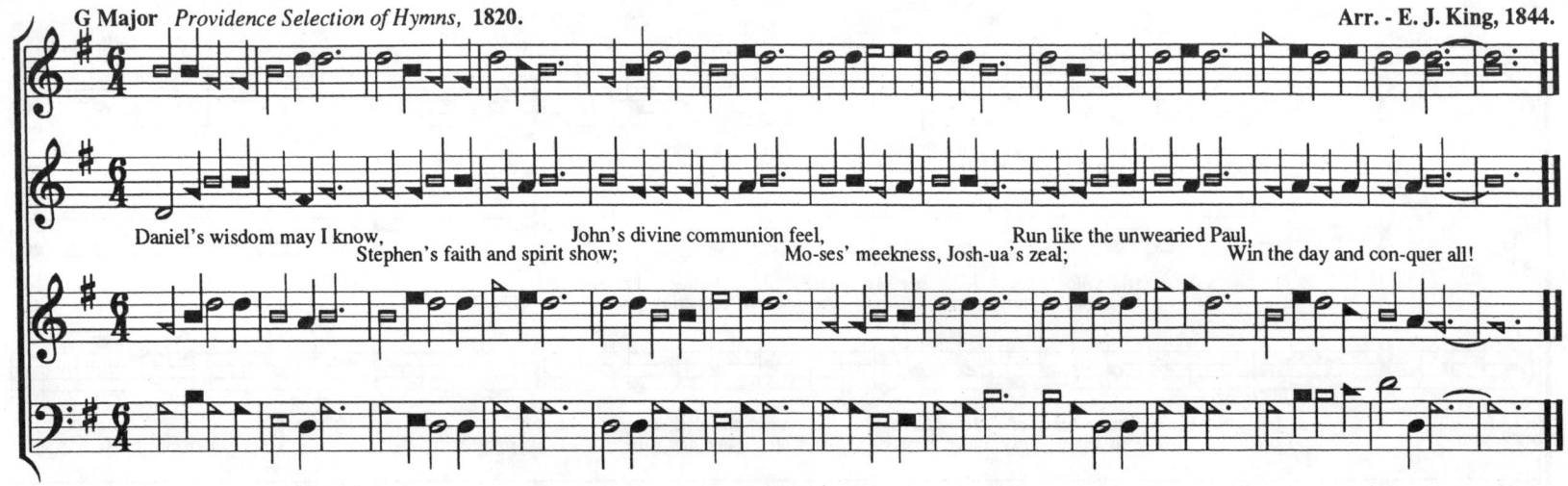

Daniel's wisdom may I know,
Stephen's faith and spirit show;
John's divine communion feel,
Mo-ses' meekness, Josh-ua's zeal;
Run like the unwearied Paul,
Win the day and con-quer all!

DESIRE FOR PIETY. L. M.

"He that saith he abideth in him ought himself also so to walk, even as he walked." -- 1 John 2:6.

C Major Anonymous B. F. White, 1844.

'Tis my de-sire with God to walk, Till the war-fare is o-ver, hal-le-lu-jah.
And with His chil-dren pray and talk, Till the war-fare is o-ver, hal-le-lu-jah. Cry A-men, pray on till the war-fare is o-ver, hal-le-lu-jah.

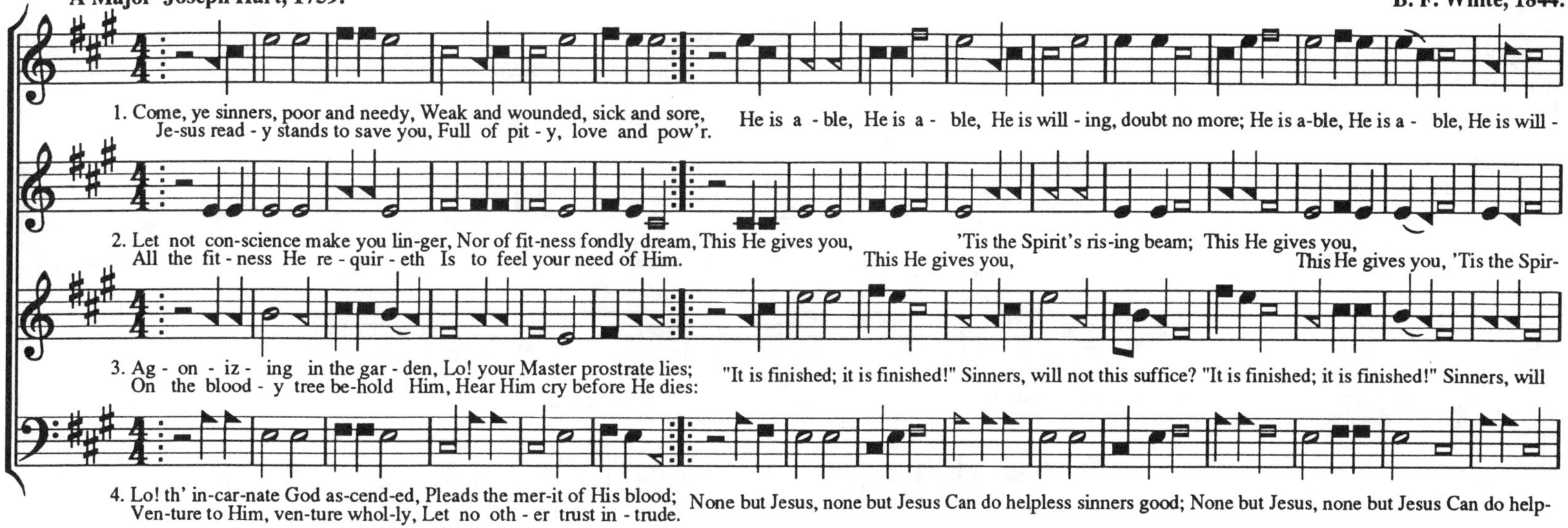

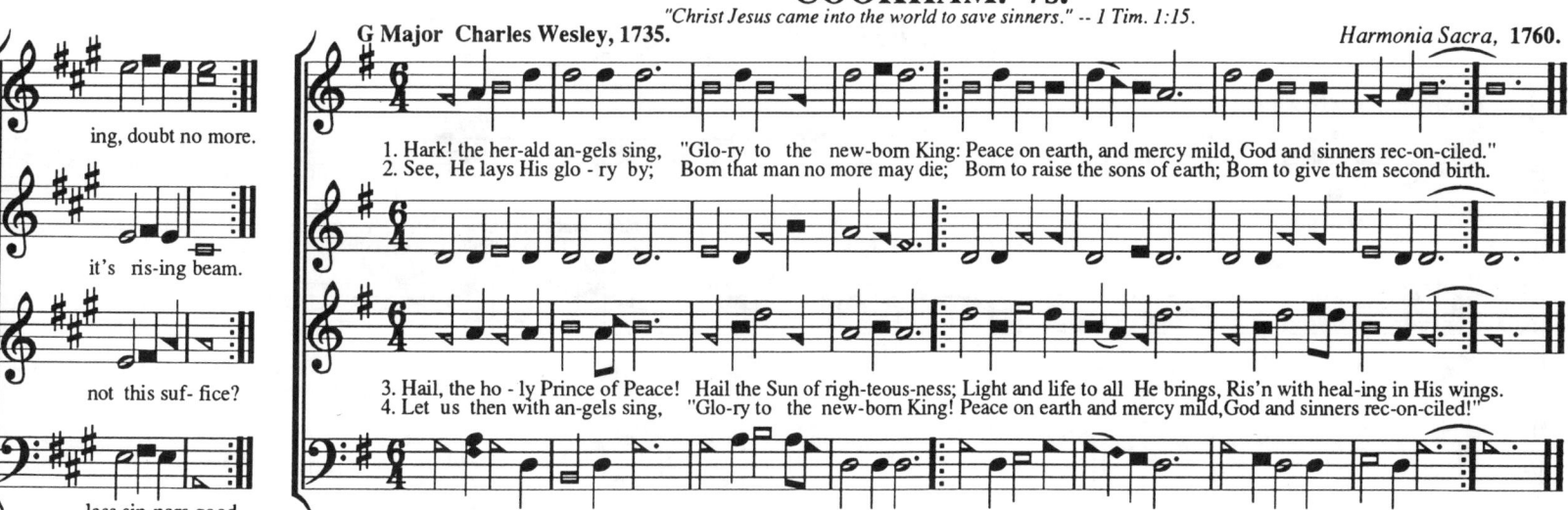

BOUND FOR CANAAN. 7s & 6s.

"Ye see him not, yet believing, ye rejoice with joy unspeakable and full of glory." -- 1 Pet. 1:8.

Bb Major John Leland, 1793.   Arr. - E. J. King, 1844.

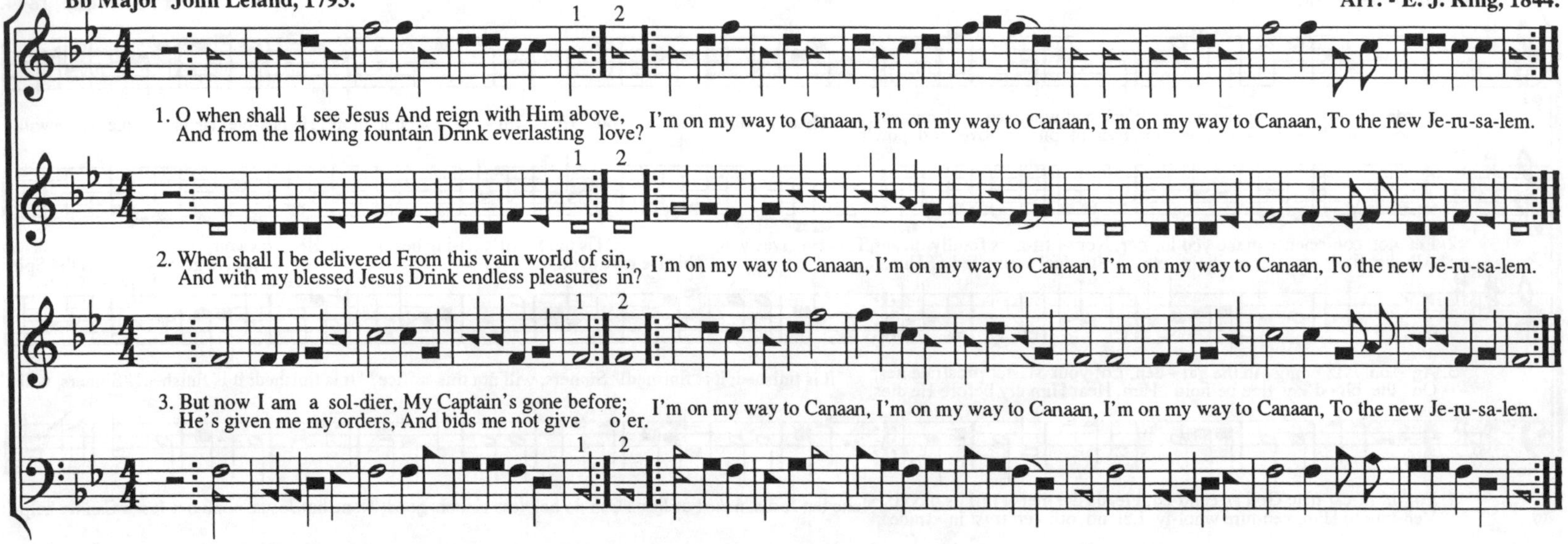

1. O when shall I see Jesus And reign with Him above, And from the flowing fountain Drink everlasting love? I'm on my way to Canaan, I'm on my way to Canaan, I'm on my way to Canaan, To the new Je-ru-sa-lem.

2. When shall I be delivered From this vain world of sin, And with my blessed Jesus Drink endless pleasures in? I'm on my way to Canaan, I'm on my way to Canaan, I'm on my way to Canaan, To the new Je-ru-sa-lem.

3. But now I am a sol-dier, My Captain's gone before; He's given me my orders, And bids me not give o'er. I'm on my way to Canaan, I'm on my way to Canaan, I'm on my way to Canaan, To the new Je-ru-sa-lem.

EDGEFIELD. 8s.

"None upon earth that I desire besides thee." -- Ps. 73:25.

F# Minor John Newton, 1779.   Arr. - J. T. White, 1844.

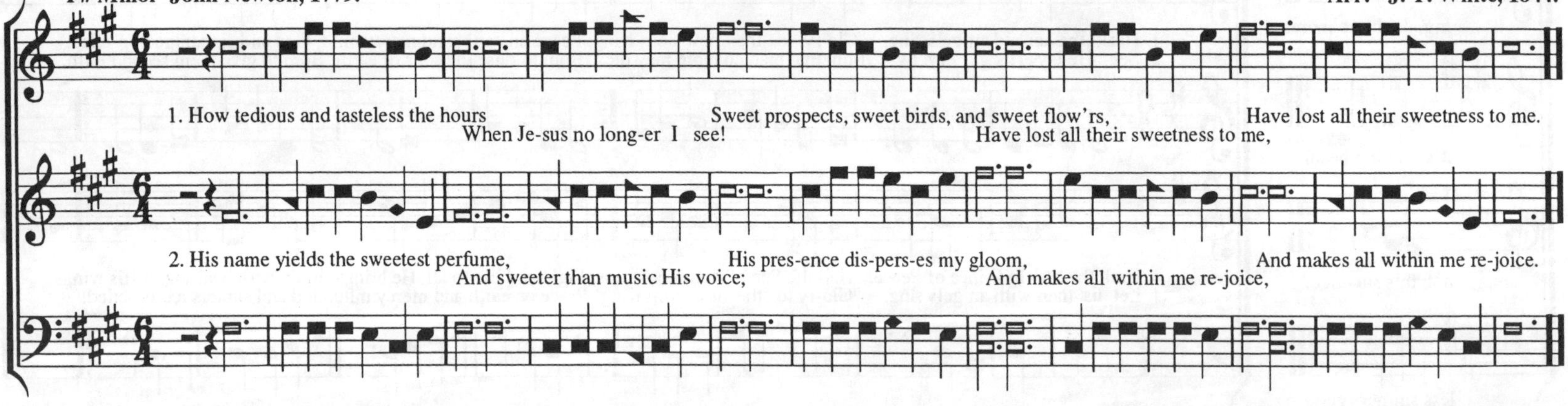

1. How tedious and tasteless the hours When Je-sus no long-er I see! Sweet prospects, sweet birds, and sweet flow'rs, Have lost all their sweetness to me, Have lost all their sweetness to me.

2. His name yields the sweetest perfume, And sweeter than music His voice; His pres-ence dis-pers-es my gloom, And makes all within me re-joice, And makes all within me re-joice.

VALE OF SORROW. P.M.
"For we are saved by hope." -- Rom. 8:24.

THE DYING MINISTER. C.M.
"In due season we shall reap, if we faint not." -- Gal. 6:9.

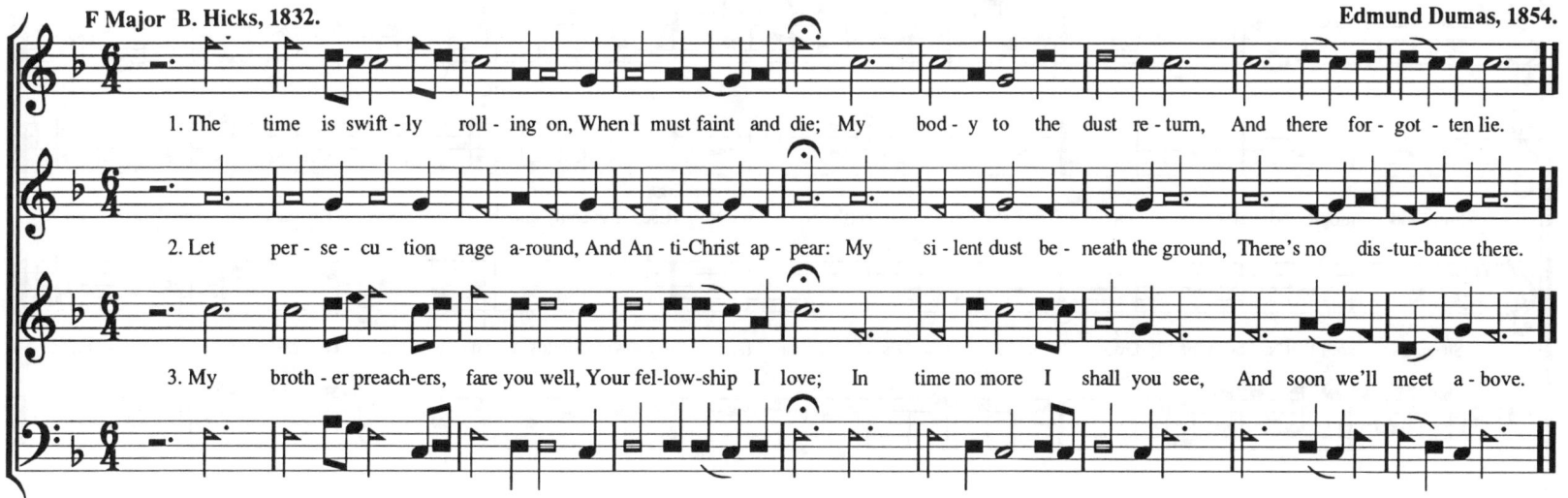

THE MORNING TRUMPET. 7s & 6s. 85

"There shall be a resurrection of the dead, both of the just and unjust." -- Acts 24:15.

F# Minor John Leland, 1793.

B. F. White, 1844.

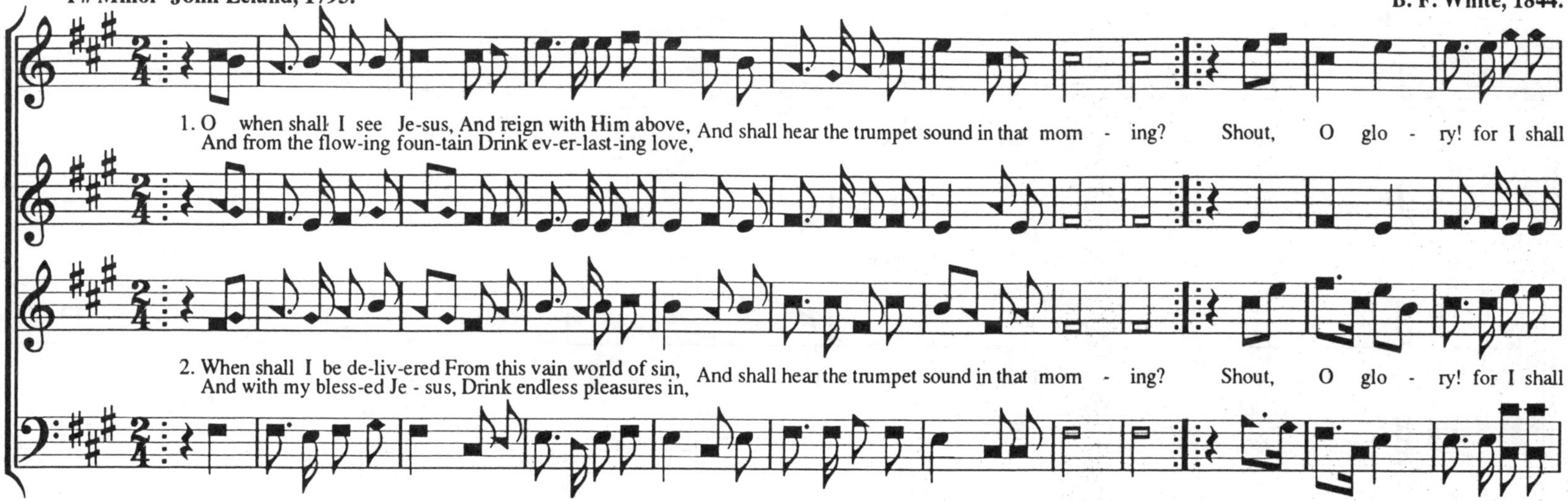

1. O when shall I see Jesus, And reign with Him above,
And from the flow-ing foun-tain Drink ev-er-last-ing love,
And shall hear the trumpet sound in that morn - ing?
Shout, O glo - ry! for I shall mount a-bove the skies,
When I hear the trum-pet sound in that morn - ing.

2. When shall I be deliv-ered From this vain world of sin,
And with my bless-ed Je - sus, Drink endless pleasures in,
And shall hear the trumpet sound in that morn - ing?
Shout, O glo - ry! for I shall mount a-bove the skies,
When I hear the trum-pet sound in that morn - ing.

3. But now I am a soldier,
My Captain's gone before; And shall...
He's given me my orders,
And bids me ne'er give o'er; And shall...
Chorus

4. His promises are faithful --
A righteous crown He'll give, And shall...
And all His valiant soldiers
Eternally shall live. And shall...
Chorus

5. Through grace I feel determined
To conquer, though I die, And shall...
And then away to Jesus
On wings of love I'll fly; And shall...
Chorus

6. Farewell to sin and sorrow,
I bid them both adieu! And shall...
And, O my friends, prove faithful,
And on your way pursue. And shall...
Chorus

7. Whene'er you meet with troubles,
And trials on your way, And shall...
Then cast your cares on Jesus,
And don't forget to pray. And shall...
Chorus

8. Gird on the gospel armor
Of faith, and hope, and love, And shall...
And when the combat's ended,
He'll carry you above. And shall...
Chorus

9. O do not be discouraged,
For Jesus is your Friend; And shall...
And if you lack for knowledge,
He'll not refuse to lend. And shall...
Chorus

10. Neither will He upbraid you,
Though often you request, And shall...
He'll give you grace to conquer,
And take you home to rest. And shall...
Chorus

POLAND. C.M.

"I become like them that go down into the pit." -- Ps. 28:1.

C# Minor Isaac Watts, 1719.
Timothy Swan, 1785.

1. God of my life, look gent-ly down, Behold the pains I feel; But I am dumb before Thy throne, Nor dare dispute Thy will.
2. I'm but a sojourner below, As all my fathers were; May I be well prepared to go When I the summons hear.
3. But if my life be spared awhile, Before my last remove, Thy praise shall be my bus'ness still And I'll declare Thy love.

LOOK OUT. P.M.

"Be not deceived; God is not mocked: for whatsoever a man soweth, that shall he also reap. -- Gal. 6:7.

A Major B. F. White, 1842.   B. F. White, 1844.

My breth-ren all, on you I call, A-rise and look a-round you.
How man-y foes, bound to op-pose, Who're wait-ing to con-found you! The gos-pel calls on Zi-on's walls, Shake off your sleep and slum-ber; A-rise and pray, we'll win the day, Tho' we are few in num-ber.

ASSURANCE. C.M.

"The ransomed of the Lord shall return and come to Zion with songs and everlasting joy upon their heads." -- Isa. 35:10.

A Major Isaac Watts.   William Billings, 1781.

BURK. 7s & 6s.

"Christ . . . abolished death, and hath brought life and immortality to light through the gospel." -- 2 Tim. 1:10.

F Major B. F. White, 1843. B. F. White, 1844.

1. The glo-r'ous light of Zi - on Is spread-ing far and wide, And sin - ners now are com - ing Un - to the gos - pel tide.
2. The glo - ry of King Je - sus Tri - um-phant doth a -rise, And sin-ners crowd a- round it With bit - ter groans and cries.

To see the saints in glo - ry, And the an-gels stand in - vit - ing, And the an - gels stand in - vit - ing To wel-come sin-ners home.

FROZEN HEART. L.M.

"Call on the Lord out of a pure heart." -- 2 Tim. 2:22.

F Major Joseph Hart, 1762.
Arr. - E. J. King, 1844.

1. Lord, shed a beam of heav'n-ly day, To melt this stub-born stone a-way; And thaw, with rays of love di-vine, This heart, this fro-zen heart of mine, This heart, this fro-zen heart of mine, This heart, this fro-zen heart of mine.

2. To hear the sor-rows Thou hast felt, All but an ad-a-mant would melt; Good-ness and wrath in vain com-bine To move this stu-pid heart of mine, To move this stu-pid heart of mine, To move this stu-pid heart of mine.

3. But One can yet per-form the deed; That One in all His grace I need; Thy Spir-it can from dross re-fine And melt this stub-born heart of mine, And melt this stub-born heart of mine, And melt this stub-born heart of mine.

4. O Breath of life, breathe on my soul! On me let streams of mer-cy roll; Now thaw with rays of love di-vine This heart, this fro-zen heart of mine, This heart, this fro-zen heart of mine, This heart, this fro-zen heart of mine.

NEVER PART. Concluded. 95

What? nev-er part a-gain? No, nev-er part a-gain, And soon shall hear the trumpet sound, And nev-er, nev-er part a-gain.

No, nev-er part a-gain, No, nev-er part a-gain, And soon shall hear the trumpet sound, And nev-er, nev-er part a-gain.

No, nev-er part a-gain, What? nev-er part a-gain? No, nev-er part a-gain, And soon shall hear the trumpet sound, And nev-er, nev-er part a-gain.

No, nev-er part a-gain, No, nev-er part a-gain, And soon shall hear the trumpet sound, And nev-er, nev-er part a-gain.

VERNON. L.M.

"No man hath seen God at any time; the only begotten Son, which is in the bosom of the Father, he hath declared him." -- John 1:18.

E Minor   Charles Wesley, 1742.   Arr. - Lucius Chapin, 1813.

1. Come, O Thou trav-el-er un-known, Whom still I hold, but can-not see; With Thee all night I mean to stay, And wres-tle till the break of day. day.
My com-pa-ny be-fore is gone, And I am left a-lone with Thee.

2. In vain Thou strug-glest to get free, I nev-er will un-loose my hold; Wres-tling, I will not let Thee go, Till I Thy name, Thy nature know. know.
Art Thou the Man that died for me? The se-cret of Thy love un-fold.

WE'LL SOON BE THERE. L.M.

"Blessed is he that cometh in the name of the Lord: Hosanna in the highest." -- Mark 11:9-10.

G Major *Mead's Collection, 1807.* Arr. - Oliver Bradfield, 1859.

Oh, who will come and go with me, We'll shout and sing, Ho-san-na, I'm bound fair Ca-naan's land to see, We'll shout and sing, Ho-san - na.

Go on, go on, we'll soon be there; We'll shout and sing, Ho-san-na; Come on, come on, we'll soon be there, We'll shout and sing, Ho-san - na.

ANIGMATION. C.M.

"The Lord redeemeth the soul of his servants: and none of them that trust in him shall be desolate." -- Ps. 34:22.

RUSSIA. L.M.

"Looking unto Jesus the author and finisher of our faith. . .(He sat) down at the right hand of the throne of God." -- Heb. 12:2.

108

WEEPING SINNERS. 7s.
"Blessed are they that mourn: for they shall be comforted." -- Matt. 5:4.

C Major *Convert's Companion, 1806.* — J. P. Reese, 1868.

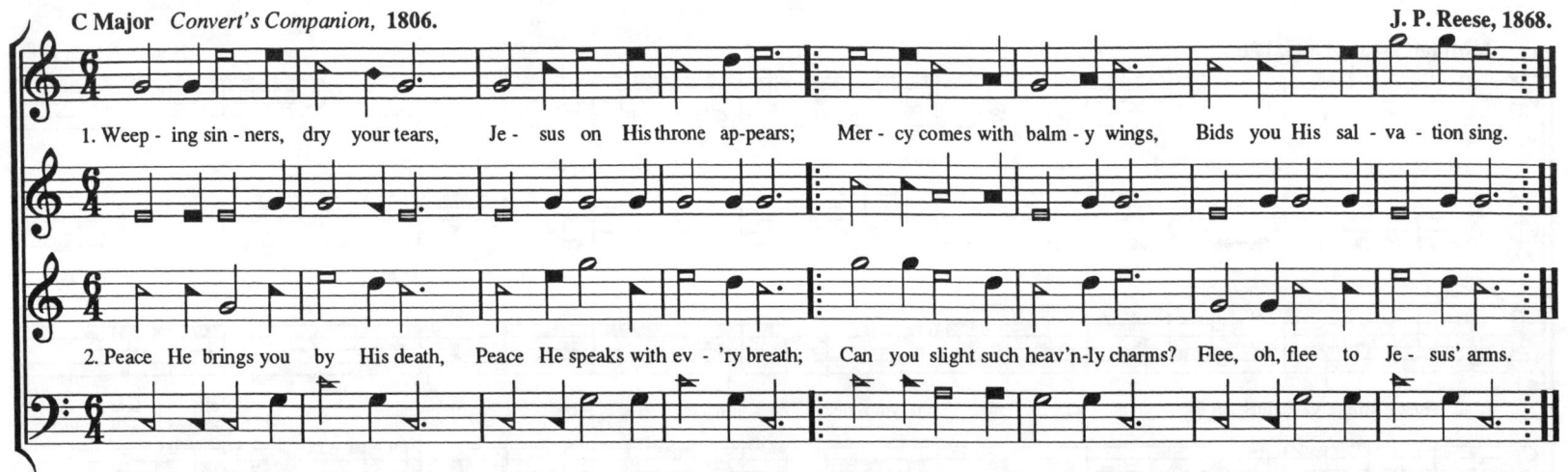

1. Weep-ing sin-ners, dry your tears, Je-sus on His throne ap-pears; Mer-cy comes with balm-y wings, Bids you His sal-va-tion sing.
2. Peace He brings you by His death, Peace He speaks with ev-'ry breath; Can you slight such heav'n-ly charms? Flee, oh, flee to Je-sus' arms.

THE TRAVELER. 7s.
"How shall we escape, if we neglect so great salvation." -- Heb. 2:3.

A Minor — Arr. - Absalom Ogletree, 1868.

1. Trav'ler haste, the night comes on, Many a shining hour is gone; Oh, come, trav'ler, haste away, Oh, come, trav'ler, haste away,
   Storm is gathering in the west, And you are so far from home. You must walk while it is day, You will find in Christ the way.
2. Far from home thy footsteps stray; Christ the life and Christ the way. Oh, come, trav'ler, haste away, Oh, come, trav'ler, haste away,
   Christ the light, yon setting sun, Ere the noon is scarce be-gun. You must walk while it is day, You will find in Christ the way.
3. Rising tempest sweeps the sky, Rains descend, the winds are high, Oh, come, trav'ler, haste away, Oh, come, trav'ler, haste away,
   Waters swell and death and fear Sets thy path no ref-uge near. You must walk while it is day, You will find in Christ the way.

MOUNT VERNON. L.M.D.
"Upon the harp with a solemn sound." -- Ps. 92:3.

JOURNEY HOME. L.M.

"I am filled with comfort, I am exceeding joyful." -- 2 Cor. 7:4.

G Major Mead's Collection, 1807.

R. F. M. Mann, 1868.

1. Oh, who will come and go with me? I'm on my jour-ney home.
   I'm bound fair Canaan's land to see, I'm on my jour-ney home.
   Oh, come and go with me; For I'm on my journey home, Home, sweet home, Bless the Lord.

2. E-ter-nal Spir-it, we con-fess, I'm on my jour-ney home.
   And sing the wonders of Thy grace, I'm on my jour-ney home.
   Oh, come and go with me; For I'm on my journey home, Home, sweet home, Bless the Lord.

3. Thy pow'r conveys our blessings down, I'm on my jour-ney home.
   From God the Fa-ther and the Son, I'm on my jour-ney home.
   Oh, come and go with me; For I'm on my journey home, Home, sweet home, Bless the Lord.

TO DIE NO MORE. L.M.

"They desire a better country, that is, a heavenly: . . . God hath prepared for them a city." -- Heb. 11:16.

A Major Isaac Watts, 1707.

Edmund Dumas, 1856.

1. Why should we start, and fear to die? What tim-'rous worms we mortals are, Death is the gate of end-less joy, And yet we dread to en-ter there.

2. Oh, if my Lord would come and meet, My soul should stretch her wings in haste, Fly fearless through death's i-ron gate, Nor feel the ter-rors as she passed.

Chorus: I'm go-ing home to Christ a-bove; I'm go-ing to the Chris-tian's rest, To die no more, to die no more, I'm go-ing home to die no more.

THE LAST WORDS OF COPERNICUS. C.M.

"They need no candle, neither light of the sun; for the Lord God giveth them light." -- Rev. 22:5.

THE PRODIGAL SON. C.M.

"Many are the afflictions of the righteous: but the Lord delivereth him out of them all." -- Ps. 34:19.

A Major John Newton, 1779.
Arr. - E. J. King, 1844.

1. Af-flic-tions, tho' they seem se-vere, Are oft in mer-cy sent: They stopped the prodigal's ca-reer, And caused him to re-pent. Oh, I die with
2. Al-though he no re-lent-ing felt Till he had spent his store, His stubborn heart began to melt When famine pinched him sore.
3. What have I gained by sin, he said, But hun-ger, shame and fear? My Father's house abounds with bread Whilst I am starving here. Oh, I die with
4. I'll go and tell him what I've done, Fall down before his face; Not wor-thy to be called his son, I'll ask a ser-vant's place.
5. He saw his son re-turn-ing back, He looked, he ran, he smiled, And threw his arms a-round the neck Of his re-bel-l'ous child.

hun-ger, here he cries, Oh! I die with hunger, here, he cries, And starve in a foreign land, My Father's house hath large supplies, And bounteous are his hands.

EDMONDS. 7s & 6s.

"But from the beginning of the creation God made them male and female." -- Mark 10:6.

F# Minor
Edmund Dumas, 1869.

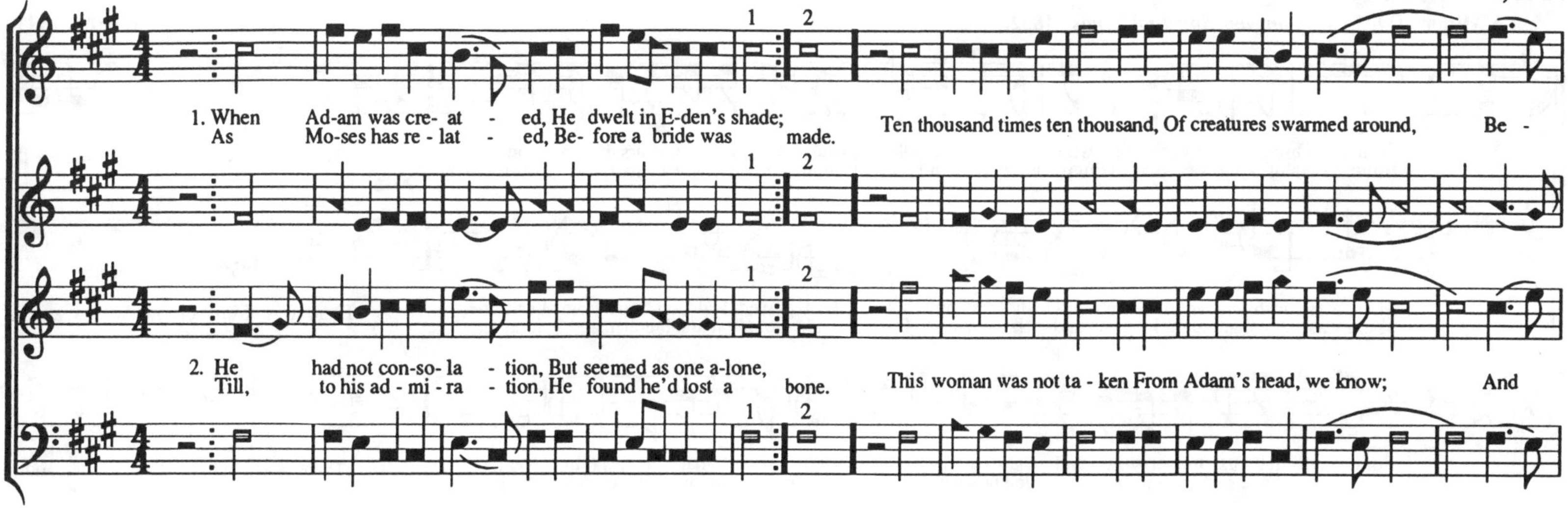

1. When Adam was created, He dwelt in Eden's shade;
As Moses has related, Before a bride was made.
Ten thousand times ten thousand, Of creatures swarmed around,
Before a bride was formed, Or any mate was found.

2. He had not consolation, But seemed as one alone,
Till, to his admiration, He found he'd lost a bone.
This woman was not taken From Adam's head, we know;
And she must not rule o'er him, It's evidently so.

3. This woman, she was taken
From near to Adam's heart,
By which we are directed
That they should never part.

The book that's called the Bible,
Be sure you don't neglect;
For in every sense of duty,
It will you both direct.

4. The woman is commanded
To do her husband's will,
In every thing that's lawful,
Her duty to fulfill.

Great was his exultation,
To see her by his side;
Great was his elevation
To have a loving bride.

5. This woman, she was taken
From under Adam's arm;
And she must be protected
From injury and harm.

This woman was not taken
From Adam's feet, we see;
And she must not be abused,
The meaning seems to be.

6. The husband is commanded
To love his loving bride;
And live as does a Christian,
And for his house provide.

The woman is commanded
Her husband to obey,
In every thing that's lawful,
Until her dying day.

UNION. P.M.

"And let thy saints shout for joy." -- Ps. 132:9.

A Minor Dupuy's Hymns and Spiritual Songs, 1832. Arr. - E. J. King, 1844.

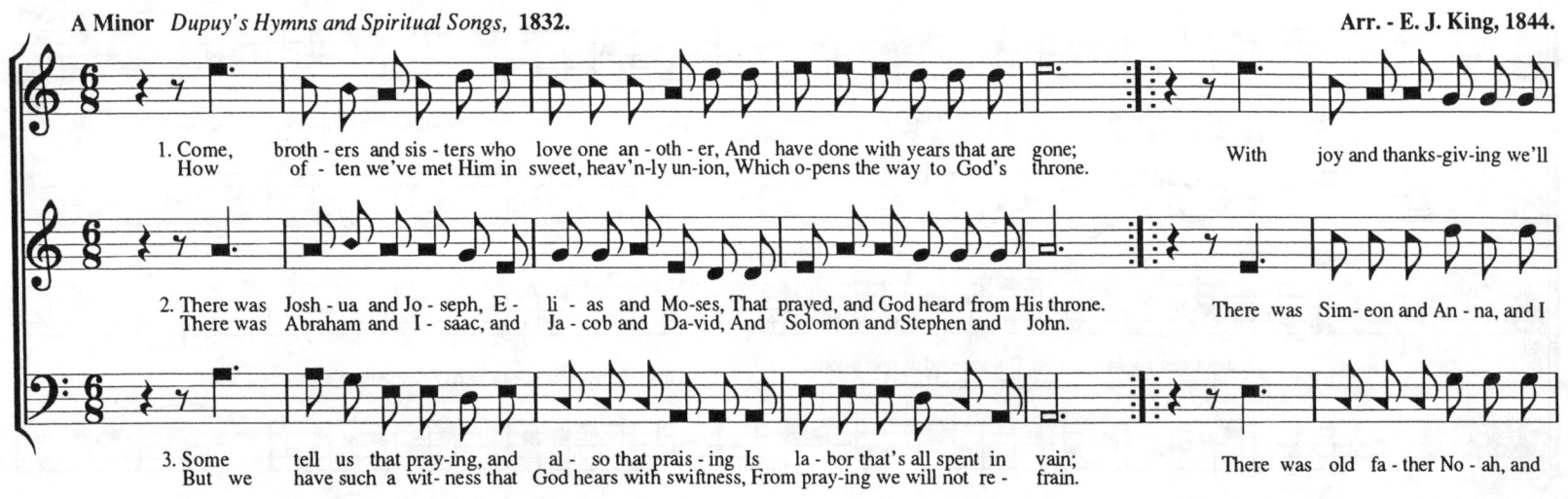

1. Come, broth-ers and sis-ters who love one an-oth-er, And have done with years that are gone; With joy and thanks-giv-ing we'll praise Him who loved us,
How of-ten we've met Him in sweet, heav'n-ly un-ion, Which o-pens the way to God's throne.

2. There was Josh-ua and Jo-seph, E-li-as and Mo-ses, That prayed, and God heard from His throne. There was Sim-eon and An-na, and I don't know how man-y,
There was Abraham and I-saac, and Ja-cob and Da-vid, And Solomon and Stephen and John.

3. Some tell us that pray-ing, and al-so that prais-ing Is la-bor that's all spent in vain; There was old fa-ther No-ah, and ten thou-sand more,
But we have such a wit-ness that God hears with swiftness, From pray-ing we will not re-frain.

That prayed as they jour-neyed a-long; Some cast a-mong li-ons, some bound with rough i-rons, Yet glory and praises they sung.
While we run the bright, shin-ing way; Tho' we part here in bod-y, we're bound for one glory, And bound for each oth-er to pray.
That witnessed that God heard them pray; There was Sam-uel and Hannah, Paul, Si-las and Pe-ter, And Dan-iel and Jo-nah, we'll say.

STOCKWOOD. 8s & 7s.

"How fair is thy love, my sister, my spouse! how much better is thy love than wine! and the smell of thine ointments than all spices! -- S. Sol. 4:10.

A Minor — Samuel F. Smith, 1832.
M. Mark Wynn, 1869.

1. Sis - ter, thou wast mild and love-ly, Gen - tle as the sum - mer breeze, Pleas - ant as the air of ev-'ning, When it flows a-mong the trees,

2. Dear - est sis - ter, thou hast left us, Here thy loss we deep - ly feel, But 'tis God that hast be - reft us; He can all our sor - rows heal.

Peace - ful be thy si - lent slum-ber, Peace-ful in the grave so low; Thou no more wilt join our num-ber, Thou no more our songs shall know.

Yet a - gain we hope to meet thee, When the day of life is fled, Then in heav'n with joy to greet thee, Where no fare - well tear is shed.

HEAVEN'S MY HOME. 11s.

"In heaven . . . we look for the Savior, the Lord Jesus Christ." -- Phil. 3:20.

G Major Arr. - R. H. Davis and J. S. Terry, 1869.   R. H. Davis and J. S. Terry, 1869.

1. Come, all my dear breth-ren, and help me to sing; I'm go-ing to Je-sus, He's heav-en's great King,
He died to a-tone for the sins of the world; His ban-ner is fly-ing, His sails are un-furled,

2. While here in the val-ley of con-flict I stay, Oh, give me sub-mis-sion, and strength as my day,
In all my af-flic-tions to Thee would I come, Re-joic-ing in hope of my glo-ri-ous home.

3. I long, dear-est Lord, in Thy beau-ties to shine, No more as an ex-ile in sor-row to pine;
And in Thy dear im-age a-rise from the tomb, With glo-ri-fied mil-lions to praise Thee at home.

Heav'n's my home, heav'n's my home, I'm go-ing to Je-sus, For heav-en's my home.

FLORENCE. C.M.

"The harvest is the end of the world." -- Matt. 13:39.

124 LOVER OF THE LORD. C.M.

"Continue ye in my love." -- John 15:9.

BABEL'S STREAMS. C.M.

"We hanged our harps upon the willows in the midst thereof." -- Ps. 137:2.

Stephen Jenks, 1811.

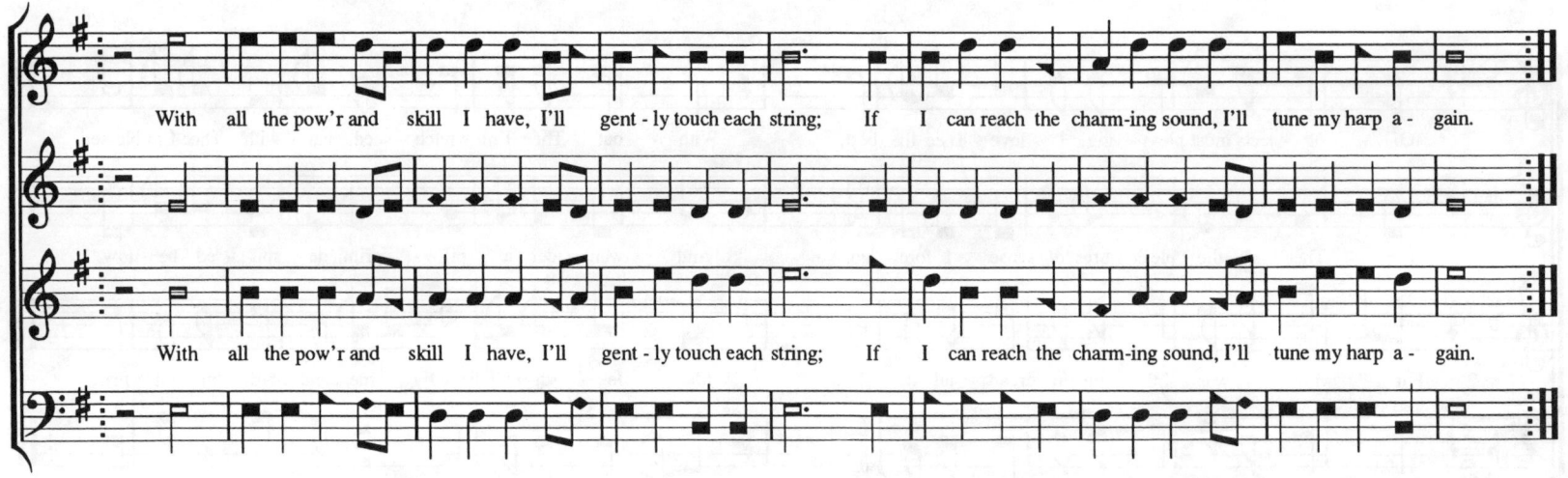

GREEN FIELDS. 8s.

"Whom have I in heaven but thee? and there is none upon earth I desire besides thee." -- Ps. 73:25.

127

G Major John Newton, 1779.

THE PROMISED LAND. C.M.

"... travelling in the greatness of his strength." -- Isa. 63:1.

HEAVENLY ARMOR. 7s & 6s.

"Let not your heart be troubled, neither let it be afraid." -- John 14:27.

1. And if you meet with trou-bles And tri-als on the way,
Then cast your care on Je-sus, And don't for-get to pray.
Gird on the heav'n-ly ar-mor Of faith, and hope, and love;
And when the com-bat's end-ed, He'll take you up a-bove.

2. Through grace I am de-ter-mined To con-quer, though I die;
And then a-way to Je-sus On wings of love I'll fly;
Fare-well to sin and sor-row, I bid you all a-dieu,
Then, O my friends, prove faith-ful, And on your way pur-sue.

MILLENNIUM 12, 12, 12, 13.

"But the end shall not be yet." -- Matt. 24:6.

F Major *Zion Songster,* **1834.** **William Walker, 1831.**

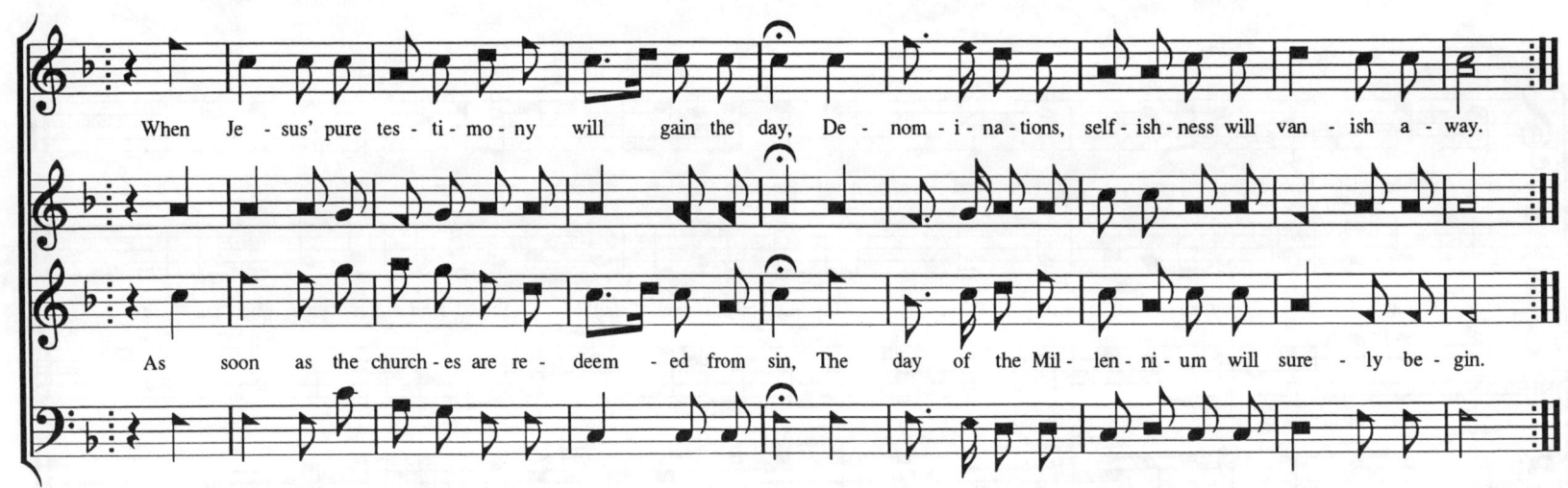

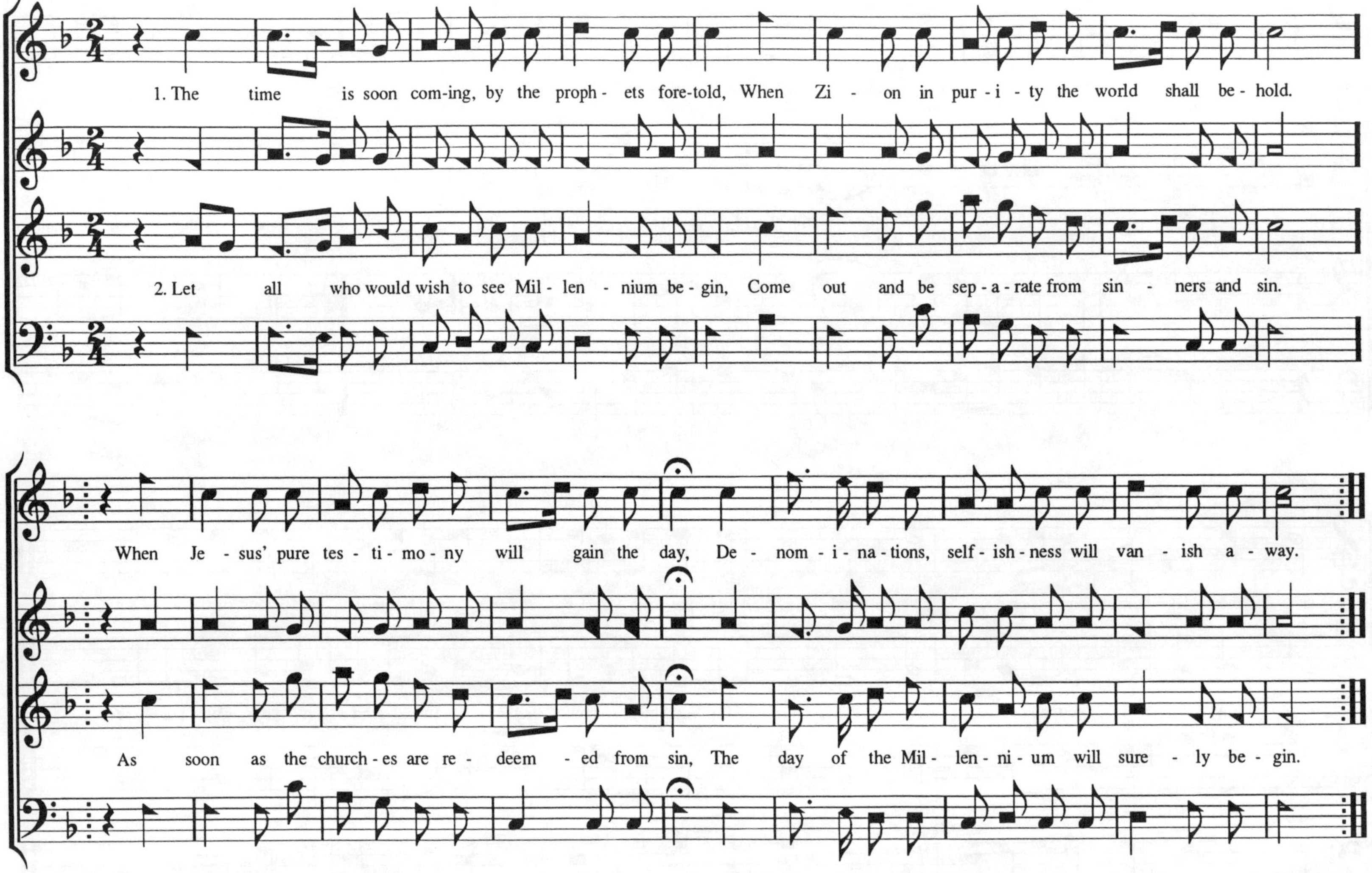

132 SINNER'S FRIEND. L.M.

"Christ Jesus came into the world to save sinners." -- 1 Tim. 1:15.

F# Minor Isaac Watts, 1709. J. P. Reese, 1869.

He dies! the friend of sinners dies! And He died on the cross for sinners, Lo! Salem's daughters weep around! And He died on the cross for sinners. I love my Lord, for He first loved me, And He died on the cross for sinners.

HEBREW CHILDREN. P.M.
"These men were cast into the midst of the burning fiery furnace." -- Dan. 3:21.

133

MORALITY. 11s.

"But I thy servant fear the Lord from my youth." -- 1 Kings 18:12.

G Major Hannah More.

1. While beauty and youth are in their full prime, And folly and fashion affect our whole time; Oh, let not the phantom our wishes engage; Let's live so in youth that we blush not in age.

2. I sigh not for beauty, nor languish for wealth, But grant me, kind Providence, virtue and health; Then, richer than kings, and far happier than they, My days shall pass swiftly and sweetly away.

3. The vain and the young may attend us a while, But let not their flatt'ry our prudence beguile. Let's covet those charms that shall never decay, Nor listen to all that deceivers can say.

LIBERTY. C.M.

"Deliver me from the oppression of man." -- Ps. 119:134.

ADORATION. C.M.
"Praise him for his mighty acts." -- Ps. 150:2.

G Major Anne Steele, 1760.   W. W. Parks, 1869.

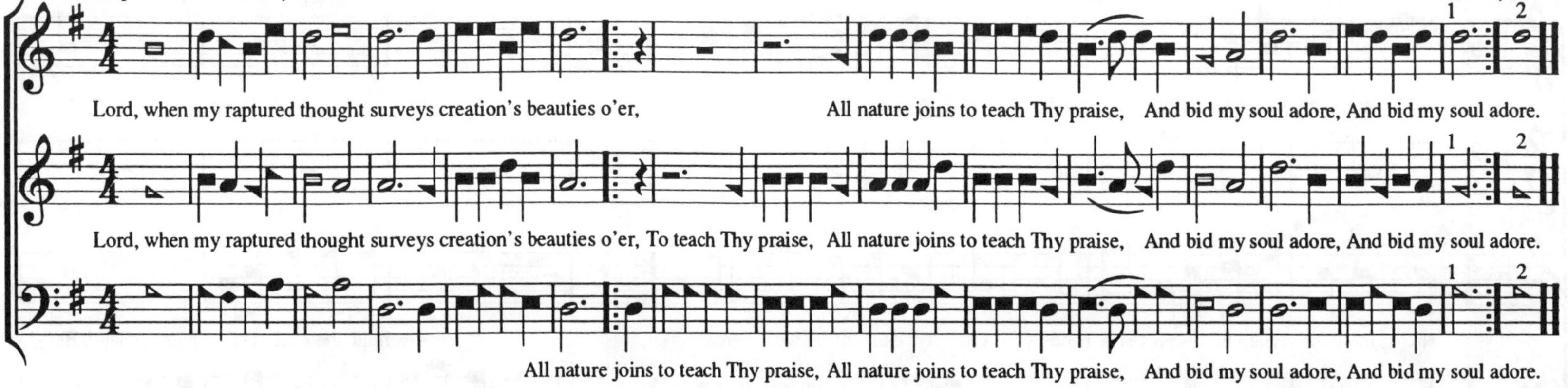

Lord, when my raptured thought surveys creation's beauties o'er, All nature joins to teach Thy praise, And bid my soul adore, And bid my soul adore.

Lord, when my raptured thought surveys creation's beauties o'er, To teach Thy praise, All nature joins to teach Thy praise, And bid my soul adore, And bid my soul adore.

All nature joins to teach Thy praise, All nature joins to teach Thy praise, And bid my soul adore, And bid my soul adore.

OGLETREE. C.M.
". . . quickened together with him, having forgiven. . ." -- Col. 2:13.

G Major Simon Browne, 1720.   S. M. Brown, 1869.

1. Fre-quent the day of God re-turns To shed its quick-'ning beams; And yet how slow de-vo-tion burns, How lan-guid are its flames.

2. In-crease, O Lord, our faith and hope, And fit us to as-cend, Where the as-sem-bly ne'er breaks up, And sab-baths nev-er end.

3. There shall we join, and nev-er tire, To sing im-mor-tal lays; And, with the bright se-raph-ic choir, Sound forth Im-man-uel's praise.

ELYSIAN. 7,6,7,6,7,7,7,7.

"There was a rainbow round about the throne, in sight like unto an emerald." -- Rev. 4:3.

1. Burst, ye emerald gates, and bring To my raptured vision 'Round the bright elysian. Lo, we lift our longing eyes, Burst, ye intervening skies, Sun of righteousness, arise; Ope the gates of Paradise.
2. Floods of everlasting light Freely flash before Him; Myriads, with supreme delight, Instantly adore Him. Angel trumps resound His fame, Lutes of lucid gold proclaim All the music of His name; Heaven echoing the theme.
3. Four-and-twenty elders rise From their princely station; Shout His glorious victories, Sing the great salvation; Cast their crowns before His throne, Cry in reverential tone, "Glory give to God alone, Holy, holy, holy One!"

140 SWEET SOLITUDE. L.M.

"The wilderness and the solitary place shall be glad for them; and the desert shall rejoice, and blossom as the rose." -- Isa. 35:1.

A Major Hannah More. *Southern Harmony*, 1835.

1. Hail, sol-i-tude, thou gen-tle queen, Of mod-est air and brow se-rene! 'Tis thou in-spires the po-et's theme, Wrapped in sweet vi-sion's air-y dream, Wrapped in sweet vision's air-y dream, Wrapped in sweet vi-sion's air-y dream.

2. With Thee the charms of life shall last, E'en when the ro-sy bloom is past, When slow-ly pac-ing time shall spread Thy sil-ver blos-som o'er my head, No more with this vain world per-plexed, Thou shalt pre-pare me for the next.

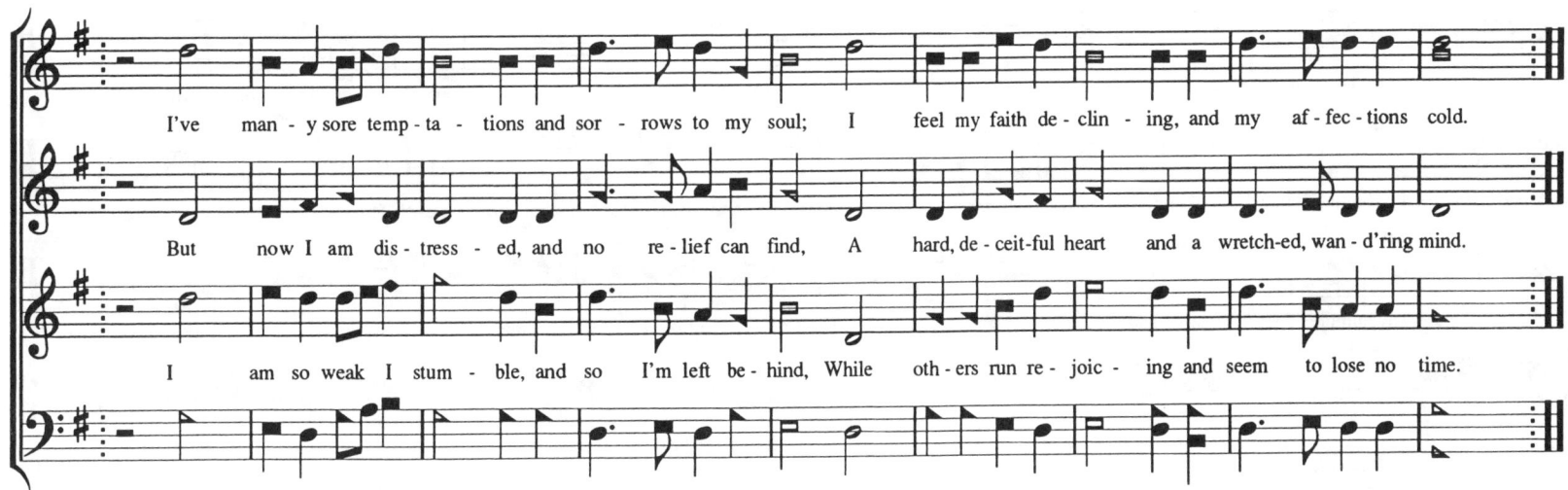

STRATFIELD. L.M.

"Heaven is my throne, and earth is my footstool: what house will ye build me? saith the Lord: or what is the place of my rest?" -- Acts 7:49.

F# Minor Isaac Watts, 1719.

Ezra Goff, 1786.

PLEYEL'S HYMN (First). C.M. 143

"Power belongeth unto God; also unto thee, O Lord, belongeth mercy: for thou renderest to every man according to his work." -- Ps. 62:11, 12.

F Major Helen Maria Williams, 1790. Ignaz Joseph Pleyel.

1. While Thee I seek, pro-tect-ing Pow'r, Be my vain wish-es stilled, And may this con-se-crat-ed hour With bet-ter hopes be filled.
2. In each e-vent of life, how clear Thy rul-ing hand I see! Each bless-ing to my soul more dear, Be-cause con-ferred by Thee.
3. When glad-ness wings my fa-vored hour, Thy love my thoughts shall fill; Re-signed when storms of sor-row lower, My soul shall meet Thy will.

Thy love the pow'r of tho't be-stowed, To Thee my tho'ts would soar; Thy mer-cy o'er my life has flowed, That mer-cy I a-dore. dore.

In ev-'ry joy that crowns my days, In ev-'ry pain I bear, My heart shall find de-light in praise, Or seek re-lief in prayer. prayer.

My lift-ed eye, with-out a tear, The gath-'ring storm shall see: My stead-fast heart shall know no fear; That heart shall rest on Thee. Thee.

144   JUBILEE. 8s & 7s.

"For the grace of God that bringeth salvation hath appeared to all men." -- Titus 2:11.

A Major   *The Baltimore Collection,* **1801**.   *Supplement to the Kentucky Harmony,* **1820**.

1. Hark! the jubilee is sounding, O the joyful news is come;
Free salvation is proclaimed In and through God's only Son.
Now we have the invitation To the meek and lowly Lamb,
Glory, honor and salvation; Christ, the Lord, is come to reign.

2. Come, dear friend, and don't neglect it,
Come to Jesus in your prime;
Great salvation, don't reject it,
O receive it, now's your time;
Now the Savior is beginning
To revive His work again.
Glory, honor, and salvation;
Christ, the Lord, is come to reign.

3. Now let each one cease from sinning,
Come and follow Christ, the way;
We shall all receive a blessing,
If from Him we do not stray;
Golden moments we've neglected,
Yet the Lord invites again!
Glory, honor, and salvation;
Christ, the Lord, is come to reign.

4. Let us run our race with patience,
Looking unto Christ the Lord,
Who doth live and reign for ever,
With His Father and our God;
He is worthy to be praised,
He is our exalted King.
Glory, honor, and salvation;
Christ, the Lord, is come to reign.

5. Come dear children, praise your Jesus
Praise Him, praise Him evermore;
May His great love now constrain us,
His great name for to adore.
O then let us join together,
Crowns of glory to obtain
Glory, honor, and salvation;
Christ, the Lord, is come to reign.

WARRENTON. 8s, 7s.

145

"...and shall lead them unto living fountains of waters." -- Rev. 7:17.

G Major Robert Robinson, 1758.   J. Williams & William Walker, 1835.

1. Come, thou fount of ev-'ry bless-ing, Tune my heart to sing thy grace;
   Streams of mer-cy nev-er ceas-ing, Call for songs of loud-est praise.
   I am bound for the kingdom, Will you go to glory with me? Hal-le-lu-jah, praise the Lord.

2. Oh, to grace how great a debt-or Dai-ly I'm con-strained to be!
   Let that grace, Lord, like a fet-ter, Bind my wan-d'ring heart to Thee.
   I am bound for the kingdom, Will you go to glory with me? Hal-le-lu-jah, praise the Lord.

3. Prone to wan-der, Lord, I feel it, Prone to leave the God I love;
   Here's my heart, Lord, take and seal it, Seal it for Thy courts a-bove.
   I am bound for the kingdom, Will you go to glory with me? Hal-le-lu-jah, praise the Lord.

SWEET AFFLICTION. 8s, 7s.

"In the world ye shall have tribulation: but be of good cheer; I have overcome the world." -- John 16:33.

F Major Samuel Pearce, 1800.   J. J. Rousseau. Arr. - Lowell Mason, 1823.

1. In the floods of trib-u-la-tion, While the bil-lows o'er me roll,
   Je-sus whis-pers con-so-la-tion, And sup-ports my faint-ing soul.
   Hal-le-lu-jah, Hal-le-lu-jah, Hal-le-lu-jah, praise the Lord!
   Hal-le-lu-jah, Hal-le-lu-jah, Hal-le-lu-jah, praise the Lord!

2. Wear-ing there a weight of glo-ry, Still the path I'll ne'er for-get,
   But ex-ult-ing cry it led me To my bless-ed Sav-ior's feet.
   Hal-le-lu-jah, Hal-le-lu-jah, Hal-le-lu-jah, praise the Lord!
   Hal-le-lu-jah, Hal-le-lu-jah, Hal-le-lu-jah, praise the Lord!

SYMPHONY. P.M.

"For the hour of his judgment is come: and worship him that made heaven, and earth, and the sea." -- Rev. 14:7.

Eb Major Isaac Watts, 1707.
Justin Morgan, 1790.

Be - hold, the Judge de-scends, His guards are nigh; Tempests and fire at tend Him down the sky; Heav'n, earth and hell draw near, let all things come To hear His jus - tice and the sin-ner's doom; But gath-er first, my saints, the Judge commands, Bring them, ye an - gels, from their dis-tant lands.

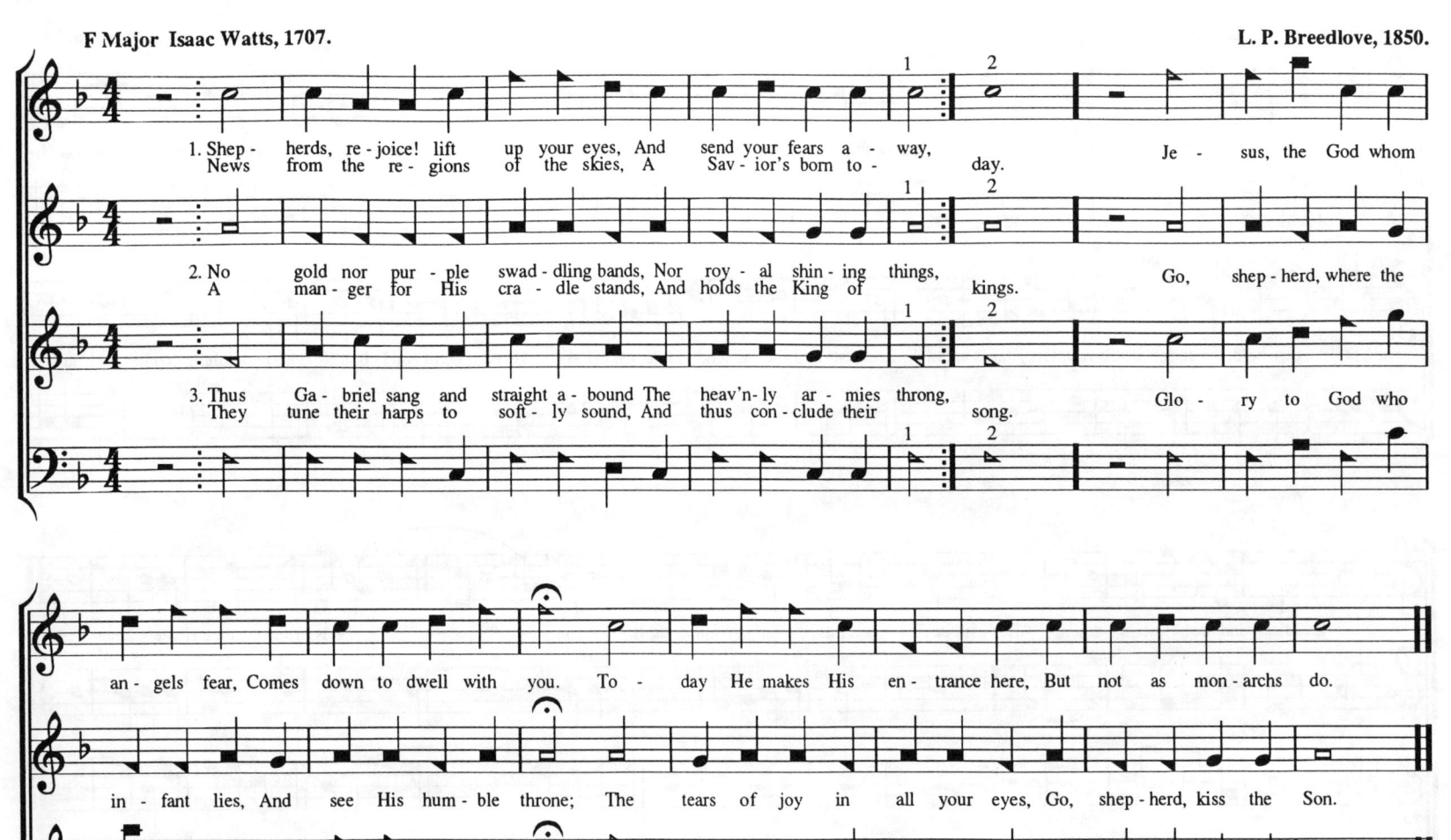

RESURRECTED. P.M.

"And they ascended up to heaven in a cloud." -- Rev. 11:12.

NORTHFIELD. C.M.

"I say unto you, Hereafter ye shall see heaven open." -- John 1:51.

Bb Major Isaac Watts, 1707.

Jeremiah Ingalls, 1800.

WONDROUS LOVE. 12,9,6,6,12,9.

"A man that hath friends..." -- Pro. 18:24.

159

F Minor Mead's *General Selection,* 1811. James Christopher, 1840.

1. What wondrous love is this! oh, my soul! oh, my soul! What wondrous love is this! oh, my soul! What wondrous love is this That caused the Lord of bliss To bear the dreadful curse for my soul, for my soul, To bear the dreadful curse for my soul.

2. When I was sinking down, sinking down, sinking down, When I was sinking down, sinking down, When I was sinking down Beneath God's righteous frown Christ laid aside His crown for my soul, for my soul, Christ laid aside His crown for my soul.

3. To God and to the Lamb I will sing, I will sing, To God and to the Lamb I will sing; To God and to the Lamb, Who is the great I Am, While millions join the theme, I will sing, I will sing, While millions join the theme, I will sing.

4. And when from death I'm free, I'll sing on, I'll sing on, And when from death I'm free, I'll sing on, And when from death I'm free, I'll sing and joyful be Throughout eternity, I'll sing on, I'll sing on, Throughout eternity I'll sing on.

160

WAR DEPARTMENT. 11s.
"A land which floweth with milk and honey..." - Num. 14:8

E Minor Anonymous
Southern Harmony, 1835.

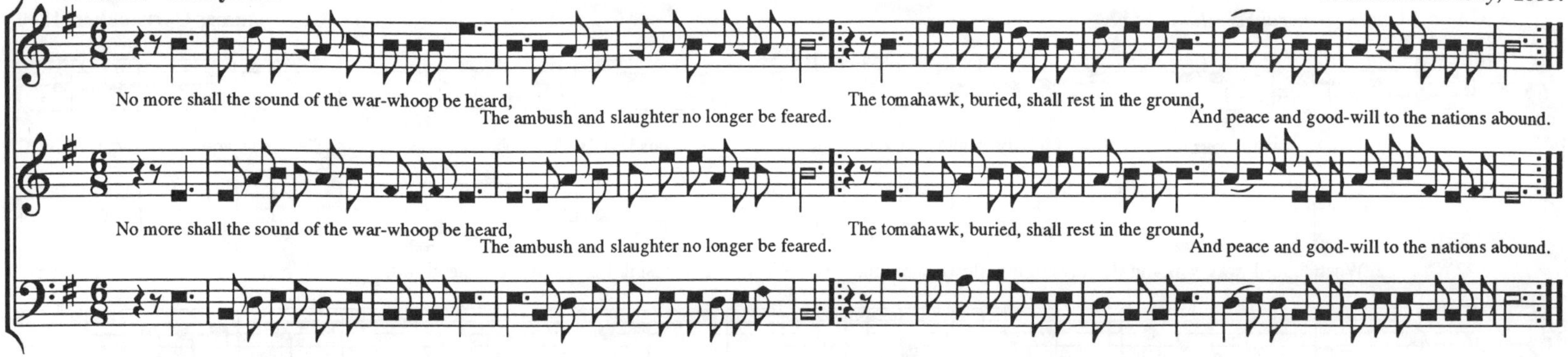

No more shall the sound of the war-whoop be heard,
The ambush and slaughter no longer be feared.
The tomahawk, buried, shall rest in the ground,
And peace and good-will to the nations abound.

TURN, SINNER, TURN. L.M.
"Be ye angry, and sin not: let not the sun go down upon your wrath." -- Eph. 4:26.

D Minor William Miller, 1809.
Arr. - E. J. King, 1844.

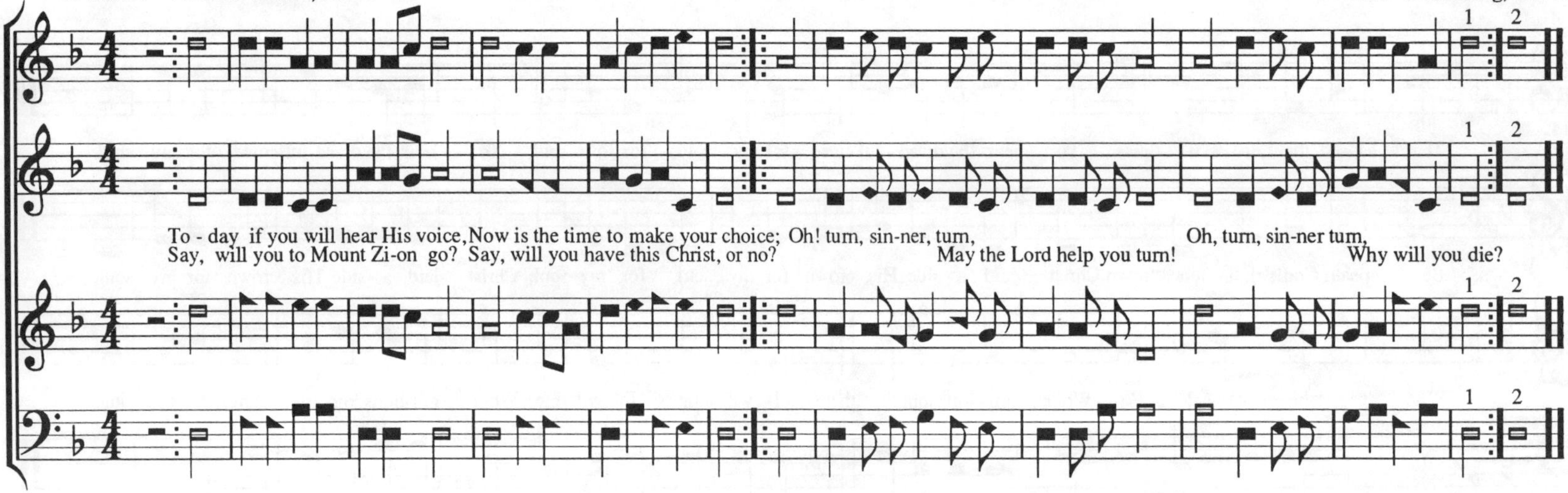

To-day if you will hear His voice, Now is the time to make your choice; Oh! turn, sin-ner, turn, Oh, turn, sin-ner turn,
Say, will you to Mount Zi-on go? Say, will you have this Christ, or no? May the Lord help you turn! Why will you die?

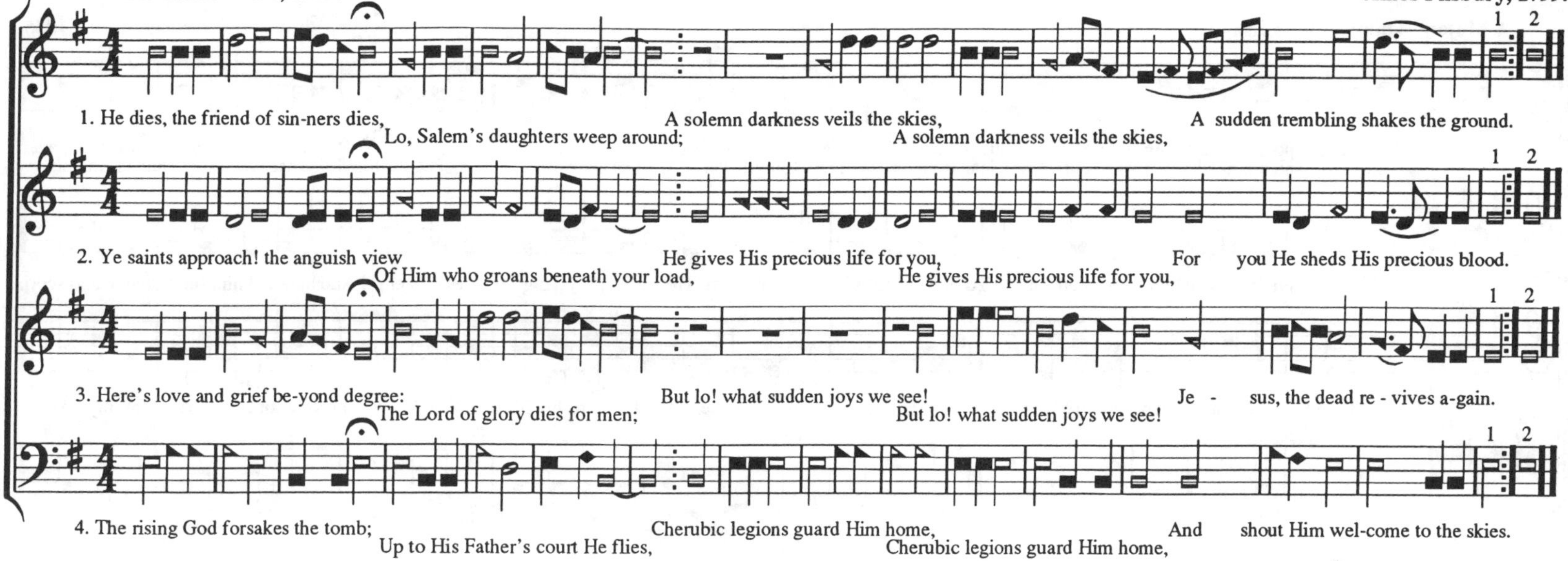

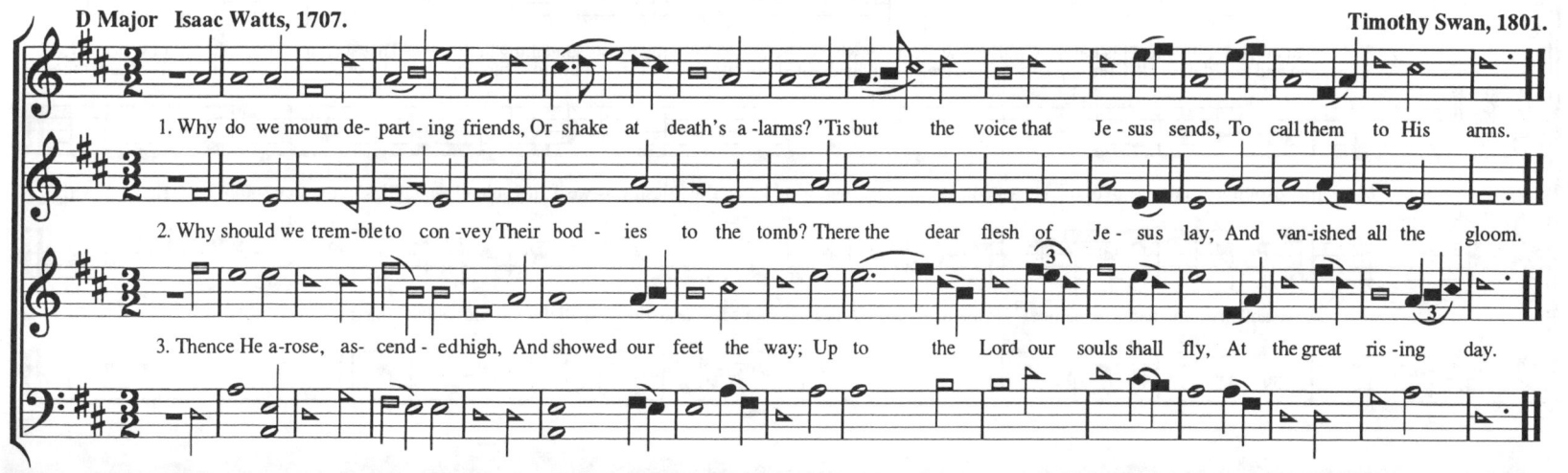

FAMILY BIBLE. 12s & 11s.

"...and the true light now shineth..." -- 1 John 2:8.

A Minor *Young Christian's Companion, 1826.*

1. How pain-ful-ly pleas-ing the fond rec-ol-lec-tion Of youth-ful con-nec-tion and in-no-cent joy, While blessed with pa-ren-tal ad-vice and af-fec-tion, Sur-round-ed with mer-cy and peace from on high. I still view the chairs of my fa-ther and moth-er, The seats of their off-spring, as ranged on each hand, And the rich-est of books, which ex-cels ev-'ry oth-er, The fam-i-ly har-mo-n'ous sweet-ness, As warmed by the hearts of the fam-i-ly band, Hath raised us from earth to that rap-tur-ous dwell-ing De-scribed in the

2. The Bi-ble, that vol-ume of God's in-spi-ra-tion, At morn-ing and ev-'ning could yield us de-light. The prayers of our fa-ther, a sweet in-vo-ca-tion, For mer-cy by day and for safe-ty at night. O hymns of thanks-giv-ing with

FAMILY BIBLE. Concluded.

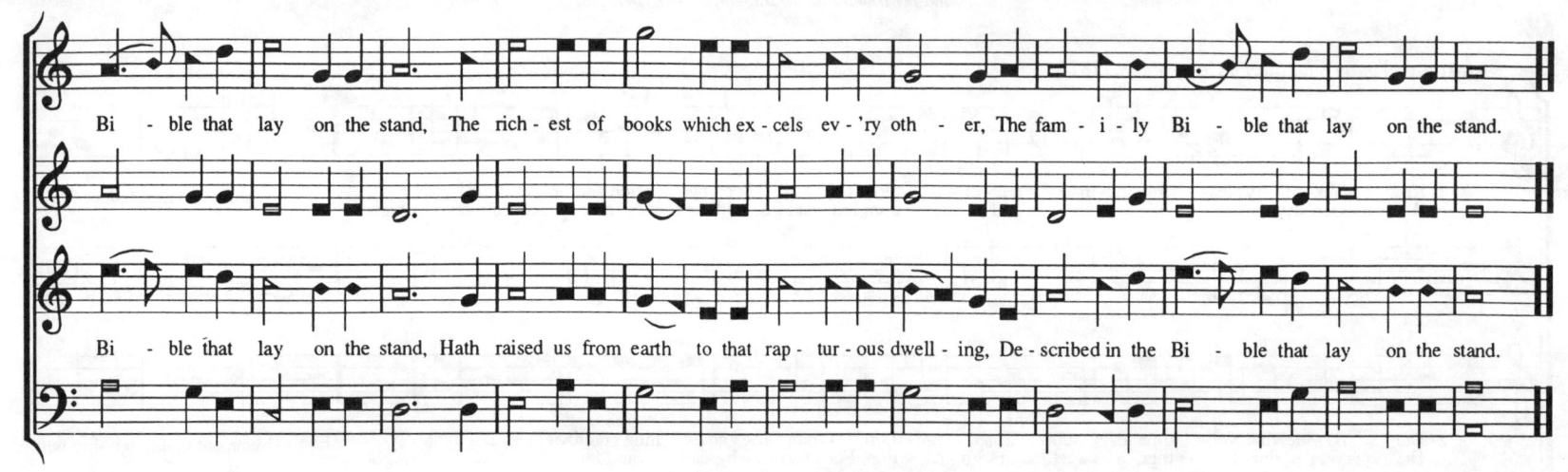

STILL BETTER. 8s & 7s.

"And the chief priests and scribes stood and vehemently accused him." -- Luke 23:10.

C Major

Israel Bradfield & J. L. Meggs, 1869.

PRAY, BRETHREN, PRAY
167

"I will pray with the spirit, and I will pray with the understanding also: I will sing with the spirit, and I will sing with the understanding also." -- 1 Cor. 14:15.

DARTMOUTH. S.M.D.

"Singing and making melody in your heart to the Lord." -- Eph. 5:19.

169

G Major Isaac Watts, 1719.

Stephen Jenks, 1803.

EXHILARATION. L.M.

"And washed us from our sins in his own blood." -- Rev. 1:5.

EXHORTATION (First). C.M.

"My voice shalt thou hear in the morning, O Lord; in the morning will I direct my prayer unto thee." -- Ps. 5:3.

PHOEBUS. C.M.D.

173

"Evening, and morning, and at noon, will I pray, and cry aloud: and he shall hear my voice." -- Ps. 55:17.

F# Minor Isaac Watts, 1719.

William Billings, 1770.

1. Lord, in the morning Thou shalt hear My voice ascending high: To Thee will I direct my prayer, To Thee lift up mine eye; Up to the hills where Christ is gone To plead for all His saints, Pre-sent-ing at His Father's throne, Pre-sent-ing at His Fa-ther's throne Our songs and our com-plaints.

2. Thou art a God before whose sight The wicked shall not stand; Sinners shall ne'er be Thy delight, Nor dwell at Thy right hand; But to Thy house will I resort, To taste Thy mer-cies there: Thy word in-to our minds in-still; Thy word in-to our minds in-still; And wor-ship in Thy fear.

PETERSBURG. L.M.

"Thy kingdom is an everlasting kingdom, and thy dominion endureth throughout all generations." -- Ps. 145:13.

D Major John Logan, 1781. William Billings, 1786.

PETERSBURG. Concluded.

175

humble spirit and contrite, Is an abode of my delight, Is an abode of my delight.

humble spirit and contrite, Is an abode of my delight, Is an abode of my delight.

HIGHLANDS OF HEAVEN. 6s & 7s.

"My kingdom is not of this world." -- John 18:36.

F Major

J. D. Arnold, 1869.

1. Sinner, go, will you go, To the highlands of heaven; Where the bright, blooming flow'rs Are their odors emitting;
Where the storms nev-er blow, And the long summer's giv-en?

D. C. — And the leaves of the bow'rs On the breezes are flitting.

2. Where the saints robed in white, Cleansed in life's flowing fountain, Where no sin, nor dismay, Neither trouble or sorrow,
Shining, beauteous and bright, Shall inhabit the mountain.

D. C. — Will be felt for to-day, Nor be feared for the morrow.

176 RAGAN. L.M.

"Precious in the sight of the Lord is the death of his saints." -- Ps. 116:15.

Arr. - W. F. Moore, 1869.

F Major

1. Fare - well, vain world, I'm going home; I be - long to this band, hal-le-lu - jah. Hal - le - lu - jah, hal - le - lu - jah, I be - long to this band, hal-le-lu - jah.
   My Sav-ior smiles and bids me come; I be - long to this band, hal-le-lu - jah.

2. Sweet an - gels beck-on me a - way; I be - long to this band, hal-le-lu - jah. Hal - le - lu - jah, hal - le - lu - jah, I be - long to this band, hal-le-lu - jah.
   To sing God's praise in endless day, I be - long to this band, hal-le-lu - jah.

BLOOMING YOUTH. C.M.

"Remember now thy Creator in the days of thy youth." -- Ecc. 12:1.

C Major Thomas Gibbons, 1769.   Henry G. Mann, 1869.

1. In the bright season of thy youth, In nature's smiling bloom, Ere age arrives, and trembling waits Its summons to the tomb, Its summons to the tomb.
   Ere age ar-rives,

2. Re-mem-ber thy Creator, God; For Him thy pow'rs employ; Make Him thy fear, thy love, thy hope, Thy portion and thy joy, Thy portion and thy joy.
   Make Him thy fear,

3. The Lord will safely guide thy course O'er life's uncertain seas. And bring thee to the peaceful shore, The heav'n prepared for thee, The heav'n prepared for thee.
   And bring thee to

178 AFRICA. C.M.

"The Lord hath comforted his people, and will have mercy upon his afflicted." -- Isa. 49:13.

Eb Major Isaac Watts, 1709. William Billings, 1770.

1. Now shall my inward joys arise, And burst into a song; Almighty love inspires my heart, And pleasure tunes my tongue.
2. God, on His thirsty Zion's hill, Some mercy drops has thrown; And solemn oaths have bound His love To show'r salvation down.
3. Why do we then indulge our fears, Suspicions and complaints? Is He a God, and shall His grace Grow weary of His saints?

VERMONT. C.M.D.

"For it is a good thing that the heart be established with grace; not with meats." -- Heb. 13:9.

E Minor Isaac Watts, 1709.

William Billings, 1778.

In vain we lav-ish out our lives, To gath-er emp-ty wind; The choic-est bless-ings earth can yield Will starve a hun-gry mind.

Come, and the Lord shall feed our souls With more sub-stan-tial meat, With such as saints in glo-ry love, With such as an-gels eat.

EXIT. L.M.

"He cometh forth like a flower, and is cut down." -- Job 14:2.

E Minor Isaac Watts, 1707.
P. Sherman, 1808.

PROTECTION (First). C.M.

"He hath shewed strength with his arm; he hath scattered the proud in the imagination of their hearts." -- Luke 1:51

SPRING. Concluded.

MONTGOMERY. C.M.

"Remember now thy Creator in the days of thy youth, while the evil days come not, nor the years draw nigh, when thou shalt say, I have no pleasure in them." -- Ecc. 12:1.

C Major Isaac Watts, 1719.
Justin Morgan, 1790.

VIRGINIA. C.M.

"He sendeth out his word, and melteth them: he causeth his wind to blow, and the waters flow." -- Ps. 147:18.

E Minor Isaac Watts
Oliver Brownson, 1782.

SCHENECTADY. Concluded. 193

shore to shore, Till suns............ shall rise and set no more. Till suns shall rise and set no more. Set no more.

praise shall sound from shore to shore, Till suns............ shall rise and set no more, Till suns shall rise and set no more. Set no more.

shore. Till suns shall rise and set no more. Till suns shall rise and set no more. Set no more.

suns shall rise and set no more............................. Till suns shall rise and set no more. Set no more.

HUNTINGTON. L.M.
"Wait on the Lord, and keep his way, and he shall exalt thee to inherit the land." -- Ps. 37:34.

A Major Isaac Watts, 1719.   Justin Morgan, 1790.

Lord, what a thought-less wretch was I to mourn and murmur and re-pine; To see the wick-ed placed on high, in pride and robes

Lord, what a thought-less wretch was I to mourn and murmur and re-pine; To see the wick-ed placed on high, in pride and robes

WORCESTER. S.M.

"Ye shall say, Blessed is he that cometh in the name of the Lord." -- Luke 13:35.

195

F Major Isaac Watts, 1707.

Abraham Wood, 1778.

How beauteous are their feet / Who stand on Zion's hill; / Who bring salvation on their tongues, / And words of peace reveal! / How charming, charming is their voice; / How sweet the tid-ings are. / Zion, behold thy Savior King, / He reigns and triumphs here!

ALABAMA. C.M.D.

"Make a loud noise, and rejoice, and sing praise." -- Ps. 98:4.

E Minor *Southern Harmony*, 1835. *Southern Harmony*, 1835.

GEORGIA. C.M.D.

"Christ died for us." -- Rom. 5:8.

E Minor *Southern Harmony, 1835.*
T. B. McGraw, 1935.

The cross of Christ in-spires my heart To sing redeeming grace, A-wake my soul and bear a part in my Re-deem-er's praise. Oh! who can be com-pared to Him Who died up-on the tree? This is my dear de-light-ful theme, That Je-sus died for me.

© 1936 copyright Sacred Harp Publishing Company, Inc.

GREEN STREET. Concluded. 199

Bring forth the roy-al di-a-dem, And crown Him Lord of all, And crown Him, Crown Him, crown Him, crown Him,

Bring forth the roy-al di-a-dem......... And crown Him Lord of all, And crown Him, Crown Him,

Bring forth the roy-al di-a-dem, And crown Him Lord of all, And crown Him Lord of all, And crown Him,

Bring forth the roy-al di-a-dem,......... And crown Him Lord of all, And crown Him, Crown Him,

Crown Him Lord of all, And crown,..................................... And crown Him Lord of all.

Crown Him Lord of all............. And crown Him, Crown Him, Crown Him Lord of all, And crown Him Lord of all.

Crown Him Lord of all............. And crown,..................................... And crown Him Lord of all.

Crown Him Lord of all, And crown Him, Crown Him, Crown Him Lord of all, And crown Him Lord of all.

EDOM. C.M.

"Who covereth the heavens with clouds, who prepareth rain for the earth, who maketh grass to grow upon the mountains." -- Ps. 147:8.

F Major Isaac Watts, 1719. Elisha West, 1797.

EDOM. Concluded. 201

blessings down To cheer the plains below; To cheer the plains be-low; He makes the grass the mountains crown; And corn in valleys grow, And corn in valleys grow.

sends His show'rs of blessings down To cheer the plains below,......... He makes the grass the mountains crown; And corn in valleys grow, And corn in valleys grow.

low,................. He makes the grass the mountains crown; He makes the grass the mountains crown; And corn in valleys grow, And corn in valleys grow.

low,.. He makes the grass the mountains crown, And corn in valleys grow,......... And corn in valleys grow.

PILGRIM. C.M.
"Thou therefore endure hardness; as a good soldier of Jesus Christ." -- 2 Tim. 2:3.

F# Minor John Adam Granade, ca. 1801.   *Missouri Harmony,* **1820.**

Come, all ye mourning pilgrims dear, Who're bound for Canaan's land, Our Captain's gone before us,   Then, pil-grims dear, pray do not fear,
Take cour - age and fight valiantly, Stand fast with sword in hand,   Our Fa-ther's on-ly Son,   But let us fol - low on.

PLEASANT HILL. C.M.D.

"Therefore shall ye keep my commandments, and do them." -- Lev. 22:31.

E Major John Fawcett, 1782.   Nicholson, 1820.

1. Religion is the chief concern Of mortals here below. More needful this than glit-t'ring wealth Or aught the world bestows; Nor reputation, food, or health Can give us such repose.
May I its great importance learn, Its sovereign virtues know. O may my heart, by grace renewed, Be my Redeemer's throne, And be my stubborn will subdued, His government to own.

2. Religion should our thoughts engage Amidst our youthful bloom; 'Twill fit us for declining age And for the awful tomb.

3. Let deep repentance, faith, and love, Be joined with godly fear; And all my conversation prove My heart to be sincere. Preserve me from the snares of sin Through my remaining days, And in me let each virtue shine, To my Redeemer's praise.

CHRISTIAN'S HOPE. P.M.

"Lord Jesus Christ, which is our hope." -- 1 Tim. 1:1.

G Major *Southern And Western Harmonist, 1845.* H. A. Parris, 1907.

1. We have our troubles here below, We're trav-'ling through this world of woe, To that bright world where loved ones go, Where all is peace and love, Where all is peace and love, To that bright world where loved ones go, Where all is peace and love.

2. We're fet-tered and chained up in clay While in this bod-y here we stay; By faith we know a world a-bove, Where all is peace and love, Where all is peace and love, By faith we know a world a-bove, Where all is peace and love.

3. I feel no way like get-ting tired, I'm trust-ing in His Ho-ly Word To guide my wea-ry feet a-bove, Where all is peace and love, Where all is peace and love, To guide my wea-ry feet a-bove, Where all is peace and love.

WHITESTOWN. L.M.

"The good seed are the children of the kingdom; but the tares are the children of the wicked one." -- Matt. 13:38.

REPENTANCE. C.M.D.

"But, except ye repent, ye shall all likewise perish." -- Luke 13:3.

F# Minor Isaac Watts, 1707.

Rollo, 1796.

DELIGHT. P.M.

"I will guide thee with mine eye." -- Ps. 32:8.

MOUNT PLEASANT. C.M.

"We have a building of God, an house not made with hands, eternal in the heavens." -- 2 Cor. 5:1.

F Major Isaac Watts, 1709. Deolph, 1793.

MOUNT PLEASANT. Concluded.

MOUNT ZION (First). S.M.

"I will lift mine eyes to the hills, from whence cometh my help." -- Ps. 121:1.

MOUNT ZION (First). Concluded.

OCEAN. C.M.D.

"Bless the Lord, all his works in all places of his dominion." Ps. 103:22.

PORTUGUESE HYMN. P.M.

"Saying, Where is he that is born King of the Jews? for we have seen his star in the east, and are come to worship him." -- Matt. 2:2.

A Major John F. Wade, c. 1743.

224 SAVE, LORD, OR WE PERISH. 12s.

"Thy faith hath saved thee; go in peace." -- Luke 7:50.

E Minor Reginald Heber, 1827. M. Mark Wynn, 1869.

1. When thro' the torn sail the wild tem-pest is stream-ing, When o'er the dark wave the red light-ning is gleam-ing.

1. When thro' the torn sail the wild tem-pest is stream-ing, When o'er the dark wave the red light-ning is gleam-ing.

Nor hope lends a ray the poor sea-man to cher-ish, We fly to our Mak-er, Save, Lord, or we per-ish.

Nor hope lends a ray the poor sea-man to cher-ish, We fly to our Mak-er, Save, Lord, or we per-ish.

Nor hope lends a ray the poor sea-man to cher-ish, We fly to our Mak-er, Save, Lord, or we per-ish.

ray the poor sea-man to cher-ish, We fly to our Mak-er, Save, Lord, or we per-ish.

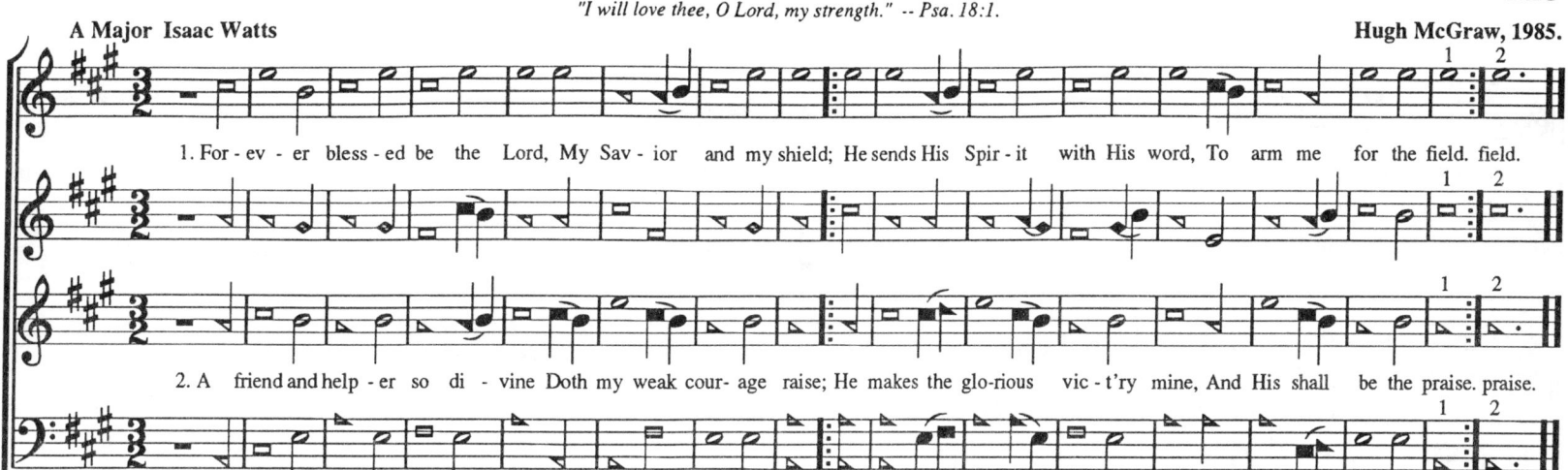

226 CHRISTMAS ANTHEM. Concluded.

ODE ON LIFE'S JOURNEY.

227

"But he forsook the counsel of the old men, which they had given him, and consulted with the young men." -- 1 Kings 12:8.

A Major

E. J. King, 1844.

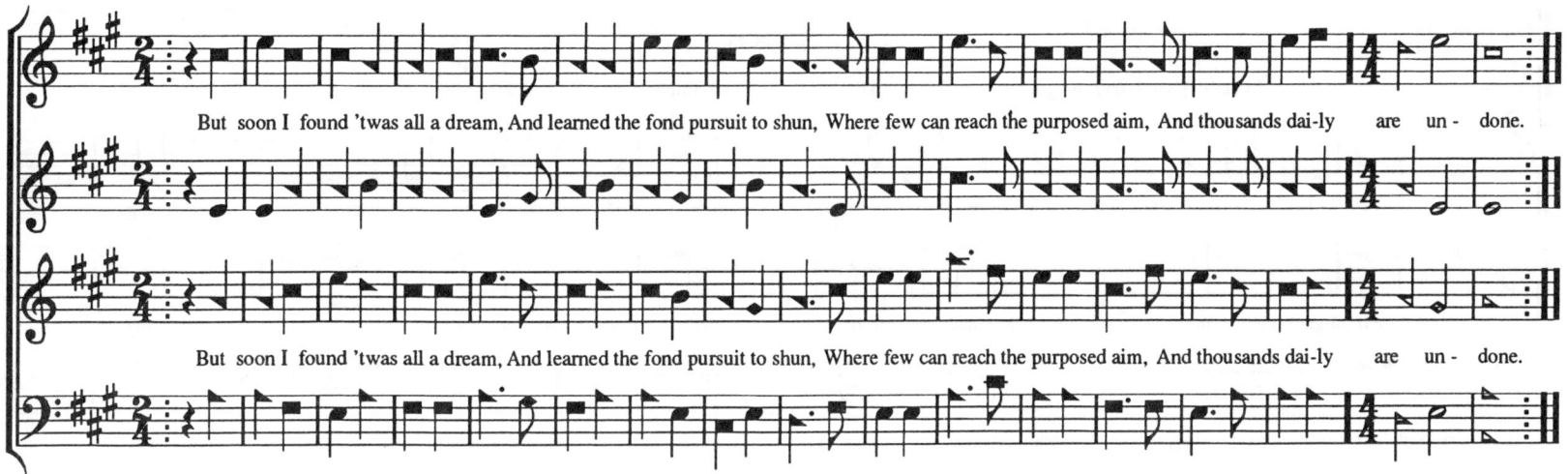

I be-gan life's jour-ney when young, And the glitt'ring prospect charmed my eyes; I saw joy af-ter joy suc-ces-sive rise A-long the ex-tend-ed plain.

I be-gan life's jour-ney when young, And the glitt'ring prospect charmed my eyes; I saw joy af-ter joy suc-ces-sive rise A-long the ex-tend-ed plain.

But soon I found 'twas all a dream, And learned the fond pursuit to shun, Where few can reach the purposed aim, And thousands dai-ly are un-done.

But soon I found 'twas all a dream, And learned the fond pursuit to shun, Where few can reach the purposed aim, And thousands dai-ly are un-done.

MARLBOROUGH. C.M.

"Be glad in the Lord, and rejoice, ye righteous: and shout for joy." -- Psa. 32:11.

C Major Isaac Watts, 1719.

Abraham Wood, 1793.

IRWINTON. C.M.D.

"Harken my beloved brethren, Hath not God chosen the poor of this world rich in faith." -- James 2:5.

CONVERTING GRACE. C.M.

"The law of the Lord is perfect, converting the soul." -- Ps. 19:7.

G Major Tate and Brady's *New Version*, 1696. R. E. Brown, Jr., 1859.

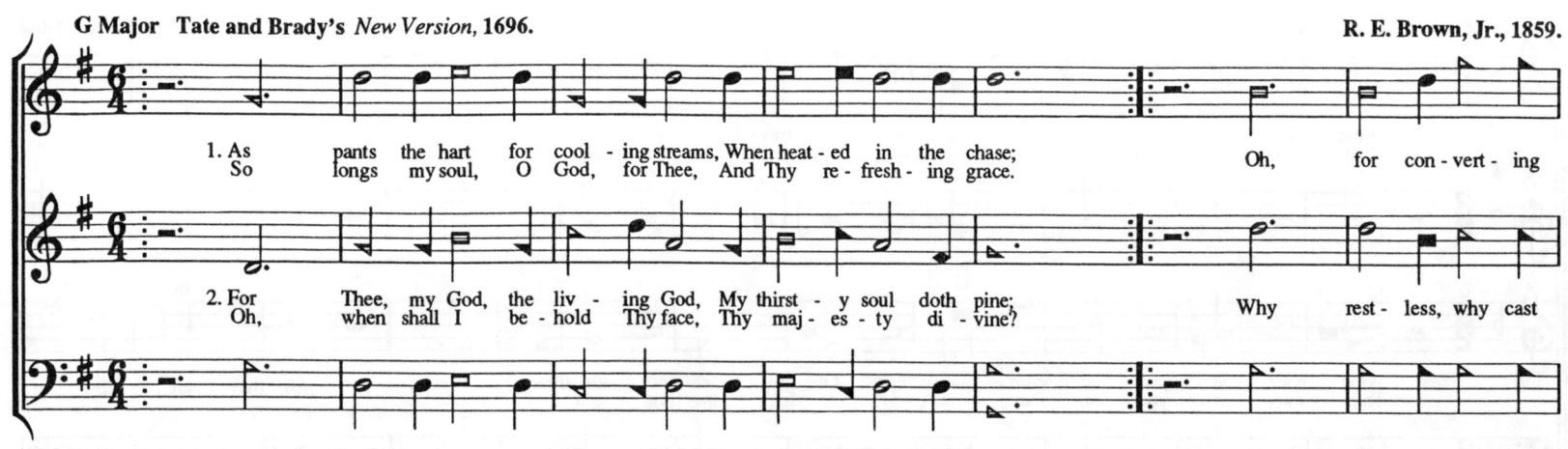

1. As pants the hart for cool-ing streams, When heat-ed in the chase;
So longs my soul, O God, for Thee, And Thy re-fresh-ing grace.

2. For Thee, my God, the liv-ing God, My thirst-y soul doth pine;
Oh, when shall I be-hold Thy face, Thy maj-es-ty di-vine?

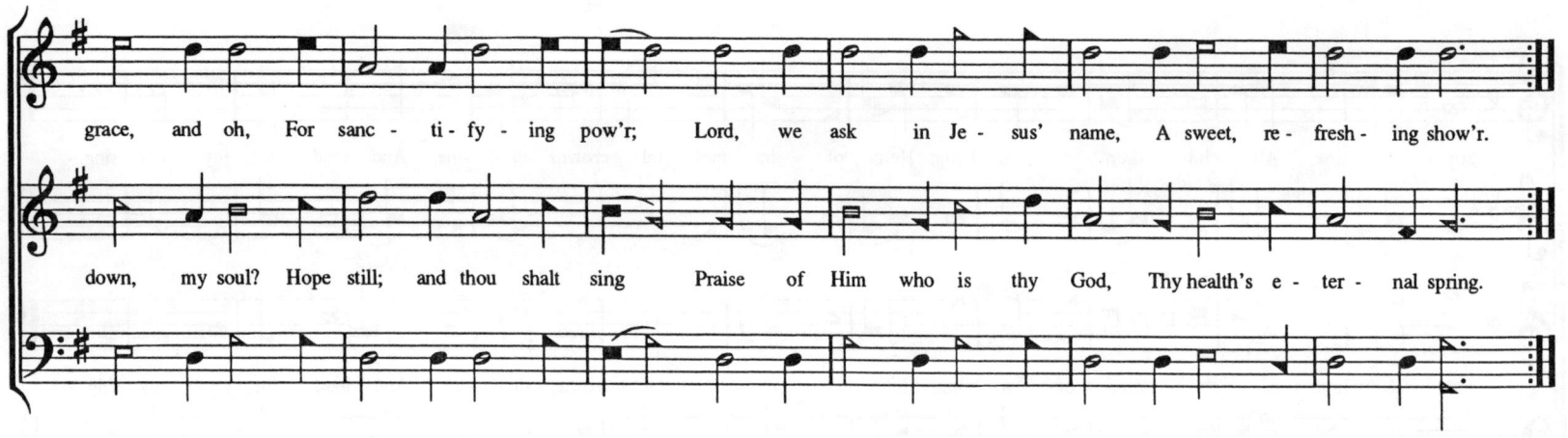

Oh, for con-vert-ing grace, and oh, For sanc-ti-fy-ing pow'r; Lord, we ask in Je-sus' name, A sweet, re-fresh-ing show'r.

Why rest-less, why cast down, my soul? Hope still; and thou shalt sing Praise of Him who is thy God, Thy health's e-ter-nal spring.

THOU ART PASSING AWAY. 11s.

"Because as the flower of the grass he shall pass away." -- James 1:10.

G Major
Arr. - George Coles.

1. Thou art pass-ing a-way, thou art pass-ing a-way, Thy life has been brief as a mid-sum-mer day;
2. Thou art pass-ing a-way from the beau-ti-ful earth, Thy much lov'd a-bode, and the land of thy birth;
3. Thou art pass-ing a-way from thy kin-dred and friends, And the last chain that bound thee, the spoil-er now rends;

Thy fore-head is pale, and thy puls-es are low, And thy once bloom-ing cheek wears an om-i-nous glow.
From its for-ests and fields, from its mur-mur-ing rills, From its beau-ti-ful plains and its herb-age-crowned hills.
And thy last tones are fall-ing on love's list-'ning ear, And now in thine eye shines the fond, part-ing tear.

232 BAPTISMAL ANTHEM.
"In those days came John the Baptist, preaching in the wilderness of Judea." -- Matt. 3:1-4.

BAPTISMAL ANTHEM. Concluded. 233

234 REVERENTIAL ANTHEM.
"Give unto the Lord the glory due unto his name." -- Ps. 96.

C Major Psalm 29:2; 96:11-13.
E. J. King, 1844.

Come in-to His courts, Wor-ship the Lord in the beau-ty of ho-li-ness.

Give un-to the Lord The glo-ry due un-to His name; Come in-to His courts, Wor-ship the Lord in the beau-ty of ho-li-ness.

Give un-to the Lord The glo-ry due un-to His name; Come in-to His courts, Wor-ship the Lord in the beau-ty of ho-li-ness.

The glo-ry due un-to His name; Come in-to His courts, Wor-ship the Lord in the beau-ty of ho-li-ness.

Fear be-fore Him all the earth, He shall judge the peo-ple right-eous-ly. Let the heav'ns re-joice, And the earth be

Fear be-fore Him all the earth, He shall judge the peo-ple right-eous-ly. Let the heav'ns re-joice, And the earth be

Fear be-fore Him all............... the earth, He shall judge the peo-ple right-eous-ly. Let the heav'ns re-joice, And the earth be

Fear be-fore Him all the earth, right-eous-ly. And the earth be

REVERENTIAL ANTHEM. Concluded. 235

glad be-fore the Lord. For He com-eth To judge the world with righteousness, And the peo-ple with His truth.

glad be-fore the Lord. To judge the world with righteousness, And the peo-ple with His truth.

glad be-fore the Lord. For He com-eth, To judge the world with righteousness, And the peo-ple with His truth.

glad be-fore the Lord. For He com-eth To judge the world with righteousness, And the peo-ple with His truth.

LONG SOUGHT HOME. C.M.

"In my father's house are many mansions: if it were not so, I would have told you." -- St. John 14:2.

C Major Anonymous, ca. 1600.   **William Bobo, 1847.**

1. Je - ru - sa - lem! my hap - py home! Oh, how I long for thee!
   When will my sor - rows have an end? Thy joys when shall I see?
   Home, sweet home, my long-sought home, My home in heav'n a - bove.

2. Thy walls are all of pre - cious stones, Most glo - r'ous to be - hold!
   Thy gates are rich - ly set with pearl, Thy streets are paved with gold.

3. My friends, I bid you all a - dieu; I leave you in God's care;
   And if I here no more see you, Go on; I'll meet you there.
   Home, sweet home, my long-sought home, My home in heav'n a - bove.

EASTER ANTHEM.

"But now is Christ risen from the dead, and become the firstfruits of them that slept." - I Cor. 15:20.

A Major Edward Young.   William Billings, 1787.

EASTER ANTHEM. Continued.

237

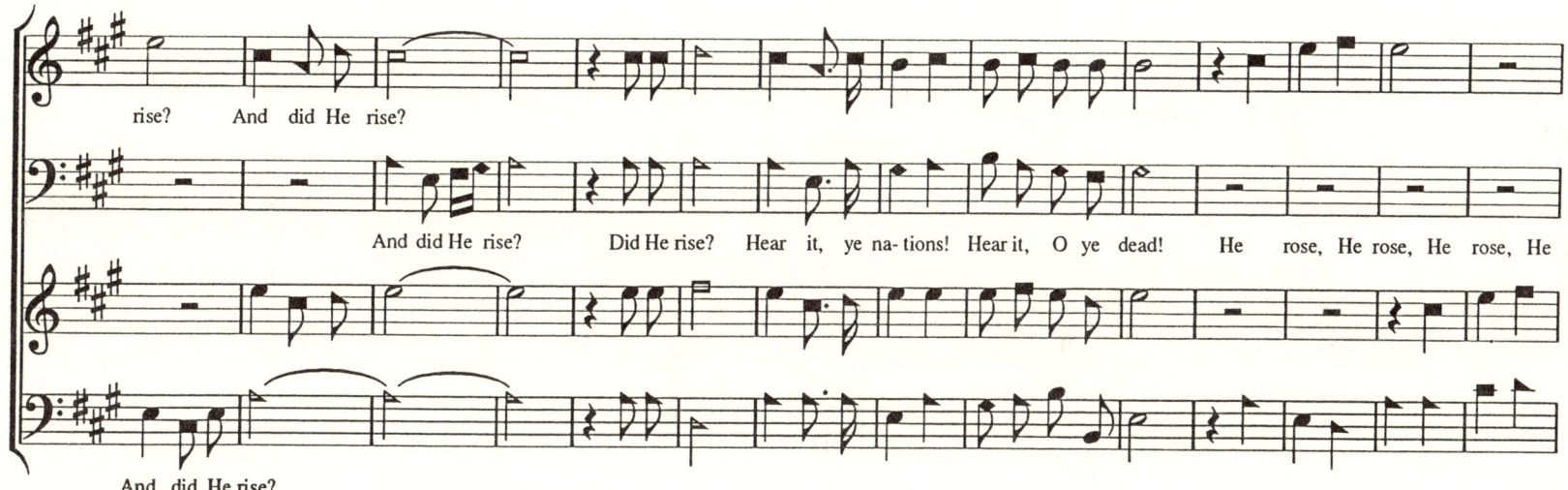

238   **EASTER ANTHEM. Continued.**

EASTER ANTHEM. Concluded.

CHRISTIAN SONG.
"Write, Blessed are the dead which die in the Lord." -- Rev. 14:13.

CHRISTIAN SONG. Concluded. 241

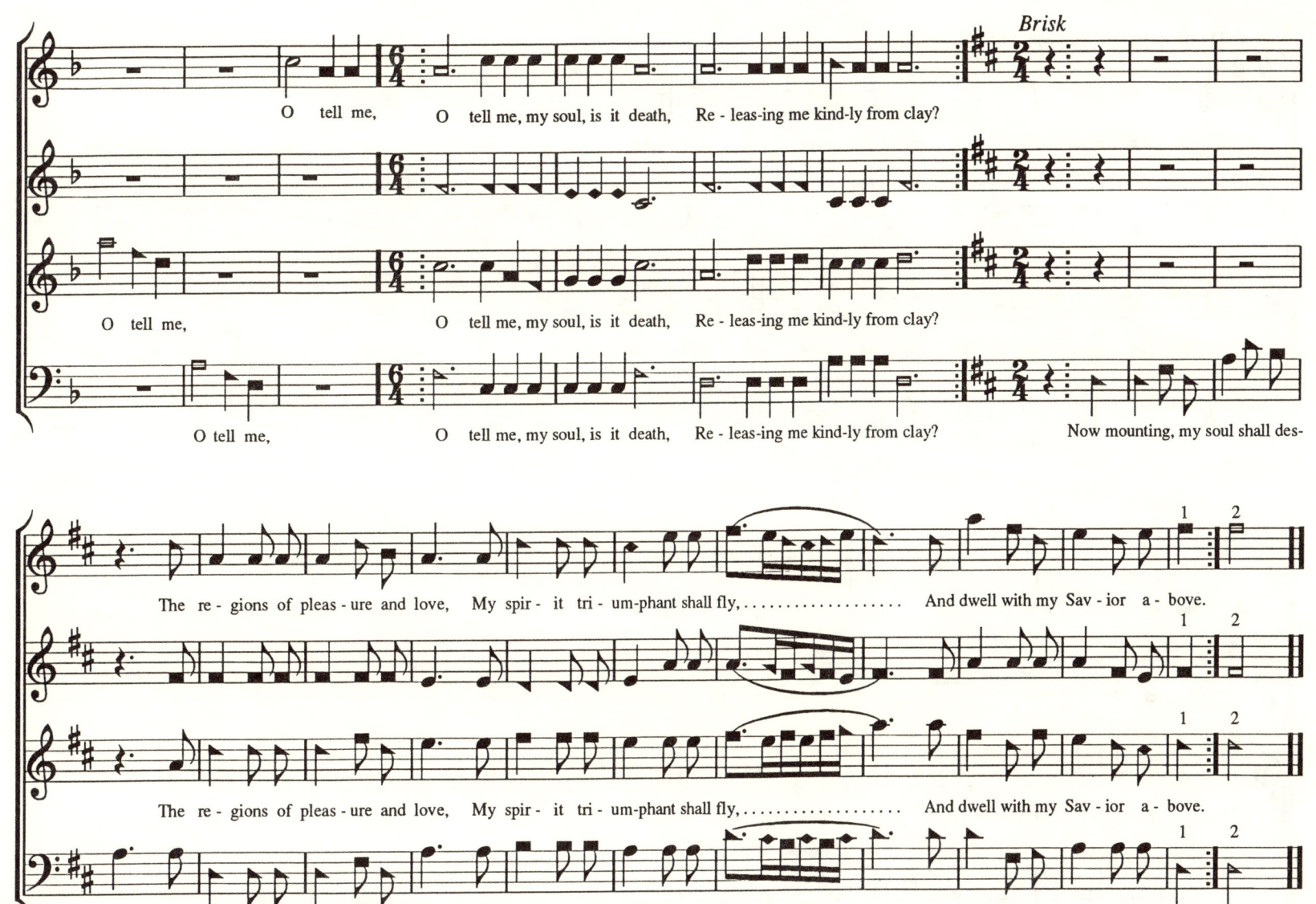

ODE ON SCIENCE. Concluded.

CLAREMONT. 7s & 8s.

"O death, where is thy sting? O grave, where is thy victory?" -- 1 Cor. 15:55.

A Minor Alexander Pope, 1712. Temple & Merrill, 1799.

CLAREMONT. Continued.

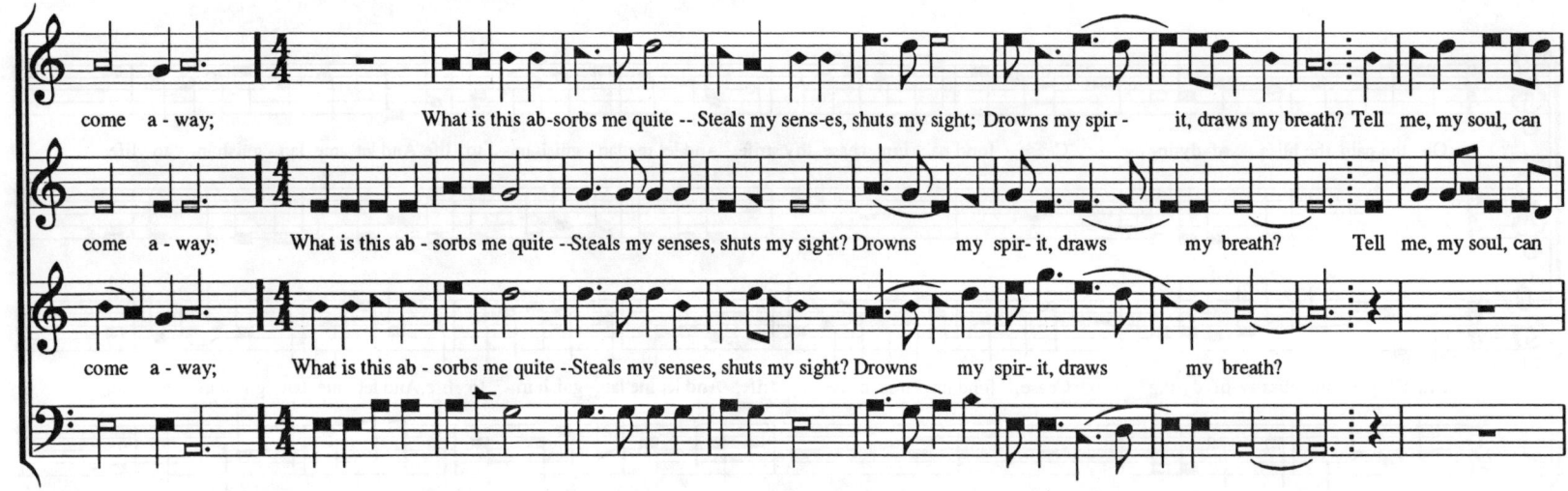

CLAREMONT. Continued. 247

this be death? Tell me, my soul, can this be death? *The*

this be death? Tell me, my soul, can this be death? Tell me, my soul, can this be death?

Tell me, my soul, can this be death? Tell me, my soul, can this be death? *The*

Soft

world recedes, it disappears, Heav'n opens on my eyes, my ears with sounds seraphic ring, My ears with

world recedes, it disappears, Heav'n opens on my eyes, my ears with sounds seraphic ring, My ears with

248

CLAREMONT. Continued.

HEAVENLY VISION.
Based on Revelation 7:9; 5:11; 4:8; 8:13; 6:15-17.

Jacob French, 1786.

HEAVENLY VISION. Continued. 251

HEAVENLY VISION. Continued.

HEAVENLY VISION. Concluded. 253

ROSE OF SHARON.

"I am the rose of Sharon, and the lily of the valleys..." -- S. Sol. 2:1-11.

William Billings, 1778

ROSE OF SHARON. Continued. 255

256 ROSE OF SHARON. Continued.

He brought me to the banqueting house, his ban-ner o-ver me was love. Stay me with flagons

He brought me to the banqueting house, his ban-ner o-ver me was love.

Comfort me with

His ban-ner o-ver me was love, He brought me to the banqueting house, his ban-ner o-ver me was love.

for I am sick, for I am sick.......... of love; I charge you, O ye daugh-ters of Je-ru-sa-lem,

for I am sick.......... of love; I charge you, O ye daugh-ters of Je-ru-sa-lem,

ap-ples, for I am sick, for I am sick.......... of love; I charge you, O ye daugh-ters of Je-ru-sa-lem,

ROSE OF SHARON. Continued.

257

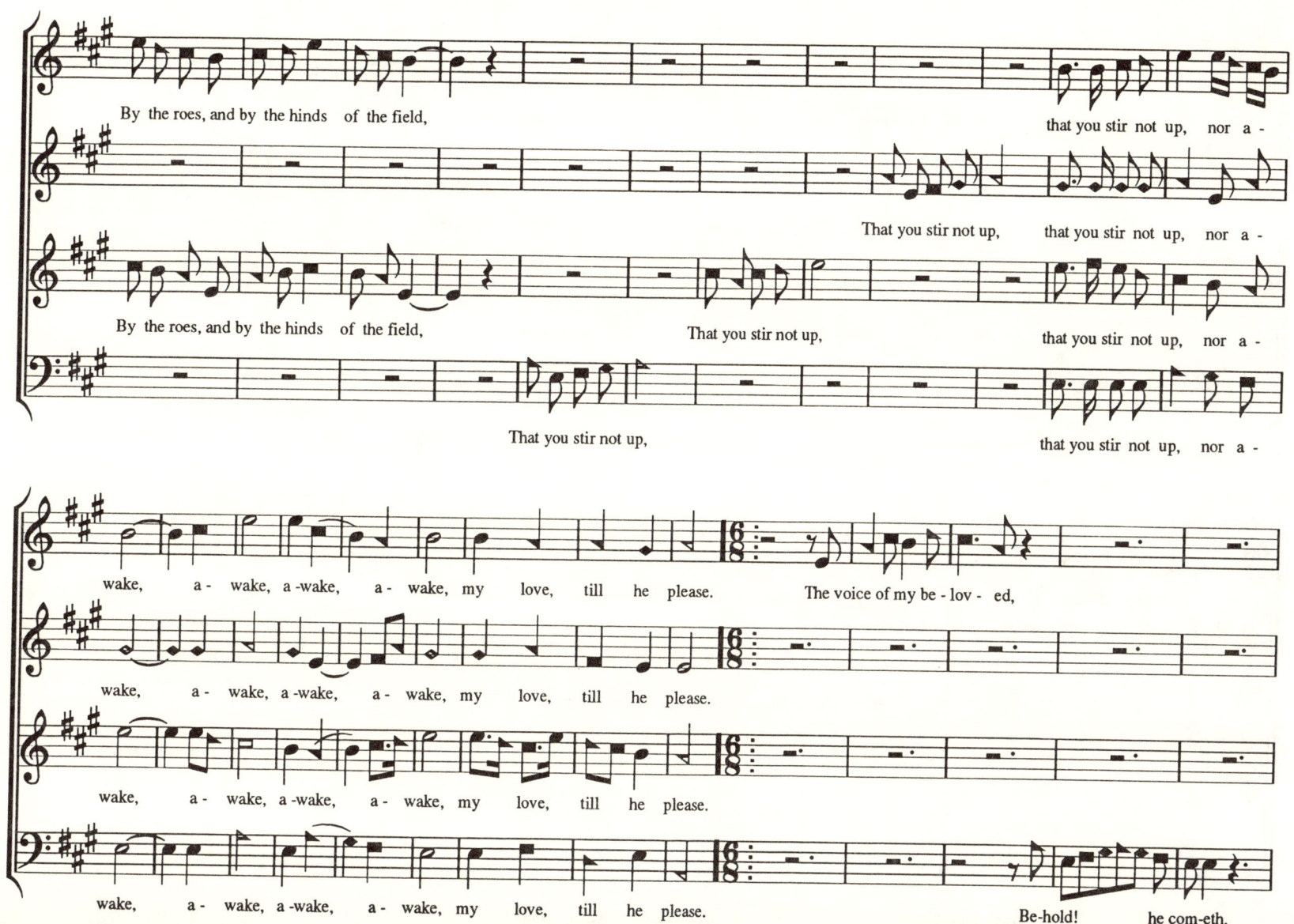

ROSE OF SHARON. Concluded. 259

FAREWELL ANTHEM.
"But let me bid them farewell." -- Luke 9:61.

A Minor Anonymous.   Jacob French, 1789.

My friends, I am go-ing a long and tedious journey, Nev-er to re-turn. I am go-ing a long and tedious journey, Never to re-turn. I am go-ing a long journey, Nev-er to re-turn; nev-er to re-turn.

My friends, I am go-ing a long and te-dious jour-ney, Nev-er to re-turn. I am go-ing, I am go-ing a long and tedious journey, Never to re-turn. I am go-ing a long jour-ney, Never to re-turn, Nev-er to re-turn, Nev-er to re-turn, Nev-er to re-

My friends, I am go-ing a long and te-dious jour-ney, Nev-er to re-turn. I am go-ing, I am go-ing a long and te-dious jour-ney, Never to re-turn. I am going a long journey, Never to return, Nev-er to re-turn, Nev-er to re-turn, Nev-er to re-

My friends, I am go-ing a - long, and te-dious jour-ney, Nev-er to re-turn. I am going a long journey, Nev-er to re-turn, I am going a long jour-ney, Never to re-turn. Nev-er to re-turn, Nev-er to re-turn,

FAREWELL ANTHEM. Continued. 261

FAREWELL ANTHEM. Concluded.

DODDRIDGE. 8,7,8,7,4,7.
263

"And if the righteous scarcely be saved, where shall the ungodly and the sinner appear?" -- 1 Peter 4:18.

A Major M. M. Wynn, 1869.
M. M. Wynn, 1869.

"Why, O sinner, me profaning...... Why," says God, "my statutes name; Why my cov'nant grace disdaining, Still my cov'nant grace proclaim! Hating counsel, Hating counsel, All my laws exposed to shame. Long in

DODDRIDGE. Concluded. 265

KINGWOOD. 8,8,6.

"Lord, make me to know mine end, and the measure of my days." - Ps. 39:4.

A Major Joshua Smith's *Divine Hymns,* 1794. Humphreys, 1820.

1. My days, my weeks, my months, my years, Fly rap-id as the whirl-ing spheres, Fly rap-id as the whirl-ing spheres, A-round the stead-y pole. Time, like the tide, its mo-tion keeps, And I must launch thro' end-less deeps, And I must launch thro' end-less deeps, Where end-less a-ges roll.

2. The grave is near the cra-dle seen, How swift the mo-ments pass be-tween, How swift the mo-ments pass be-tween, And whis-per as they fly, Un-think-ing man, re-mem-ber this, Though fond of sub-lu-nar-y bliss, Though fond of sub-lu-nar-y bliss, That you must groan and die.

3. My soul, at-tend the sol-emn call, Thine earth-ly tent must short-ly fall, Thine earth-ly tent must short-ly fall, And thou must take thy flight Be-yond the vast ex-pan-sive blue, To sing a-bove, as an-gels do, To sing a-bove, as an-gels do, Or sing in end-less night.

PARTING FRIENDS (First). P.M.

"For I am now ready to be offered, and . . . my departure is at hand." -- 2 Tim. 4:6.

Arr. - John G. McCurry, 1842.

F# Minor

Fare - well, my friends, I'm bound for Ca-naan, I'm trav-'ling through the wil-der-ness; I go a - way, be - hind to leave you;
Your com - pa - ny has been de - light - ful, You, who doth leave my mind dis-tressed.

Per - haps nev - er to meet a - gain, But if we nev - er have the plea-sure, I hope we'll meet on Ca-naan's land.

DAVID'S LAMENTATION.

"And as he went, thus he said, O my son Absalom! my son, my son Absalom! Would God I had died for thee, O Absalom, my son, my son! -- 2 Sam. 18:33.

William Billings, 1778.

BEAR CREEK. L.M.

269

"The chariots of God are twenty thousand, even thousands of angels." -- Ps. 67:17.

E Major Isaac Watts, 1719.

William Billings, 1778.

CONFIDENCE. L.M.D.

"Repentance toward God, and faith toward our Lord Jesus Christ." -- Acts 20:21.

A Major Charles Wesley, 1742.   J. R. Turner, 1850.

A-way, my un-be-liev-ing fear; Fear shall in me no more have place; But shall I there-fore let Him go,
My Sav-ior doth not yet ap-pear; He hides the bright-ness of His face;

And base-ly to the tempt-er yield? No, in the strength of Je-sus, no! I nev-er will give up my shield.

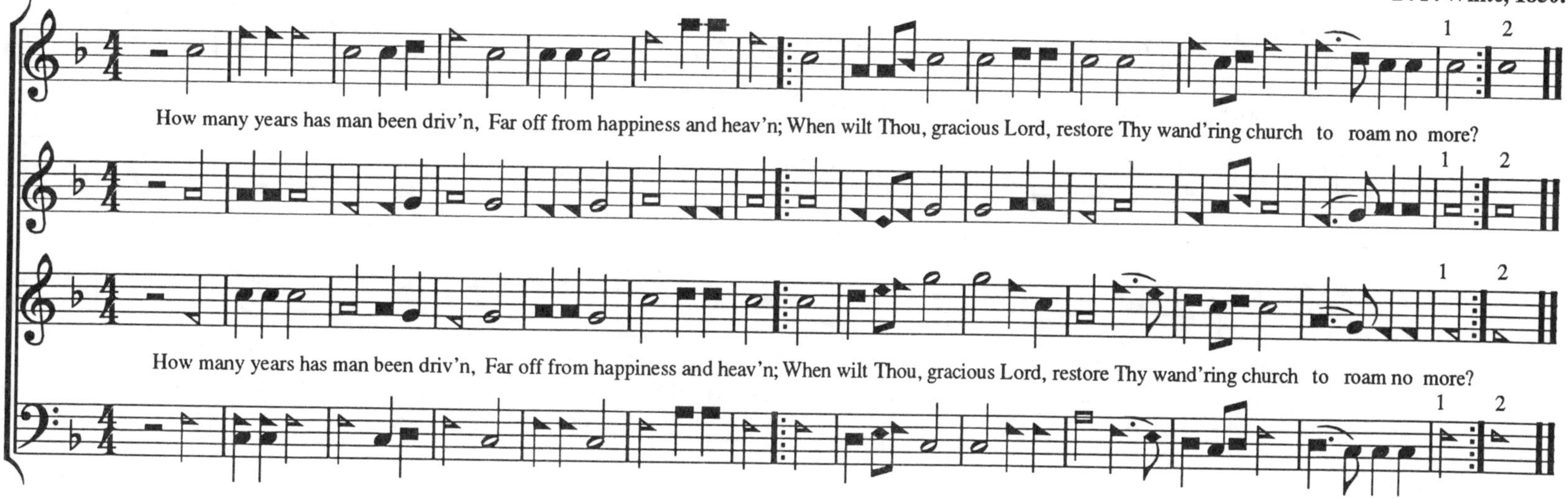

272 EXHORTATION. (Second) L. M.

"Flee also youthful lusts." -- 2 Tim. 2:22.

A Minor Isaac Watts, 1709.   Eliakim Doolittle, 1800.

Now, in the heat of youth-ful blood, Re-mem-ber your Cre-a-tor God, Be-hold the months come hast'ning on, When you shall say, My joys are gone.

Now, in the heat of youth-ful blood, Re-mem-ber your Cre-a-tor God, Be-hold the months come hast'ning on, When you shall say, My joys are gone. When you shall say, My joys are gone.

Be-hold the months come hast'ning on, When you shall say, My joys are gone, When you shall say, My joys are gone.

Behold the months come hast'ning on, When you shall say, My joys are gone. Be-hold the months come hast'ning on, When you shall say, My joys are gone.

you shall say, My joys are gone. Be-hold the months come hast-'ning on, When you shall say, My joys are gone.

274

THE GOLDEN HARP. L.M.

"Yea, upon the harp will I praise thee." -- Ps. 43:4.

F Minor *Sacred Harp, 1869.*
J. P. Reese, 1869

1. Fare-well, vain world, I'm go-ing home To play on the Gold-en Harp. To play on the Gold-en Harp, To play on the Gold-en Harp.
My Sav-ior smiles and bids me come To play on the Gold-en Harp.

Cho.- I want to be where Je-sus is, To play on the Gold-en Harp.

2. Sweet an-gels beck-on me a-way To play on the Gold-en Harp. To play on the Gold-en Harp, To play on the Gold-en Harp.
To sing God's praise in end-less day To play on the Gold-en Harp.

ROLL JORDAN. L.M.

"Blow the trumpet among the nations, prepare the nations." -- Jer. 51:27.

G Major Charles Wesley, 1758 Alt.
A. W. and John G. McCurry, 1855.

1. He comes! He comes! the Judge severe, Roll, Jor-dan, roll; I want to go to heav'n, I do, Hallelujah, Lord, We'll praise the Lord in heav'n above, Roll, Jordan, roll.
The seventh trum-pet speaks Him near, Roll, Jor-dan, roll;

2. His lightnings flash, His thunders roll, Roll, Jor-dan, roll; I want to go to heav'n, I do, Hallelujah, Lord, We'll praise the Lord in heav'n above, Roll, Jordan, roll.
How wel-come to the faith-ful soul! Roll, Jor-dan, roll;

ANTIOCH. L.M.

"For I know that my Redeemer liveth, and that he shall stand at the latter day upon the earth." -- Job 19:25.

1. I know that my Redeemer lives, Glory, Hallelujah!
What comfort this sweet sentence gives, Glory, Hallelujah!

2. He lives to bless you with His love; Glory, Hallelujah!
He lives to plead my cause above; Glory, Hallelujah!

3. He lives to crush the fiends of hell; Glory, Hallelujah!
He lives and doth within me dwell; Glory, Hallelujah!

Shout on, pray on, we're gaining ground, Glory, hallelujah! The dead's alive, and the lost is found, Glory, hallelujah!

278

LOVE SHALL NEVER DIE C.M.

"Mercy unto you, and peace, and love, be multiplied." -- Jude 1:2.

F Minor Isaac Watts, 1709.
Toney Smith, 1987.

1. Long have I sat be-neath the sound Of Thy sal-va-tion, Lord, And still how weak my faith is found And knowl-edge of Thy word. word.
2. How cold and fee-ble is my love! How neg-li-gent my fears! How long my hopes of joys a-bove, How few af-fec-tions there. there.
3. Show my for-get-ful feet the way That leads to joys on high, Where knowl-edge grows with-out de-cay And love shall nev-er die. die.

TRAVELING PILGRIM. L.M.

"Man goeth to his long sought home." -- Ecc. 15:5.

E Minor H. S. Reese, 1850.
H. S. Reese, 1850.

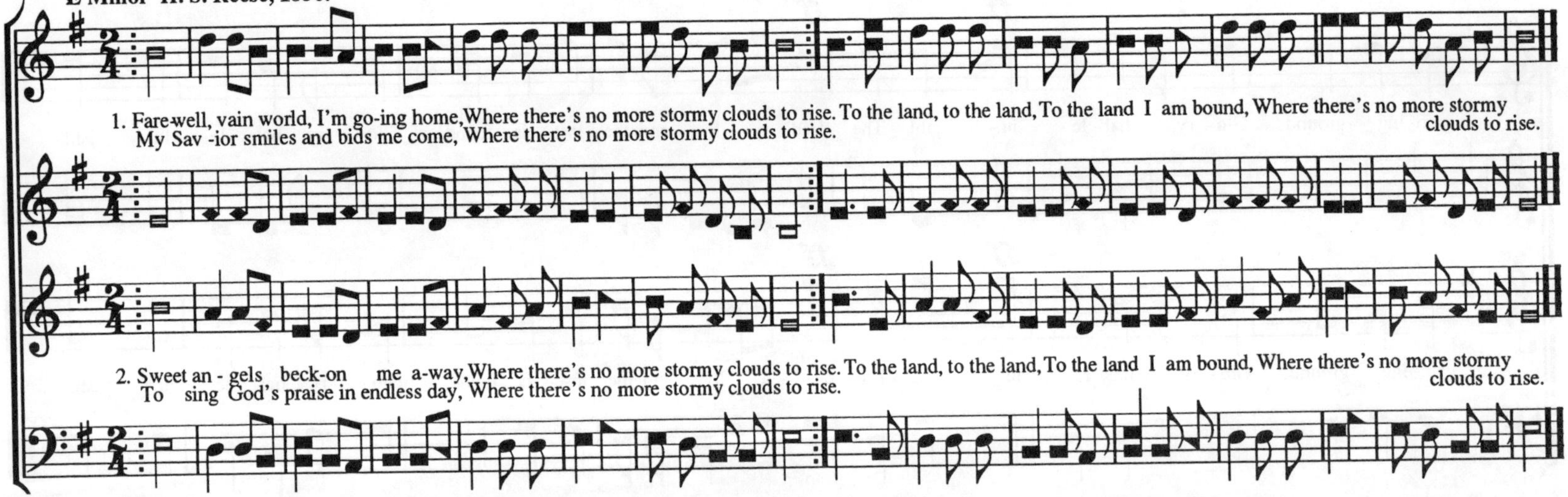

1. Fare-well, vain world, I'm go-ing home, Where there's no more stormy clouds to rise. To the land, to the land, To the land I am bound, Where there's no more stormy clouds to rise.
My Sav-ior smiles and bids me come, Where there's no more stormy clouds to rise.

2. Sweet an-gels beck-on me a-way, Where there's no more stormy clouds to rise. To the land, to the land, To the land I am bound, Where there's no more stormy clouds to rise.
To sing God's praise in endless day, Where there's no more stormy clouds to rise.

280 WESTFORD. L.M.

"Therefore sprang there even of one, and him as good as dead, so many as the stars of the sky in multitude, and as the sand which is by the seashore innumerable." -- Heb. 11:12.

Bb Major Isaac Watts, 1707.   Daniel Read, 1785.

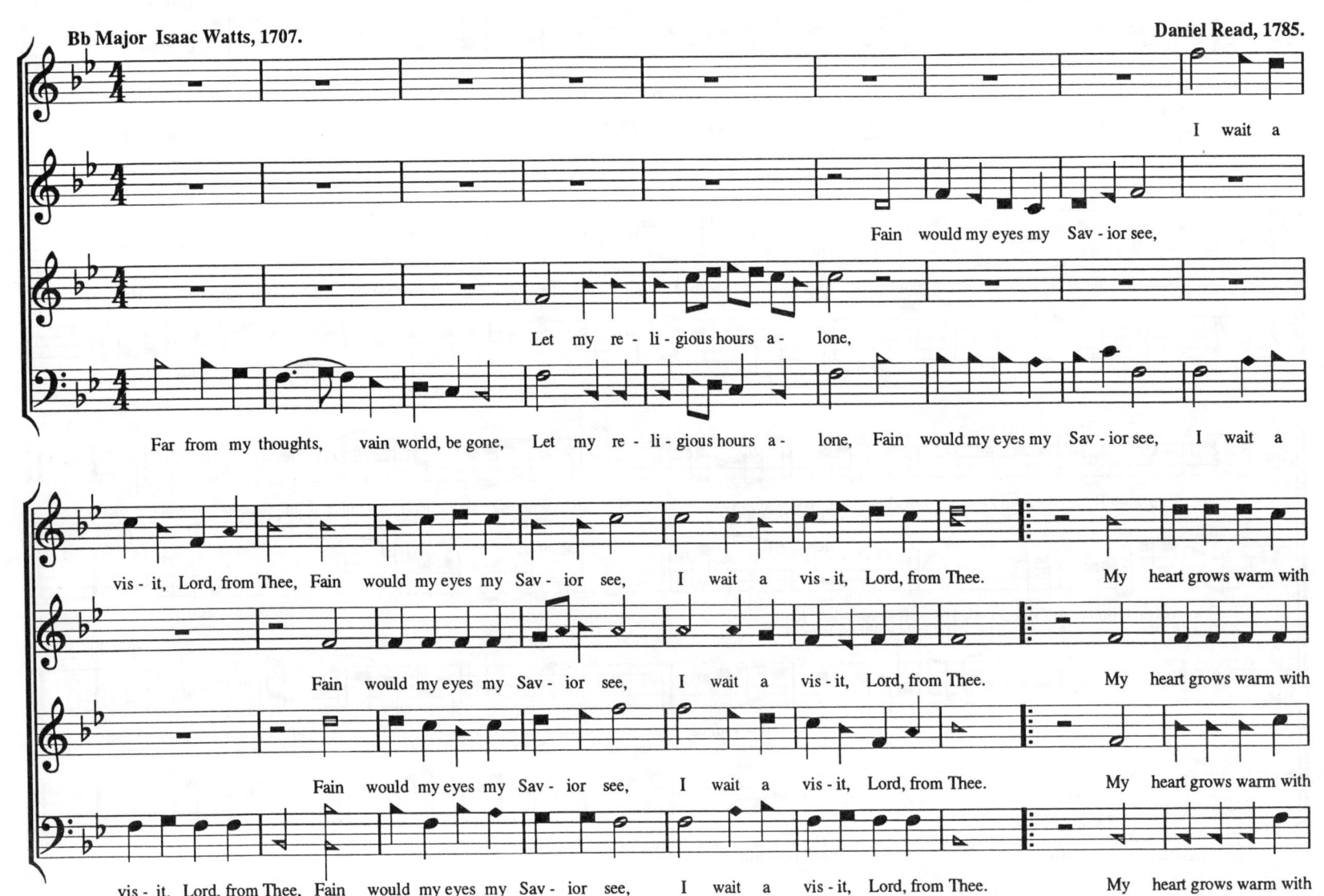

WESTFORD. Concluded.

GARDEN HYMN. 8,8,6.

"Thou that dwellest in the gardens, the companions harken to thy voice." -- S. of Sol. 8:13.

G Major

Supplement to the *Kentucky Harmony,* 1826.

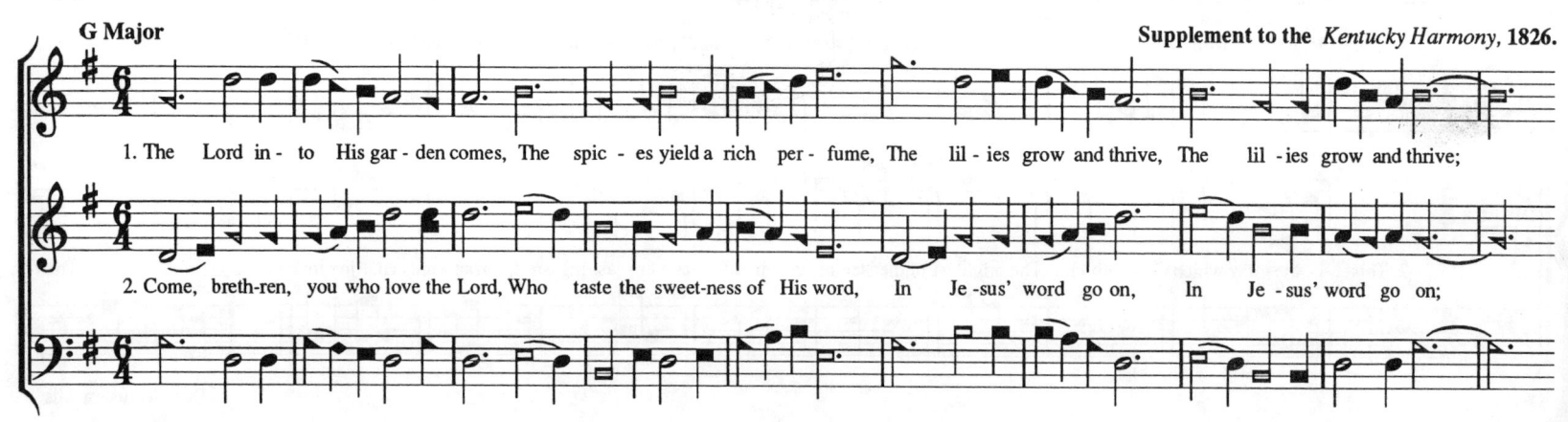

1. The Lord in-to His gar-den comes, The spic-es yield a rich per-fume, The lil-ies grow and thrive, The lil-ies grow and thrive;
2. Come, breth-ren, you who love the Lord, Who taste the sweet-ness of His word, In Je-sus' word go on, In Je-sus' word go on;

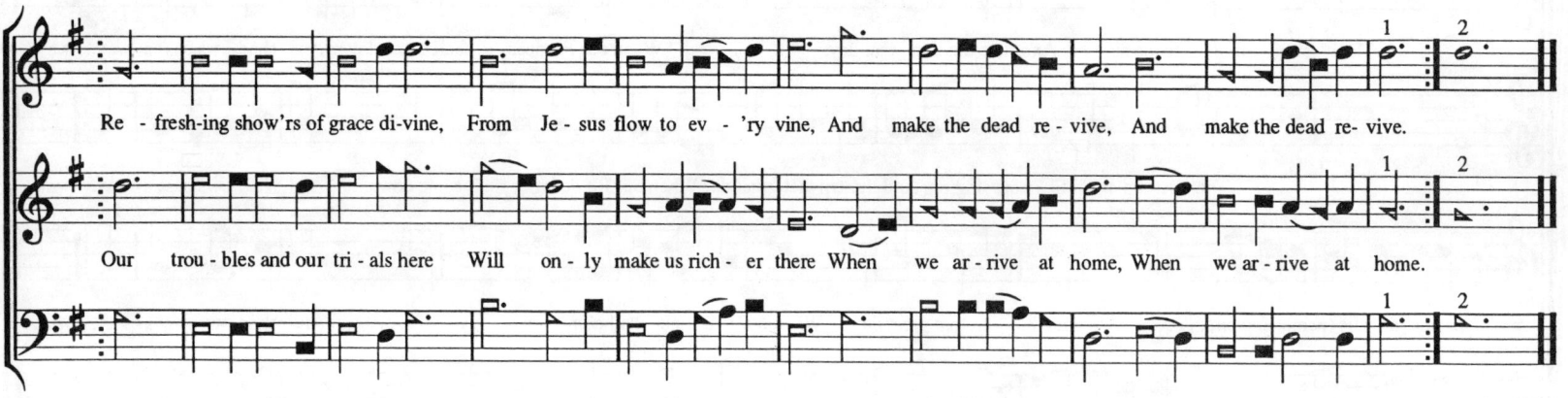

Re-fresh-ing show'rs of grace di-vine, From Je-sus flow to ev-'ry vine, And make the dead re-vive, And make the dead re-vive.

Our trou-bles and our tri-als here Will on-ly make us rich-er there When we ar-rive at home, When we ar-rive at home.

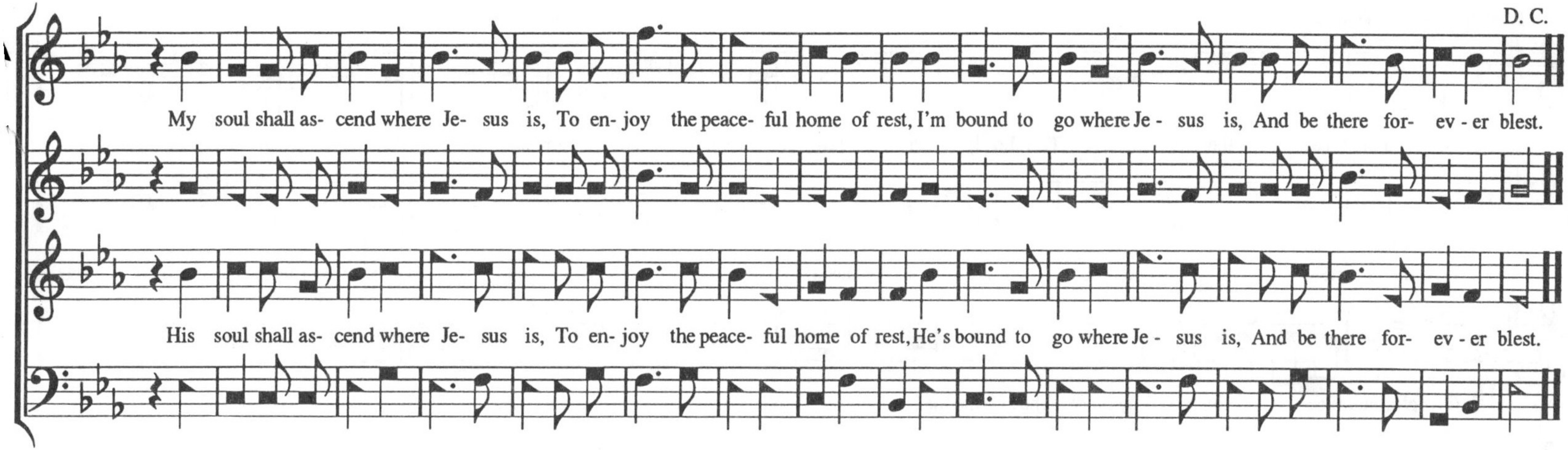

ROCKY ROAD. Concluded. 295

D.C.

My soul shall as-cend where Je-sus is, To en-joy the peace-ful home of rest, I'm bound to go where Je-sus is, And be there for-ev-er blest.

His soul shall as-cend where Je-sus is, To en-joy the peace-ful home of rest, He's bound to go where Je-sus is, And be there for-ev-er blest.

ODEM (First). C.M.

"... repent ye, and believe the gospel." -- Mark 1:15.

G Major Isaac Watts, 1707.   Leon McGraw, 1935.

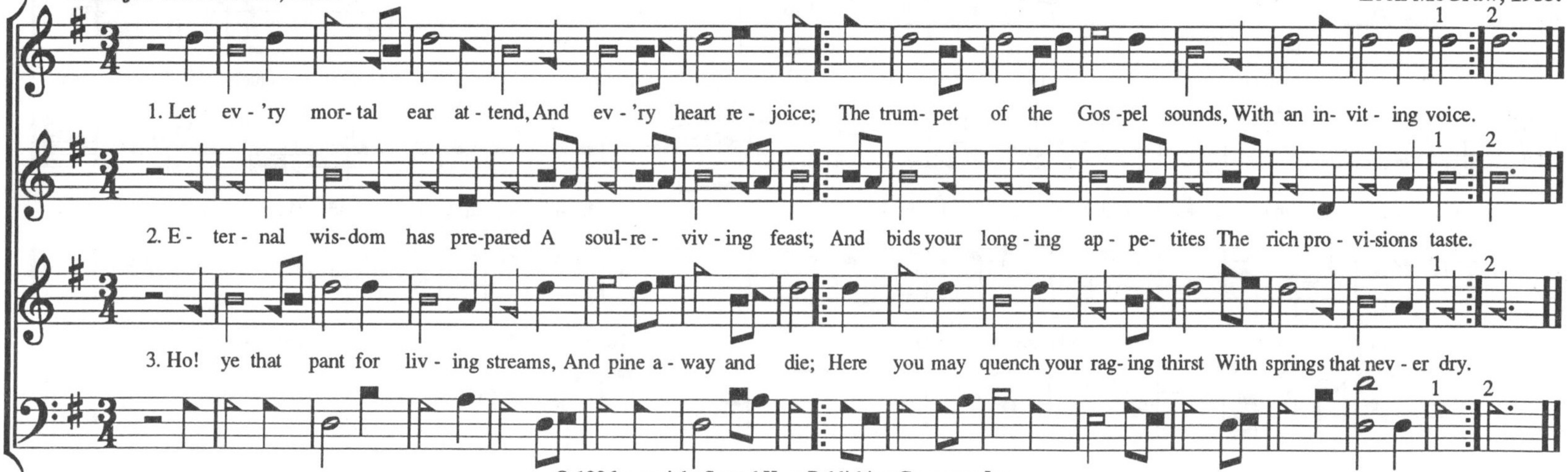

1. Let ev-'ry mor-tal ear at-tend, And ev-'ry heart re-joice; The trum-pet of the Gos-pel sounds, With an in-vit-ing voice.

2. E-ter-nal wis-dom has pre-pared A soul-re-viv-ing feast; And bids your long-ing ap-pe-tites The rich pro-vi-sions taste.

3. Ho! ye that pant for liv-ing streams, And pine a-way and die; Here you may quench your rag-ing thirst With springs that nev-er dry.

© 1936 copyright Sacred Harp Publishing Company, Inc.

298 PROVIDENCE. C.M.

"To give light to them that sit in darkness and in the shadow of death, to guide our feet into the way of peace. -- Luke 1:79.

A Major Isaac Watts, 1719. C. Curtis, 1820.

CALVARY. C.M.

"But the natural man receiveth not the things of the Spirit of God." -- 1 Cor. 2:14.

A Minor Isaac Watts, 1707. **Daniel Read, 1785.**

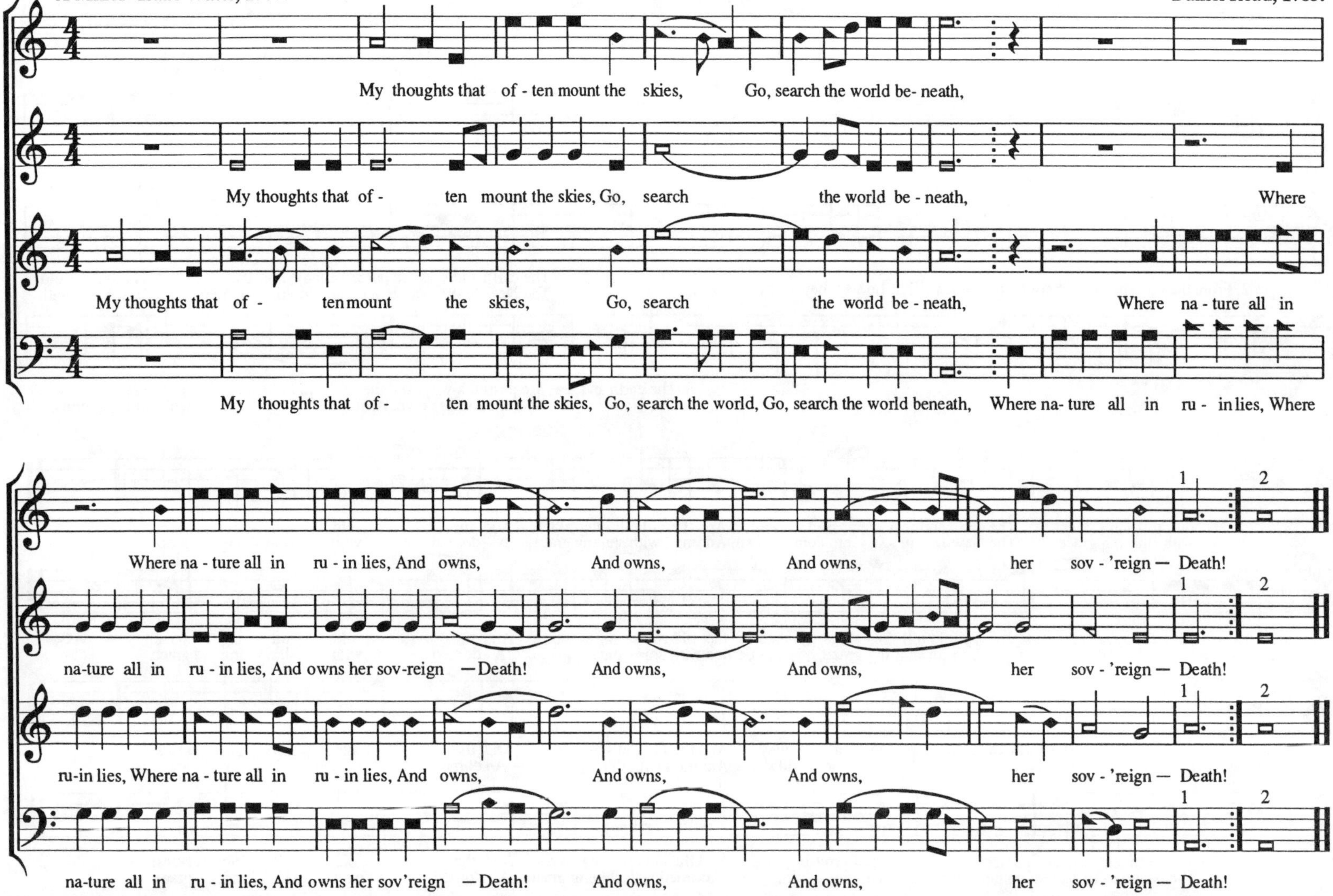
My thoughts that of - ten mount the skies, Go, search the world be- neath,
My thoughts that of - ten mount the skies, Go, search the world be - neath, Where
My thoughts that of - ten mount the skies, Go, search the world be - neath, Where na - ture all in
My thoughts that of - ten mount the skies, Go, search the world, Go, search the world beneath, Where na- ture all in ru - in lies, Where
Where na - ture all in ru - in lies, And owns, And owns, And owns, her sov - 'reign — Death!
na-ture all in ru - in lies, And owns her sov-reign —Death! And owns, And owns, her sov - 'reign — Death!
ru-in lies, Where na - ture all in ru - in lies, And owns, And owns, And owns, her sov - 'reign — Death!
na-ture all in ru - in lies, And owns her sov'reign —Death! And owns, And owns, her sov - 'reign — Death!
1
2

LOGAN. S.M.
"Whose builder and maker is God." -- Heb. 11:10.

LOGAN. Concluded.

303

move,..... O may we in Thy bos-om rest, The bosom of Thy love, So death will soon dis-robe us all Of what we here possess, Of what we here possess. sess.

.... O may we in Thy bos-om rest, The bosom of Thy love, So death will soon dis-robe us all Of what we here possess, Of what we here possess. sess.

HEAVENLY LAND. C.M.
"Thine eyes...shall behold the land." -- Isa. 33:17.

F Major Isaac Watts, 1707.

Jeff Sheppard, 1987.

1. There is a land of pure de-light, Where saints im-mor-tal reign. In-fi-nite day ex-cludes the night, And plea-sures ban-ish pain. pain.

2. There ev-er-last-ing springs a-bide, And nev-er with-'ring flow'rs. Death, like a nar-row sea, di-vides This heav'n-ly land from ours. ours.

© 1991 copyright Sacred Harp Publishing Company, Inc.

MORGAN. C.M.

"My doctrine shall be as the small rain upon the tender herd, and as the showers upon the grass." -- Deut. 32:2.

MORGAN. Continued.

305

306 — MORGAN. Concluded.

He makes the grass the moun-tains crown, And corn in val-leys grow, And corn in val-leys grow.

He makes the grass the moun-tains crown, And corn in val-leys grow.

grass the moun-tains crown, And corn in val-leys grow, And corn in val-leys grow.

moun-tains crown, And corn in val-leys grow, And corn in val-leys grow.

OXFORD. C.M.D.

"For unto us a child is born, unto us a son is given." -- Isa. 9:6.

A Major Isaac Watts, 1707. *Juvenile Harmony*, Arr.-John Massengale, 1850.

1. Shep-herds, re-joice! Lift up your eyes, And send your fears a-way: News from the re-gion of the skies — A

2. No gold nor pur-ple swad-dling bands, Nor roy-al shin-ing things, A man-ger for His cra-dle stands, And

OXFORD. Concluded.

308. PARTING FRIENDS (Second). C.M.D.

"And to wait for his son from heaven." -- 1 Thess. 1:10.

E Minor Charles Wesley, c. 1749.
E. L. King, 1850.

What is there here to court my stay, And keep me back from home,
When an-gels beck-on me a-way, And Je-sus bids me come? Shall I re-gret my part-ing friends here in this vale con-fined? Nay, but wher-e'er my soul as-cends, They will not stay be-hind.

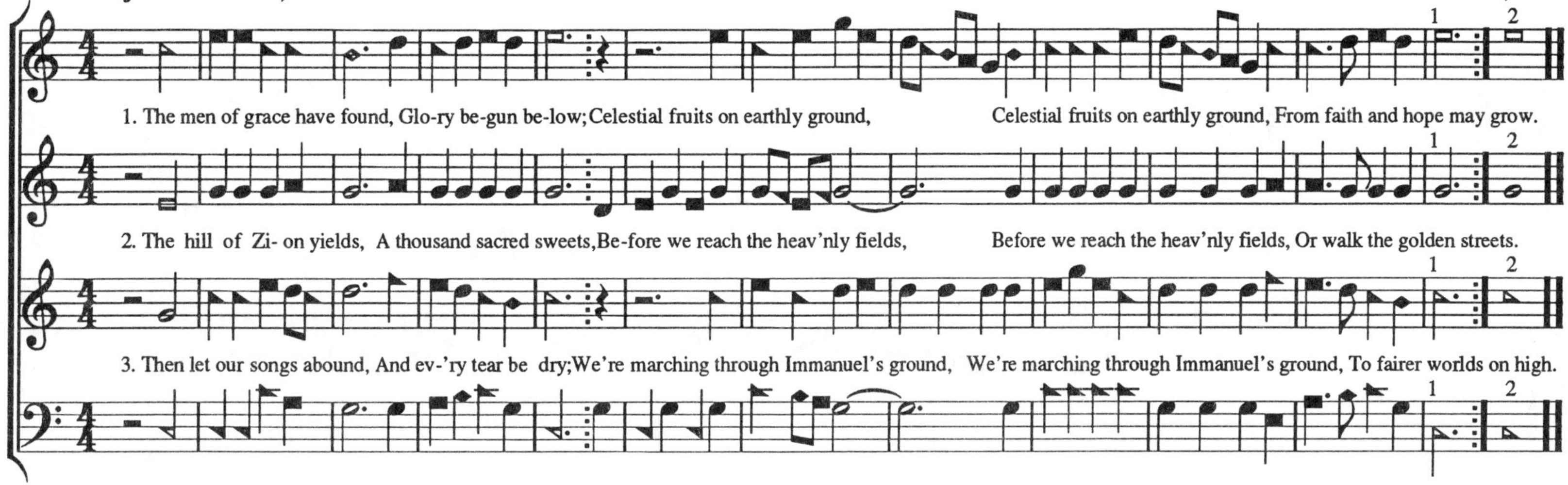

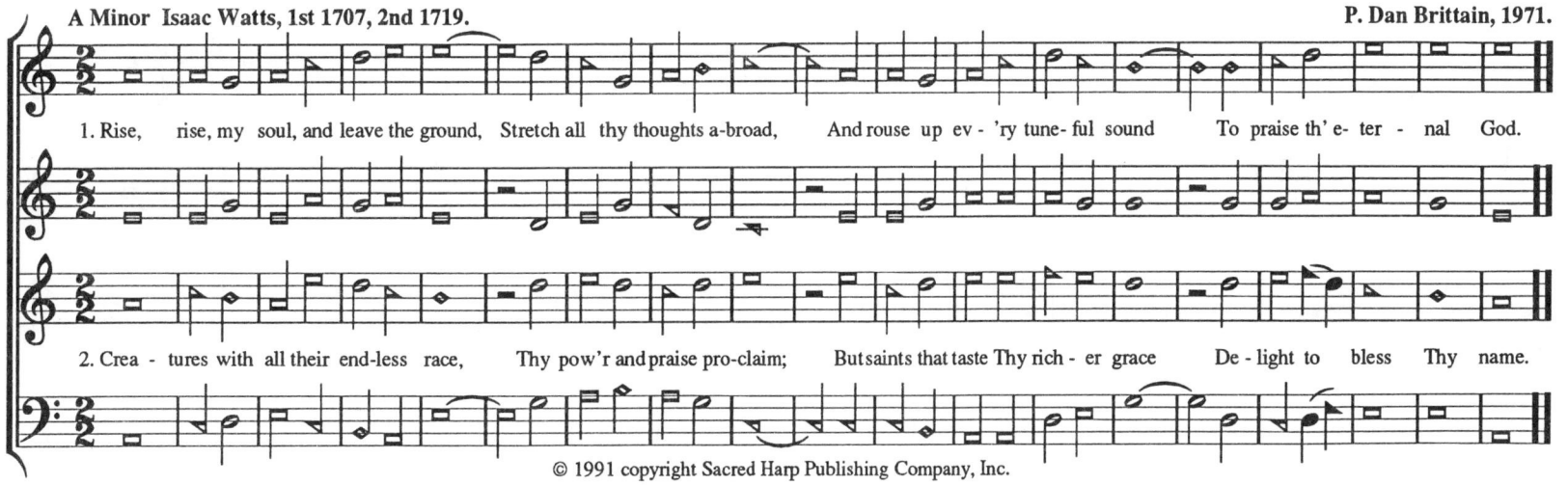

314 CLEBURNE. C.M.

"A royal diadem in the hands of thy God." -- Isa. 62:3.

G Major Edward Perronet, 1779.   S. M. Denson, 1908.

1. All hail the pow'r of Jesus' name, Let angels prostrate fall; Bring forth the royal diadem, And crown Him Lord of all.

2. Ye chosen seed of Israel's race, A remnant weak and small, Hail Him who saves you by His grace, And crown Him Lord of all.

And crown Him Lord of all........ And crown Him Lord of all, Bring forth the royal diadem, And crown Him Lord of all. all.

And crown Him Lord of all........ And crown Him Lord of all, Hail Him who saves you by His grace, And crown Him Lord of all. all.

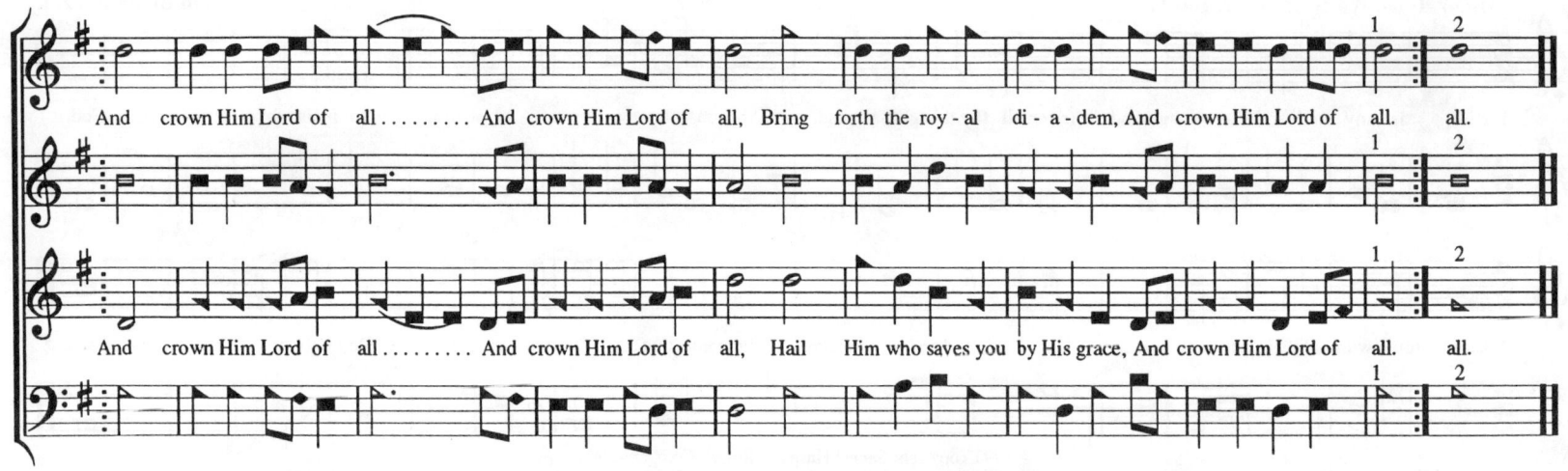

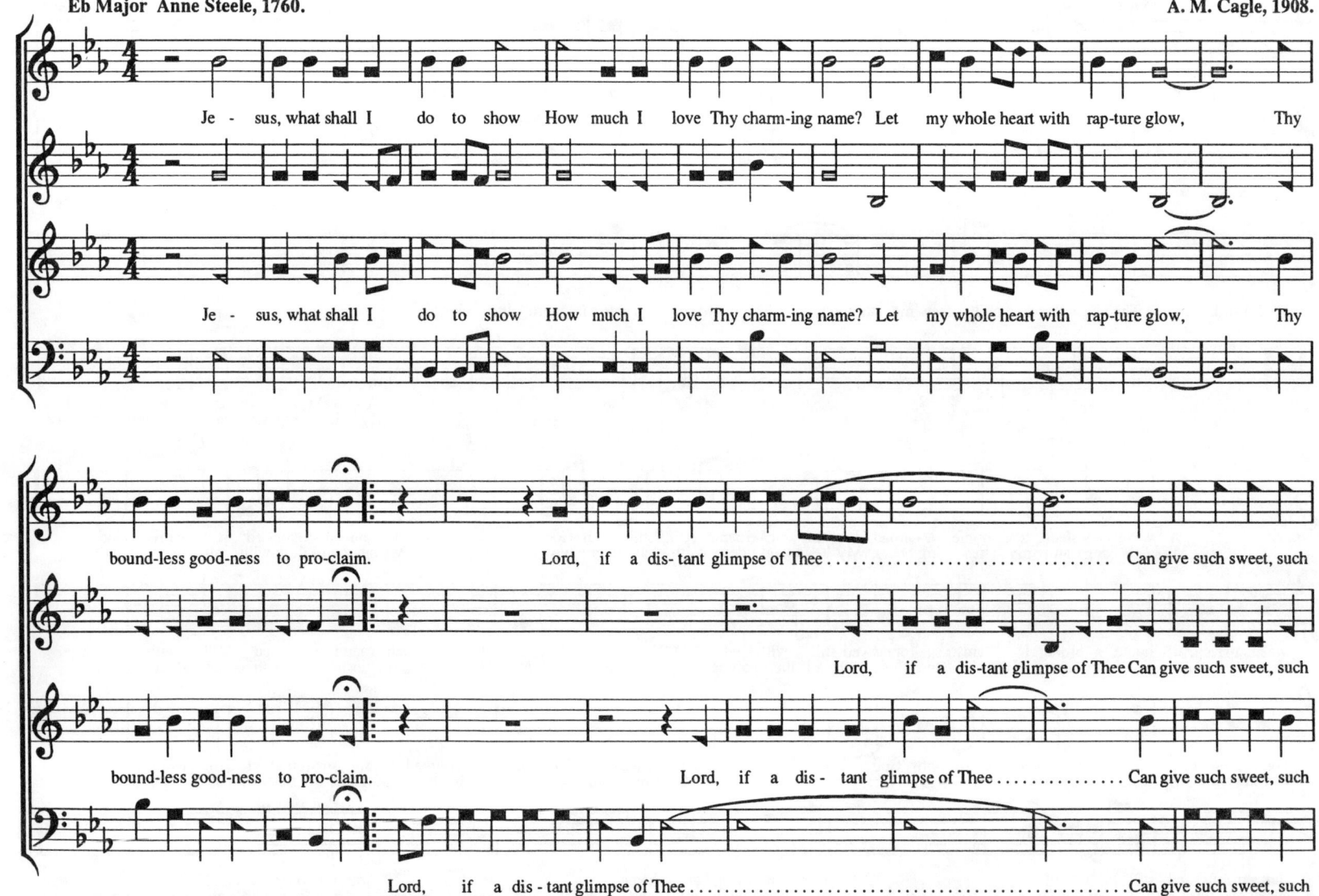

NEW HOPE. Concluded. 317

vast de-light............ What must the joy, the tri-umph be............ To dwell for-ev-er in Thy sight. sight.

vast de-light............ What must the joy, the tri-umph be............ To dwell for-ev-er in Thy sight. sight.

JACKSON. L.M.
"They were strangers and pilgrims on the earth." -- Heb. 11:13.

G Major Mercer's *Cluster*, 1810. M. F. McWhorter, 1908

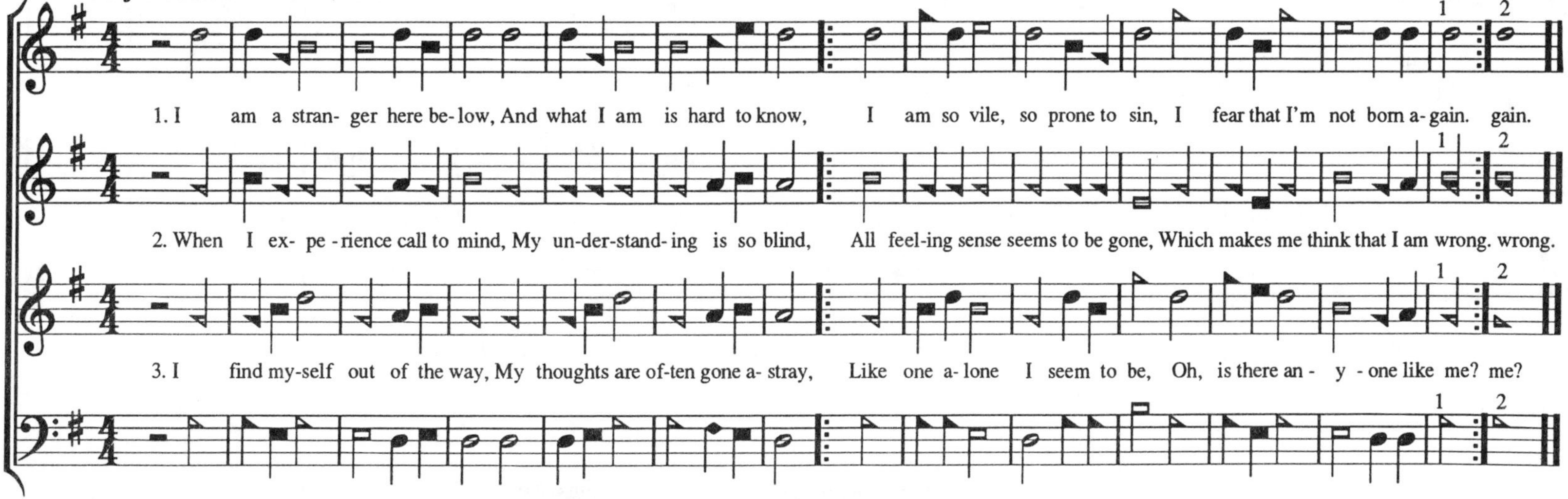

1. I am a stran-ger here be-low, And what I am is hard to know, I am so vile, so prone to sin, I fear that I'm not born a-gain. gain.

2. When I ex-pe-rience call to mind, My un-der-stand-ing is so blind, All feel-ing sense seems to be gone, Which makes me think that I am wrong. wrong.

3. I find my-self out of the way, My thoughts are of-ten gone a-stray, Like one a-lone I seem to be, Oh, is there an-y-one like me? me?

PRESENT JOYS. L.M.

"Confidence in God." -- John 5:14.

F Major Joseph Cottle. **A. M. Cagle, 1908.**

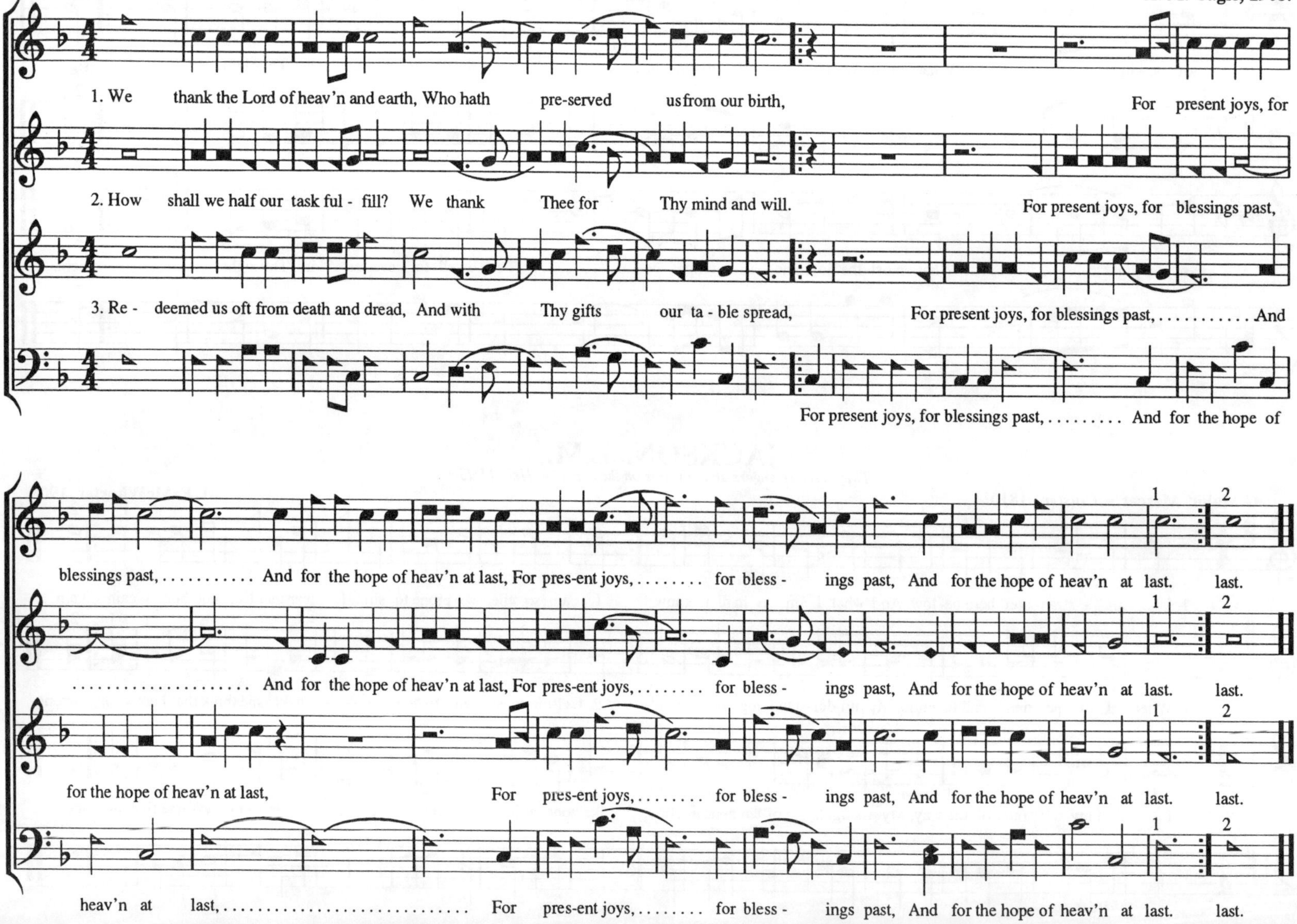
1. We thank the Lord of heav'n and earth, Who hath pre-served us from our birth, For present joys, for
2. How shall we half our task ful - fill? We thank Thee for Thy mind and will. For present joys, for blessings past,
3. Re - deemed us oft from death and dread, And with Thy gifts our ta - ble spread, For present joys, for blessings past, ... And
For present joys, for blessings past, ... And for the hope of
blessings past, ... And for the hope of heav'n at last, For pres-ent joys, ... for bless - ings past, And for the hope of heav'n at last. last.
. . . . And for the hope of heav'n at last, For pres-ent joys, ... for bless - ings past, And for the hope of heav'n at last. last.
for the hope of heav'n at last, For pres-ent joys, ... for bless - ings past, And for the hope of heav'n at last. last.
heav'n at last, ... For pres-ent joys, ... for bless - ings past, And for the hope of heav'n at last. last.

FUNERAL ANTHEM.
"Blessed are the dead which die in the Lord." - Rev. 14:13.

F# Minor Rev. 14:13.

William Billings, 1778.

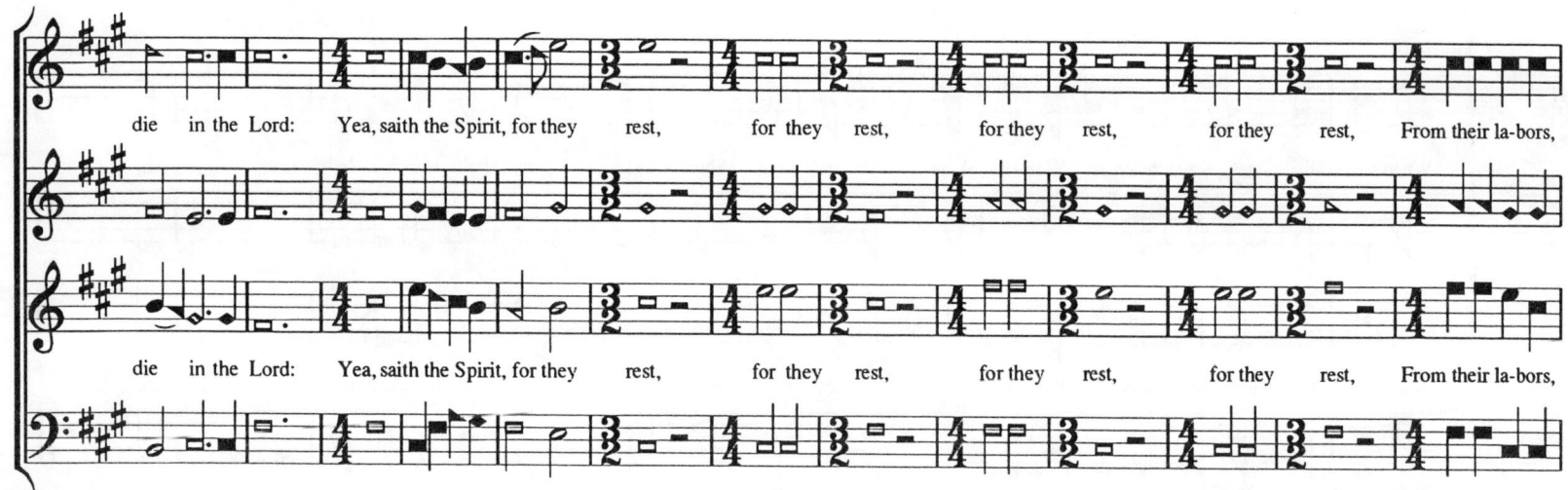

FUNERAL ANTHEM. Concluded.

321

NEWNAN. C.M.D.
"But except ye repent, ye shall all likewise perish." -- Luke 13:3.

F Major Joseph Hart, 1759.

J. P. Reese, 1859.

Vain man, thy fond pur-suits for-bear, Re-pent, thy end is nigh,
Death at the farth-est can't be far, O think be-fore thou die,
Re-flect, thou hast a soul to save, Thy sins, how high they mount.
D. C. - What are thy hopes be-yond the grave? How stands that dark ac-count?

SOLDIER OF THE CROSS. C.M.

"Endure hardships as a soldier of Jesus Christ." -- 2 Tim. 2:3.

WEARY PILGRIM. 7s, 9s.

"And ye shall find rest unto your souls." -- Matt. 11:29.

E Minor Caleb Jarvis Taylor, 1803.

Leonard P. Breedlove, 1850.

1. Come, and taste, a-long with me, The wea-ry pil-grim's con-so-la-tion;
Boundless mer-cy, run-ning free, The earn-est of com-plete sal-va-tion;
Joy and peace in Christ I find, My heart to Him is all re-signed.

2. When the world and flesh would rise, And strive to draw me from my Sav-ior,
Stran-gers slight, or friends de-spise, I then more high-ly prize His fa-vor,
Friends, be-lieve me when I tell, If Christ be pres-ent all is well.

The ful-ness of His pow'r I prove, The sweetness of re-deem-ing love!
Je-sus is the pil-grim's por-tion, Love as boundless as the o-cean.

The world and flesh in vain may rise; I all their ef-forts do de-spise;
In the world I've trib-u-la-tion, But in Christ sweet con-so-la-tion.

INVITATION. L.M.

"He is able also to save them to the uttermost that come unto God by him." -- Heb. 7:25.

D Major Isaac Watts, 1709. Jacob Kimball, 1784.

Hark! the Re-deem-er from on high, Sweet-ly in-vites His fav'rites nigh, From caves of darkness and of doubt, He gently speaks and calls us out.

Come, my be-lov-ed, haste a-way, Cut short the hours of thy de-lay; Fly like a youth-ful hart or roe, O-ver the hills where spic-es grow.

330 HORTON. C.M.

"... because as a flower of the grass he shall pass away." -- James 1:10.

F Minor Frances Maria Cowper, 1792. Paine Denson, 1935.

1. My span of life will soon be gone, The pass-ing mo-ments say; As length'ning shad-ows o'er the mead Pro-claim the close of day.
2. My Christian friends to whom I speak, I have a crown in view; My sin-ner friends, now will you seek, How stands the case with you?
3. The love of Christ con-strain-eth me, Sin's e-vil ways to shun, And in the paths of right-eous-ness, My race with pa-tience run.
4. The cross of Christ in-spires my heart To sing re-deem-ing grace; A-wake, my soul, and bear a part In my Re-deem-er's praise.
5. How long, dear Sav-ior, Oh, how long? Shall this bright hour de-lay? Fly swift a-round, ye wheels of time, And bring the prom-ised day.
6. When we've been there ten thousand years, Bright shin-ing as the sun, We've no less days to sing God's praise, Than when we first be-gun.

© 1936 copyright Sacred Harp Publishing Company, Inc.

FELLOWSHIP. S.M.

"If any man suffer as a Christian, let him not be ashamed." -- 1 Peter 4:16.

E Minor John Fawcett, 1782. Paine Denson, 1935.

1. Blest be the tie that binds Our hearts in Christian love; The fel-low-ship of kin-dred minds Is like to that a-bove.
2. We share our mu-tual woes, Our mu-tual bur-dens bear, And of-ten for each oth-er flows The sym-pa-thiz-ing tear.
3. When we as-sun-der part, It gives us in-ward pain; But we shall still be joined in heart, And hope to meet a-gain.

© 1936 copyright Sacred Harp Publishing Company, Inc.

332

SONS OF SORROW. 8s, 7s.

"The earth mourneth and fadeth away, the world languisheth and fadeth away." -- Isa. 24:4.

E Minor Anonymous   Arr. - William Houser, 1848.

1. Hail ye sighing sons of sorrow; Learn with me, your certain doom; See all nature fading, dying, Silent, all things seem to mourn; Life from vegetation flying, Calls to mind the mould'ring urn.
Learn with me your fate tomorrow —Dead, perhaps, laid in the tomb!

2. Oft the autumn tempest rising, Makes the lofty forest nod; And our sov'reign sole Creator Lives eternal in the sky, While we mortals yield to nature, Bloom awhile, then fade and die.
Scenes of nature, how surprising, Read in nature, Nature's God.

3. Fast my sun of life's declining, Soon 'twill set in dismal night; Cease then trembling, fearing, sighing, Death will break the sullen gloom; Soon my spirit, flut'ring, flying, Shall be borne beyond the tomb.
But my hopes, pure and refining, Rest in future life and light.

SAWYER'S EXIT. 9,8.

"Precious in the sight of the Lord is the death of his saints." -- Ps. 116:15.

A Major S. B. Sawyer, 1850.
Arr. - John Massengale, 1850.

1. How bright is the day when the Christian Re-ceives the sweet message to come, To rise to the man-sions of glo-ry, And be there for-ev-er at
2. The an-gels stand read-y and wait-ing, The mo-ment the spir-it is gone, To car-ry it up-ward to heav-en, And wel-come it safe-ly at
3. The saints that have gone up be-fore us, All raise a new shout as we come, And sing hal-le-lu-jah the loud-er To wel-come the trav-el-ers

home, And be there for-ev-er at home, And be there for-ev-er at home; To rise to the man-sions of glo-ry, And be there for-ev-er at home.
home, And wel-come it safe-ly at home, And wel-come it safe-ly at home; To car-ry it up-ward to heav-en, And wel-come it safe-ly at home.
home, To wel-come the travelers home, To wel-come the trav-el-ers home, And sing hal-le-lu-jah the loud-er, To wel-come the trav-el-ers home.

342 THE OLD-FASHIONED BIBLE. 12s & 11s.

"And this is the law which Moses set before the children of Israel." -- Deut. 4:44.

A Major *Young Christian's Companion, 1826.* L. P. Breedlove, 1850.

1. How painfully pleasing the fond recollection Of youthful connection and innocent joy; While blessed with parental advice and affection, Surrounded with mer-cy and peace from on high. I still view the chairs of my father and mother, Their offspring, as seated and ranged on each hand; And the richest of books, which ex-

2. My parents, though dear, are safe landed in glory, Escaped to the mansions of heavenly rest, Where ser-aphs and angels repeat the glad sto-ry Of Je-sus' great mer - cy to sin-ners con-fessed. They range the bless'd fields on the banks of the river, Surveying the breadth of Immanuel's land; And they love Him and praise Him for-

THE OLD FASHIONED BIBLE. Concluded. 343

cels ev-'ry oth-er, The fam-i-ly Bi-ble that lay on the stand! The old-fashion'd Bible, The dear, blessed Bible! The fam-i-ly Bi-ble that lay on the stand!

ev-er and ev-er, The fam-i-ly Bi-ble that lay on the stand! The old-fashion'd Bible, The dear, blessed Bible! The fam-i-ly Bi-ble that lay on the stand!

HAPPY HOME. L.M.
"Righteous into life eternal." -- Matt. 25:46.

J. P. Reese, 1859.

A Major

1. O yes, my Sav-ior I will trust,
And though my bod-y turns to dust, Oh, what a hap-py time, when the Christians all get home, And we'll shout and praise the Lamb in glo-ry!

2. My spir-it shall fly out and sing,
E-ter-nal prais-es to my King, Oh, what a hap-py time, when the Christians all get home, And we'll shout and praise the Lamb in glo-ry!

THE AMERICAN STAR. 12s & 11s.
"I will make thee a nation." -- Deut. 9:14.

D Minor John McCreery

Arr. - D. P. White, 1850.

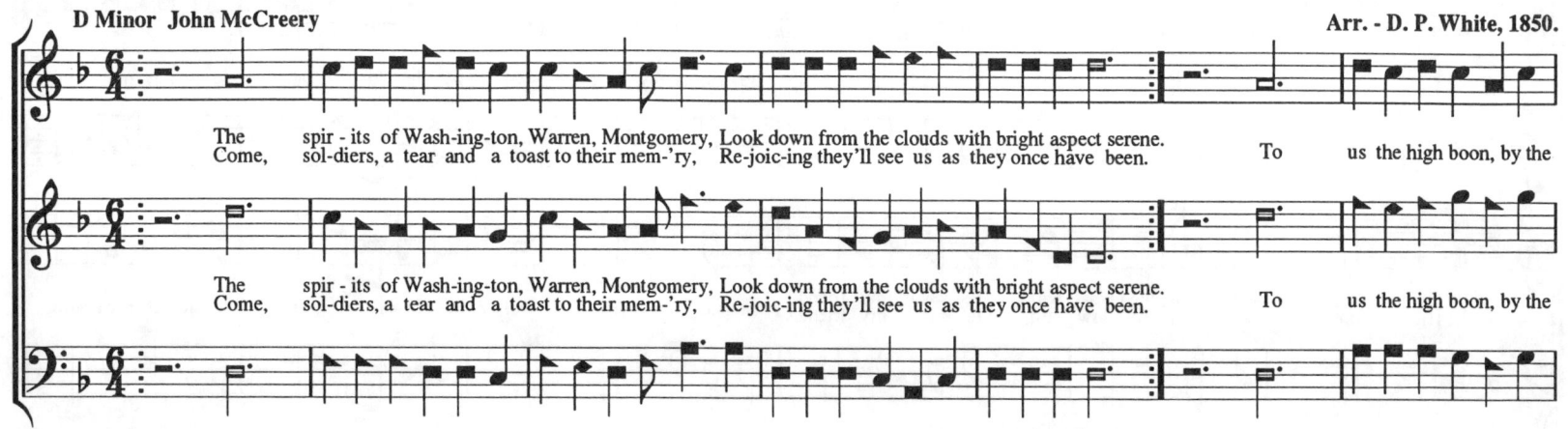
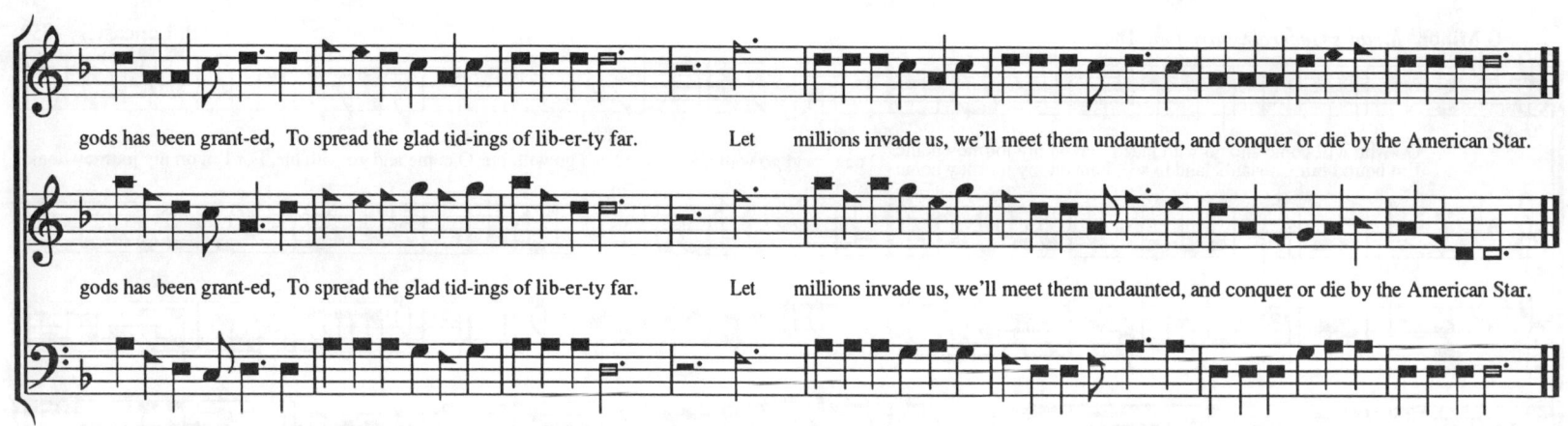

CHRISTIAN'S FAREWELL. P.M.

"Cast me not away from thy presence; and take not thy Holy Spirit from me." -- Ps. 51:11.

347

Bb Major *Primitive Hymns*

Raymond C. Hamrick, 1989.

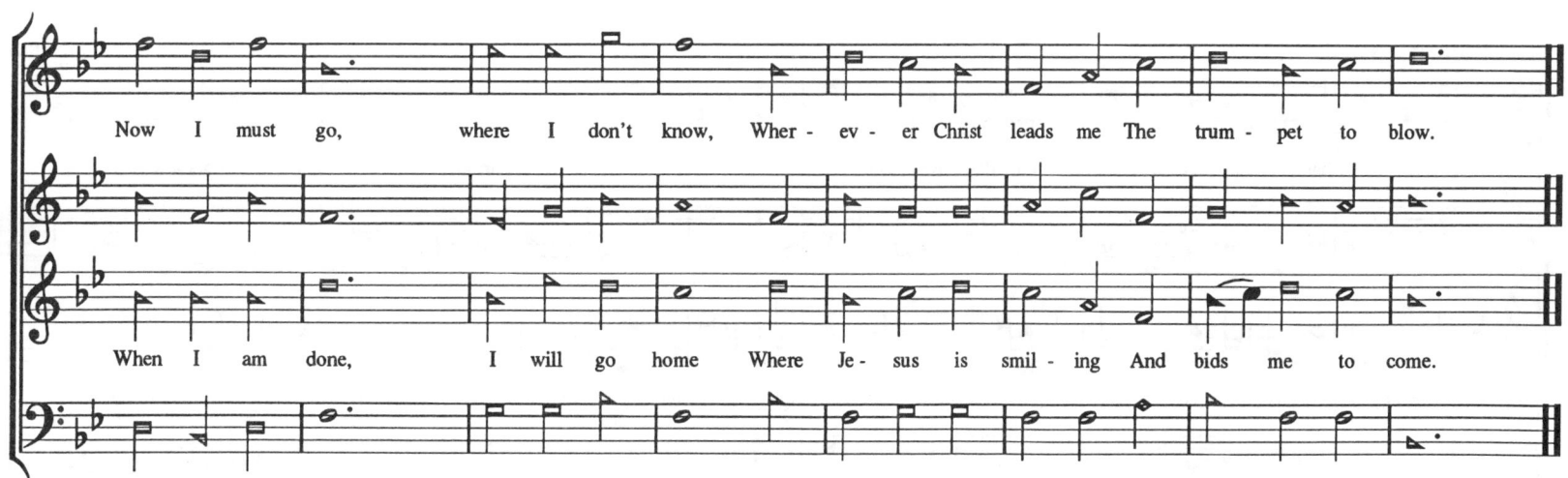

1. Breth-ren, fare-well, I do you tell, I'm sor-ry to leave, I love you so well.
2. Here I have worked, la-bored a-while, But la-bor is sweet if Je-sus doth smile.

Now I must go, where I don't know, Wher-ev-er Christ leads me The trum-pet to blow.
When I am done, I will go home Where Je-sus is smil-ing And bids me to come.

© 1991 copyright Sacred Harp Publishing Company, Inc.

348 AINSLIE. C.M.
"For dust thou art, and unto dust shalt thou return." -- Gen. 3:19.

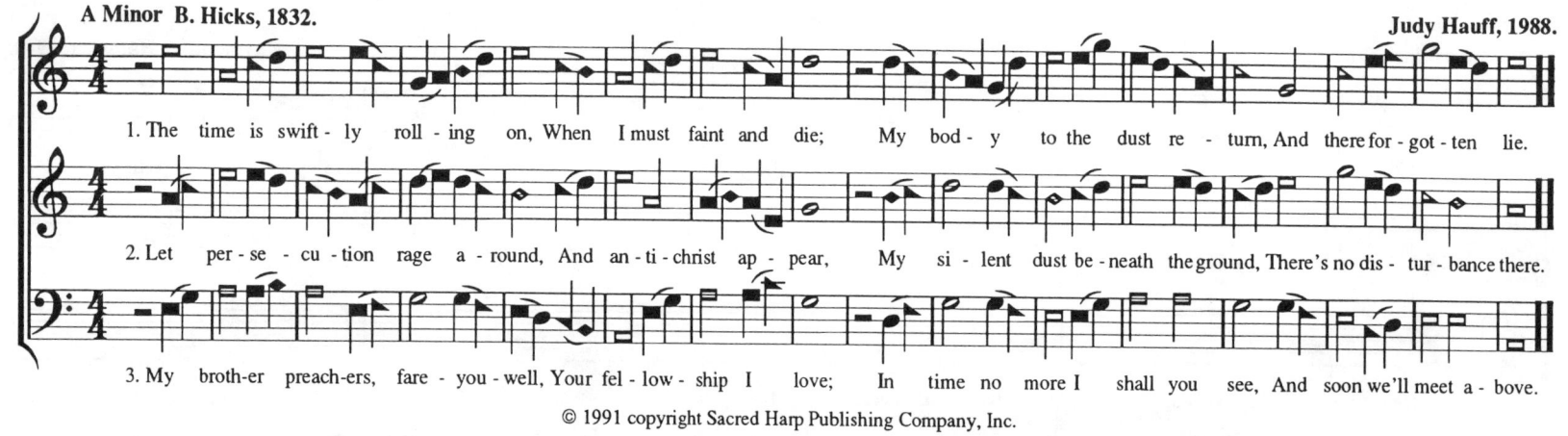

1. The time is swift-ly roll-ing on, When I must faint and die; My bod-y to the dust re-turn, And there for-got-ten lie.
2. Let per-se-cu-tion rage a-round, And an-ti-christ ap-pear, My si-lent dust be-neath the ground, There's no dis-tur-bance there.
3. My broth-er preach-ers, fare-you-well, Your fel-low-ship I love; In time no more I shall you see, And soon we'll meet a-bove.

© 1991 copyright Sacred Harp Publishing Company, Inc.

FLEETING DAYS. C.M.
"He cometh forth like a flower, and is cut down." -- Job 14:2.

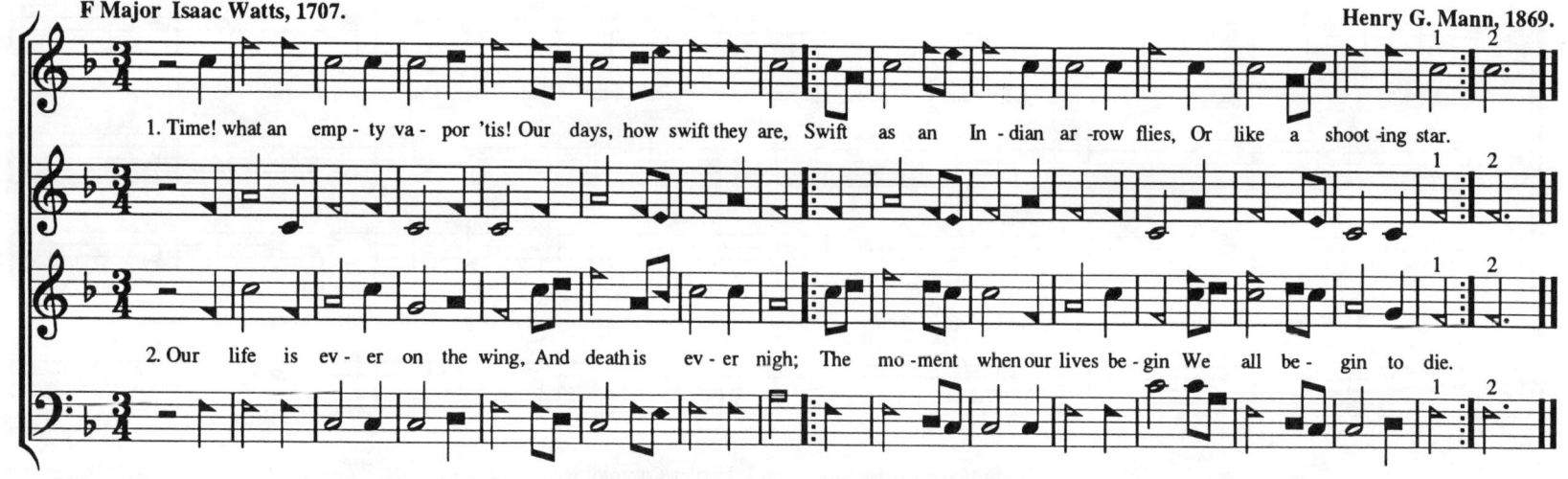

1. Time! what an emp-ty va-por 'tis! Our days, how swift they are, Swift as an In-dian ar-row flies, Or like a shoot-ing star.
2. Our life is ev-er on the wing, And death is ev-er nigh; The mo-ment when our lives be-gin We all be-gin to die.

PITTSFORD. C.M.

"Praise the Lord with harp: sing unto him." -- Ps. 33:2.

351

SWANTON. L.M.

352

"Our soul waiteth for the Lord: he is our help and our shield." -- Ps. 33:20.

E Major Isaac Watts, 1707.

Hezekiah Moors, 1809.

McGRAW. L.M.

353

"Every day will I bless you and praise your Name for ever and ever." -- Ps. 145:2.

F Major Isaac Watts, 1719.

P. Dan Brittain, 1971.

My God, my King, Thy var-ious praise Shall fill the rem — nant of my days;

My God, my King, Thy var-ious praise Shall fill the rem — nant of my days; Thy

My God, my King, Thy var-ious praise Shall fill the rem — nant of my days; Thy grace em - ploy my

My God, my King, Thy var-ious praise Shall fill the rem — nant of my days; Thy grace em - ploy my hum-ble tongue, Thy

Thy grace em - ploy my humble tongue, Till death, till death, till death........ and glo — ry raise the song. song.

grace em- ploy my humble tongue, my hum-ble tongue, Till death, till death, till death........ and glo — ry raise the song. song.

hum-ble tongue, Thy grace employ my hum-ble tongue, Till death, till death, till death........ and glo — ry raise the song. song.

grace em - ploy............. my hum-ble tongue, Till death, till death, till death........ and glo — ry raise the song. song.

© 1991 copyright Sacred Harp Publishing Company, Inc.

354

LEBANON. C.M.

"And all things, whatsoever ye shall ask in prayer, believing, ye shall receive." -- Matt. 21:22.

A Major Anne Steele, 1756.　　　　　　　　　　　　　　　　　　　　　　　　　J. Monroe Denton, 1980.

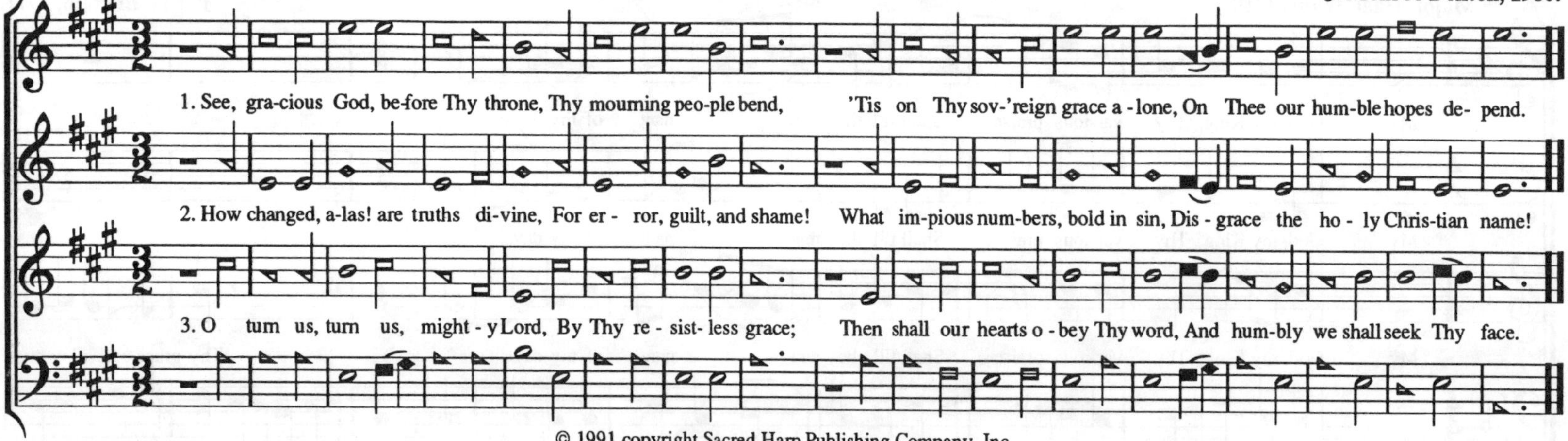

1. See, gracious God, before Thy throne, Thy mourning people bend, 'Tis on Thy sov-'reign grace alone, On Thee our humble hopes depend.
2. How changed, alas! are truths divine, For error, guilt, and shame! What impious numbers, bold in sin, Disgrace the holy Christian name!
3. O turn us, turn us, mighty Lord, By Thy resistless grace; Then shall our hearts obey Thy word, And humbly we shall seek Thy face.

© 1991 copyright Sacred Harp Publishing Company, Inc.

HAPPY LAND. H.M.

"Then shall every man have the praise of God." -- 1 Cor. 4:5.

F Major Andrew Young, 1838.　　　　　　　　　　　　　　　　　　　　　　　　　Arr. - L. P. Breedlove, 1850.

1. There is a happy land, far, far away, Where saints in glory stand, bright, bright as day; O how they sweetly sing, Worthy is our Savior, King, Loud let His praises ring, Praise, praise for aye.
2. Come to that happy land, come, come away, Why will ye doubting stand, why yet delay; O we shall happy be When from sin and sorrow free, Lord, we shall live with Thee, Blest, blest for aye.
3. Bright in that happy land beams ev'ry eye, Kept by a Father's hand, love cannot die; Then shall His kingdom come, Saints shall share a glor'ous home, And bright above the sun We'll reign for aye.

ANTHEM ON THE SAVIOR.

"For unto you is born this day in the city of David a Savior, which is Christ the Lord." - Luke 2:11.

355

A Minor *Sacred Harp,* **1850.** B. F. White, 1850.

My friends, come lis-ten a-while, And I will tell you a sto-ry A-bout our lov-ing Sav-ior; He came of low es-tate, was re-ject-ed by His own, Was

born of the Vir-gin Ma - ry, And was cra-dled in a man-ger. The next we hear of this bless-ed Sav-ior, He was go-ing a-bout do-ing good; And

356 ANTHEM ON THE SAVIOR. Continued.

ANTHEM ON THE SAVIOR. Concluded. 357

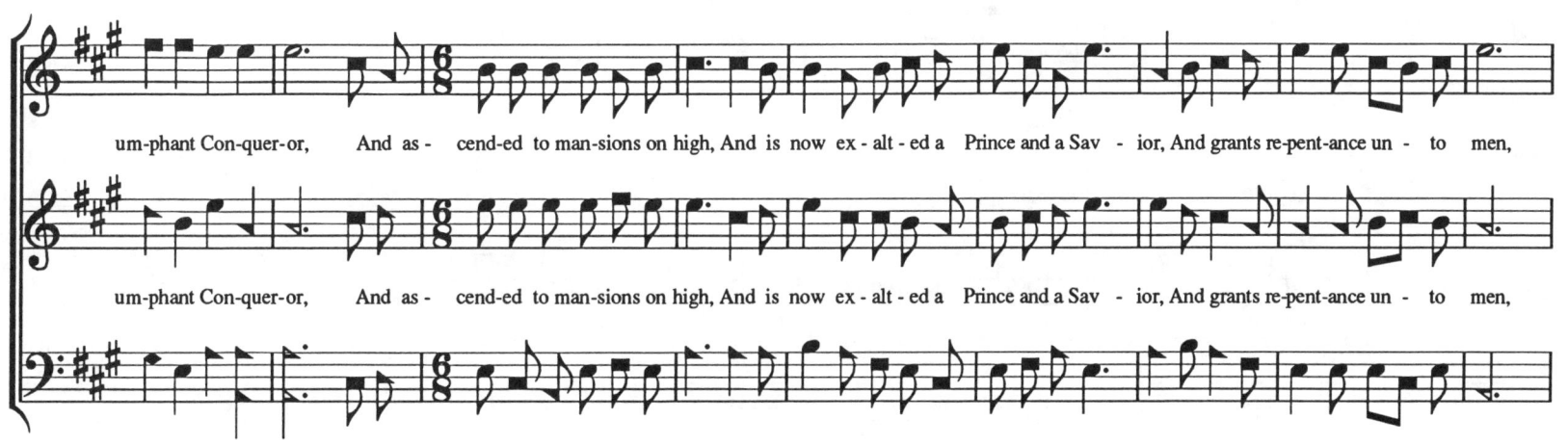

um-phant Con-quer-or, And as-cend-ed to man-sions on high, And is now ex-alt-ed a Prince and a Sav-ior, And grants re-pent-ance un - to men,

Then let us praise Him, Then let us praise Him, Then let us praise Him, Mag-ni-fy and a-dore, World with-out end. A-men.

MURILLO'S LESSON. Concluded. 359

THE BRIDE'S FAREWELL. 8,7.
"And they lifted up their voice, and wept again: but Ruth clave unto her." -- Ruth 1:14.

D Major Miss M. L. Beevor, ca. 1840

H. S. Reese, 1869.

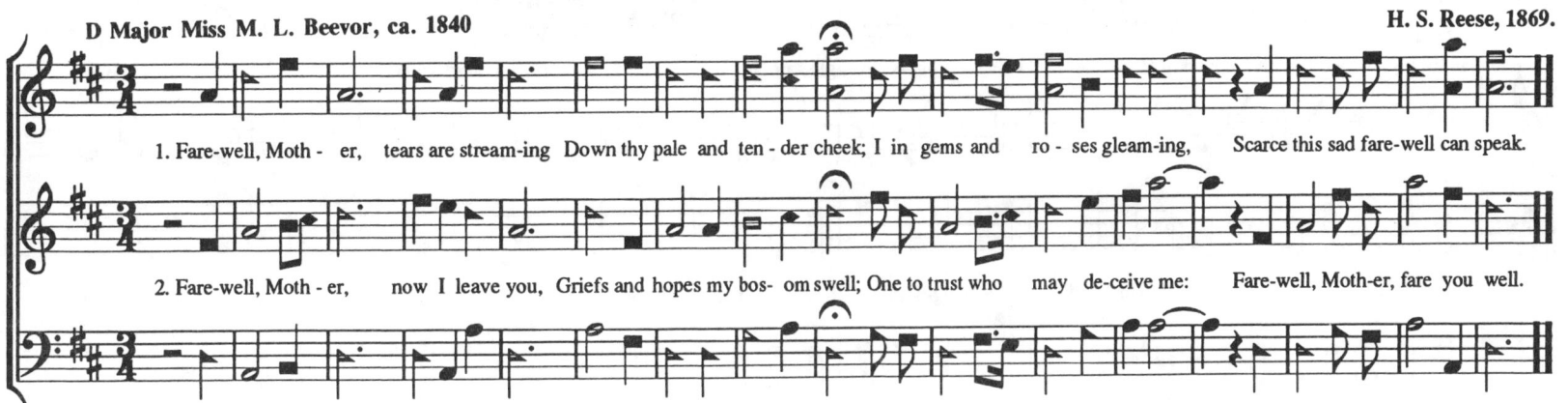

1. Fare-well, Moth-er, tears are stream-ing Down thy pale and ten-der cheek; I in gems and ro-ses gleam-ing, Scarce this sad fare-well can speak.

2. Fare-well, Moth-er, now I leave you, Griefs and hopes my bos-om swell; One to trust who may de-ceive me: Fare-well, Moth-er, fare you well.

LOVING JESUS. Concluded.

362

Glo-ry, glo-ry, hon-or, praise and pow-er, Glo-ry, glo-ry to the Lord! Glo-ry, glo-ry to the Lord!

Glo-ry, hon-or, praise and pow-er Be un-to the Lamb for-ev-er! Glo-ry, glo-ry to the Lord! Glo-ry, glo-ry to the Lord!

Glo-ry, glo-ry, hon-or, praise and pow-er, Glo-ry, glo-ry to the Lord! Glo-ry, glo-ry to the Lord!

Glo-ry, hon-or, praise and pow-er Be un-to the Lamb for-ev-er! Glo-ry, glo-ry to the Lord! Glo-ry, glo-ry to the Lord!

NORWICH. C.M.

"These things have I spoken unto you, that my joy might remain in you, and that your joy might be full." -- John 15:11.

Bb Major Isaac Watts, 1707.

D. P. White, 1850.

Oh, the de-lights, the heav'n-ly joys, The glo-ries of the place Where Je-sus sheds the bright-est beams, Where Je-sus sheds the

Where

Oh, the de-lights, the heav'n-ly joys, The glo-ries of the place Where Je-sus sheds the brightest beams, Where

Oh, the de-lights, the heav'n-ly joys, The glo-ries of the place Where Je-sus sheds the

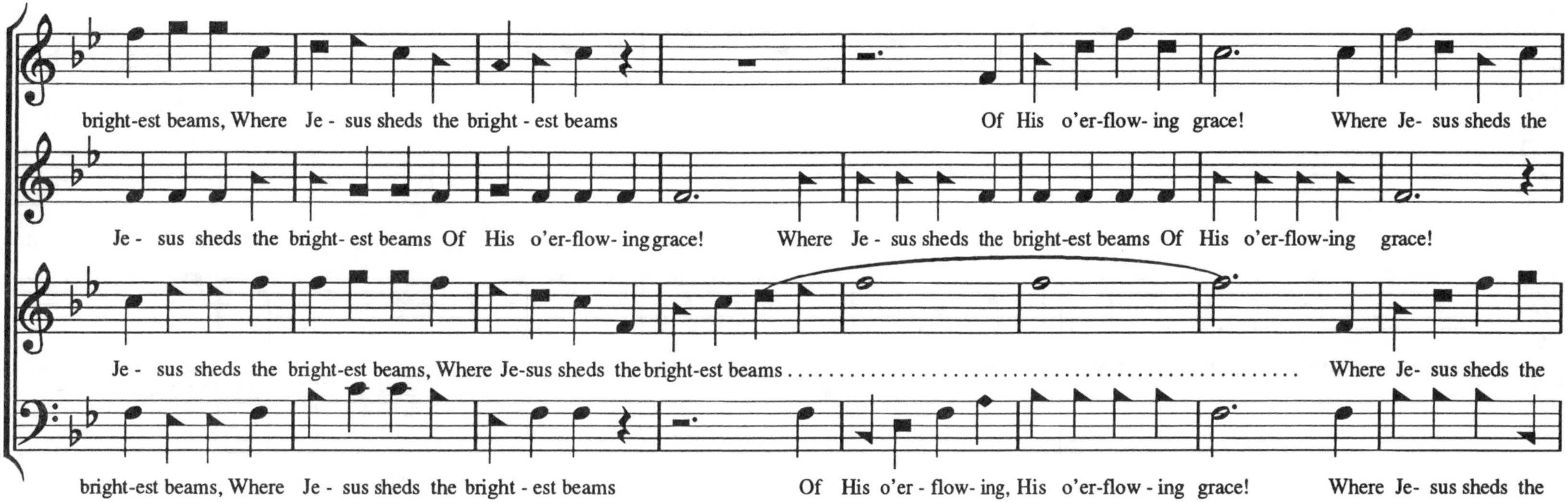

NORWICH. Continued. 363

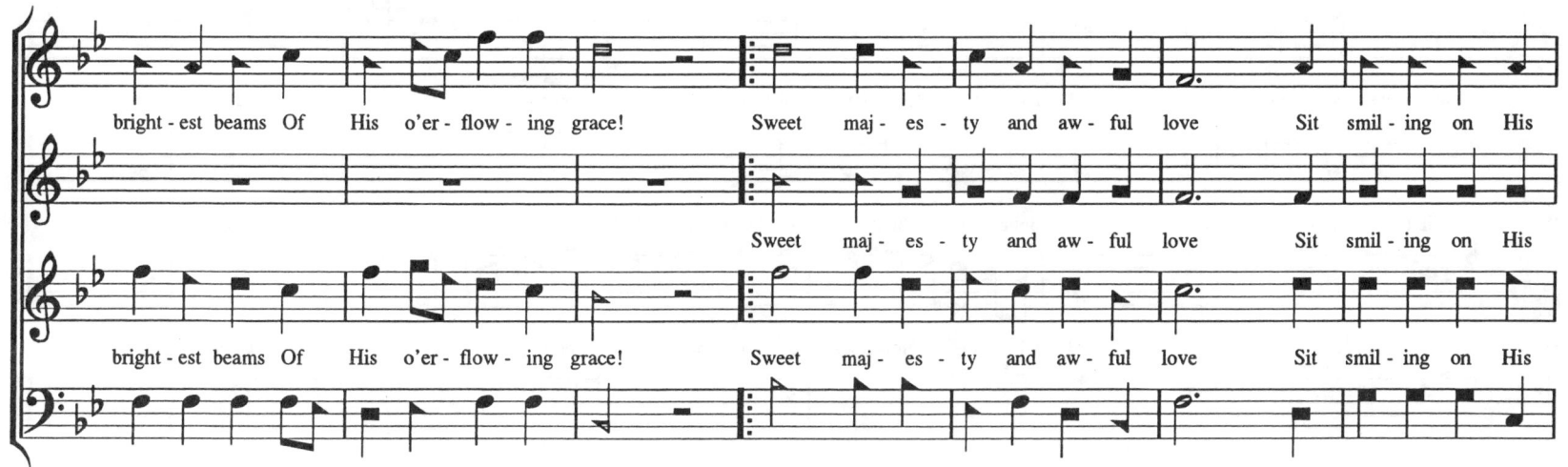

364 NORWICH. Concluded.

brow, And all the glorious, all the glorious ranks above At

brow, And

brow, And all the glorious ranks above, And all the glorious ranks above At humble distance

brow, And all the glorious ranks above At humble distance bow..............

humble distance bow; And all the glorious ranks above At hum.......... ble distance bow.

all the glorious ranks above, At humble distance bow, At hum.......... ble distance bow.

bow,..................... And all the glorious ranks above At hum.......... ble distance bow.

SOUTHWELL. 8,8,6.

"Jesus said, It is finished: and he bowed his head and gave up the ghost." -- John 19:30.

E Major Samuel Stennett, 1787.   Elihu Carpenter, 1786.

'Tis fin-ished, 'tis fin-ished, 'tis fin-ished, 'tis fin-ished, The Re-deem-er said, And meek-ly bowed His dy-ing

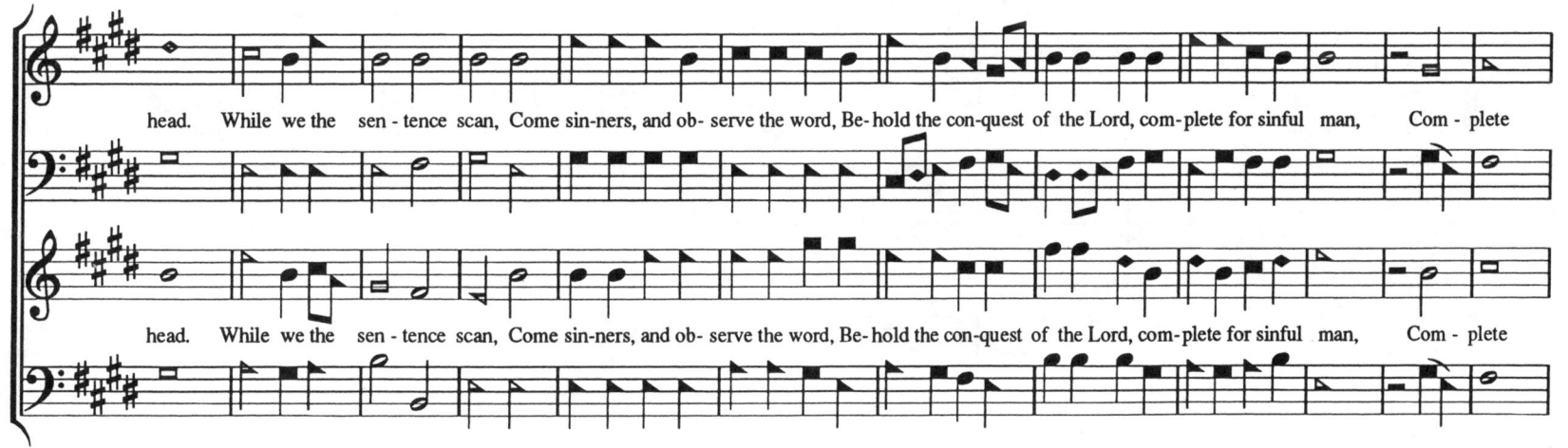

head. While we the sen-tence scan, Come sin-ners, and ob-serve the word, Be-hold the con-quest of the Lord, com-plete for sinful man, Com-plete

SOUTHWELL. Concluded.

HEAVENLY DOVE. C.M.

"I saw the Spirit descending from heaven like a dove, and it abode upon him." -- John 1:32.

371

F Major Isaac Watts, 1707.

Abraham Maxim, 1802. Arr. - Absalom Ogletree, 1859.

LOVE THE LORD. C.M.

"A man that hath friends..." -- Prov. 18:24.

F# Minor Isaac Watts, 1707.

J. P. Reese, 1859.

A - las and did my Sav - ior bleed, And did my sov - 'reign die? O who is like Je - sus?
Would He de - vote that sa - cred head For such a worm as I?

hal - le - lu - jah, Praise ye the Lord; There's none like Je - sus, hal - le - lu - jah, Love and serve the Lord.

HELP ME TO SING. P.M.

"Sing unto him, sing psalms unto him." -- Ps. 105:2.

A Minor *Dover Selection,* 1828. B. F. White, 1859.

Ye souls who are bound unto Canaan, Come join in and help me to sing The prais-es of my lov-ing Je-sus, My Proph-et, my Priest, and my King.

His name is most sweet-ly me-lo-dious, 'Twill help you most swiftly to move, While Je-sus Him-self is the lead-er, We're bound by the cords of His love.

HEAVENLY PORT. C.M.

"Thine eyes shall behold the land that is very far off." -- Isa. 33:17.

A Major Samuel Stennett, 1787. **Edmund Dumas, 1859.**

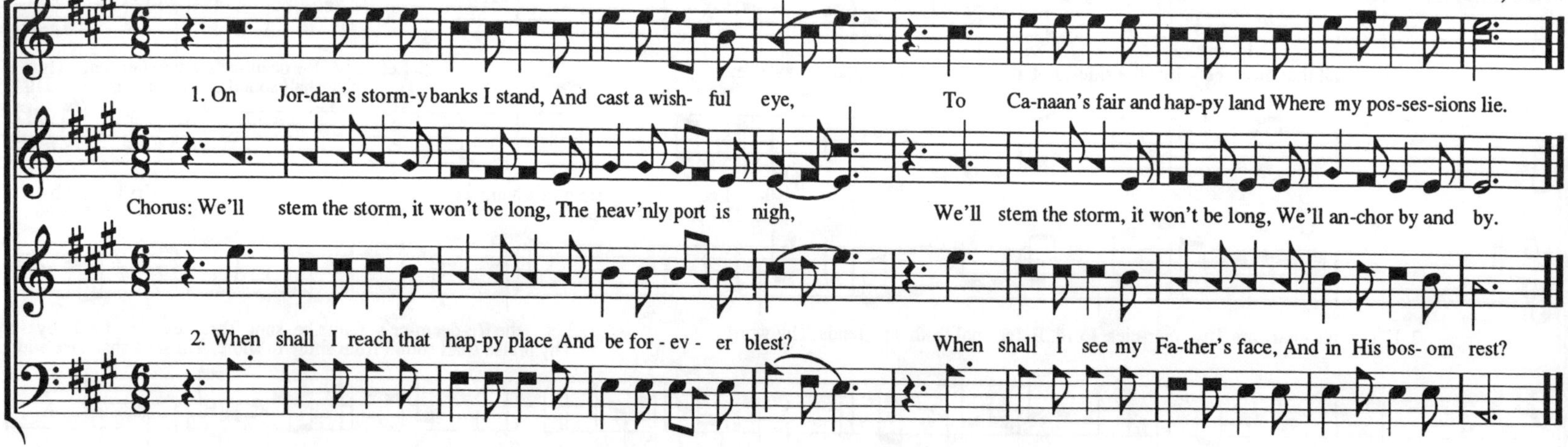
1. On Jor-dan's storm-y banks I stand, And cast a wish- ful eye, To Ca-naan's fair and hap-py land Where my pos-ses-sions lie.
Chorus: We'll stem the storm, it won't be long, The heav'nly port is nigh, We'll stem the storm, it won't be long, We'll an-chor by and by.
2. When shall I reach that hap-py place And be for - ev - er blest? When shall I see my Fa-ther's face, And in His bos- om rest?

NEVER TURN BACK. L.M.

"Our heart is not turned back, neither have our steps declined from the way." -- Ps. 44:18.

G Minor Anonymous **Arr. - J. P. Reese & F. E. Parkerson, 1869.**

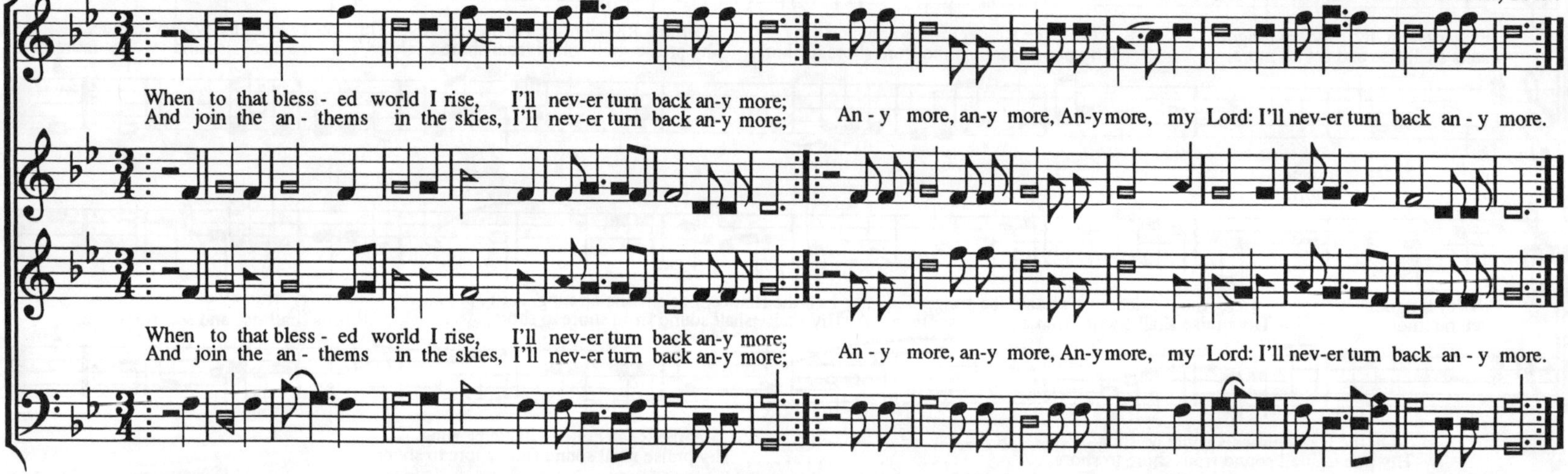
When to that bless - ed world I rise, I'll nev-er turn back an-y more;
And join the an - thems in the skies, I'll nev-er turn back an-y more; An - y more, an-y more, An-y more, my Lord: I'll nev-er turn back an - y more.
When to that bless - ed world I rise, I'll nev-er turn back an-y more;
And join the an - thems in the skies, I'll nev-er turn back an-y more; An - y more, an-y more, An-y more, my Lord: I'll nev-er turn back an - y more.

LAWRENCEBURG. Concluded. 381

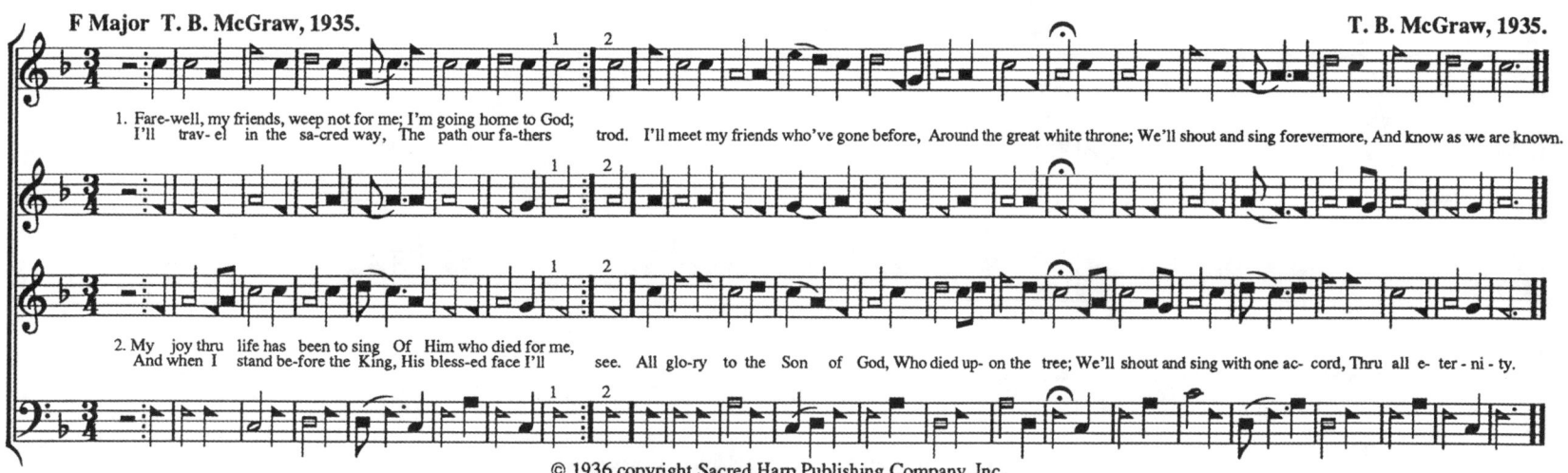

SING ON. C.M.D.
"... singing with grace in your hearts to the Lord." -- Col. 3:16.

F Major T. B. McGraw, 1935.   T. B. McGraw, 1935.

1. Fare-well, my friends, weep not for me; I'm going home to God; I'll trav-el in the sa-cred way, The path our fa-thers trod. I'll meet my friends who've gone before, Around the great white throne; We'll shout and sing forevermore, And know as we are known.

2. My joy thru life has been to sing Of Him who died for me, And when I stand be-fore the King, His bless-ed face I'll see. All glo-ry to the Son of God, Who died up-on the tree; We'll shout and sing with one ac-cord, Thru all e-ter-ni-ty.

© 1936 copyright Sacred Harp Publishing Company, Inc.

382 COSTON. C.M.D.

"...be ye kind one to another..." -- Eph. 4:32.

F Major *The Baltimore Collection, 1803.* T. J. Denson, 1935.

Dear friends, farewell! I do you tell, Since you and I must part; I go my way, and here you stay, But still we're joined in heart. Your love to me has been most free, Your con-ver-sa-tion sweet; How can I bear to journey where With you I can-not meet? How can I bear to jour-ney where With you I can-not meet? meet?

Your love to me has been most free,

© 1936 copyright Sacred Harp Publishing Company, Inc.

PANTING FOR HEAVEN. 8s.

". . . man should both hope and quietly wait for the salvation of the Lord." -- Lam. 3:26.

Eb Major Maria DeFleury, 1791. **S. M. Brown, 1869.**

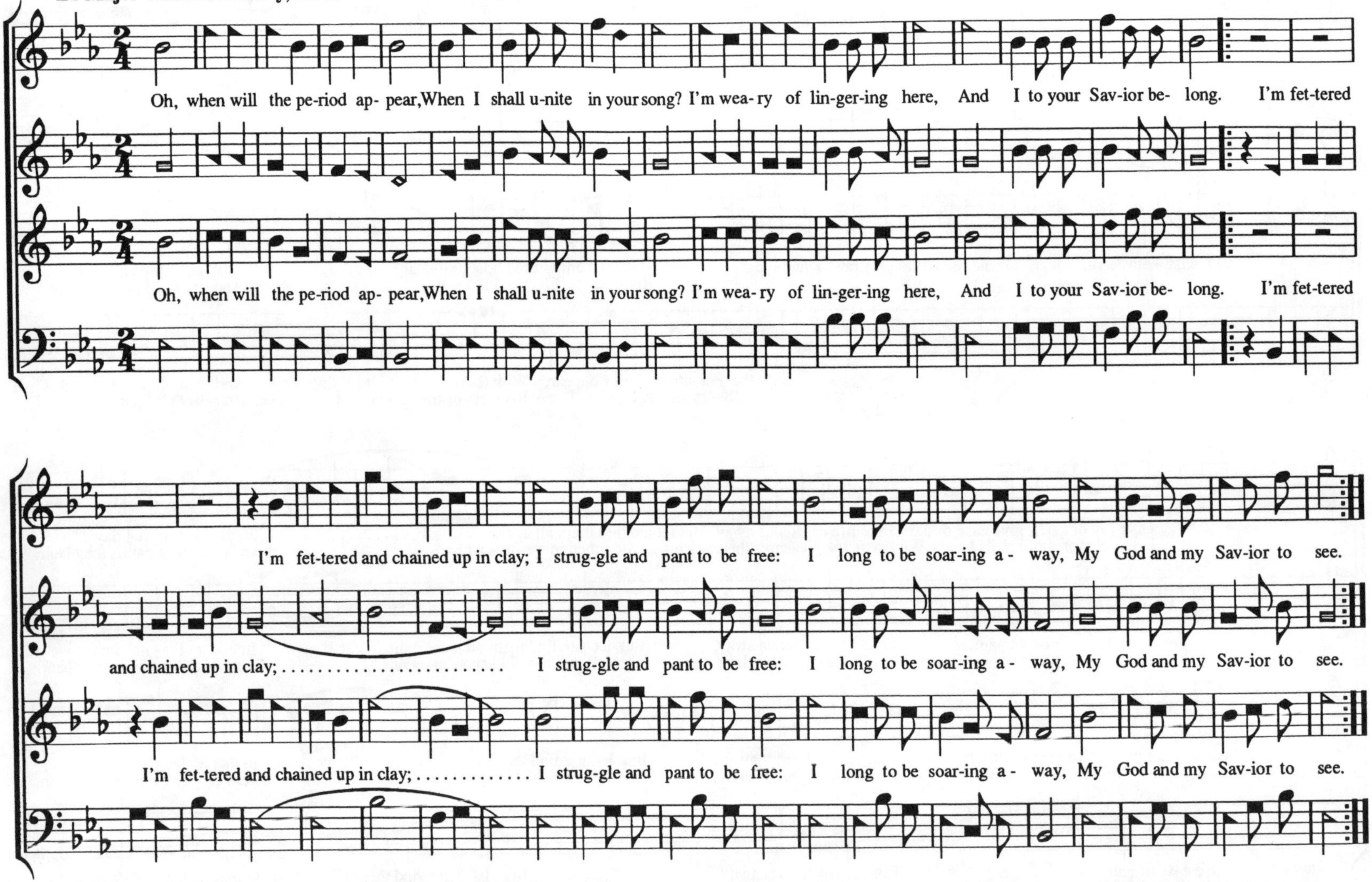
Oh, when will the pe-riod ap- pear, When I shall u-nite in your song? I'm wea-ry of lin-ger-ing here, And I to your Sav-ior be- long. I'm fet-tered
Oh, when will the pe-riod ap- pear, When I shall u-nite in your song? I'm wea-ry of lin-ger-ing here, And I to your Sav-ior be- long. I'm fet-tered
I'm fet-tered and chained up in clay; I strug-gle and pant to be free: I long to be soar-ing a - way, My God and my Sav-ior to see.
and chained up in clay; . . . . I strug-gle and pant to be free: I long to be soar-ing a - way, My God and my Sav-ior to see.
I'm fet-tered and chained up in clay; . . . . I strug-gle and pant to be free: I long to be soar-ing a - way, My God and my Sav-ior to see.

FREDERICKSBURG. C.M.

"...with the voice together shall they sing..." -- Isa. 52:8.

O. H. Frederick, 1935.

© 1936 copyright Sacred Harp Publishing Company, Inc.

390 NEW PROSPECT. C.M.

"Yea, saith the Spirit, that they may rest from their labors." -- Rev. 14:13.

W. S. Turner, 1866.

1. O land of rest, for thee I sigh: When will the moment come When I shall lay my armor by, And dwell in peace at home,............ And dwell in peace at home.

2. No tranquil joy on earth I know, No peaceful, sheltering dome; This world's a wilderness of woe, This world is not my home,............ O this is not my home.

3. Our tears shall all be wiped away When we have ceased to roam, And we shall hear our Father say, Come dwell with me at home,............ Come dwell with me at home,

THE MESSIAH'S PRAISE. P.M.

"Every man have praise of God." -- 1 Cor. 4:5.

F Major Benjamin Rhodes, 1787. **R. F. M. Mann & James A. Sparks, 1869.**

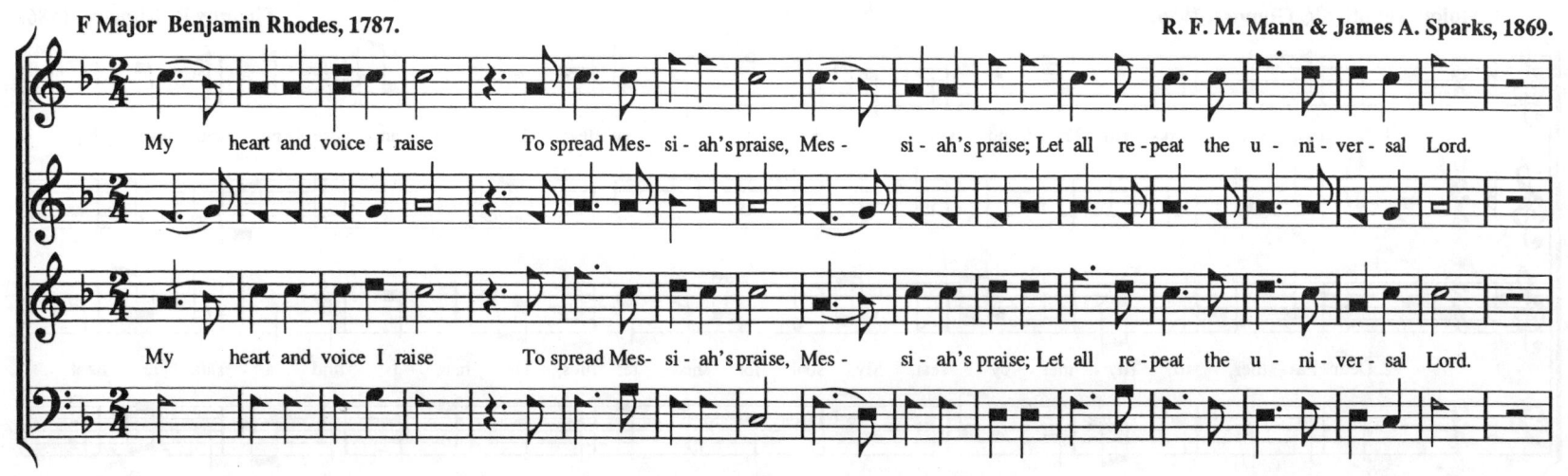

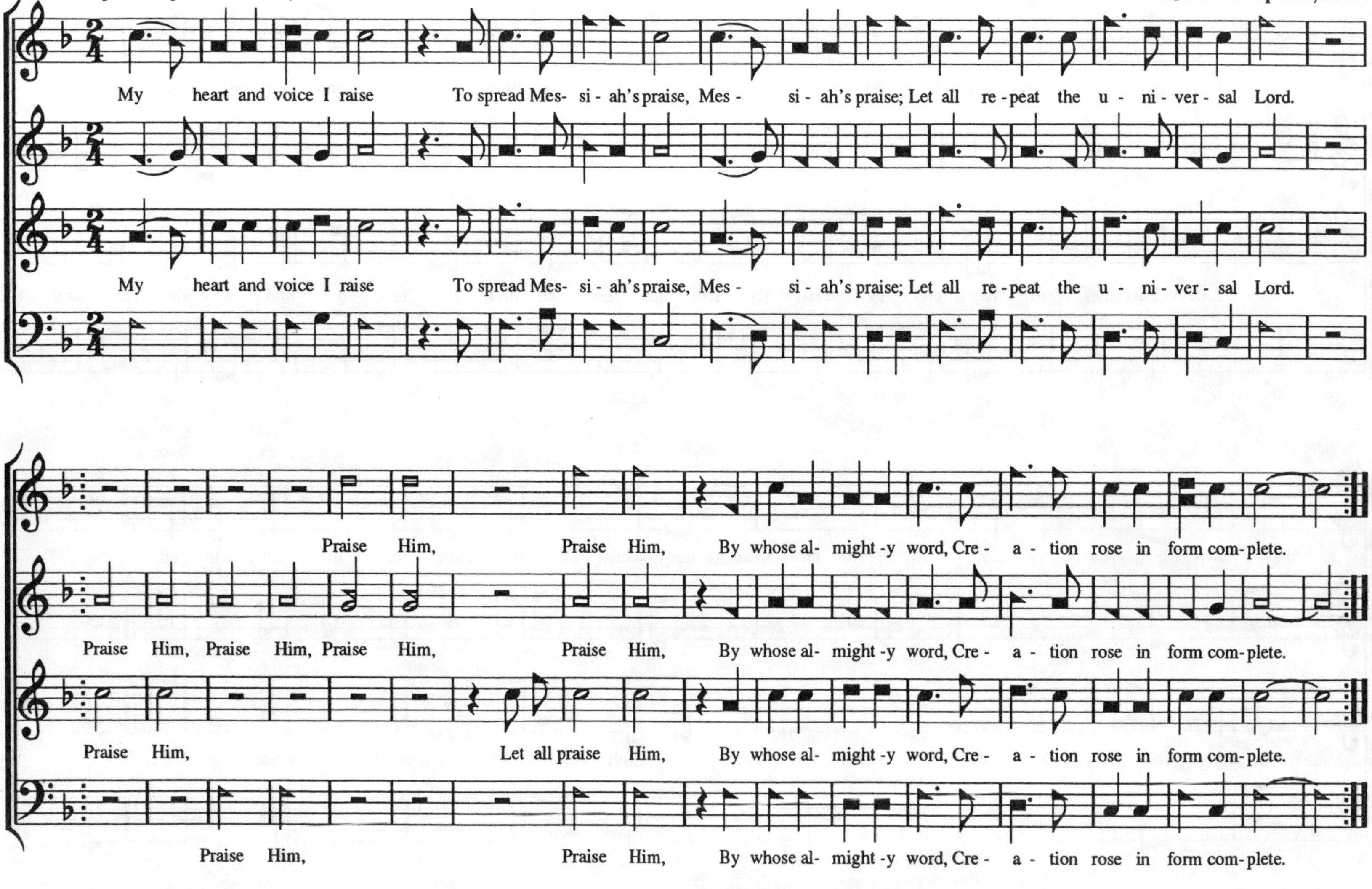

My heart and voice I raise To spread Mes- si - ah's praise, Mes - si - ah's praise; Let all re - peat the u - ni - ver - sal Lord.
My heart and voice I raise To spread Mes- si - ah's praise, Mes - si - ah's praise; Let all re - peat the u - ni - ver - sal Lord.
Praise Him, Praise Him, By whose al- might -y word, Cre - a - tion rose in form com- plete.
Praise Him, Praise Him, Praise Him, Praise Him, By whose al- might -y word, Cre - a - tion rose in form com- plete.
Praise Him, Let all praise Him, By whose al- might -y word, Cre - a - tion rose in form com- plete.
Praise Him, Praise Him, By whose al- might -y word, Cre - a - tion rose in form com- plete.

THE DYING BOY. C.M.D.

"Jesus saw her weeping . . . and was troubled." -- John 11:33.

398

F Major

H. S. Reese, 1859.

I'm dy-ing, Moth-er, dy-ing now, Please raise my ach-ing head,
And fan my heat-ed, burn-ing brow, Your boy will soon be dead.
Turn o'er my pil-low once a-gain, And kiss my fe-vered cheek;
I'll soon be freed from all the pain, For now I am so weak.

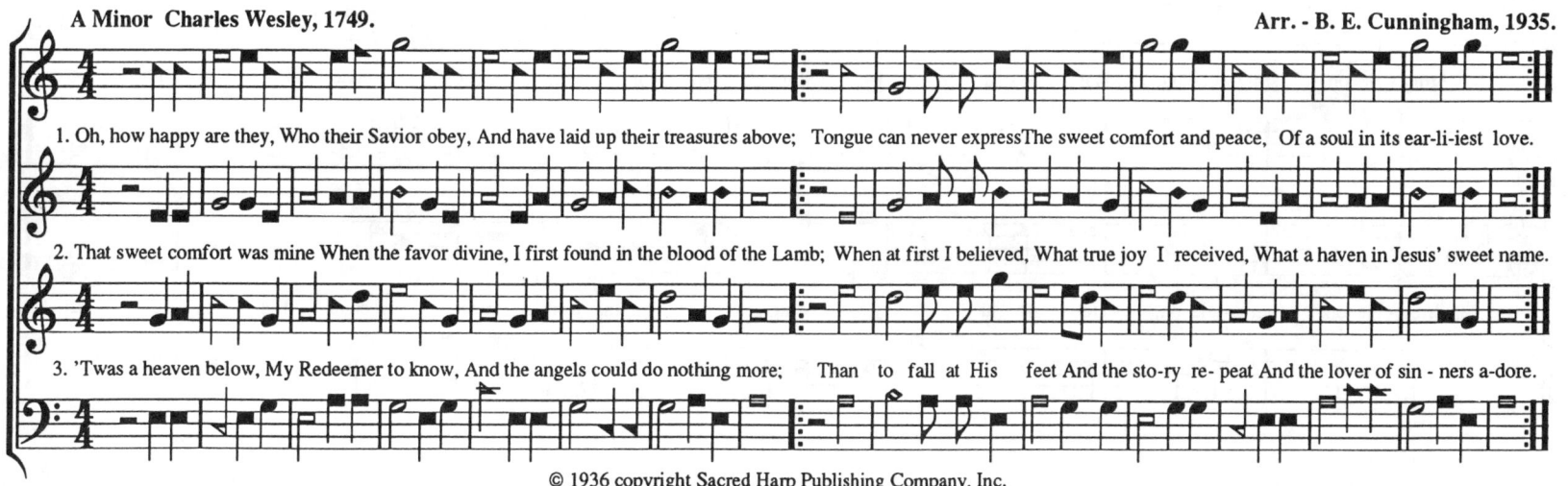

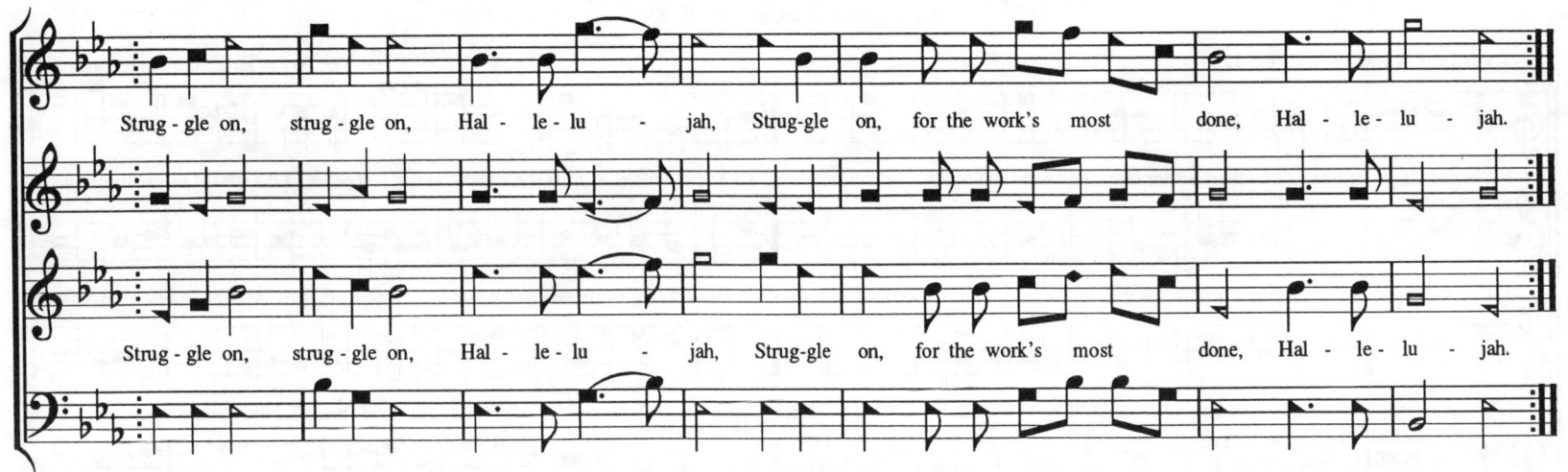

CUBA. 9s,8s.

"Go ye therefore and teach all nations." -- Matt. 28:19.

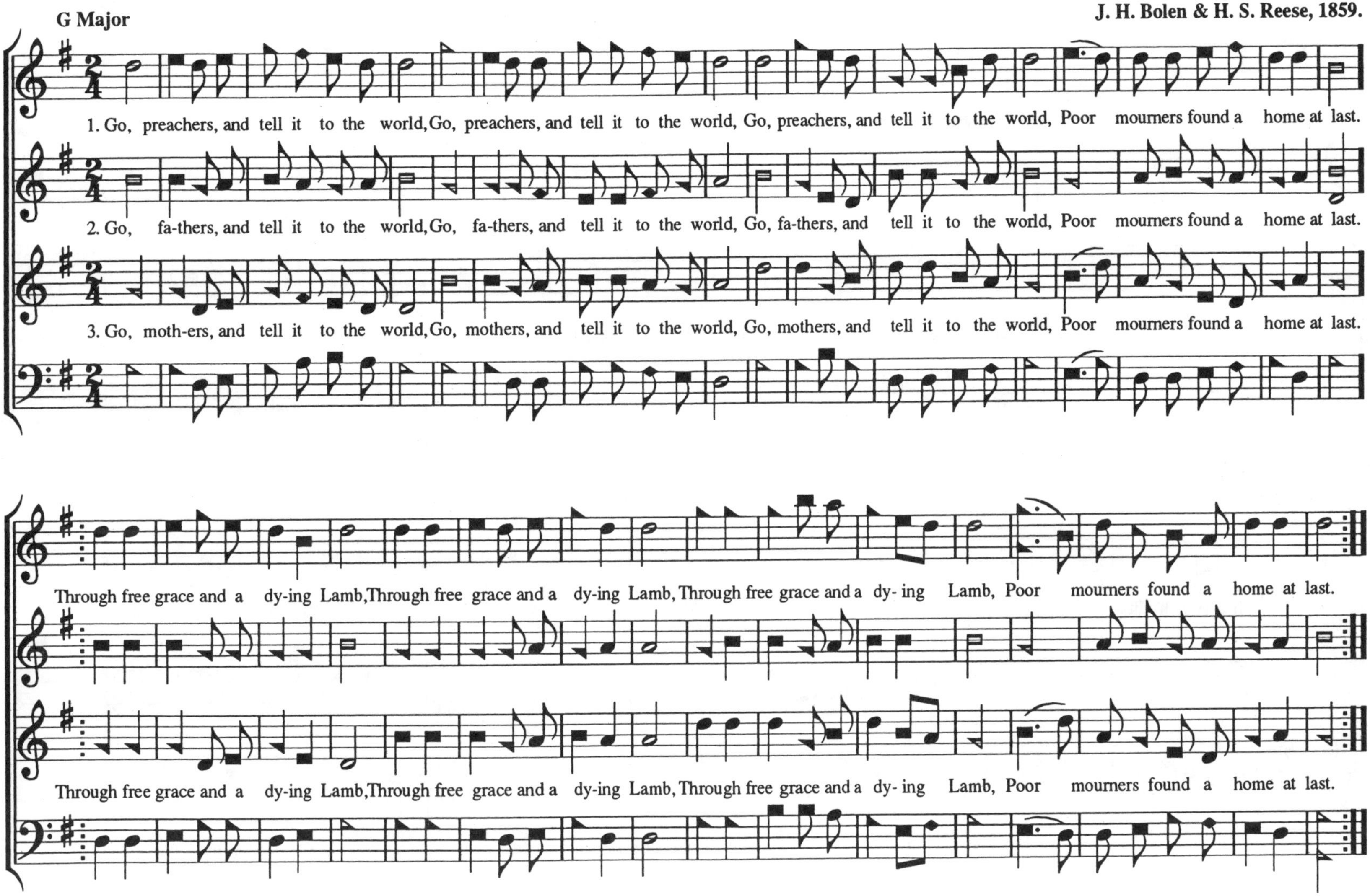
G Major
J. H. Bolen & H. S. Reese, 1859.
1. Go, preachers, and tell it to the world, Go, preachers, and tell it to the world, Go, preachers, and tell it to the world, Poor mourners found a home at last.
2. Go, fa-thers, and tell it to the world, Go, fa-thers, and tell it to the world, Go, fa-thers, and tell it to the world, Poor mourners found a home at last.
3. Go, moth-ers, and tell it to the world, Go, mothers, and tell it to the world, Go, mothers, and tell it to the world, Poor mourners found a home at last.
Through free grace and a dy-ing Lamb, Through free grace and a dy-ing Lamb, Through free grace and a dy- ing Lamb, Poor mourners found a home at last.
Through free grace and a dy-ing Lamb, Through free grace and a dy-ing Lamb, Through free grace and a dy- ing Lamb, Poor mourners found a home at last.

HEAVENLY REST. C.M.

"Then shall ye also appear with him in glory." -- Col. 3:4.

406 NEW HARMONY. 8s,7s.

"For in him we live, and move, and have our being." -- Acts 17:28.

G Major *Sacred Harp, 1859.*
M. L. A. Lancaster, 1859.

1. I want to live a Christian here, I want to die a-shouting,
I want to feel my Savior near, While soul and body's parting.
I want to see bright angels stand And waiting to receive me,
To bear my soul to Canaan's land, Where Christ has gone before me.

2. My heart is often made to mourn Because I'm faint and feeble,
And when my Savior seems to frown, My soul is fill'd with trouble.
But when He doth again return, And I repent my folly,
'Tis then I after glory run, And still my Jesus follow.

3. I have my bitter and my sweet While through this world I travel,
Sometimes I shout and often weep, Which makes my foes to marvel.
But let them think and think again, I feel I'm bound for heaven;
I hope I shall with Jesus reign, I therefore still will praise Him.

CHARLTON. C.M.

"For I have learned, in whatsoever state I am, therewith to be content." -- Phil. 4:11.

Eb Major Francis Maria Cowper, 1792. L. P. Breedlove, 1859.

1. My span of life will soon be gone, The passing moments say, As length'ning shadows o'er the mead Proclaim the close of day.

2. Ere first I drew this vital breath, From nature's prison free, Crosses in number, measure, weight, Were written, Lord, for me.

O that my heart might dwell aloof From all created things, And learn that wisdom from above, Whence true contentment springs.

But Thou my Shepherd, Friend, and Guide, Hast led me kindly on, Taught me to rest my fainting head On Christ, "the Cornerstone".

410 THE DYING CALIFORNIAN. 8s & 7s.

"For he that is dead is freed from sin." -- Rom. 6:7.

A Major Kate Harris, 1850.   Ball & Drinkard, 1859.

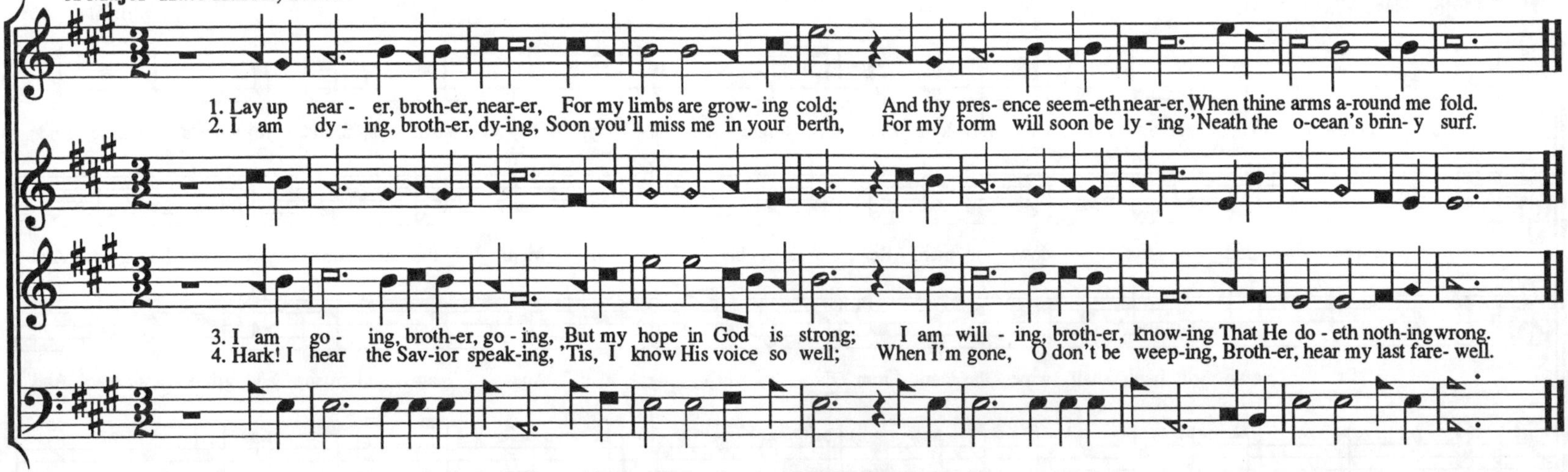

1. Lay up near-er, broth-er, near-er, For my limbs are grow-ing cold; And thy pres-ence seem-eth near-er, When thine arms a-round me fold.
2. I am dy-ing, broth-er, dy-ing, Soon you'll miss me in your berth, For my form will soon be ly-ing 'Neath the o-cean's brin-y surf.
3. I am go-ing, broth-er, go-ing, But my hope in God is strong; I am will-ing, broth-er, know-ing That He do-eth noth-ing wrong.
4. Hark! I hear the Sav-ior speak-ing, 'Tis, I know His voice so well; When I'm gone, O don't be weep-ing, Broth-er, hear my last fare-well.

MUTUAL LOVE. 7s & 6.

"... we shall also reign with Him." -- 2 Tim. 2:12.

G Major John Leland, 1793.   William Walker, 1835.

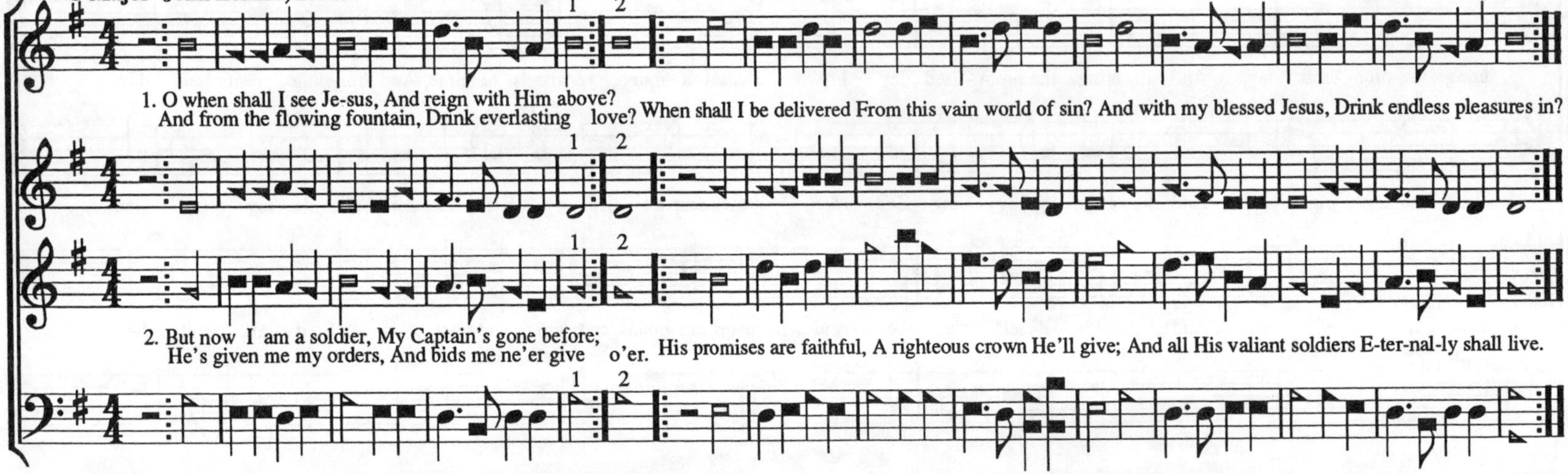

1. O when shall I see Je-sus, And reign with Him above? And from the flowing fountain, Drink everlasting love? When shall I be delivered From this vain world of sin? And with my blessed Jesus, Drink endless pleasures in?
2. But now I am a soldier, My Captain's gone before; He's given me my orders, And bids me ne'er give o'er. His promises are faithful, A righteous crown He'll give; And all His valiant soldiers E-ter-nal-ly shall live.

THE LOVED ONES. 11,8.

"A wise son maketh a glad father: but a foolish man despiseth his mother." -- Prov. 15:20.

Arr. - E. T. Pound, 1859.

414 THE LOVED ONES. Concluded.

old, his locks in-ter-min-gled with grey; His foot-steps are fee-ble, Once fear-less and bold, Thy fa-ther is pass-ing a-way.

old, his locks in-ter-min-gled with grey; His foot-steps are fee-ble, Once fear-less and bold, Thy fa-ther is pass-ing a-way.

PARTING FRIEND. C.M.D.
"A friend loveth at all times." -- Prov. 17:17.

Arr. - J. C. Graham, 1859.

G Major

The time must come when we must part, When we must say fare-well; When I am gone and far a-way, I still will think of thee.
To part with you gives to my heart A sting no one can tell.

I'll think of thee both night and day, O then re-mem-ber me.

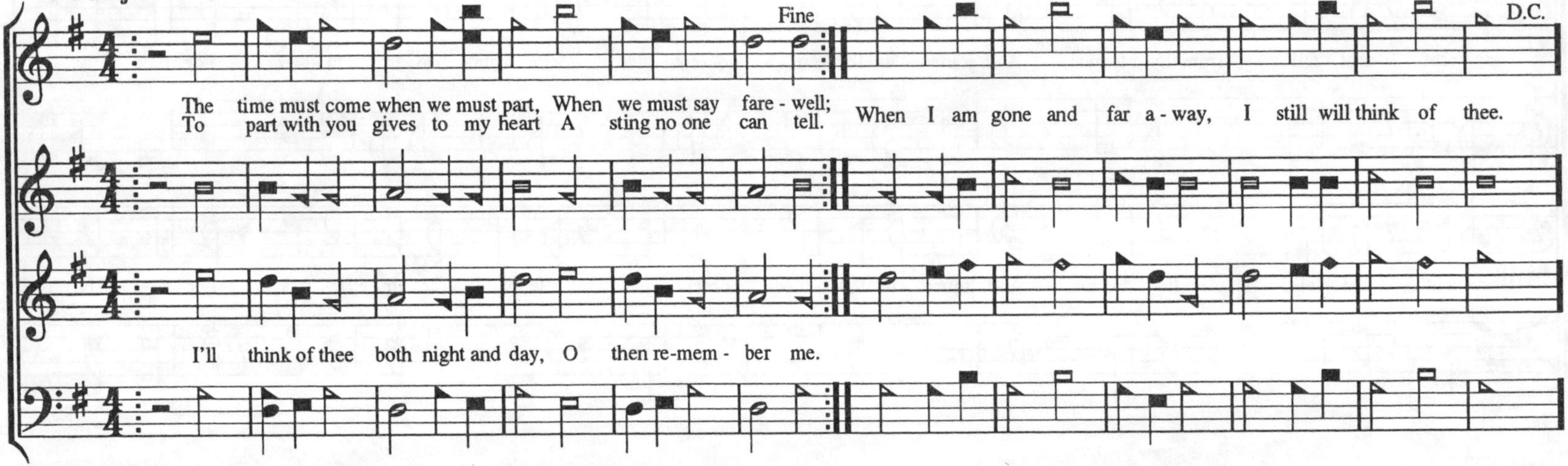

WEEPING PILGRIM.

"And the voice of weeping shall be no more heard in her, nor the voice of crying." -- Isa. 5:19.

417

J. P. Reese, 1859.

MELANCHOLY DAY. C.M.D.

419

"The fool hath said in his heart, there is no God." -- Ps. 14:1.

F# Minor Isaac Watts, 1709.

H. S. Reese, 1859.

420 MELANCHOLY DAY. Concluded.

lifts her eyes, For guilt, a heav-y chain, Still drags her downward from the skies, To darkness, fire and pain. dark-ness, fire and pain.

heav-y chain, Still drags her downward from the skies, To dark-ness, fire and pain, To dark-ness, fire and pain. and pain.

For guilt, a heav-y chain, Still drags her downward from the skies, To dark-ness, fire and pain. and pain.

heav-y chain, Still drags her downward from the skies, To dark-ness, fire and pain, To dark-ness, fire and pain. and pain.

BISHOP. C.M.
"But I trust in the Lord that I also myself shall come shortly." -- Phil. 2:24.

F Major Octavia Bishop McGraw, 1935. T. B. McGraw, 1935.

1. Our Father's gone to that bright land, He dwells with Christ, the King; And with the saints of old doth stand, While all the an-gels sing.
2. A-round dear Moth-er's bed we stood And watched her dy-ing face; While Je-sus bade her spir-it come And take a heav'n-ly place.
3. Their forms on earth no more we see, They're hid-den from our view; Their mem-'ries lin-ger still with me, As no-ble, good and true.
4. Could we but stand and view that goal, 'Twould dry our brin-y tears; True love and joy there to be-hold, Would ban-ish all our fears.

© 1936 copyright Sacred Harp Publishing Company, Inc.

GRANTVILLE. C.M. 423

"That we may obtain mercy, and find grace to help in time of need." -- Heb. 4:16.

F# Minor Isaac Watts, 1707.
J. P. Reese, 1859.

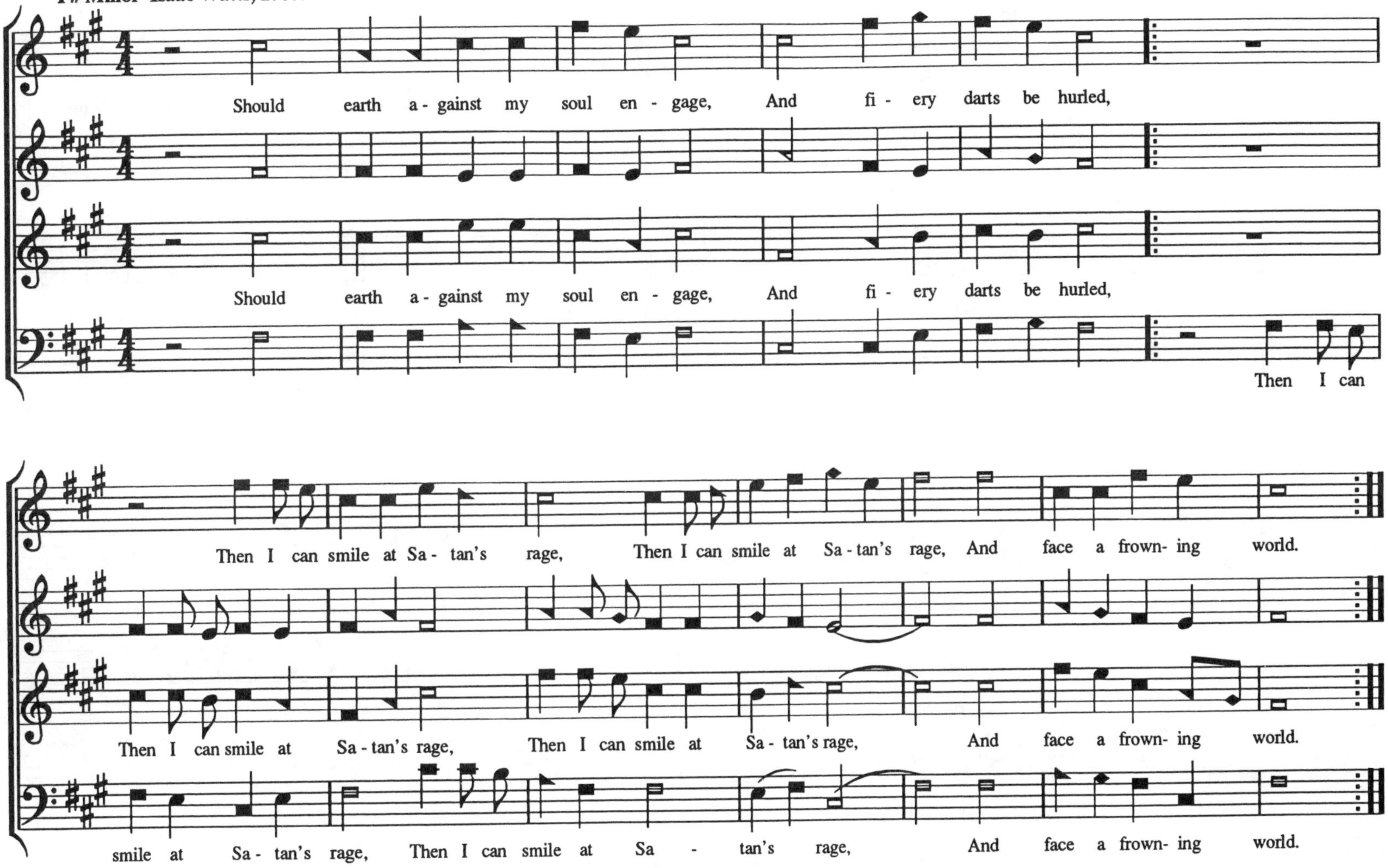

Should earth against my soul engage, And fiery darts be hurled,
Then I can smile at Satan's rage, Then I can smile at Satan's rage, And face a frowning world.

SWEET UNION. Concluded.

425

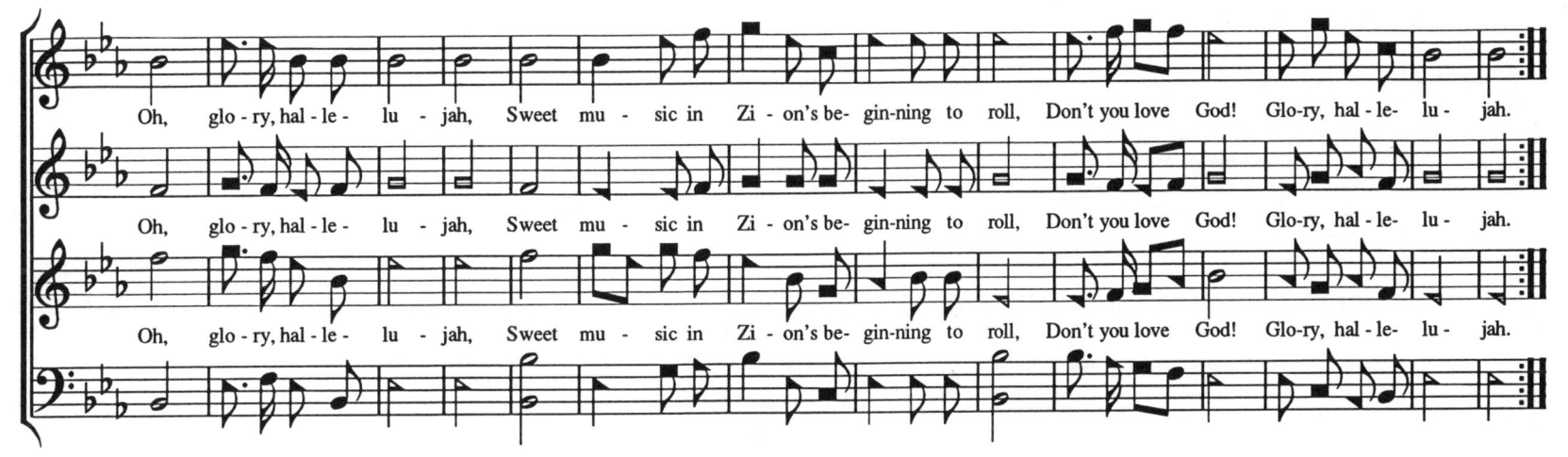

GOLDEN STREETS. P.M.

"We are journeying unto the place." -- Num. 10:29.

J. L. Pickard, 1859.

426 KELLEY. C.M.D.

"For ye yourselves are taught of God to love one another." -- 1 Thes. 4:9.

G Major Amanda Burdette Denson, 1908. Amanda Burdette Denson, 1908.

My Christian friends, to whom I speak, I have a crown in view.
My sinner friends, now will you seek, How stands the case with you?
I know there is a paradise, The saints all bid us come.

D. C. - And He who reigns rules earth and sky, O heaven is my home. I know there is a paradise, The saints all bid us come.

JASPER. C.M.

"I will sing unto the Lord as long as I live." -- Ps. 104:33.

F Major Ottiwell Heginbotham, 1794. T. J. Denson, 1907.

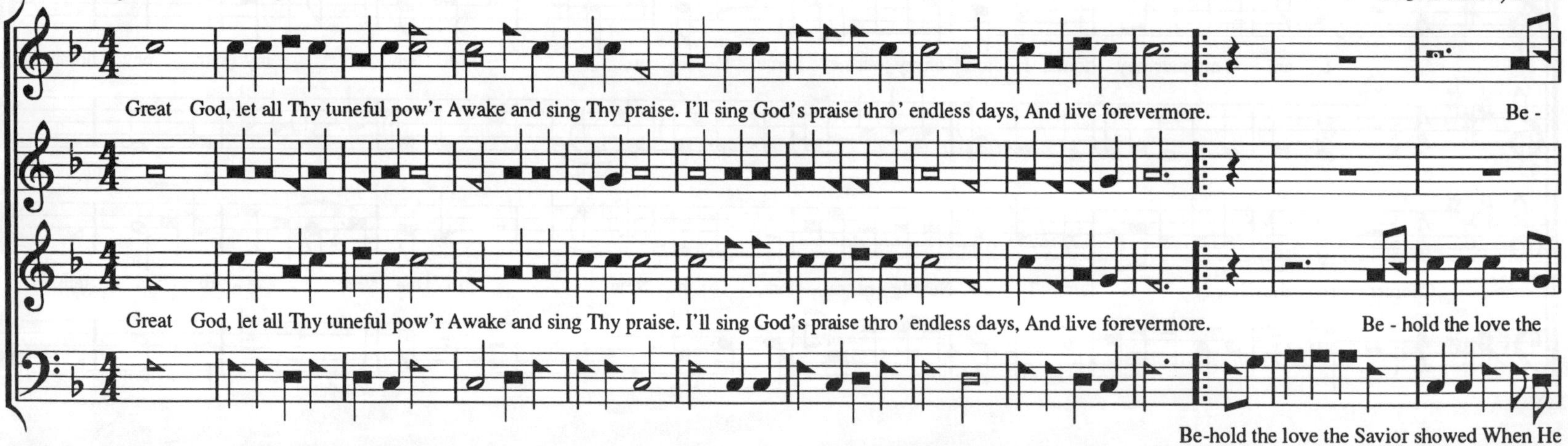

Great God, let all Thy tuneful pow'r Awake and sing Thy praise. I'll sing God's praise thro' endless days, And live forevermore. Be-

Great God, let all Thy tuneful pow'r Awake and sing Thy praise. I'll sing God's praise thro' endless days, And live forevermore. Be-hold the love the

Be-hold the love the Savior showed When He

JASPER. Concluded.

CHRISTIAN'S DELIGHT. L.M.

"He will not forsake thee, neither destroy thee." -- Deut. 4:31.

F# Minor Samuel Ecking, 1778.

Arr. - William L. Williams, 1859.

1. Peace, troubled soul, thou need not fear, Jesus says He will be with us to the end.
Thy Great Provider still is near,

2. Who fed thee last, will feed thee still, Jesus says He will be with us to the end.
Be calm and sink into His will,

3. The Lord, who built the earth and sky, Jesus says He will be with us to the end.
In mercy stoops to hear thy cry,

4. His promise all may freely claim, Jesus says He will be with us to the end.
Ask, and receive in Jesus' name,

And He has been with us, And He yet is with us, And He's promised to be with us to the end.

ARBACOOCHEE. C.M.D.

Typical of Christ' s love for the church -- Isa. 63:9.

F# Minor Isaac Watts, 1719. **S. M. Denson, 1908.**

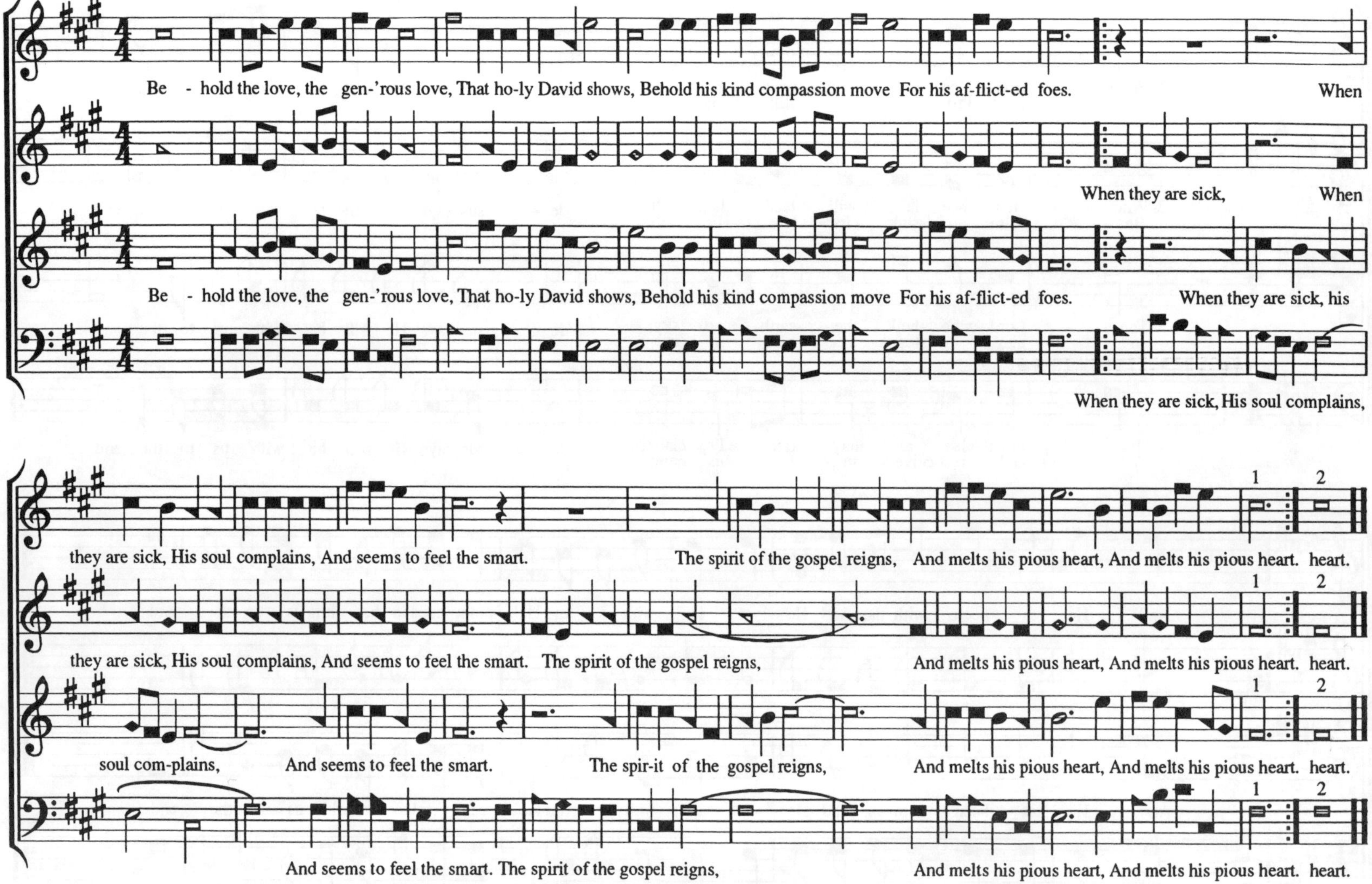
Be - hold the love, the gen-'rous love, That ho-ly David shows, Behold his kind compassion move For his af-flict-ed foes.
When
When they are sick,
When
Be - hold the love, the gen-'rous love, That ho-ly David shows, Behold his kind compassion move For his af-flict-ed foes.
When they are sick, his
When they are sick, His soul complains,
they are sick, His soul complains, And seems to feel the smart.
The spirit of the gospel reigns, And melts his pious heart, And melts his pious heart. heart.
1
2
they are sick, His soul complains, And seems to feel the smart. The spirit of the gospel reigns,
And melts his pious heart, And melts his pious heart. heart.
soul com-plains, And seems to feel the smart.
The spir-it of the gospel reigns,
And melts his pious heart, And melts his pious heart. heart.
And seems to feel the smart. The spirit of the gospel reigns,
And melts his pious heart, And melts his pious heart. heart.

NEW BETHANY. L.M.

431

"Before the mountains were. . . or thou hadst formed the earth and the world, even from everlasting to everlasting, thou art God." -- Ps. 90:2.

F Major Harriet Auber, 1829.

B. F. White, Jr., 1869.

432 CHEVES. L.M.
"My grace is sufficient for thee." -- 2 Cor. 12:9.

F Major *Baptist Hymn Book,* **1825.** Oliver Bradfield, 1857.

McKAY. C.M.D.

"And he showed me a pure river of water of life, clear as crystal, proceeding out of the throne of God and the Lamb." -- Rev. 22:1.

A Minor Samuel Stennett, 1787. S. M. Denson, 1908.

FILLMORE. L.M.
"I will sing unto the Lord as long as I live." -- PS. 104:33.

F Major Ottiwell Heginbotham, 1794.   J. P. Reese, 1869.

Great God, let all my tune-ful pow'rs A-wake, and sing Thy might-y name; Thy hand re-volves my circling hours, Thy hand from whence my be-ing came. Thus will I sing till na-ture cease, Till sense and lan-guage are no more, And af-ter death Thy boundless grace Through

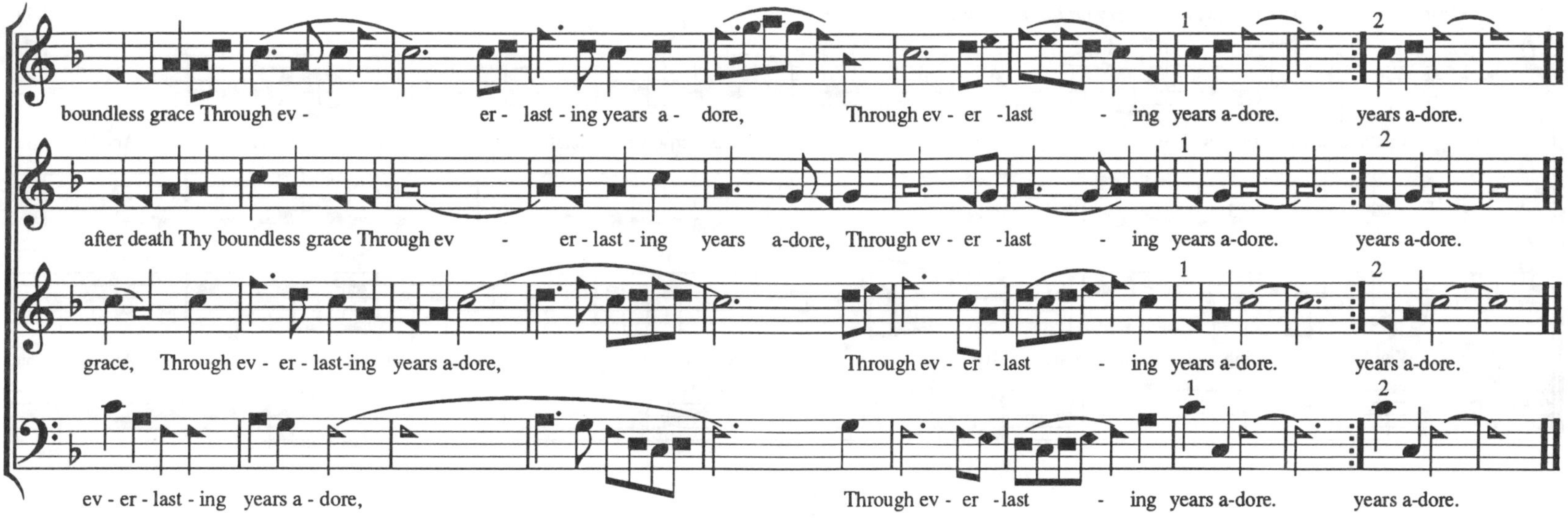

FILLMORE. Concluded. 435

boundless grace Through ev - er - last-ing years a - dore, Through ev - er - last - ing years a-dore. years a-dore.

after death Thy boundless grace Through ev - er - last-ing years a-dore, Through ev - er - last - ing years a-dore. years a-dore.

grace, Through ev - er - last-ing years a-dore, Through ev - er - last - ing years a-dore. years a-dore.

ev - er - last-ing years a - dore, Through ev - er - last - ing years a-dore. years a-dore.

SACRED REST. L.M.
"Solemn Sound." -- Ps. 92:2.

F Major Isaac Watts, 1719.   W. D. Jones, 1869.

Sweet is the day of sa - cred rest, No mor - tal care shall fill my breast; Oh, may my heart in tune be found, Like Da-vid's harp of sol - emn sound.

Sweet is the day of sa - cred rest, No mor - tal care shall fill my breast; Oh, may my heart in tune be found, Like Da-vid's harp of sol - emn sound.

436 MORNING SUN. L.M.D.

"Remember now thy Creator in the days of thy youth, while the evil days come not, nor the years draw nigh." -- Ecc. 12:1.

Eb Major *New England Sunday School Hymn Book,* **1830.** S. M. Denson, 1911.

Youth, like the spring, will soon be gone, By fleet-ing time or con-quering death; Your morn-ing sun may set at noon, And leave you ev-er in the dark. Your spar-kling eyes and bloom-ing cheeks Must with-er like the blast-ed rose; The cof-fin,

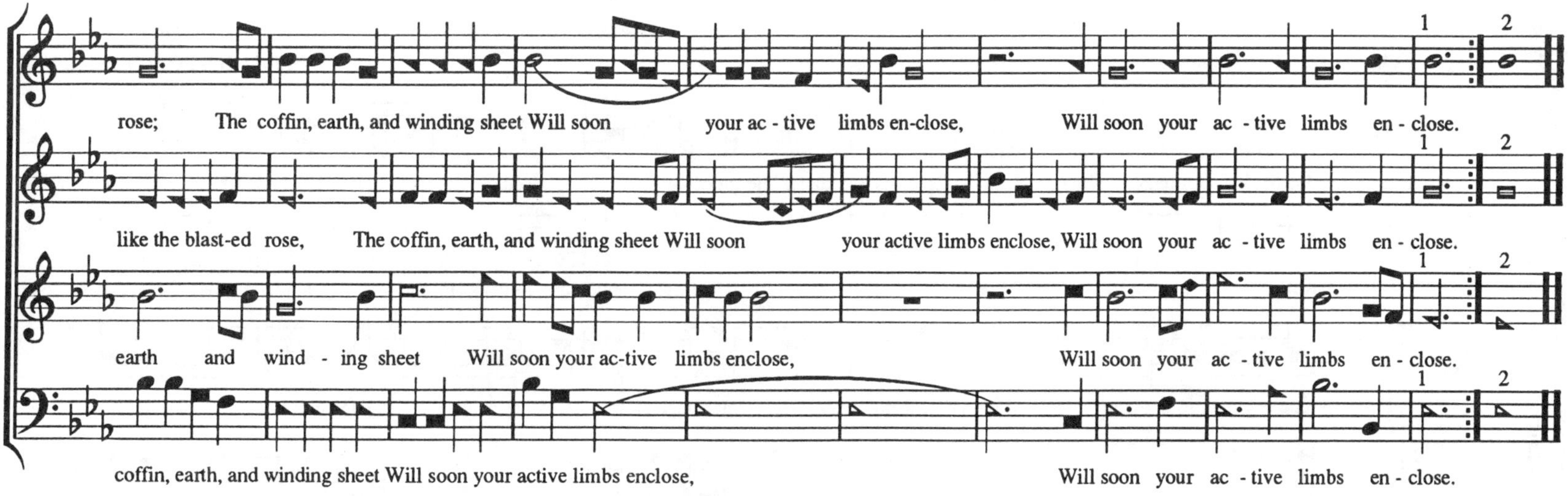

MORNING SUN. Concluded. 437

rose; The coffin, earth, and winding sheet Will soon your ac-tive limbs en-close, Will soon your ac-tive limbs en-close.

like the blast-ed rose, The coffin, earth, and winding sheet Will soon your active limbs enclose, Will soon your ac-tive limbs en-close.

earth and wind-ing sheet Will soon your ac-tive limbs enclose, Will soon your ac-tive limbs en-close.

coffin, earth, and winding sheet Will soon your active limbs enclose, Will soon your ac-tive limbs en-close.

SIDNEY. C.M.D.
"I am the good shepherd: the good shepherd giveth his life for his sheep." -- John 10:11.

F Major Isaac Watts, 1719.   S. Whitt Denson, 1908.

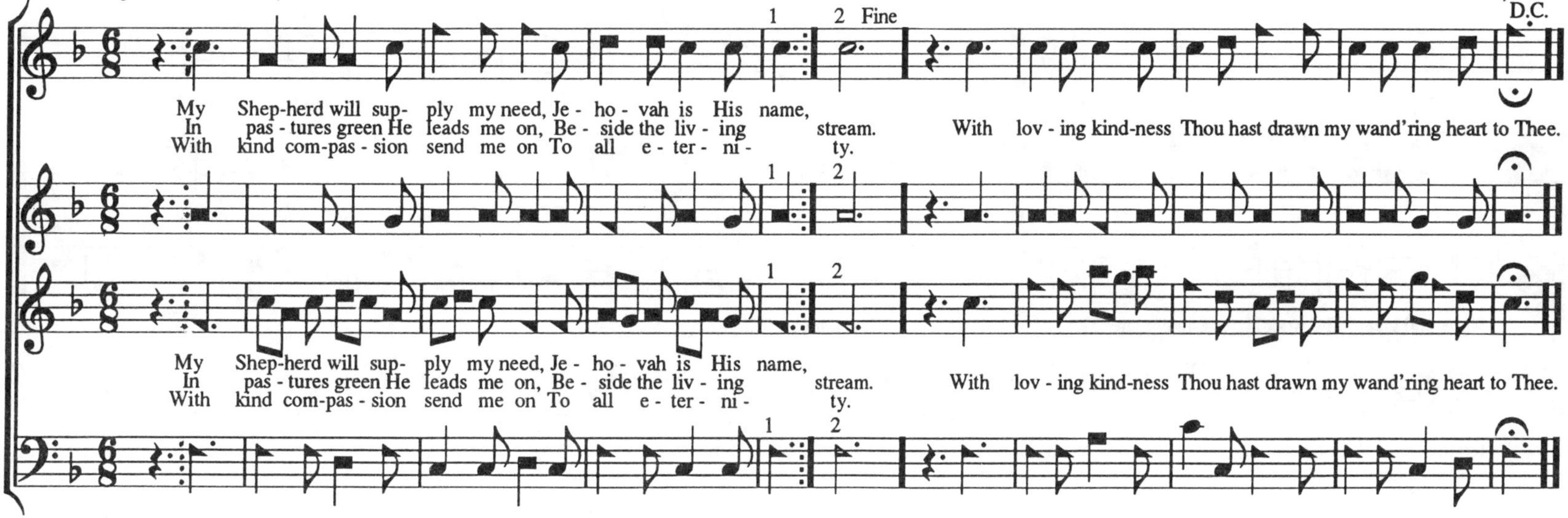

My Shep-herd will sup-ply my need, Je-ho-vah is His name,
In pas-tures green He leads me on, Be-side the liv-ing stream. With lov-ing kind-ness Thou hast drawn my wand'ring heart to Thee.
With kind com-pas-sion send me on To all e-ter-ni-ty.

JORDAN (Second). C.M.D.

"Thine eyes shall behold the land." -- Isa. 33:17.

F Major Samuel Stennett, 1787. **A. M. Cagle, 1908.**

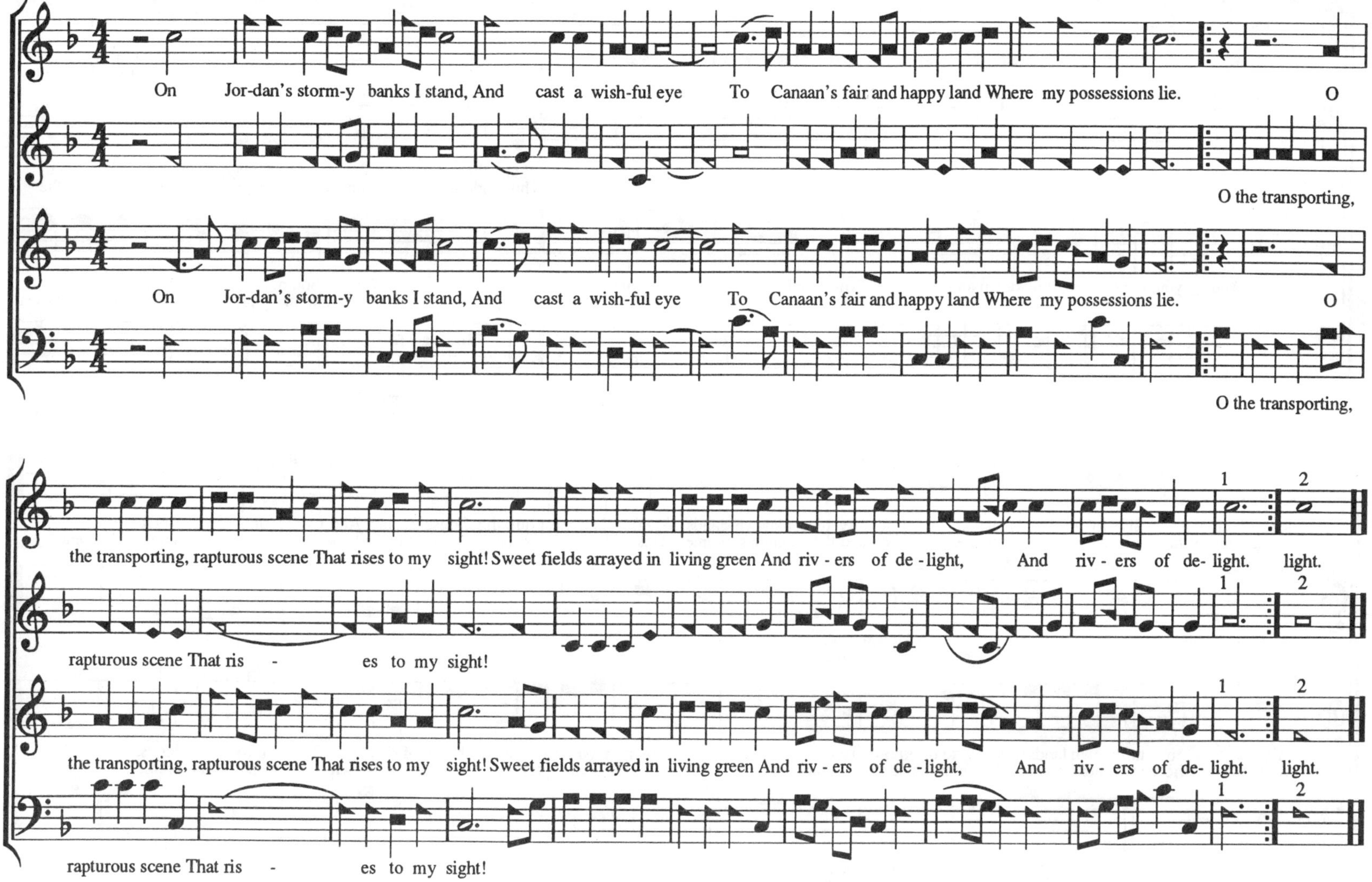
On Jor-dan's storm-y banks I stand, And cast a wish-ful eye To Canaan's fair and happy land Where my possessions lie. O
O the transporting,
On Jor-dan's storm-y banks I stand, And cast a wish-ful eye To Canaan's fair and happy land Where my possessions lie. O
O the transporting,
the transporting, rapturous scene That rises to my sight! Sweet fields arrayed in living green And riv - ers of de - light, And riv - ers of de- light. light.
rapturous scene That ris - es to my sight!
the transporting, rapturous scene That rises to my sight! Sweet fields arrayed in living green And riv - ers of de - light, And riv - ers of de- light. light.
rapturous scene That ris - es to my sight!
1
2

NORTH SALEM. C.M.

"But truly as the Lord liveth, and as thy soul liveth, there is but a step between me and death." -- 1 Sam. 20:3.

E Minor — Isaac Watts, 1707. — Stephen Jenks, 1799.

NEW JORDAN. Concluded. 443

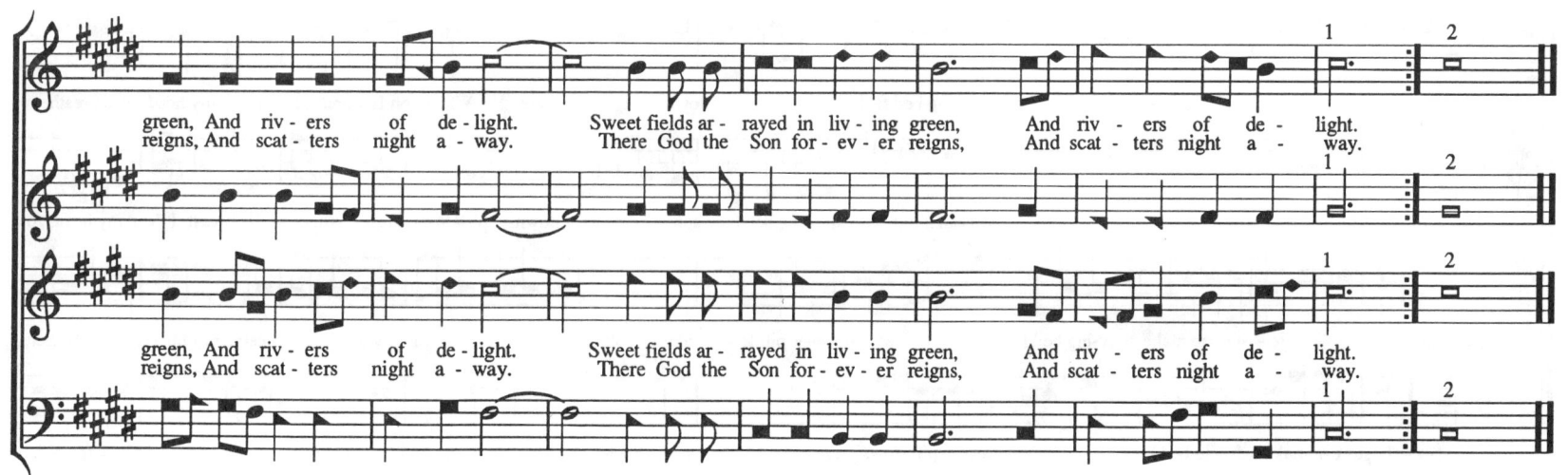

444 ALL SAINTS NEW. L.M.

"Let me die the death of the righteous, and let my last end be like his." -- Num. 23:10.

D Minor Isaac Watts, 1707.
Amariah Hall, 1791.

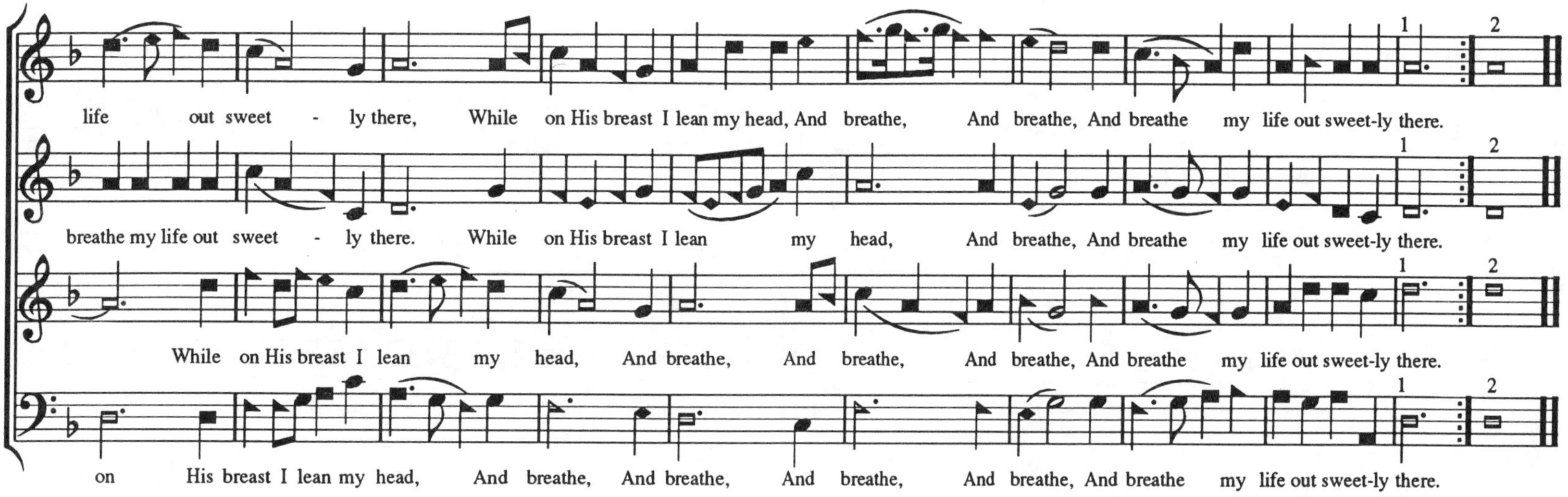

ALL SAINTS NEW. Concluded. 445

life out sweet-ly there, While on His breast I lean my head, And breathe, And breathe, And breathe my life out sweet-ly there.

breathe my life out sweet-ly there. While on His breast I lean my head, And breathe, And breathe my life out sweet-ly there.

While on His breast I lean my head, And breathe, And breathe, And breathe, And breathe my life out sweet-ly there.

on His breast I lean my head, And breathe, And breathe, And breathe, And breathe, And breathe my life out sweet-ly there.

PASSING AWAY. C.M.

"It is appointed unto man once to die, but after this the judgment." -- Heb. 9:27.

C Major   Charles Wesley, 1763.   John A. Watson, 1872.

1. And must I be to judgment brought, And answer in that day
   For ev-'ry vain and i-dle thought And ev-'ry word I say?

We are passing a-way, We are pass-ing a-way, We are passing a-way, To that great judgment day.

2. Yes, ev-'ry se-cret of my heart Shall shortly be made known;
   And I receive my just de-sert For all that I have done.

We are passing a-way, We are pass-ing a-way, We are passing a-way, To that great judgment day.

3. How careful, then, ought I to be; With what religious fear,
   Who such a strict account must give For my behavior here.

We are passing a-way, We are pass-ing a-way, We are passing a-way, To that great judgment day.

448

CONSECRATION. 8s.
"Present your bodies a living sacrifice, holy, acceptable unto God." -- Rom. 12:1.

F# Minor William S. Turner, 1866.

William S. Turner, 1866.

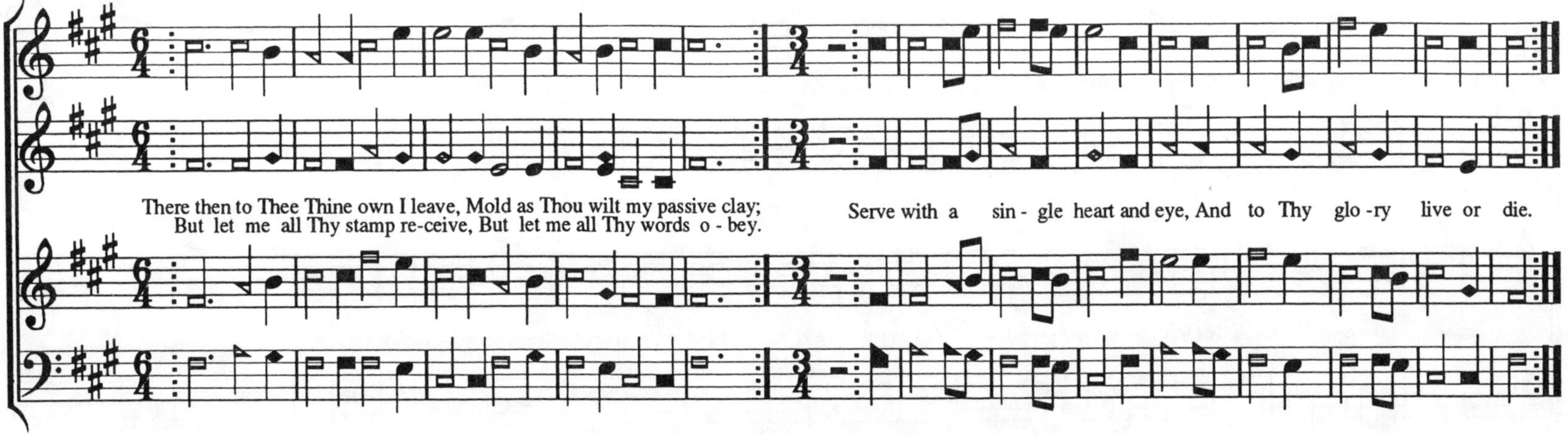

There then to Thee Thine own I leave, Mold as Thou wilt my passive clay;
But let me all Thy stamp re-ceive, But let me all Thy words o-bey.

Serve with a sin-gle heart and eye, And to Thy glo-ry live or die.

THE GRIEVED SOUL. 7,6.
"For he doth not afflict willingly, nor grieve the children of men." -- Lam. 3:33.

A Major Joseph Hart, 1759.

M. A. Hendon, 1859.

Come, my soul and let us try For a lit-tle sea-son.
Ev-'ry bur-den to lay by, Come and let us rea-son.

What is this that casts thee down? Who are those that grieve thee?

Chorus: Speak and let the worst be known? Speak-ing may re-lieve thee.

MARY'S GRIEF AND JOY. 7s. 451

"Magdalene, and Mary the mother of James, and Salome, had bought sweet spices, that they might come and anoint him." -- Mark 16:1.

D Major John Newton, 1779.
J. P. Webster, Arr. - B. F. White, 1869.

Ma-ry to her Sav-ior's tomb Hast-ed at the ear-ly dawn; Spice she brought and sweet per-fume, But the Lord she loved was gone.

For a-while she weep-ing stood, Struck with sor-row and sur-prise; Shed-ding tears, a plen-teous flood, For her heart sup-plied her eyes.

452 MARY'S GRIEF AND JOY. Concluded.

Oh, my Savior, oh, my Savior, Where has my Savior gone? Oh, my Savior, here's my Savior; He has risen from the tomb.

MARTIN. 7s.
"A hiding place from the wind." -- Isa. 32:2.

F Major Charles Wesley, 1738. S. B. Marsh, 1836.

1. Jesus, Lover of my soul, Let me to Thy bosom fly,
While the nearer waters roll, While the tempest still is high! Hide me, O my Savior, hide, Till the storm of life is past;
D.C. - Safe into the haven guide; O receive my soul at last.

2. Other refuge have I none, Hangs my helpless soul on Thee:
Leave, ah! leave me not alone, Still support and comfort me; All my trust on Thee is stayed, All my help from Thee I bring,
D.C. - Cover my defenseless head With the shadow of Thy wing.

3. Wilt Thou not regard my call? Wilt Thou not accept my prayer?
Lo! I faint, I sink, I fall Lo! on Thee I cast my care. Reach me out Thy gracious hand, While I of Thy strength receive,
D.C. - Hoping against hope I stand, Dying, and behold I live!

THE BETTER LAND. P.M.

"But now they desire a better country..." -- Heb. 11:16.

Bb Major O. A. Parris, 1935.

O. A. Parris, 1935.

1. The road to glo-ry seems so long, And sor-rows of-ten take my song. I'm go-ing to a bet-ter land, I'm go-ing to a bet-ter land,
2. From Je-sus' side I will not stray, I know He'll guide me all the way. I'm go-ing to a bet-ter land, I'm
3. I know it is not ver-y far, To heav-en where my trea-sures are. I'm go-ing to a bet-ter land, Where troubles are un-

known, All sor-row will be gone, We'll sing a-round the throne in sweet accord, A-dor-ing Je-sus, our dear Lord. Lord.

© 1936 copyright Sacred Harp Publishing Company, Inc.

TOLLING BELL. 10s, 4s.
"Weep not for me." -- Luke 23:28.

459

A Major John Ellis, 1838. R. F. M. Mann, 1868.

Shed not a tear o'er your friend's ear-ly bier;
Smile when the slow toll-ing bell you shall hear, When I am gone, When I am gone. Weep not for me when you stand round my grave,
Think who has died His be-lov-ed to save, Think of the crown all the ran-somed shall wear, When I am gone, I am gone.

WHERE THERE'S NO TROUBLE AND SORROW. L.M.D.

465

"...Rest from thy sorrow..." -- Isa. 14:3.

F Major

Doris W. DeLong, 1960.

I have my troubles here below As the nar-row way I fol-low, But there's a land of peace and rest, Where there's no trou-ble or sor - row.

Yes, my loved ones now are o - ver there, and I know I soon will fol - low, I'll see my Sav - ior in that land where there's no trou-ble or sor - row.

© 1960 copyright Sacred Harp Publishing Company, Inc.

HAYNES CREEK. Concluded. 467

bent, And God has showered His bless-ing down As oft, as of - ten as we went.

LISBON. S.M.
"And Jesus came and touched them . . ." -- Matt. 17:7.

Bb Major Isaac Watts, 1719.   Arr. from Daniel Read, 1785.

1. Wel- come, sweet day of rest, That saw the Lord a - rise; Wel - come to this re - viv-ing breast And these re-joic- ing eyes.

2. The King Him-self comes near, To feast His saints to - day; Here we may sit and see Him here, And love, and praise, and pray.

BRISTOL. L.M.D.

"O magnify the Lord with me, and let us exalt his name together." -- Ps. 34:4.

F Major Joseph Addison, 1712.

Timothy Swan, 1785.

BRISTOL. Concluded. 469

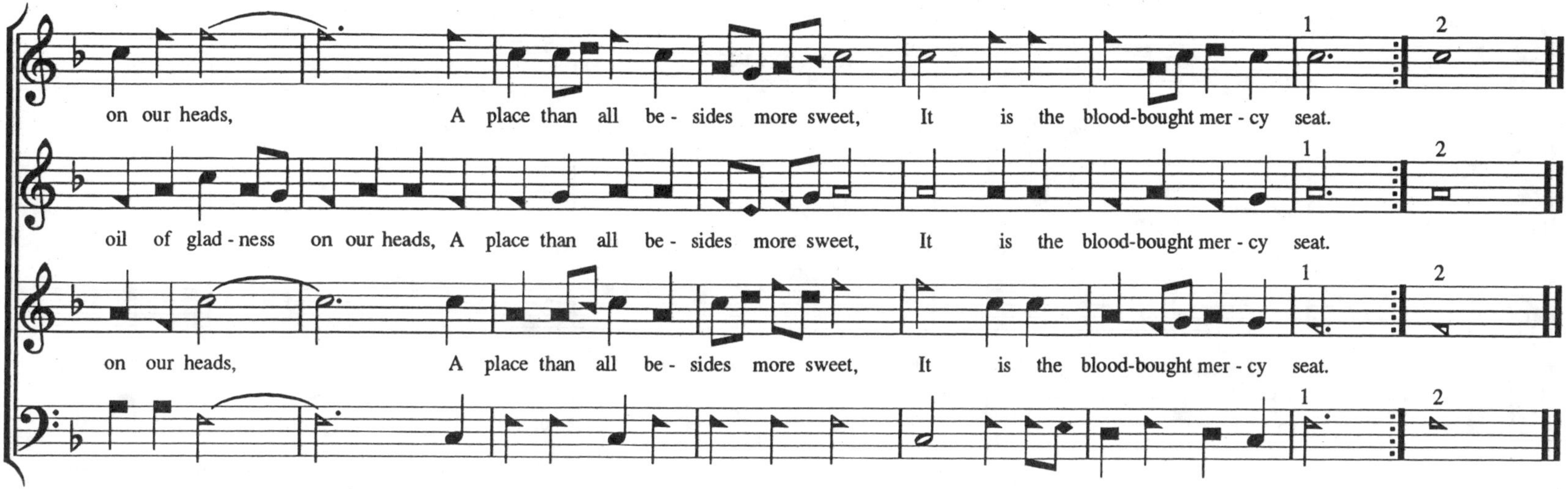

THE MERCY SEAT. Concluded. 471

on our heads, A place than all besides more sweet, It is the blood-bought mercy seat.

oil of gladness on our heads, A place than all besides more sweet, It is the blood-bought mercy seat.

on our heads, A place than all besides more sweet, It is the blood-bought mercy seat.

THE SAVIOR'S NAME. C.M.
"Sing aloud unto God our strength..." -- Ps. 81:1.

F Major Frederick Whitfield, 1855. T. B. McGraw, 1960.

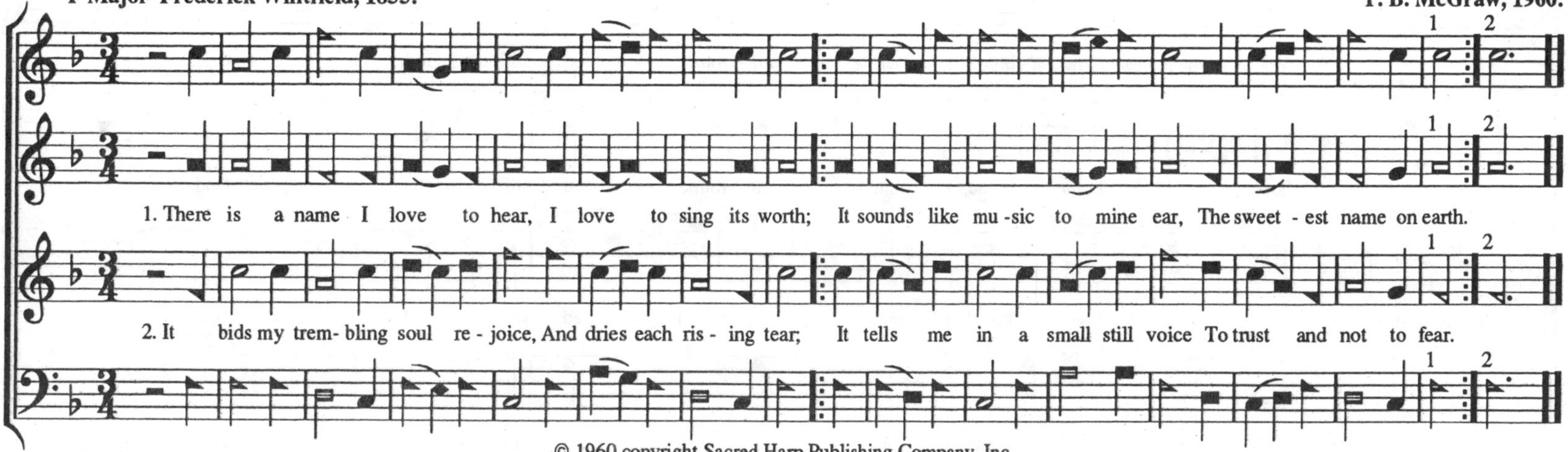

1. There is a name I love to hear, I love to sing its worth; It sounds like music to mine ear, The sweetest name on earth.

2. It bids my trembling soul rejoice, And dries each rising tear; It tells me in a small still voice To trust and not to fear.

© 1960 copyright Sacred Harp Publishing Company, Inc.

472 AKIN. L.M.

"Thou hast kept close guard before me and behind, and hast spread thy hand over me." -- Ps. 139:5.

C Major Isaac Watts, 1719.
P. Dan Brittain, 1971.

Within Thy circling pow'r I stand, On ev'ry side I find Thy hand; Awake, asleep, at home, abroad, I am surrounded still with God.

© 1991 copyright Sacred Harp Publishing Company, Inc.

478 MY RISING SUN. C.M.

"... great is the mystery of godliness." -- 1 Tim. 3:16.

F Major William Cowper, 1774.

C. H. Gilliland, 1960.

1. God moves in a mys-terious way His wonders to perform; He plants His footsteps in the sea And rides upon the storm. My sor-rows will be
2. He forms the sinful man a-new, Sub-dues the love of sin; He takes a-way the heart of stone And plants His grace with-in. Ap- plies re-deem-ing

In darkest night when He appears My sorrows will be
He came from Heav'n our souls to save, Applies redeeming

gone, He is my soul's sweet morning star, And He's my rising sun. He is my soul's sweet morn-ing star, And He's my ris-ing sun. sun.
blood, Bids all our guilt and fears removed, Leaves us at peace with God. Bids all our guilt and fears re-moved, Leaves us at peace with God. God.

© 1960 copyright Sacred Harp Publishing Company, Inc.

CHESTER. L.M.

"There is one glory of the sun, and another glory of the moon, and another glory of the stars: for one star differeth from another star in glory." -- 1 Cor. 15:41.

F Major Philip Doddridge, 1755.   William Billings, 1770.

1. Let the high heav'ns your songs in-vite, These spa-cious fields of bril-liant light,
Where sun and moon and plan-ets roll, And stars that glow from pole to pole.

2. Sun, moon and stars con-vey Thy praise Round the whole earth and nev-er stand,
So when Thy truth be-gan its race, It touched and glanced on ev-'ry hand.

NOVAKOSKI. S.M.

"Therefore my heart sings to you without ceasing." -- Ps. 30:13.

E Minor Isaac Watts, 1707.
P. Dan Brittain, 1989.

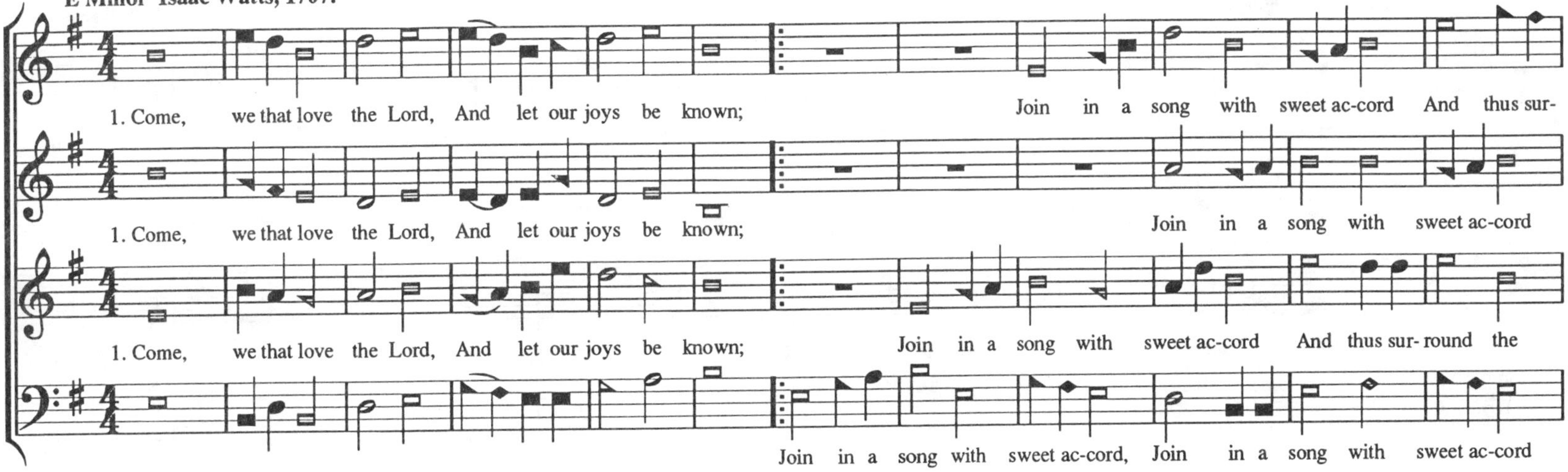

2. Let those refuse to sing
   Who never knew our God;
   But children of the heav'nly King
   May speak their joys abroad.

3. Then let our songs abound,
   And ev'ry tear be dry;
   We're marching thro' Immanuel's ground
   To fairer worlds on high.

© 1991 copyright Sacred Harp Publishing Company, Inc.

ETERNAL LIGHT. C.M.

"...Ye shall not be ashamed..." -- Isa. 45:17.

483

F Major Isaac Watts, 1707.

H. N. McGraw, 1960.

1. I'm not a-shamed to own my Lord, or to de-fend His cause, Main-tain the hon-or of His Word, the glo-ry of His cross.
2. Firm as His throne His promise stands and He can well se-cure What I've com-mit-ted to His hands till the de-ci-sive hour.

I know His name, His name is all my trust, Nor will He put my soul to shame, nor let my hope be lost.
My worthless name before His Father's face, And in the new Je-ru-sa-lem ap-point my soul a place.

Je-sus, my God, I know His name, His name is all my trust, Nor will He put my soul to shame, nor let my hope be lost.
Then He will own My worthless name before His Father's face, And in the new Je-ru-sa-lem ap-point my soul a place.

Je-sus, my God, I know His name, His name is all my trust,
Then He will own my worthless name be-fore His Fa-ther's face,

© 1960 copyright Sacred Harp Publishing Company, Inc.

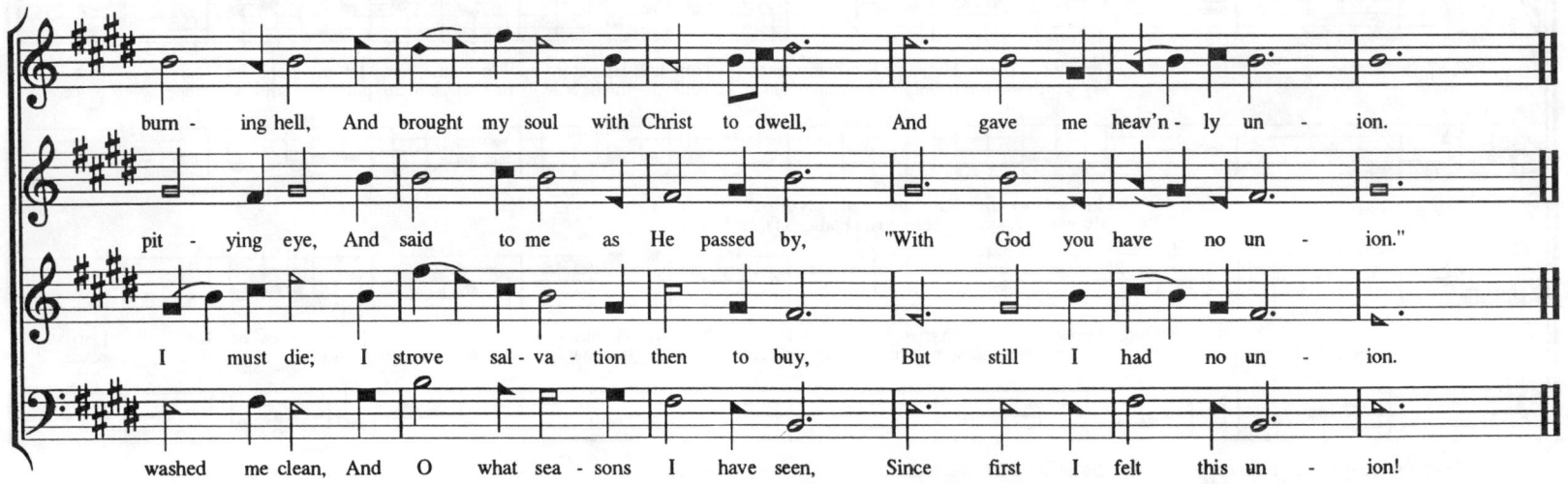

BENEFICENCE. L.M.D.

"...Thou blessed of the Lord..." -- Gen. 24:31.

BENEFICENCE. Concluded.   487

SOLDIER'S DELIGHT. L.M.
"I will praise the Lord..." -- Ps. 7:17.

F# Minor C. O. Woodard, 1918.   T. P. Woodard, 1918.

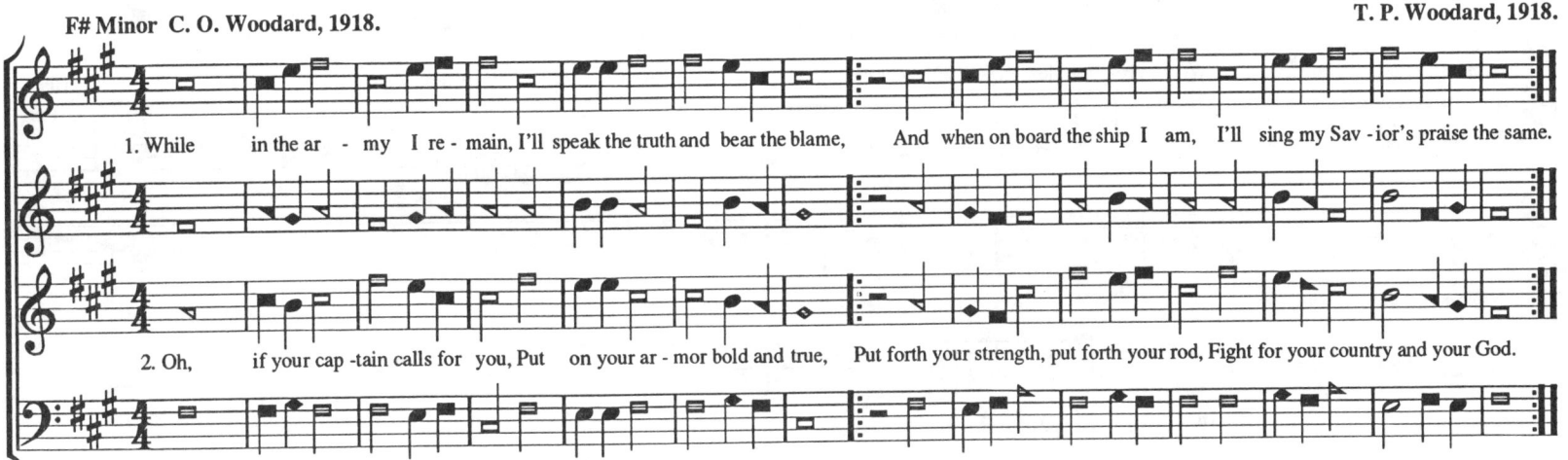

1. While in the ar - my I re - main, I'll speak the truth and bear the blame, And when on board the ship I am, I'll sing my Sav - ior's praise the same.

2. Oh, if your cap - tain calls for you, Put on your ar - mor bold and true, Put forth your strength, put forth your rod, Fight for your country and your God.

488 AS WE GO ON. L.M.

"...always abounding in the work of the Lord..." -- 1 Cor. 15:58.

F Major O. H. Handley, 1959.   O. H. Handley, 1959.

© 1960 copyright Sacred Harp Publishing Company, Inc.

AS WE GO ON. Concluded.

love, O Lord, It guides us as we go a-long To join that great ce-les-tial band, To sing Thy praise for-ev-er-more. more.

love, O Lord, It guides us as we go a-long To join that great ce-les-tial band, To sing Thy praise for-ev-er-more. more.

It guides us as we go a-long

THE SAVIOR'S CALL. S.M.

"Rejoice with me; for I have found my sheep which was lost." -- Luke 15:6.

G Major *Lyra Catholica,* 1851. Elphrey Heritage, 1869.

1. Come, wan-d'ring sheep, oh, come! I'll bind thee to my breast, I'll bear thee to my home, And lay thee down to rest.
2. I saw thee stray for-lorn, And heard thee faint-ly cry, And on the tree of scorn, For thee I deign to die.
3. I shield thee from a-larms, And wilt thou not be blest? I bear thee in my arms; Thou bear me in thy breast.

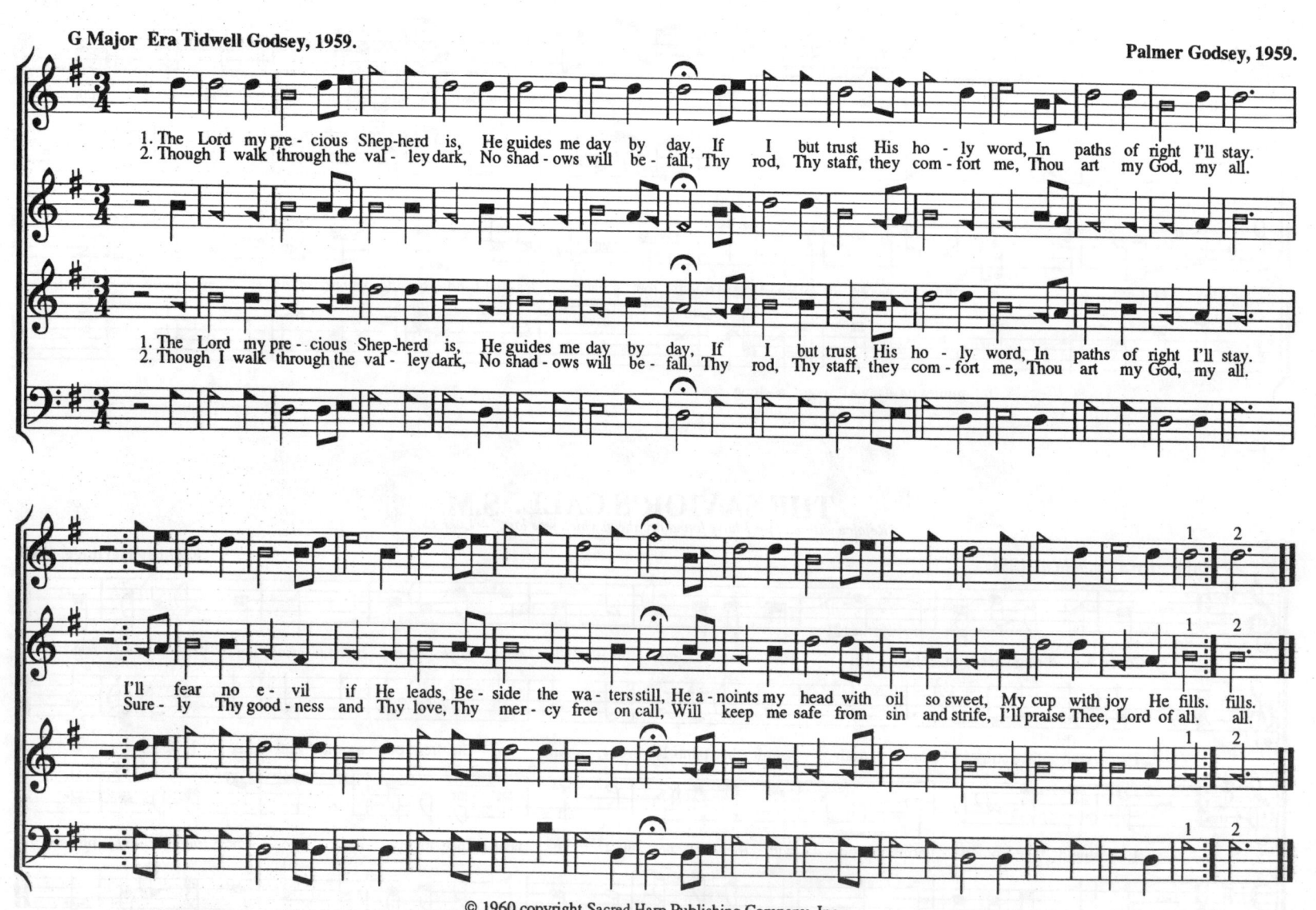

INVOCATION. Concluded. 493

pleasure sing, of pleasure sing; Loud hallelujahs shall address The honors of her King.

pleasure sing; Loud hallelujahs shall address The honors of her King.

AMANDA RAY. C.M.
"He that is our God is the God of salvation." -- Ps. 68:20.

Eb Major Frances R. Havergal, 1878.
S. Whitt Denson, 1960.

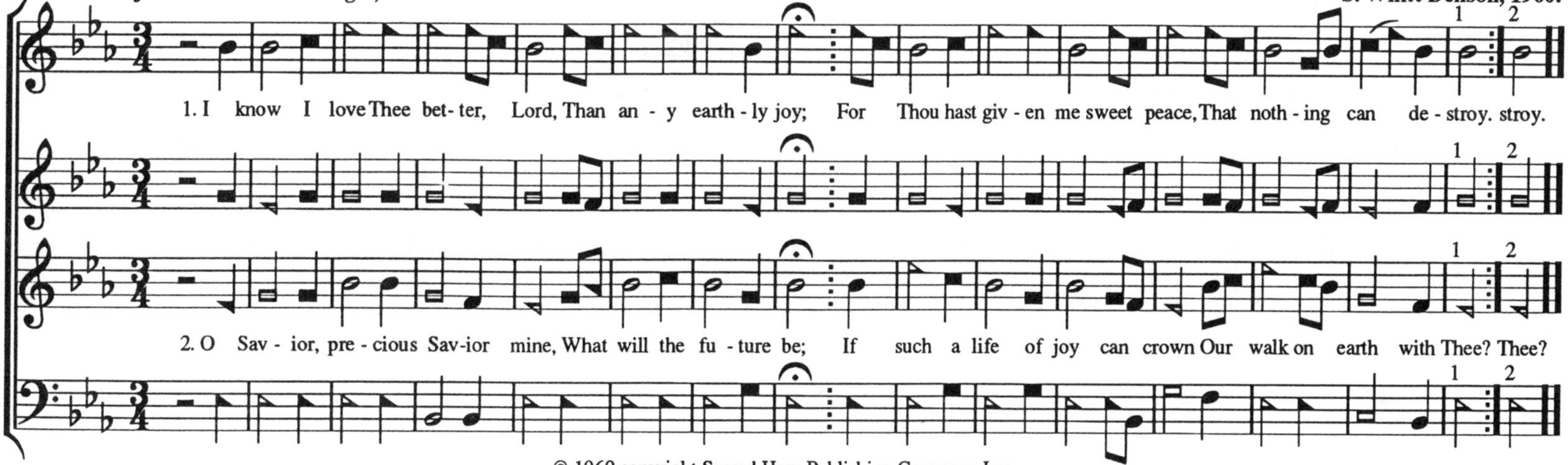

1. I know I love Thee better, Lord, Than any earthly joy; For Thou hast given me sweet peace, That nothing can destroy.

2. O Savior, precious Savior mine, What will the future be; If such a life of joy can crown Our walk on earth with Thee?

© 1960 copyright Sacred Harp Publishing Company, Inc.

THE RESURRECTION DAY. Concluded. 499

AT REST. S.M.
"...And I will give you rest." -- Matt. 11:28.

F Major James Montgomery, 1825. 3rd verse - Floyd M. Frederick, 1960.

Floyd M. Frederick, 1960.

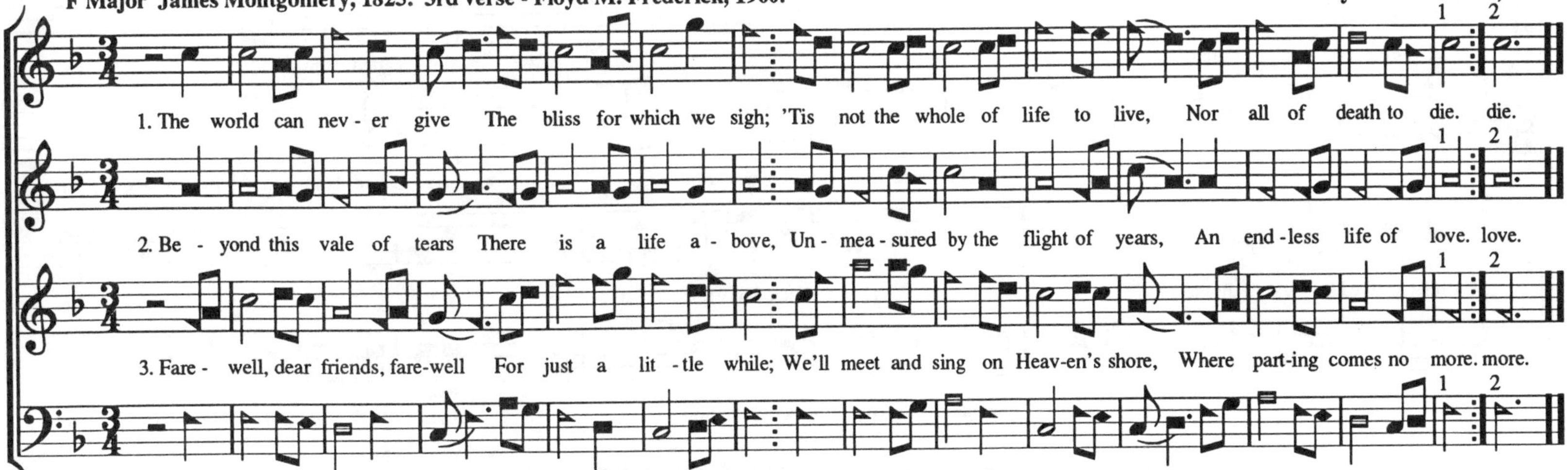

1. The world can nev-er give The bliss for which we sigh; 'Tis not the whole of life to live, Nor all of death to die. die.

2. Be-yond this vale of tears There is a life a-bove, Un-mea-sured by the flight of years, An end-less life of love. love.

3. Fare-well, dear friends, fare-well For just a lit-tle while; We'll meet and sing on Heav-en's shore, Where part-ing comes no more. more.

© 1960 copyright Sacred Harp Publishing Company, Inc.

LIVING HOPE. Concluded. 501

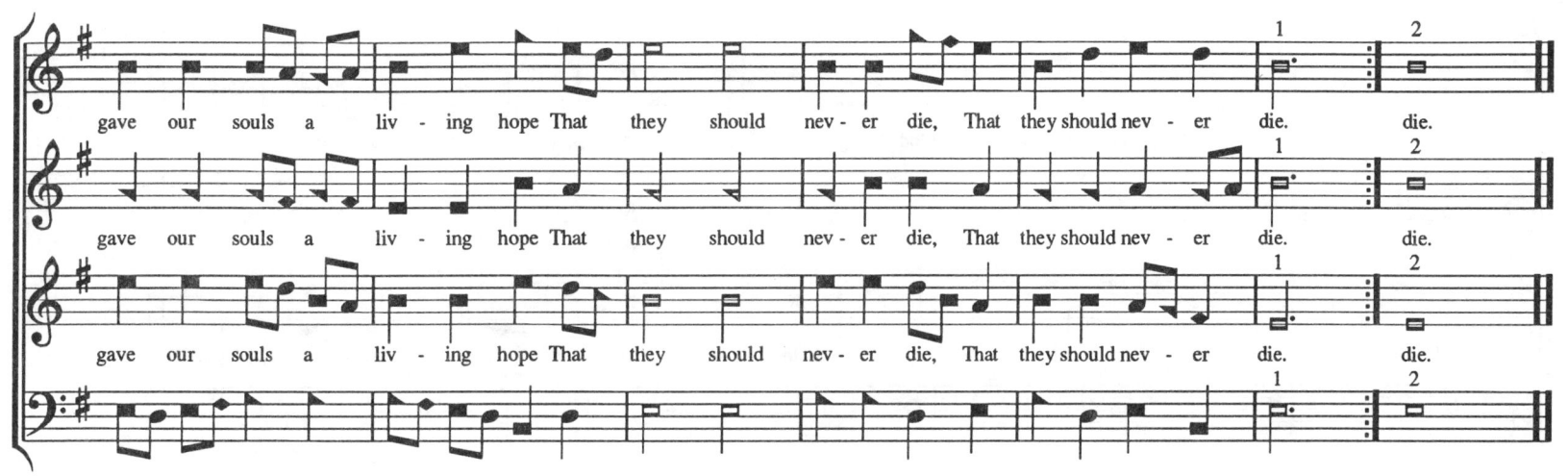

O'LEARY. S.M.

"But the day of the Lord will come as a thief in the night." -- 2 Peter 3:10.

G Major Philip Doddridge, 1755.
Theodore Mercer, 1990.

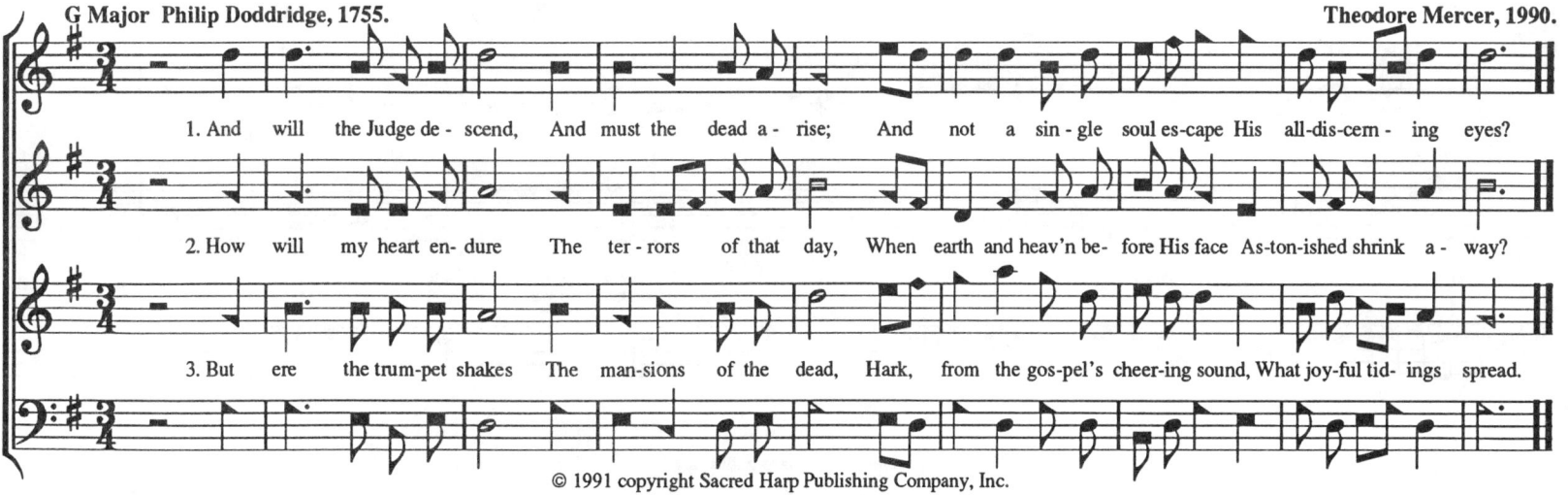

1. And will the Judge descend, And must the dead arise; And not a single soul escape His all-discerning eyes?
2. How will my heart endure The terrors of that day, When earth and heav'n before His face Astonished shrink away?
3. But ere the trumpet shakes The mansions of the dead, Hark, from the gospel's cheering sound, What joyful tidings spread.

© 1991 copyright Sacred Harp Publishing Company, Inc.

A CHARGE TO KEEP. Concluded. 503

O may it all my pow'rs engage To do my Master's will, To do my Master's will. will.

As-sured, if I my trust be-tray, I shall for-ev-er die, I shall for-ev-er die. die.

LLOYD. S.M.

"For he that is mighty hath done to me great things ..." -- Luke 1:49.

F Major Isaac Watts, 1719.

Raymond C. Hamrick, 1980.

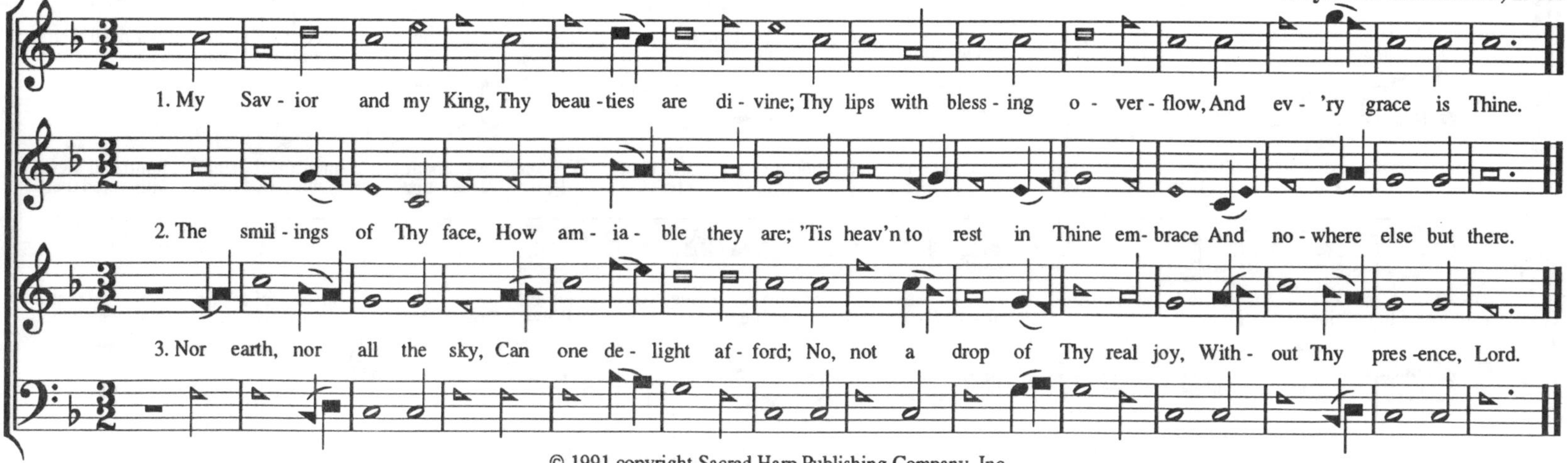

1. My Savior and my King, Thy beauties are divine; Thy lips with blessing o-ver-flow, And ev'ry grace is Thine.
2. The smil-ings of Thy face, How am-ia-ble they are; 'Tis heav'n to rest in Thine em-brace And no-where else but there.
3. Nor earth, nor all the sky, Can one de-light af-ford; No, not a drop of Thy real joy, With-out Thy pres-ence, Lord.

© 1991 copyright Sacred Harp Publishing Company, Inc.

SERMON ON THE MOUNT. Continued.

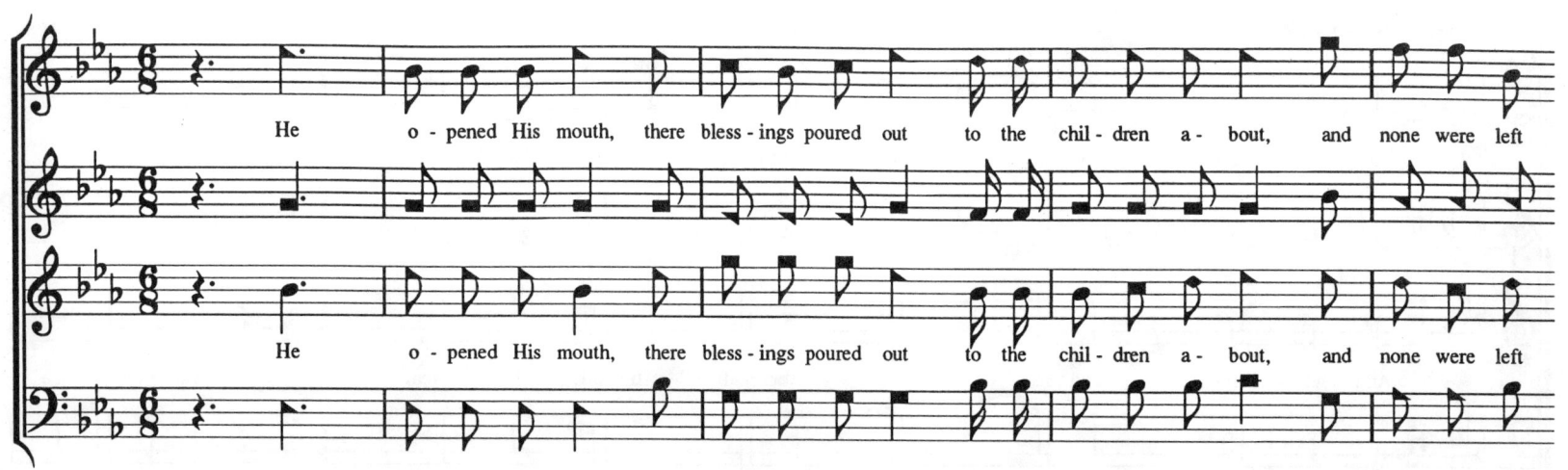

SERMON ON THE MOUNT. Concluded. 509

CORLEY. 7s.

"I have set the Lord always before me..." -- Ps. 16:8.

G Major Marcus M. Wells, 1858.

John Wilson, 17th century. Arr. - Richard L. DeLong, 1988.

1. Ho-ly Spir-it, faith-ful guide, Ev-er near the Chris-tian's side;
Gent-ly lead us by the hand, Pil-grims in a bar-ren land;
Wea-ry souls for-e'er re-joice While they hear that sweet-est voice,
Whis-per soft-ly, "Fol-low me, I'll guide thee home."

2. Ev-er pres-ent, tru-est friend, Ev-er near Thine aid to lend,
Leave us not to doubt and fear, Grop-ing on in dark-ness drear;
Wea-ry souls for-e'er re-joice While they hear that sweet-est voice,
Whis-per soft-ly, "Fol-low me, I'll guide thee home."

© 1991 copyright Sacred Harp Publishing Company, Inc.

JOYFUL. C.M.

"Watch ye, stand fast in the faith, quit you like men, be strong." -- 1 Cor. 16:13.

513

Bb Major Isaac Watts, 1724.
Arr. - B. F. White, 1844.

1. Am I a sol-dier of the cross—a fol-l'wer of the Lamb?
And shall I fear to own His cause, or blush to speak His name? Must I be car-ried to the skies on flow-'ry beds of ease? While oth-ers fought to win the prize, or sailed through blood-y seas?

2. Are there no foes for me to face? Must I not stem the flood?
Is this vile world a friend to grace, To help me on to God? Sure I must fight if I would reign; In-crease my cour-age, Lord; I'll bear the toil, en-dure the pain, Sup-port-ed by Thy word.

JOYFUL. Concluded.   515

FEDERAL STREET. L.M.
"Let thy will be done." -- Matt. 10:9.

Ab Major Isaac Watts, 1709.   H. K. Oliver, 1832.

1. My dear Re-deem-er and my Lord, I read my du-ty in Thy Word; But in Thy life the law ap-pears, Drawn out in liv-ing char-ac-ters.
2. Such was Thy truth and such Thy zeal, Such def-'rence to Thy Fa-ther's will; Such love and meekness so di-vine, I would transcribe and make them mine.
3. Cold mountains and the mid-night air Witnessed the fer-vor of Thy prayer; The des-ert Thy temp-ta-tions knew, Thy con-flict and Thy vic-t'ry, too.
4. Be Thou my pat-tern; make me bear More of Thy gra-cious im-age here; Then God, the Judge, shall own my name A-mong the fol-l'wers of the Lamb.

HEAVENLY ANTHEM. Continued. 519

HEAVENLY ANTHEM. Concluded.

PARTING FRIENDS (Third). C.M.

"Sing forth the honor of his name..." -- Ps. 66:2.

E Major *Primitive Hymns*, 1858. R. A. Conant, 1959.

© 1960 copyright Sacred Harp Publishing Company, Inc.

YE HEEDLESS ONES. Concluded. 523

move slow-ly on, Still gaz-ing on the spires of grass, With which your graves are o - ver-grown. grown.

move slow-ly on

on, Still gaz-ing on the spires of grass, With which your graves are o - ver-grown. grown.

PLEYELS HYMN (Second). 7s.
"He shall pray unto God..." -- Job 33:26.

A Major John Newton, 1779.
Ignaz Joseph Pleyel.

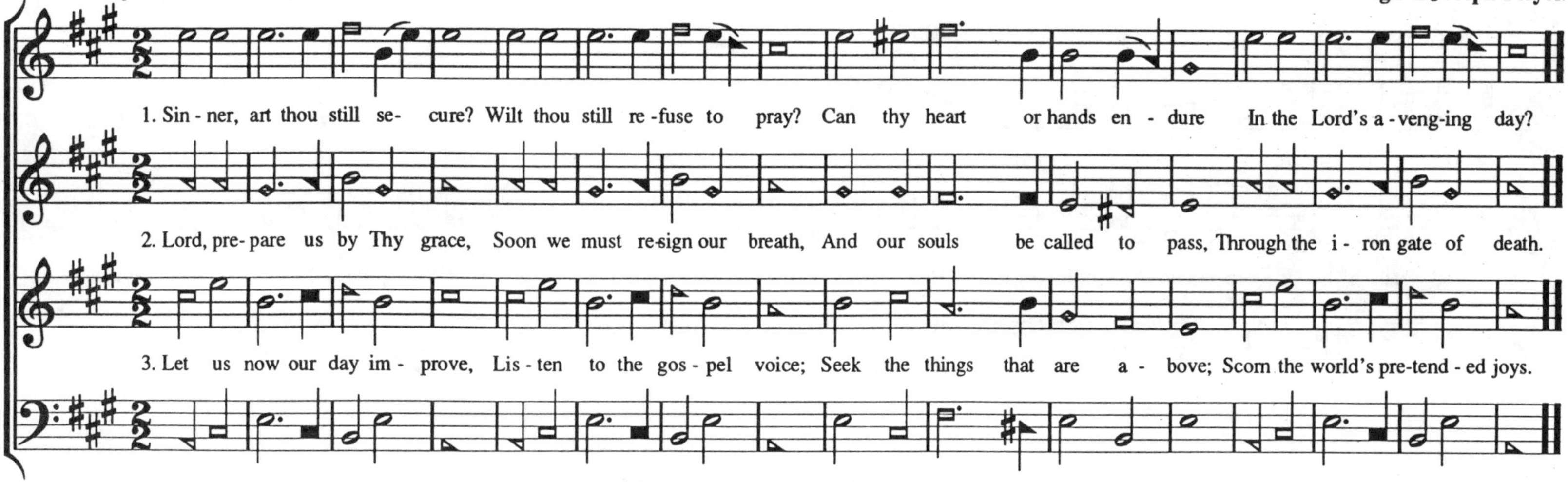

1. Sin-ner, art thou still se-cure? Wilt thou still re-fuse to pray? Can thy heart or hands en-dure In the Lord's a-veng-ing day?

2. Lord, pre-pare us by Thy grace, Soon we must re-sign our breath, And our souls be called to pass, Through the i-ron gate of death.

3. Let us now our day im-prove, Lis-ten to the gos-pel voice; Seek the things that are a-bove; Scorn the world's pre-tend-ed joys.

524 THE 23rd PSALM.

"The Lord is my shepherd . . ." -- Ps. 23:1.

F Major Psalm 23
Paine Denson, 1950.

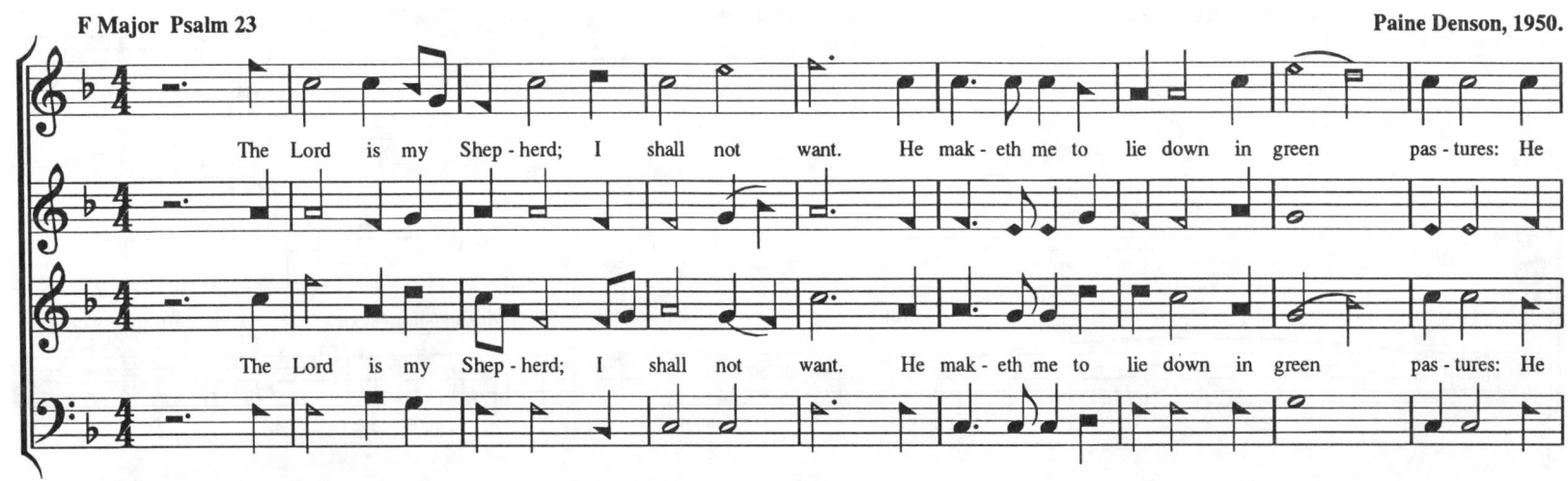

© 1960 copyright Sacred Harp Publishing Company, Inc.

THE 23rd PSALM. Continued.

THE 23rd PSALM. Concluded.

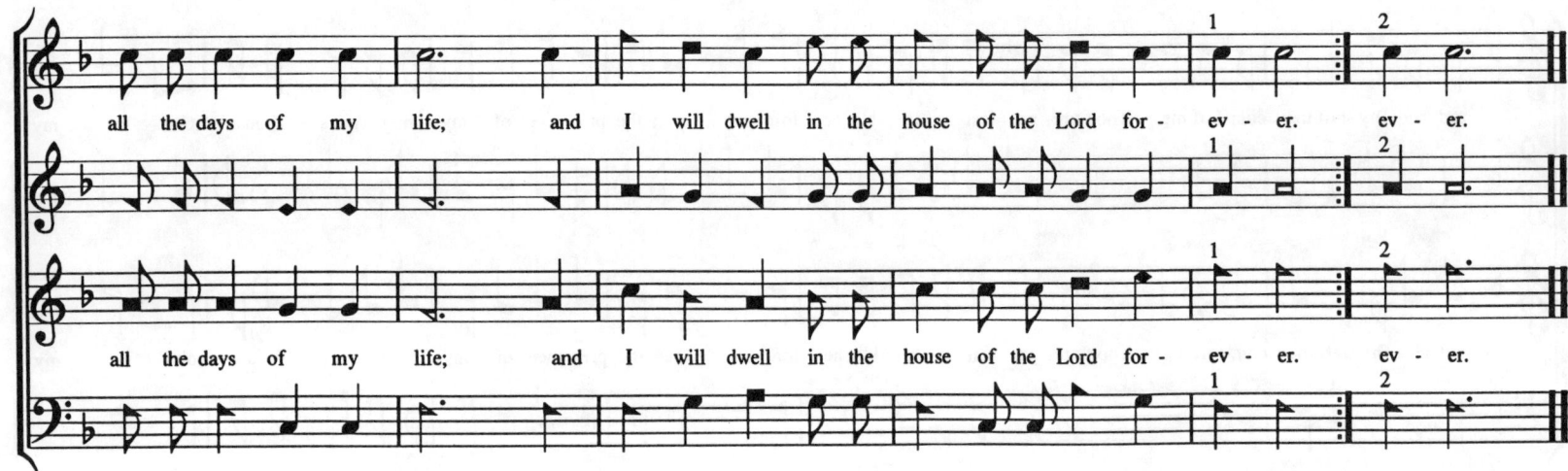

MY LIFE AND BREATH. C.M.

"...That hath redeemed my soul..." -- 1 King 1:29.

Eb Major Samuel Stennett, 1787. Hugh W. McGraw, 1959.

1. He saw me sink-ing in dis-tress, And flew to my re-lief, For me He bore the shame-ful cross, And car-ried all my grief.

2. To Heav'n, the place of His a-bode, He brings my wea-ry feet; Shows me the glo-ries of my God, And makes my joys com-plete.

To Him I owe my life and breath, And all the joys I have, He makes me tri-umph o-ver death, And saves me from the grave. grave.

© 1960 copyright Sacred Harp Publishing Company, Inc.

528 SHOWERS OF BLESSINGS. C.M.

"O sing unto the Lord a new song..." -- Ps. 96:1.

Bb Major Isaac Watts, 1719. Joseph Stone, 1793. Arr. - A. A. Blocker, 1959.

© 1960 copyright Sacred Harp Publishing Company, Inc.

SHOWERS OF BLESSINGS. Concluded.

A GLAD NEW SONG. Concluded. 531

(lyrics under staves:)

calmed my trou-bled soul, Since Je - sus calmed my trou-bled soul, And bore my sins a - way. way.
saint-ed hosts a - bove, With all the saint-ed hosts a - bove, Be - fore the great I Am. Am.

trou-bled soul, And bore my sins a - way, Since Je - sus calmed my trou-bled soul, And bore my sins a - way. way.
hosts a - bove, Be - fore the great I Am, With all the saint-ed hosts a - bove, Be - fore the great I Am. Am.

soul, Since Je - sus calmed my trou-bled soul, And bore my sins a - way. way.
bove, With all the saint-ed hosts a - bove, Be - fore the great I Am. Am.

DURA. L.M.

"The Lord is far from the wicked, but he heareth the prayer..." -- Prov. 15:29.

F Major Dura Ann Campbell Blackmon. H. M. Blackmon, 1959.

Dear Lord, for-give my sins, I pray, And lead me in the nar-row way, O Lord, give me strength day by day, Have mer-cy, Lord, for this I pray. pray.

Dear Lord, for-give my sins, I pray, And lead me in the nar-row way, O Lord, give me strength day by day, Have mer-cy, Lord, for this I pray. pray.

Dear Lord, for-give my sins, I pray, And lead me in the nar-row way, O Lord, give me strength day by day, Have mer-cy, Lord, for this I pray. pray.

© 1960 copyright Sacred Harp Publishing Company, Inc.

PEACE AND JOY. Concluded. 533

NEW GEORGIA. Concluded. 535

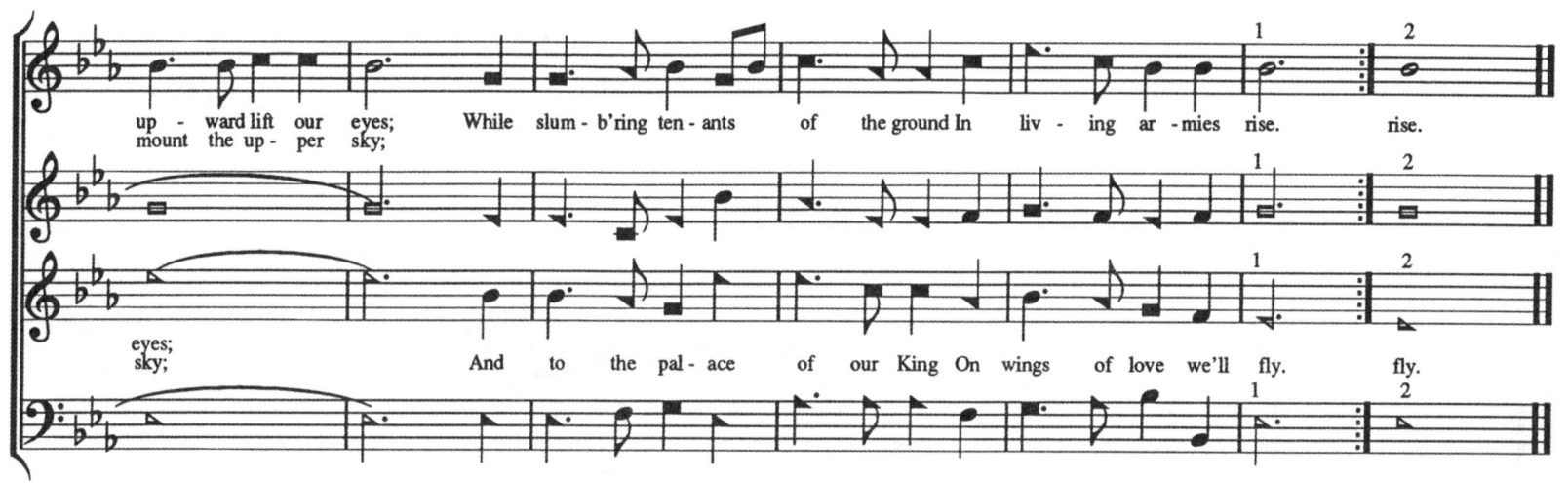

SHAWMUT. S.M.
"For thy mercy is great above the heavens..." -- Ps. 108:4.

D Major Charles Wesley, 1759.   Lowell Mason

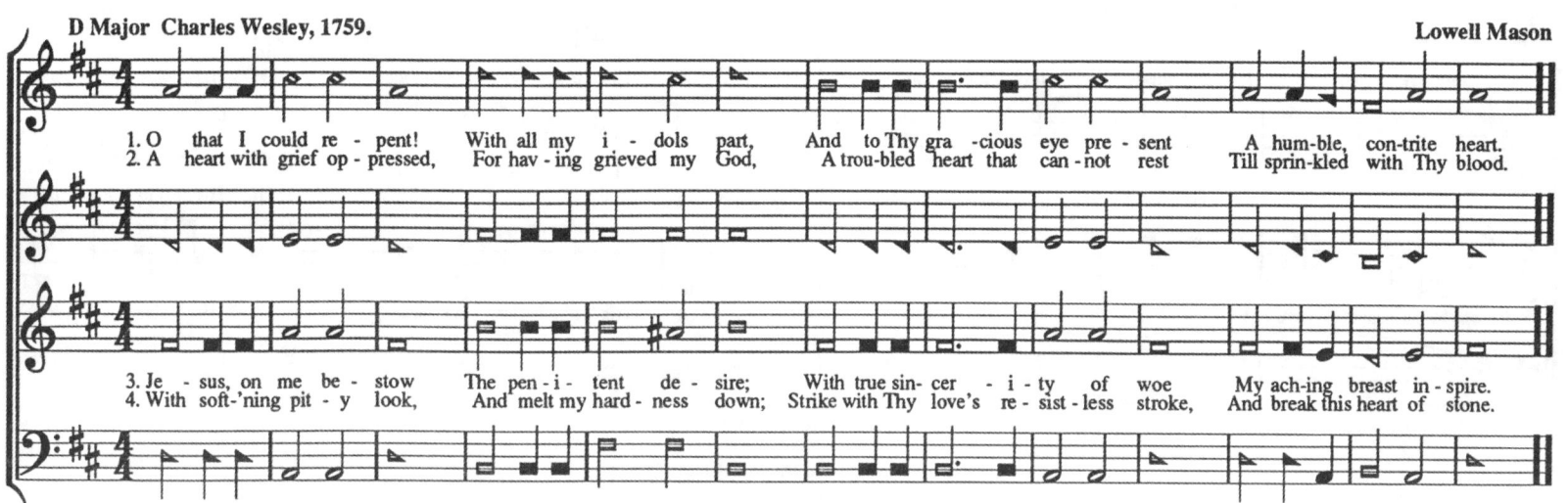

536

SWEET MAJESTY. C.M.D.

"Rejoicing in hope, patient in tribulation..." -- Rom. 12:12.

E Minor Isaac Watts, 1707.

A. M. Cagle, 1959.

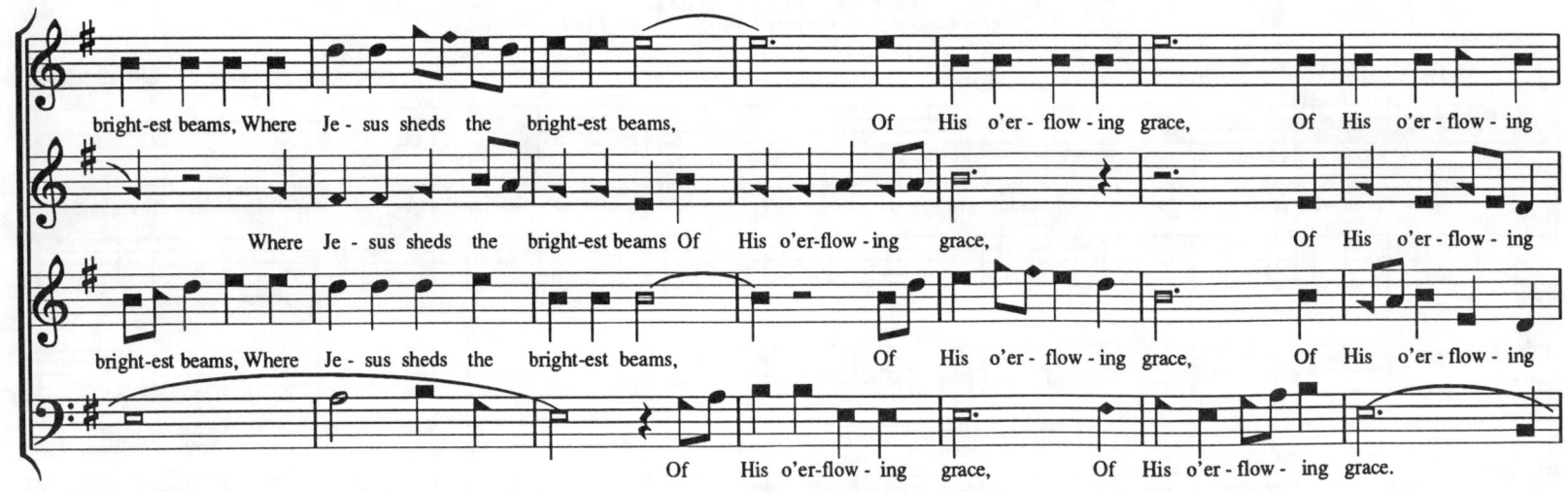

© 1960 copyright Sacred Harp Publishing Company, Inc.

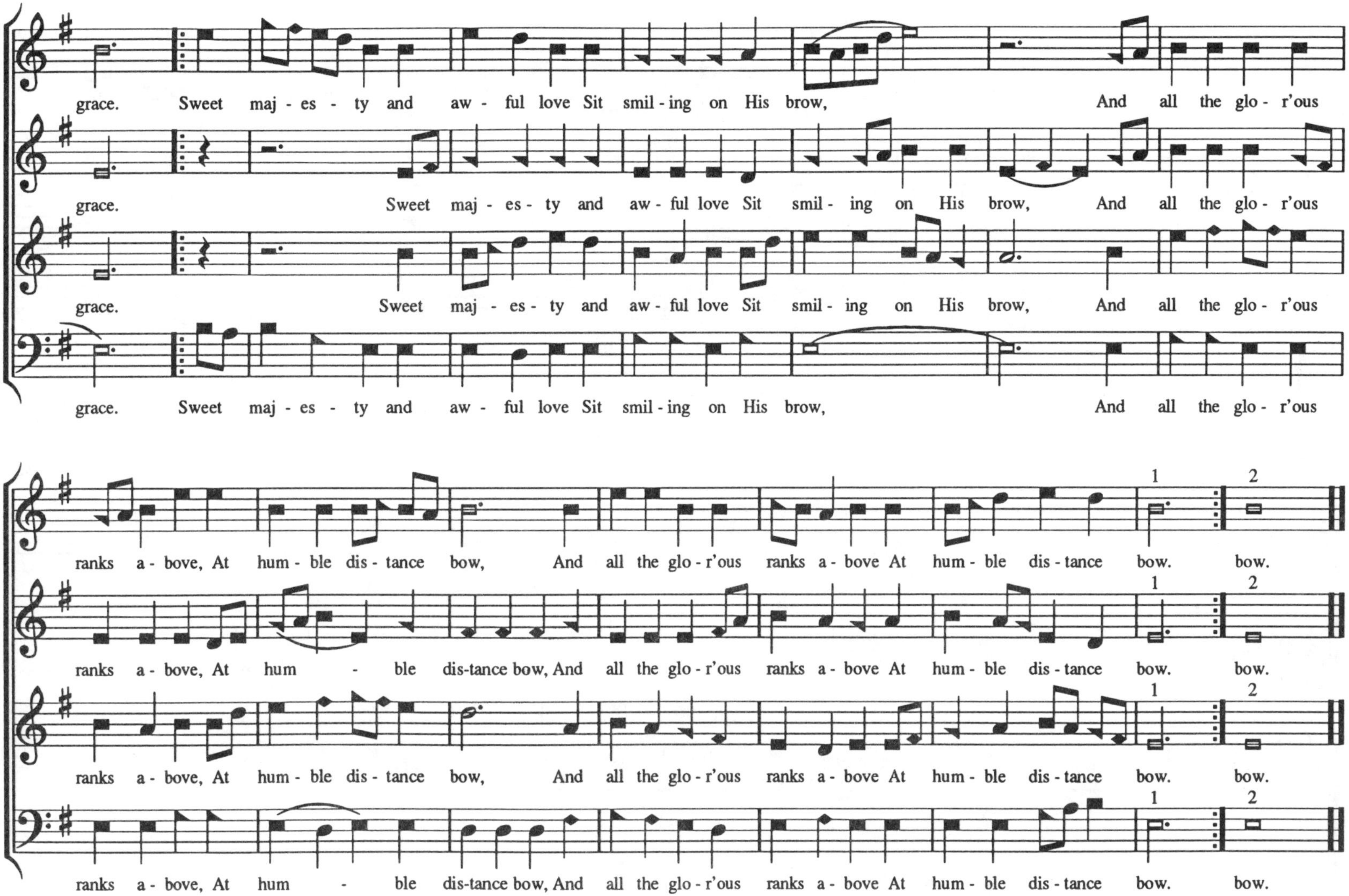

SWEET MAJESTY. Concluded. 537

grace. Sweet majesty and awful love Sit smiling on His brow, And all the glor'ous ranks above, At humble distance bow, And all the glor'ous ranks above At humble distance bow. bow.

HAMPTON. Concluded. 539

And let His praise from ev-'ry hill Rise tune - ful to the neigh - b'ring sky. sky.
From all be-low, and all a-bove, Loud hal - le - lu - jahs to the Lord. Lord.

SUPPLICATION. L.M.
"...We thank thee, and praise thy glorious name." -- 1 Chr. 29:13.

E Minor E. Foy Frederick.   Floyd M. Frederick, 1959.

1. Glo - ry to Thee, my God on high, For all the bless-ings of this life; Oh, let Thy mer - cy fill my heart, And let all fears from me de - part. part.
2. Oh, let Thy thought and praise a - rise In grate-ful an - thems in the skies; Take Thou my soul when life is o'er To live with Thee for - ev - er - more. more.

© 1960 copyright Sacred Harp Publishing Company, Inc.

544 THOU ART GOD. Concluded.

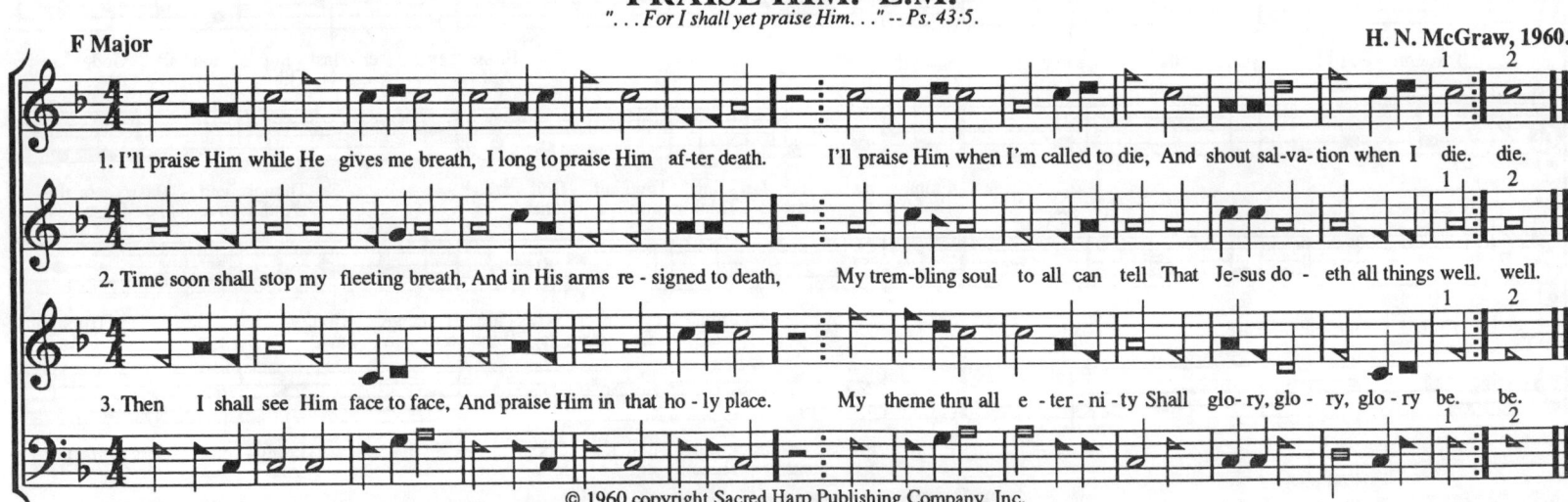

PRAISE HIM. L.M.
"...For I shall yet praise Him..." -- Ps. 43:5.

F Major

H. N. McGraw, 1960.

1. I'll praise Him while He gives me breath, I long to praise Him after death. I'll praise Him when I'm called to die, And shout salvation when I die.
2. Time soon shall stop my fleeting breath, And in His arms resigned to death, My trembling soul to all can tell That Jesus doeth all things well.
3. Then I shall see Him face to face, And praise Him in that holy place. My theme thru all eternity Shall glory, glory, glory be.

© 1960 copyright Sacred Harp Publishing Company, Inc.

THE PILGRIM'S WAY. 8s & 7s.

"... they were strangers and pilgrims..." -- Heb. 11:13.

Irene Parker Denson, 1959.

© 1960 copyright Sacred Harp Publishing Company, Inc.

546 MY BRIGHTEST DAYS. C.M.

"It is God that girdeth me with strength, and maketh my way perfect." -- Ps. 18:32.

Bb Major Isaac Watts, 1707. O. A. Parris, 1959.

1. My God, the spring of all my joys, The life of my delights, The glory of my brightest days, And comfort of my nights.
2. In darkest shades if He appears, My dawning is begun, He is my soul's sweet morning star, And He's my rising sun.

© 1960 copyright Sacred Harp Publishing Company, Inc.

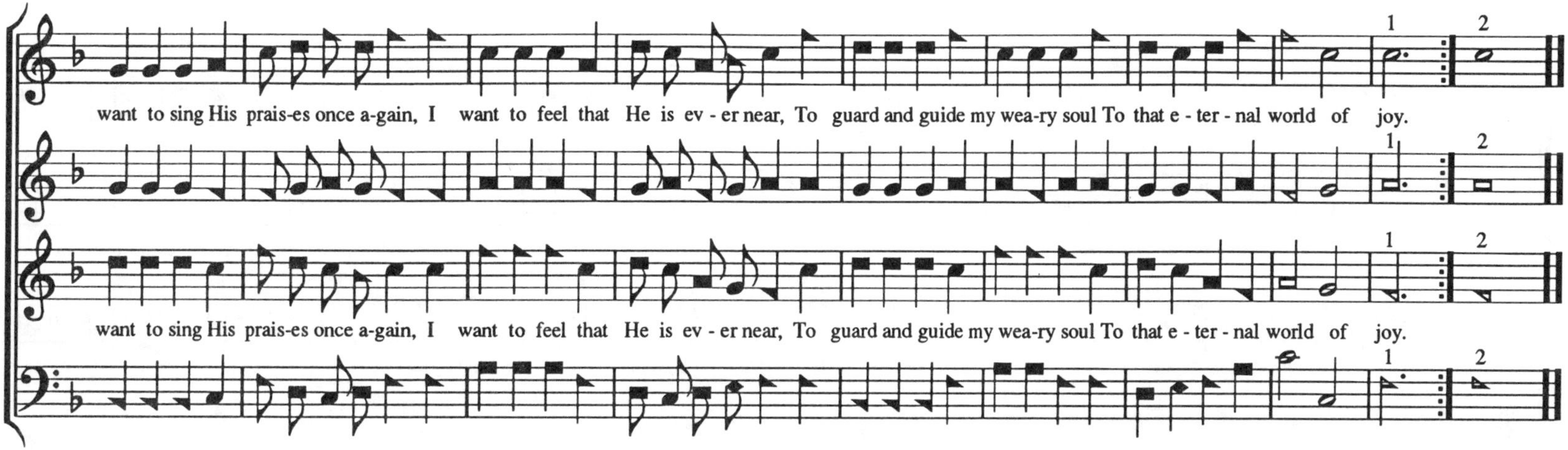

WOOTTEN. Concluded. 549

want to sing His prais-es once a-gain, I want to feel that He is ev-er near, To guard and guide my wea-ry soul To that e-ter-nal world of joy.

want to sing His prais-es once a-gain, I want to feel that He is ev-er near, To guard and guide my wea-ry soul To that e-ter-nal world of joy.

PHILLIPS FAREWELL. L.M.
"The Spirit of God hath made me, and the breath of the Almighty hath given me life." -- Job 33:4.

D Major George Phillips, 1962.   Hugh McGraw, 1962.

1. My days on earth are al-most gone, The things I want can not be won; It is the Lord that free-ly gives, It's where He lives I want to live.

2. It is one thing I sure-ly know, It is to heav'n I want to go To sing His praise where an-gels sing, To praise my Lord and Sav-ior King.

3. My life has been to sing God's praise In hope of the e-ter-nal days; I mean to do the best I can And meet you in the prom-ised land.

4. My friends have been so good to me, And where you go I want to be; My love for you no tongue can tell, Dear lov-ing friends, so fare you well.

© 1991 copyright Sacred Harp Publishing Company, Inc.

550 BLISSFUL DAWNING. C.M.

"Blessed be God..." -- 2 Cor. 1:3.

F Major Isaac Watts, 1707.

A. M. Cagle, 1959.

My God, the spring of all my joys, The life of my delight, The glory of my brightest days, And comfort of my nights.

In darkest shades if Thou appear, My blissful dawning is begun, is begun.

© 1960 copyright Sacred Harp Publishing Company, Inc.

BLISSFUL DAWNING. Concluded. 551

Thou art my soul's bright morn-ing star, And Thou my ris - ing sun, And Thou my ris-ing sun. sun.

is be-gun, Thou art my soul's bright morn-ing star, And Thou my ris - ing sun, And Thou my ris - ing sun. sun.

Thou art my soul's bright morn-ing star, And Thou my ris - ing sun, And Thou my ris - ing sun. sun.

And Thou my ris - ing sun, And Thou my ris - ing sun. sun.

JACOB'S VISION. 11s & 12s.

"...And set it up for a pillow..." -- Gen. 28:18.

F Major Hymns, Evangelical Association, 1850. Arr. - Margaret Wright, 1959.

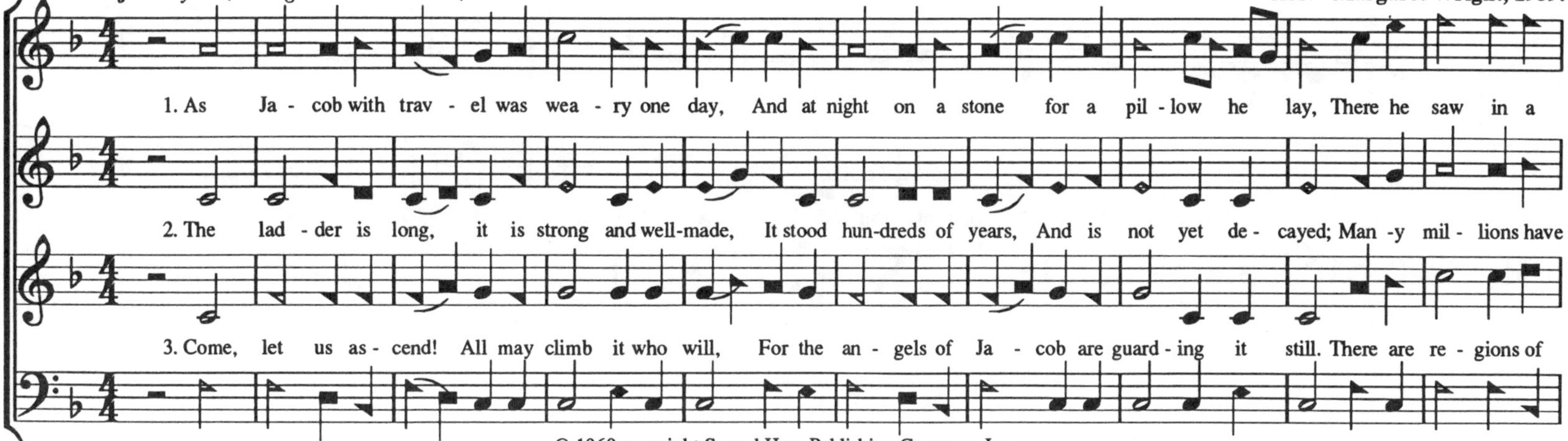

1. As Ja-cob with trav-el was wea-ry one day, And at night on a stone for a pil-low he lay, There he saw in a

2. The lad-der is long, it is strong and well-made, It stood hun-dreds of years, And is not yet de-cayed; Man-y mil-lions have

3. Come, let us as-cend! All may climb it who will, For the an-gels of Ja-cob are guard-ing it still. There are re-gions of

© 1960 copyright Sacred Harp Publishing Company, Inc.

552 JACOB'S VISION. Concluded.

554 ANTHEM ON THE BEGINNING. Continued.

ANTHEM ON THE BEGINNING. Continued. 555

556 ANTHEM ON THE BEGINNING. Concluded.

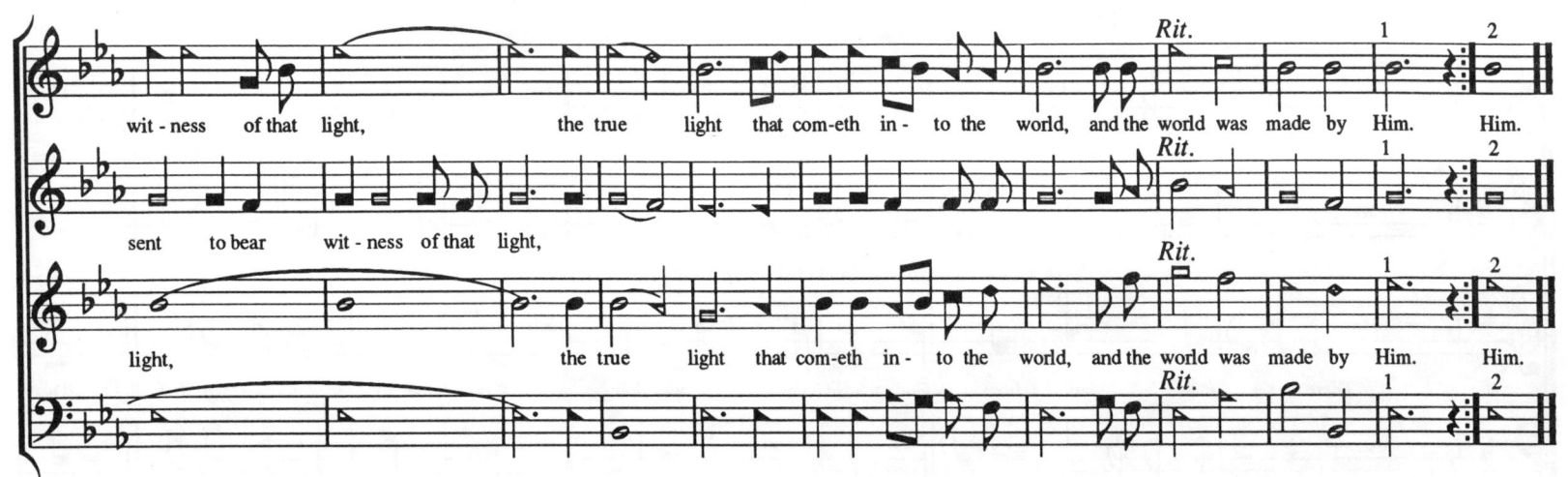

PORTLAND. L.M.
"Upon the harp with a solemn sound." -- Ps. 92:3.

F Major Isaac Watts, 1719. Abraham Maxim, 1802.

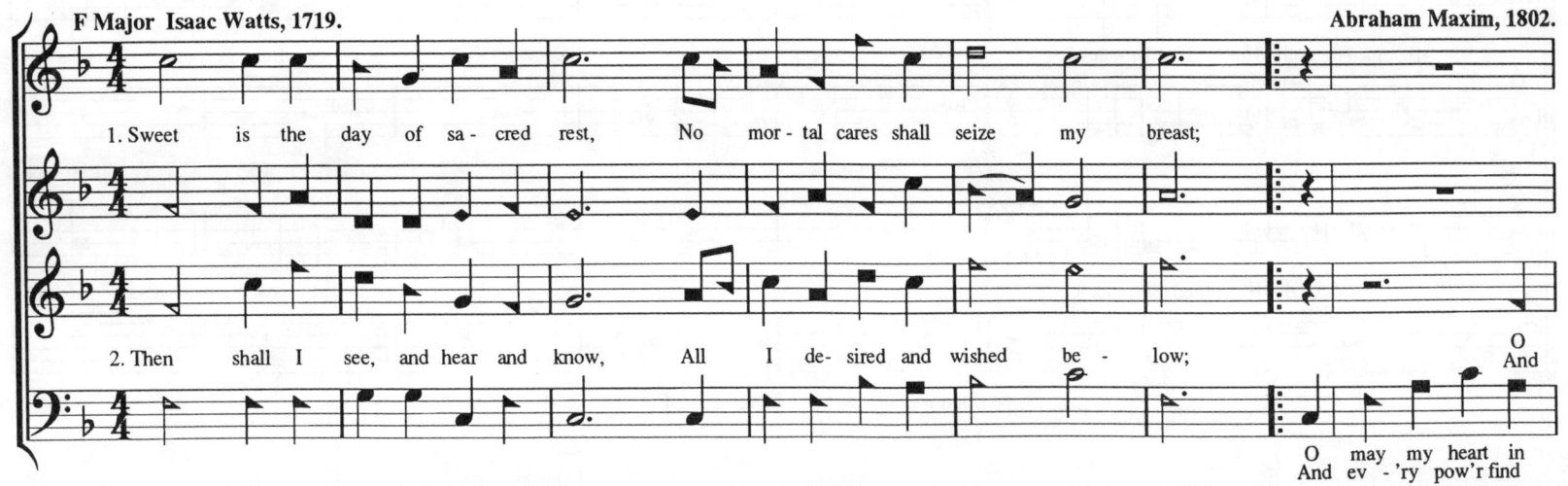

PORTLAND. Concluded.

LIVING STREAMS. Continued. 559

560 LIVING STREAMS. Concluded.

me a ta-ble Thou hast spread Be-fore the fac-es of my foes; With oil Thou dost a-noint my head, My cup is full and o-ver-flows. flows.

Thou hast spread Be-fore the fac-es of my foes; With oil Thou dost a-noint my head, My cup is full and o-ver-flows. flows.

Thou hast spread Be-fore the fac-es of my foes; With oil Thou dost a-noint my head, My cup is full and o-ver-flows. flows.

me a ta-ble Thou hast spread Be-fore the fac-es of my foes; With oil Thou dost a-noint my head, My cup is full and o-ver-flows. flows.

MY HOME (Second). P.M.
"... so shall we ever be with the Lord." -- 1 Thess. 4:17.

F Major Anonymous   H. R. Avery, 1959.

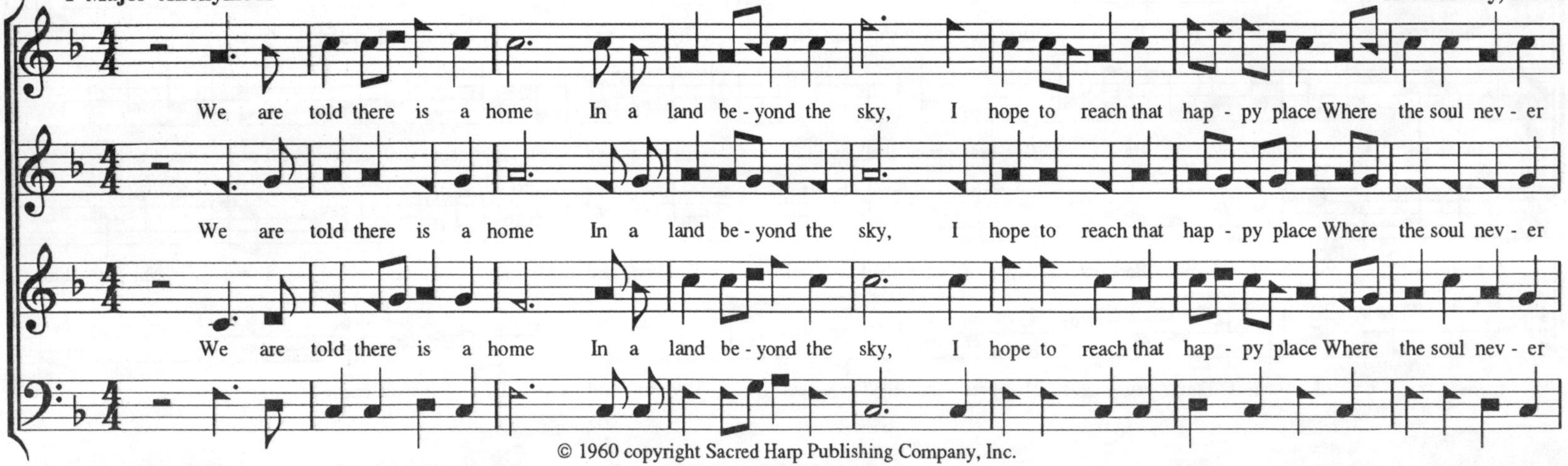

We are told there is a home In a land be-yond the sky, I hope to reach that hap-py place Where the soul nev-er

We are told there is a home In a land be-yond the sky, I hope to reach that hap-py place Where the soul nev-er

We are told there is a home In a land be-yond the sky, I hope to reach that hap-py place Where the soul nev-er

© 1960 copyright Sacred Harp Publishing Company, Inc.

MY HOME. Concluded. 561

INFINITE DELIGHT. Concluded. 563

ZION. Concluded. 565

that delight-ful shore, But all will be peace, joy, and love With Christ for-ev-er-more. more.

THE HILL OF ZION. S.M.
"Seek the Lord, and his strength: seek his face evermore." -- Ps. 105:4.

A Major Isaac Watts, 1707.   B. F. White, 1859.

1. The Hill of Zi-on yields a thou-sand sa-cred sweets, Be-fore we reach the heav'n-ly fields, Or walk the gold-en streets.

2. Then let our songs a-bound, And ev-'ry tear be dry; We're march-ing through Im-man-uel's ground To fair-er worlds on high.

THE GREAT DAY. P.M.

"They shall give account therof in the day of judgment." -- Matt. 12:36.

567

A Minor

Arr. - J. P. Reese, 1859.

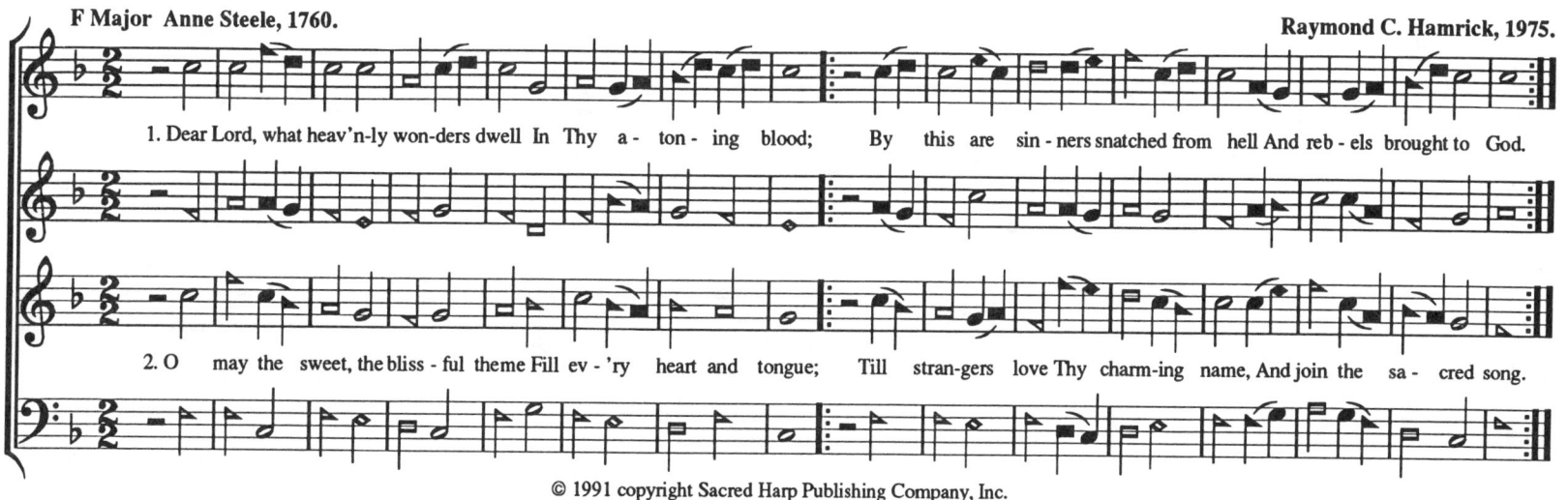

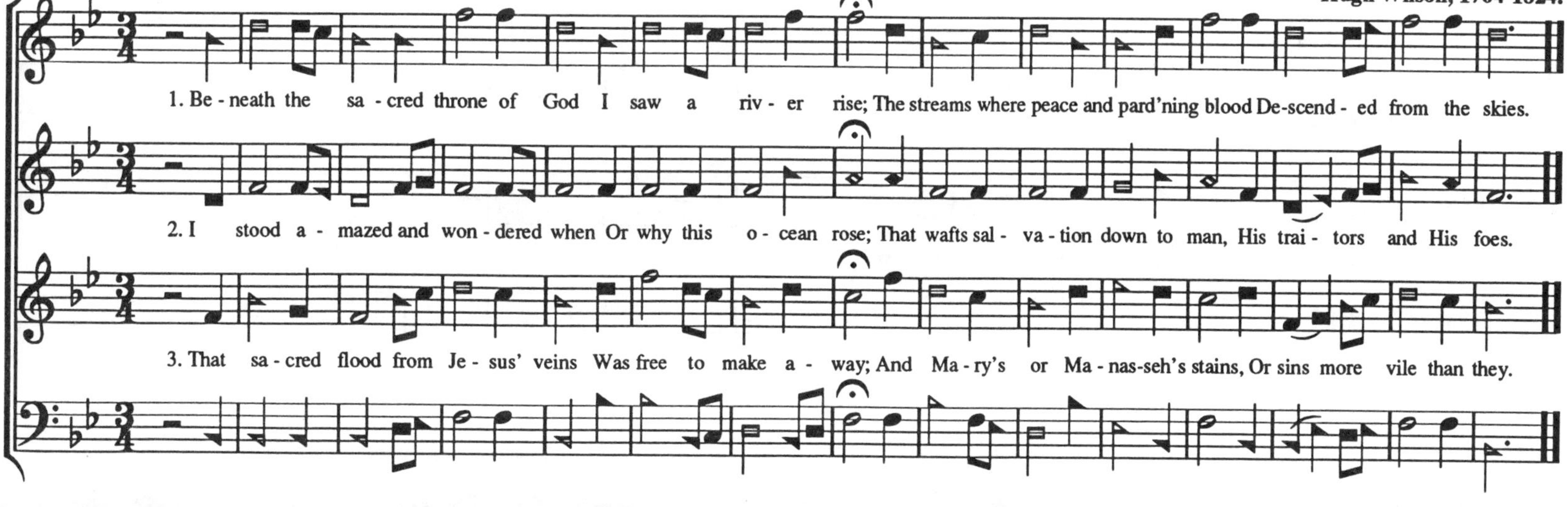

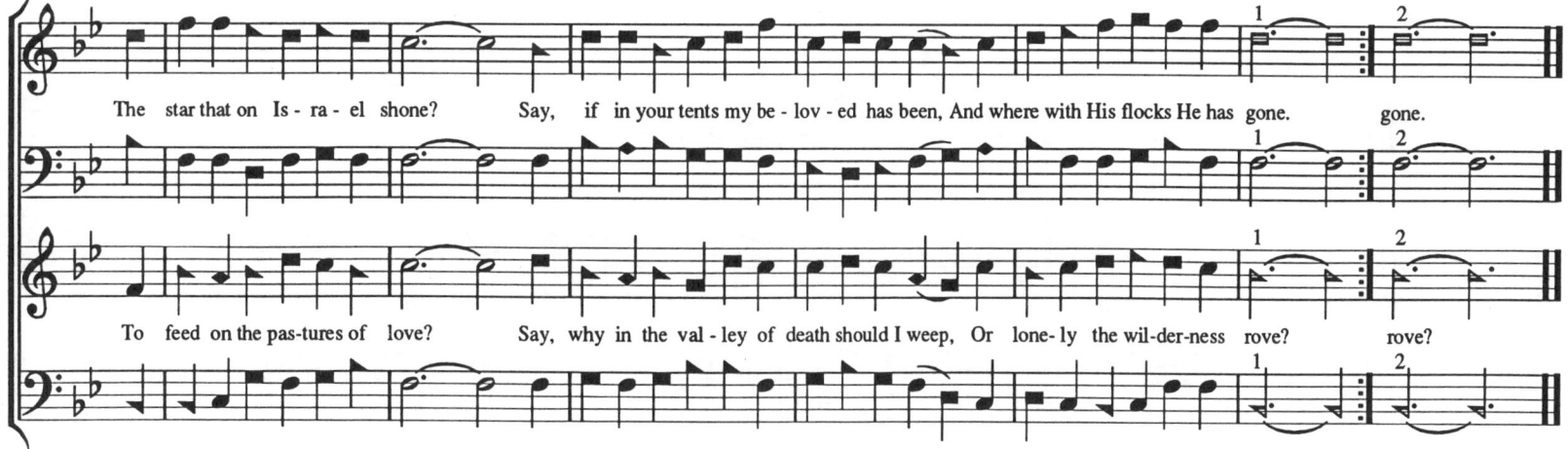

INDEX OF FIRST LINES

A charge to keep I have (A CHARGE TO KEEP)	502
A few more days on earth (STONY POINT)	368
A few more days on earth to spend (THE CHRISTIAN'S HOPE)	134
A home in heaven! What a joyful thought (HOME IN HEAVEN)	41
A poor wayfaring man of grief (DUANE STREET)	164
A story most lovely I'll tell (THE LOVELY STORY)	104
A throne of grace, then let us go (HAYNES CREEK)	466
Afflictions, tho' they seem severe (THE PRODIGAL SON)	113
Alas and did my Savior bleed! Alas, and did my Saviour bleed (VICTORIA)	290
Alas and did my Savior bleed, And did my sovereign die (LOVE THE LORD)	375
(WEEPING SAVIOR)	310
All hail the pow'r of Jesus' name (CLEBURNE)	314
(CORONATION)	63
(GREEN STREET)	198
(NEW AGATITE)	485
Am I a soldier of the Cross (CHRISTIAN SOLDIER)	57
(JOYFUL)	513
(LIVING LAMB)	309
(SOLDIER OF THE CROSS)	325
Amazing grace! how sweet the sound (JEWETT)	105
(NEW BRITAIN)	45
And am I born to die (IDUMEA)	47
(WORLD UNKNOWN)	428
And if you meet with troubles (HEAVENLY ARMOR)	129
And let this feeble body fail (ANIMATION)	103
(HALLELUJAH)	146
And must I be to judgement brought (PASSING AWAY)	445
And now, my friends, both old and young (DELONG)	516
(FAREWELL TO ALL)	69
And seeing, and seeing (SERMON ON THE MOUNT)	507
And will the judge descend (O'LEARY)	501
Angels in shining order stand (ALABAMA)	196
Arise, my soul my joyful powrs (INVOCATION)	492
As down a lone valley with cedars o'erspread (MURILLO'S LESSON)	358
As Jacob with travel was weary one day (JACOB'S VISION)	551
As on the cross the Savior hung (THE CONVERTED THIEF)	44
As pants the hart (CONVERTING GRACE)	230
Awake dear brother, sister, friend (CONSOLATION)	367
Awake my heart, arise my tongue (CHRIST OUR SONG)	386
Awake, my soul in joyful lays (SWEET UNION)	424
Awake, my soul to joyful lays (LOVING-KINDNESS)	275
Away, my unbelieving fear (CONFIDENCE)	270
Be kind to thy father (THE LOVED ONES)	413
Before the hills in order stood (THOU ART GOD)	543
Before the rosy dawn of day (ENFIELD)	184
Behold the judge descends (SYMPHONY)	151
Behold the love, the generous love (ARBACOOCHEE)	430
Behold the love, —the gen'rous love (SARDINIA)	296
Behold the morning sun (SOUNDING JOY)	391
Behold the Savior of mankind (BEHOLD THE SAVIOR)	292
Bells are ringing, what's the matter (FIRE ALARM)	25
Beneath the sacred throne of God (SACRED THRONE)	569
Beside the gospel pool (GOSPEL POOL)	34
Bleeding hearts defiled by sin (NATICK)	497
Blest be the everlasting God (LIVING HOPE)	500
Blest be the tie that binds (FELLOWSHIP)	330
Blest Jesus while in mortal flesh (SHARPSBURG)	39
Blow ye the trumpet blow (LENOX)	40
Brethren, farewell, I do you tell (CHRISTIAN'S FAREWELL)	347
Brethren, we have come to worship (HOLY MANNA)	59
Broad is the road that leads to death (WINDHAM)	38
Burst, ye emerald gates (ELYSIAN)	139
By Babel's streams we sat and wept (BABEL'S STREAMS)	126
Children of the heavenly King (THE MARCELLAS)	405
Come, all my dear brethren and help me to sing (HEAVEN'S MY HOME)	119
Come all ye mourning pilgrims dear (PILGRIM)	201
Come and taste, along with me (WEARY PILGRIM)	326
Come brothers and sisters who love one another (UNION)	116
Come, Holy Spirit, come (ABBEVILLE)	33
Come, Holy Spirit, heav'n'ly dove (HEAVENLY DOVE)	371
Come, humble sinner, in whose breast (FAIRFIELD)	29
(NEVER PART)	94
Come let us join our friends above (ARNOLD)	285
Come let us join with one accord (SABBATH MORNING)	283
Come, let us raise our voices high (MORNING PRAYER)	411
Come life, come death (JESUS IS MY FRIEND)	345
Come, little children, now we may partake (LOUISIANA)	207
Come my soul and let us try (THE GRIEVED SOUL)	448
Come, O Thou traveler unknown (VERNON)	95
Come on my fellow pilgrims (SARDIS)	460
Come on my friends and go with me (WHERE CEASELESS AGES ROLL)	505
Come, saints and sinners, hear me tell (HEAVENLY UNION)	484
Come sound his praise abroad (DARTMOUTH)	169

(SILVER STREET)	311
Come, sound His praise abroad (ST. THOMAS)	34
Come tell of your ship (THE HAPPY SAILOR)	388
Come, thou fount of every blessing (FAMILY CIRCLE)	333
(OLNEY)	135
(RESTORATION)	312
(WARRENTON)	145
Come, Thy fount of ev'ry blessing (REST FOR THE WEARY)	154
Come, wand'ring sheep, oh, come! (THE SAVIOR'S CALL)	489
Come, we that love the Lord (NOVAKOSKI)	481
Come we who love the Lord (WEBSTER)	31
Come, ye sinners, poor and needy (BEACH SPRING)	81
Come ye that love the Lord (ALBION)	52
Convinced as a sinner, to Jesus I come (THE ROCK THAT IS HIGHER THAN I)	496
Daniel's wisdom may I know (HOLINESS)	76
Dark and thorny is the desert (THE PILGRIM'S WAY)	545
David the King was grieved and moved (DAVID'S LAMENTATION)	268
Dear friends, farewell! I do you tell (COSTON)	382
(MINISTER'S FAREWELL)	69
Dear Lord, forgive my sins, I pray (DURA)	531
Dear Lord, what heavn'ly wonders (EMMAUS)	569
Dear people we have met today (DAYS OF WORSHIP)	60
Death, like an over-flowing stream (MORTALITY)	50
Death, like an overflowing stream (EXIT)	181
Death, 'tis a melancholy day (MELANCHOLY DAY)	419
(TRIBULATION)	29
Did Christ o'er sinners weep? (WEEPING SAVIOR)	33
Do not I love thee, O my Lord? (DETROIT)	39
Early, my God, without delay (MONTGOMERY)	189
Ere mountains rear'd their forms sublime (NEW BETHANY)	431
Far from my thoughts, vain world, be gone (WESTFORD)	280
Farewell my friends, I'm bound for Canaan (PARTING FRIENDS)	267
Farewell, dear brothers, fare you well (SISTER'S FAREWELL)	55
Farewell, farewell to all below (ARKANSAS)	271
Farewell, farewell, farewell, my friends (PILGRIM'S FAREWELL)	185
Farewell, mother, tears are beaming (THE BRIDE'S FAREWELL)	359
Farewell, my dear brethren (IMANDRA)	45
Farewell, my friends, weep not for me (SING ON)	381
Farewell, my loving friends, farewell (TRAVELING ON)	208
Farewell, vain world! I'm going home. I am bound to die (SERVICE OF THE LORD)	80
Farewell, vain world! I'm going home. I belong to this band (RAGAN)	176
Farewell, vain world! I'm going home. My Savior smiles (I'M GOING HOME)	282
Farewell, vain world! I'm going home. To play on the golden (THE GOLDEN HARP)	274
Farewell, vain world! I'm going home. Where there's no more (TRAVELING PILGRIM)	278
Fight on my soul (FIGHT ON)	385
Forever blessed be the Lord (REYNOLDS)	225
Forgive the song that falls so low (COWPER)	168
Frequent the day of God returns (OGLETREE)	138
From all that dwell below the skies, Let the Creator's praise (ETERNAL PRAISE)	377
(SCHENECTADY)	192
From all that dwell below the skies, Let the Redeemer's praise (BRIDGEWATER)	276
From ev'ry stormy wind that blows (THE MERCY SEAT)	470
Gently glides the stream of life (ELDER)	450
Give me a calm, a thankful heart (A THANKFUL HEART)	475
Give unto the lord the glory (REVERENTIAL ANTHEM)	234
Glorious things of thee are spoken (JEFFERSON)	148
Glory to thee, My God on high (SUPPLICATION)	539
Go and tell his disciples (JESUS ROSE)	156
Go, preachers, and tell it to the world (CUBA)	401
God of my life, look gently down (POLAND)	86
God moves in a mysterious way (MY RISING SUN)	478
God, my supporter, and my hope (PROTECTION)	187
Grace! 'tis a charming sound (NINETY-THIRD PSALM)	31
Grace, 'tis a most delightful theme (CHEVES)	432
Great God, attend, while Zion sings (BALLSTOWN)	217
Great God, let all my tuneful pow'rs awake (FILLMORE)	434
Great God, let all Thy tuneful pow'r (JASPER)	426
Great God, the heav'n's well-order'd frame (NEW LEBANON)	202
Hail the day so long expected (BABYLON IS FALLEN)	117
Hail, solitude, thou gentle queen (SWEET SOLITUDE)	140
Hail ye sighing sons of sorrow (SONS OF SORROW)	332
Hark! from the tombs a doleful sound (PLENARY)	162
Hark! how the gospel trumpet sounds! (GOSPEL TRUMPET)	99
Hark, the glad sound! (RAYMOND)	441
Hark! the herald angels sing (COOKHAM)	81
Hark! the jubilee is sounding (JUBILEE)	144
Hark! the Redeemer from on high (INVITATION)	327
He come! He comes! The Judge severe (ROLL JORDAN)	274
He comes, he comes! to judge the world (MESSIAH)	131
He dies, the friend of sinners dies, Lo! Salem's daughters (MORNING)	163
(SALEM)	68
He dies, the friend of sinners dies, And He died on the cross (SINNERS FRIEND)	132
He saw me sinking in distress (MY LIFE AND BREATH)	527

Here's my heart, my loving Jesus (LOVING JESUS) — 361
His hoary frost, his fleecy snow (WINTER) — 38
Hither, ye faithful, haste with songs (PORTUGUESE HYMN) — 223
Holy Lord, we worhip Thee (LORD, WE ADORE THEE) — 477
Holy Spirit, faithful guide (CORLEY) — 510
Hosanna to Jesus, my soul's filled with praises (THE ROYAL BAND) — 360
How beauteous are their feet (SHEPPARD) — 464
   (WORCESTER) — 195
How charming is the place (NIDRAH) — 540
How bright is the day when the Christian (SAWYERS EXIT) — 338
How firm a foundation (BELLEVUE) — 72
How happy's every child of grace (THE CHILD OF GRACE) — 77
How happy are the souls above (HEAVENLY REST) — 403
How long, dear Savior, O how long (NORTHFIELD) — 155
   (PROMISED DAY) — 409
How many years has man been driv'n (RESTORATION) — 271
How painfully pleasing the fond recollection (FAMILY BIBLE) — 165
   (THE OLD FASHIONED BIBLE) — 342
How pleasant 'tis to see kindred and friends agree (SHARON) — 212
How pleased and blest was I (AMITY) — 150
How shall the young secure their hearts (MARS HILL) — 517
How sweet the name of Jesus sounds (ORTONVILLE) — 68
How tedious and tasteless the hours (EDGEFIELD) — 82
   (GREEN FIELDS) — 127

I am a great complainer (COMPLAINER) — 141
I am a poor wayfaring stranger (WAYFARING STRANGER) — 457
I am a stranger here below (JACKSON) — 317
I am on my journey home (GOLDEN STREETS) — 425
I am the rose of sharon (ROSE OF SHARON) — 254
I began life's journey when young (ODE OF LIFE'S JOURNEY) — 227
I beheld, and lo a great multitude (HEAVENLY VISION) — 250
I came to the place where the lone pligrim lay (THE LONE PILGRIM) — 341
I find myself placed in a state of probation (THE CHRISTIAN WARFARE) — 179
I have my troubles here below (WHEN THERE'S NO TROUBLE AND SORROW) — 46
I heard a great voice from heav'n (FUNERAL ANTHEM) — 320
I know I love Thee better Lord (AMANDA RAY) — 493
I know that my Redeemer lives (ANTIOCH) — 277
I love my blessed Savior (CARNSVILLE) — 109
I need God's blessings while I live (FREDERICKSBURG) — 389
I soon shall view the promised land (WOOTTEN) — 548
I want a sober mind (SOAR AWAY) — 455
I want to go to heav'n I do (I WANT TO GO TO HEAVEN) — 568
I want to live a Christian here (NEW HARMONY) — 406

I would see Jesus (I WOULD SEE JESUS) — 75
If angels sung a Savior's birth (MILFORD) — 273
If our fathers want to go (JESTER) — 331
I'll praise Him while He gives me breath (PRAISE HIM) — 544
I'll sing my Savior's grace (THE CHRISTIAN'S NIGHTLY SONG) — 416
I'm dying, mother, dying now (THE DYING BOY) — 398
I'm enlisted on the road (ROCKY ROAD) — 294
I'm not ashamed to own my Lord (ARLINGTON) — 73
   (THE ENQUIRER) — 74
   (ETERNAL LIGHT) — 483
In humble notes our faith adores (PITTSFORD) — 351
In the beginning was the word (ANTHEM ON THE BEGINNING) — 553
In the bright season of thy youth (BLOOMING YOUTH) — 176
In the cross of Christ I glory (PEACE AND JOY) — 532
In the floods of tribulation (SWEET AFFLICTION) — 145
In those days came John the Baptist (BAPTISMAL ANTHEM) — 232
   (THE LAMB OF GOD) — 572
In vain we lavish out our lives (VERMONT) — 180
I've a long time heard that there will be a judgment (THE GREAT DAY) — 567
I've learn'd to sing a glad new song (A GLAD NEW SONG) — 530

Jerusalem! my happy home! (LONG SOUGHT HOME) — 235
Jesus, and shall it ever be (CORINTH) — 32
Jesus Christ is risen today (EASTER MORN) — 415
Jesus grant us all a blessing (MULLINS) — 323
   (SHOUTING SONG) — 80
Jesus, I my cross have taken (MONROE) — 370
Jesus left His home on high (OH WHAT LOVE) — 491
Jesus, Lover of my soul (MARTIN) — 452
Jesus, my all, to heaven is gone, And I don't expect (DONE WITH THE WORLD) — 88
Jesus, my all, to heaven is gone, Glory Hallelujah (NORTH PORT) — 324
Jesus, my all, to heaven is gone, He whom I fix my hopes (JERUSALEM) — 53
Jesus, my all, to heaven is gone, Save, mighty Lord (SAVE, MIGHTY LORD) — 70
Jesus, my shepherd, friend and guide (ALEXANDER) — 393
Jesus, Thou art the sinner's friend (PISGAH) — 58
Jesus, what shall I do to show (NEW HOPE) — 316

Lay up nearer, brother, nearer (THE DYING CALIFORNIAN) — 410
Let every creature join to praise (NEWBURGH) — 182
Let ev'ry mortal ear attend (ODEM) — 295
Let sinners take their course (FLORIDA) — 203
Let the high heav'ns your songs invite (CHESTER) — 479
Life is the time to serve the Lord (WELLS) — 28
Lift up your heads, Immanuel's friends (THE GOOD OLD WAY) — 213

Lo, what a glorious sight appears (NEW JERUSALEM)	299
Long have I sat beneath the sound (LOVE SHALL NEVER DIE)	278
Look up my soul with cheerful eyes (THE GREAT REDEEMER)	511
Lord, how divine thy comforts are (OUR HUMBLE FAITH)	463
Lord, I cannot let Thee go (KING OF PEACE)	74
Lord, in the morning thou shalt hear (EXHORTATION)	171
(HOLCOMBE)	77
(PHOEBUS)	173
Lord, shed a beam of heavenly day (FROZEN HEART)	93
Lord, we come before thee now (GAINSVILLE)	70
(HUMILITY)	50
Lord, what a thoughtless wretch was I (GREENWICH)	183
(HUNTINGTON)	193
Lord, when my raptured thought (ADORATION)	138
Lord, when Thou didst ascend on high (BEAR CREEK)	269
Love divine, all love excelling (LOVE DIVINE)	30
Lovers of pleasure more than God (LOVER OF THE LORD)	124
Mary to her Savior's tomb (MARY'S GRIEF AND JOY)	451
May the grace of Christ our Savior (COLUMBIANA)	56
Mercy, O thou Son of David (CHARLESTOWN)	52
(FRIENDSHIP)	458
(VILLULIA)	56
'Mid scenes of confusion and creature complaints (SWEET HOME)	161
Mine eyes are now closing to rest (CHRISTIAN SONG)	240
Must Jesus bear the cross alone (A CROSS FOR ME)	349
My brethren all, on you I call (LOOK OUT)	90
My Christian friends, in bonds of love (PARTING HAND)	62
My Christian friends to whom I speak (KELLEY)	426
My days, my weeks, my months, my years (KINGWOOD)	266
My days on earth are almost gone (PHILLIPS FAREWELL)	549
My dear Redeemer and my Lord (FEDERAL STREET)	515
My father's gone to view that land (RESURRECTED)	153
My friends, come listen a while (ANTHEM ON THE SAVIOR)	355
My friends, I am going on a long journey (FAREWELL ANTHEM)	260
My God, my King, thy various praise (McGRAW)	353
My God, my life, my love (BOYLSTON)	147
My God, the spring of all my joys (BLISSFUL DAWNING)	550
(MY BRIGHTEST DAYS)	546
My heart and voice I raise (THE MESSIAH'S PRAISE)	394
My hope is in the lord (I'LL SEEK HIS BLESSINGS)	542
My sands of life are running fast (MULBERRY GROVE)	482
My Savior and my King (LLOYD)	503
My shepherd is the Lord most high (LIVING STREAMS)	558
My shepherd will supply my need (SIDNEY)	427
My soul, be on thy guard (LABAN)	147
(ROCKPORT)	372
My soul come meditate the day (NORTH SALEM)	440
My soul forsakes her vain delight (LEANDER)	71
My soul repeat his praise (AMERICA)	36
My span of life will soon be gone (CHARLTON)	407
(HORTON)	330
(SPAN OF LIVE)	379
My spirit looks to God alone (RUSSIA)	107
(SAMARIA)	26
My thoughts, that often mount the skies (CALVARY)	300
No burning heats by day (DELIGHT)	216
No more beneath th'opressive hand (LIBERTY)	137
No more shall the sound of the war-whoop be heard (WAR DEPARTMENT)	160
Not many years their rounds shall roll (THE CHRISTIAN'S FLIGHT)	177
Now, in the heat of youthful blood (EXHORTATION)	272
Now, let our works and virtue show (AS WE GO ON)	488
Now shall my inward joys arise (AFRICA)	178
Now shall my soul be lifted high (ASSURANCE)	91
O come loud anthems let us sing (OLD HUNDRED)	49
O come, O come away (O COME AWAY)	334
O for a breeze of heav'nly love (CANAAN'S LAND)	101
O for a closer walk with God (BETHEL)	27
O, for a shout of sacred joy (MALBOROUGH)	228
O for a thousand tongues to sing (MOUNT ZION)	88
(NEW BETHEL)	395
O, for a thousand tongues to sing (NATIVITY)	350
O land of rest, for thee I sigh (LAND OF REST)	285
(NEW PROSPECT)	390
O, may our humble spirits stand (INFINITE DELIGHT)	562
O ring the bells in heaven high (THE MARRIAGE IN THE SKIES)	438
O, tell me no more of this world's vain store (SEND A BLESSING)	369
O that I could repent! (SHAWMUT)	535
O the transporting, rapturous scene (McKAY)	433
O what of all my sufferings here (ETERNAL DAY)	383
O when shall I see Jesus (BOUND FOR CANAAN)	82
O who will come and go with me (I'M ON MY JOURNEY HOME)	345
(JOURNEY HOME)	111
O who will come and go with me? I am bound (SWEET CANAAN)	87
O who will come and go with me, We'll shout and sing (WE'LL SOON BE THERE)	97
O yes, my Savior I will trust (HAPPY HOME)	343

Oh, could I speak the matchless worth (NOTES ALMOST DIVINE)	396
Oh, for a heart to praise my God (BURDETTE)	422
(PRAISE GOD)	328
Oh, how charming (CHRISTMAS ANTHEM)	225
Oh, how happy are they (HAPPY CHRISTIAN)	399
Oh, if my Lord should come and meet (LAWRENCEBURG)	380
Oh, if my Lord would come and meet (ALL SAINTS NEW)	444
Oh if my soul was formed for woe (REPENTANCE)	214
Oh, Jesus, my Savior, I know that thou art mine (EXPRESSION)	125
Oh! may I worthy prove to see (EXHILARATION)	170
Oh once I had a glorious view (COLUMBUS)	67
Oh, Resurrection day (THE RESURRECTION DAY)	498
Oh, sing to me of heav'n (SING TO ME OF HEAVEN)	312
Oh! sing with me of social spheres (O SING WITH ME)	374
Oh, that I knew the secret place (THE THRONE OF GRACE)	476
Oh the delights, the heavenly joys (NORWICH)	362
(SWEET MAJESTY)	536
Oh when shall I see Jesus (ECSTASY)	106
(MUTUAL LOVE)	410
(RELIGION IS A FORTUNE)	319
(THE MORNING TRUMPET)	85
Oh, when will the period appear (PANTING FOR HEAVEN)	384
Oh, why should I wander a stranger from Thee (PENITENCE)	571
On Jordan's stormy banks I stand (HEAVENLY PORT)	378
(JORDAN)	439
(MY HOME)	51
(NEW JORDAN)	442
(SWEET PROSPECT)	65
(THE PROMISED LAND)	128
Our bondage, it shall end by and by (SAINTS BOUND FOR HEAVEN)	35
Our cheerful voices let us raise (PARTING FRIENDS)	521
Our father's gone to that bright land (BISHOP)	420
Our God, our help in ages past (ETERNAL HOME)	336
Our praying time will soon be o'er (STRUGGLE ON)	400
Peace, troubled soul, thou need not fear (CHRISTIAN'S DELIGHT)	429
Pray, brethren, pray (PRAY, BRETHREN, PRAY)	167
Rejoice! the lord is King (CARMARTHEN)	473
Religion is the chief concern (PLEASANT HILL)	205
Remember, Lord, our mortal state (GRANVILLE)	547
Rise, my soul, and stretch thy wings (AMSTERDAM)	84
(INVOCATION)	131
Rise, rise, my soul, and leave the ground (COBB)	313
Salvation, O the joyful sound (PRIMROSE)	47
Savior visit thy plantation (RETURN AGAIN)	335
Say, now ye lovely social band (CLAMANDA)	42
See how the Scriptures are fulfilling (FULFILLMENT)	102
See how the wicked kingdom (ESSAY)	157
See the happy faces waiting (THE BLESSED LAMB)	54
See the Lord of glory dying (LENA)	210
See what a living stone the builders did refuse (STAFFORD)	78
See, gracious God, before Thy throne (LEBANON)	354
Shall we ever meet again at the house (LET US SING)	46
Shed not a tear o'er your friend's earthly bier (TOLLING BELL)	459
(WHEN I AM GONE)	339
Shepherds rejoice! lift up your eyes (OXFORD)	306
(SHEPHERDS REJOICE)	152
Should earth against my soul engage (GRANTVILLE)	423
Show pity, Lord; O Lord, forgive (CUSSETA)	73
Sing, O ye ransomed of the lord (SACRED MOUNT)	456
Sinner art thou still secure (PLEYEL'S HYMN)	523
Sinner, go, will you go (HIGHLANDS OF HEAVEN)	175
Sister, thou wast mild and lovely (STOCKWOOD)	118
So fades the lovely blooming flow'r (DISTRESS)	32
Soft, soft music is stealing (SOFT MUSIC)	323
Sweet is the day of sacred rest (DEVOTION)	48
(PORTLAND)	556
(SACRED REST)	435
Sweet rivers of redeeming love (SWEET RIVERS)	61
Teach me to do my duty (STILL BETTER)	166
That man is blessed who stands (BENEFICENCE)	486
The chariot! the chariot! (THE TRUMPET)	149
The cross of Christ inspires my heart (CROSS OF CHRIST)	123
(GEORGIA)	197
The day is past and gone (EVENING SHADE)	209
(LOGAN)	302
The glorious light of Zion (BURK)	92
The glorious plan of man's redemption (MAN'S REDEMPTION)	322
The God we worship now (AYLESBURY)	28
The happy day will soon appear (SWEET MORNING)	421
The heavens declare the glory of god (HEAVNELY ANTHEM)	518
The Hill of Zion yields a thousand sacred sweets (MOUNT ZION)	220
(THE HILL OF ZION)	565
The Lord descended from above (MAJESTY)	291
The Lord into His garden comes (NASHVILLE)	64
The Lord into His garden comes (GARDEN HYMN)	284

The Lord is leading me today (HOMEWARD BOUND)	373
The Lord is my shepherd (THE 23RD PSALM)	524
The Lord is ris'n indeed (EASTER ANTHEM)	236
The Lord my pasture shall prepare (PROTECTION)	402
The Lord my precious shepherd is (MY SHEPHERD GUIDES)	490
The Lord will happiness divine (CAMBRIDGE)	287
The men of grace have found glory (CONCORD)	313
The mighty hand of God doth reign (NEW GEORGIA)	534
The morning sun shines from the east (ODE ON SCIENCE)	242
The road to glory seems so long (THE BETTER LAND)	454
The scatter'd clouds are fled at last (SPRING)	188
The spacious firmament on high (BRISTOL)	468
The spirits of Washington, Warren, Montgomery (THE AMERICAN STAR)	346
The time is soon coming (MILLENNIUM)	130
The time is swiftly rolling on (AINSLIE)	348
(FAREWELL TO ALL)	570
(THE DYING MINISTER)	83
The time must come when we must part (PARTING FRIEND)	414
The voice of my beloved sounds (SWANTON)	352
The world can never give (AT REST)	499
There is a fountain filled with blood (THE FOUNTAIN)	397
There is a happy land, far, far away (HAPPY LAND)	354
There is a house not made with hands (HOLLY SPRINGS)	453
(MOUNT PLEASANT)	218
(REES)	418
There is a holy city (HOLY CITY)	101
There is a land of pure delight (GREENSBOROUGH)	289
(HEAVENLY LAND)	303
(INFINITE DAY)	446
(JORDAN)	66
(MANCHESTER)	392
There is a name I love to hear (THE SAVIOR'S NAME)	471
There is a place where my hopes are stay'd (FATHERLAND)	449
There then to thee thine own I leave (CONSECRATION)	448
There upon the cross of Calvary (REDEMPTION)	480
They crucified the Savior (WEEPING MARY)	408
Thou art gone to the grave (FUNERAL THOUGHT)	158
Thou art passing away (THOU ART PASSING AWAY)	231
Thou Man of grief, remember me (KEDRON)	48
Through every age, eternal God (STRATFORD)	142
Thus far the Lord has led me on. Thus far his power (HEBRON)	566
Thus saith the high and lofty One (PETERSBURG)	174
Thy words the raging winds control (VIRGINIA)	191
Thy works of glory, mighty Lord (OCEAN)	222
Time! what an empty vapor 'tis (FLEETING DAYS)	348
'Tis by Thy strength the mountains stand (RAINBOW)	344
'Tis finished, 'tis finished (SOUTHWELL)	365
'Tis my desire with God to walk (DESIRE FOR PIETY)	76
To leave my dear friends (THE BOWER OF PRAYER)	100
Today, if you will hear his voice (TURN, SINNER, TURN)	160
Today the Savior calls (WARNING)	213
Trav'ler haste, the night comes on (THE TRAVELLER)	108
Unshaken as the sacred hill (MOUNT DESERT)	474
Vain man, thy fond pursuits (NEWNAN)	321
Vital spark of heav'nly flame (CLAREMONT)	245
Wake, all ye soaring things (HARMONY)	172
Wake, O my soul, and hail the morn (NEW HOSANNA)	412
We are told there is a home (MY HOME)	560
We have our troubles here below (CHRISTIAN'S HOPE)	206
We thank the Lord of heav'n and earth (PRESENT JOYS)	318
Weary soldiers of the cross (BIG CREEK)	494
Weeping sinners, dry your tears (WEEPING SINNERS)	108
Welcome sweet day of rest (LISBON)	467
Welcome, welcome every guest (CANNON)	24
Well may thy servants mourn (THE CHURCH'S DESOLATION)	89
What is there here to court my stay (PARTING FRIENDS)	308
What poor despised company (IRWINTON)	229
What shall I do (FAITH AND HOPE)	462
What shall I render to my God (PROVIDENCE)	298
What ship is this that will take us all home (THE OLD SHIP OF ZION)	79
What solemn sound the ear invades (MOUNT VERNON)	110
What wondrous love is this! (WONDROUS LOVE)	159
What's this that in my soul is rising? (MERCY'S FREE)	337
What's this that steals (ALL IS WELL)	122
When Adam was created (EDMONDS)	115
When converts first begin to sing (THE YOUNG CONVERT)	24
When for eternal worlds we steer (VAIN WORLD ADIEU)	329
When God reveal'd his gracious name (CONVERSION)	297
When I can read my title clear (AKERS)	293
(NINETY-FIFTH)	36
(PRIMROSE HILL)	43
(SAINTS DELIGHT)	114
When I survey the wondrous cross (WONDROUS CROSS)	447
When Noah with his favored few (THE ARK)	506
When the midnight cry began (THE MIDNIGHT CRY)	495

When the sun, or the light (THE SPIRIT SHALL RETURN)	512
When Thou, my righteous Judge (HAPPY MATCHES)	96
When thro' the torn sail (SAVE, LORD, OR WE PERISH)	224
When to that blessed world I rise (NEVER TURN BACK)	378
When we our wearied limbs to rest (WOOD STREET)	504
Where are the Hebrew children? (HEBREW CHILDREN)	133
Where nothing dwelt but beasts of prey (WHITESTOWN)	211
Where prophet's word and martyr's blood (HARPETH VALLEY)	573
While beauty and youth are in their full prime (MORALITY)	136
While in the army I remain (SOLDIER'S DELIGHT)	487
While in the vale of sorrow (VALE OF SORROW)	83
While shepherds watch'd their flocks by night (SHERBURNE)	186
While shepherds watched their flocks by night (SHINING STAR)	461
While thee I seek, Protecting Pow'r (PLEYEL'S HYMN)	143
While trav'ling down life's weary road (ZION)	564
While trav'ling thru the world below (HEAVENLY HOME)	286
(PENICK)	387
Why do we mourn departing friends (CHINA)	163
Why, O sinner, me profaning (DODDRIDGE)	263
Why should our tears in sorrow flow (HOME OF THE BLEST)	541
Why should we at our lot complain (DULL CARE)	98
Why should we start and fear to die? (PROSPECT)	30
(ROLL ON)	275
(TO DIE NO MORE)	111
Will God forever cast us off (MEAR)	49
With songs and honors sounding loud (EDOM)	200
(GREENLAND)	301
(MORGAN)	304
(SHOWERS OF BLESSINGS)	528
Within Thy circling pow'r I stand (AKIN)	472
(IMMENSITY)	315
Wonderful things of men are said (ODEM)	340
Ye fleeting charms of earth farewell (WHITE)	288
Ye flow'ry plains, proclaim His skill (HAMPTON)	538
Ye golden lamps of Heav'n, farewell (THE LAST WORDS OF COPERNICUS)	112
Ye heedless ones who wildly stroll (YE HEEDLESS ONES)	522
Ye, little flock whom Jesus feeds (THE SHEPHERD'S FLOCK)	279
Ye objects of sense, and enjoyments of time (THE DYING CHRISTIAN)	123
Ye souls who are bound unto Canaan (HELP ME TO SING)	376
Ye weary, heavy laden soul (THE WEARY SOUL)	72
Yes, my native land, I love thee (CAN I LEAVE YOU?)	385
You may tell them father (WEEPING PILGRIM)	417
Young ladies, all attention give (ESTER)	37
Young people all attention give, And hear what I do say (NEW TOPIA)	215
Young people all attention give, And hear what I shall say (LIVERPOOL)	37
Young people all attention give, While I address (MISSION)	204
Young people hear me as your friend (THE DYING FRIEND)	399
Youth, like the spring (MORNING SUN)	436
(YOUTH WILL SOON BE GONE)	404

GENERAL INDEX

-A-
A Charge to Keep	502
A Cross for Me	349
A Glad New Song	530
A Thankful Heart	475
Abbeville	33
Adoration	138
Africa	178
Ainslie	348
Akers	293
Akin	472
Alabama	196
Albion	52
Alexander	393
All Is Well	122
All Saints New	444
Amanda Ray	493
America	36
Amity	150
Amsterdam	84
Animation	103
Anthem on the Beginning	553
Anthem on the Savior	355
Antioch	277
Arbacoochee	430
Arkansas	271
Arlington	73
Arnold	285
As We Go On	488
Assurance	91
At Rest	499
Aylesbury	28

-B-
Babel's Streams	126
Babylon Is Fallen	117
Ballstown	217
Baptismal Anthem	232
Beach Spring	81
Bear Creek	269
Behold the Savior	292
Bellevue	72
Beneficence	486
Bethel	27
Big Creek	494
Bishop	420
Blissful Dawning	550
Blooming Youth	176
Bound for Canaan	82
Boylston	147
Bridgewater	276
Bristol	468
Burdette	422
Burk	92

-C-
Calvary	300
Cambridge	287
Can I Leave You?	385
Canaan's Land	101
Carmarthen	473
Carnsville	109
Chambers	120
Charlestown	52
Charlton	407
Chester	479
Cheves	432
China	163
Christ Our Song	386
Christian Soldier	57
Christian Song	240
Christian's Delight	429
Christian's Farewell	347
Christian's Hope	206
Christmas Anthem	225
Clamanda	42
Claremount	245
Cleburne	314
Cobb	313
Columbiana	56
Columbus	67
Complainer	141
Concord	313
Confidence	270
Consecration	448
Consolation	367
Conversion	297
Converting Grace	230
Cookham	81
Corinth	32
Corley	510
Coronation	63
Coston	382
Cowper	168
Cross Of Christ	123
Cuba	401
Cusseta	73

-D-
Dartmouth	169
David's Lamentation	268
Days of Worship	60
Delight	216
DeLong	516
Desire for Piety	76
Detroit	39
Devotion	48
Distress	32
Doddridge	263
Done with the World	88
Duane Street	164
Dull Care	98
Dura	531

-E-
Easter Anthem	236
Easter Morn	415
Ecstasy	106
Edgefield	82
Edmonds	115
Edom	200
Elder	450
Elysian	139
Emmaus	569

Enfield	184
Essay	157
Ester	37
Eternal Day	383
Eternal Home	336
Eternal Light	483
Eternal Praise	377
Evening Shade	209
Exhilaration	170
Exhortation (first)	171
Exhortation (second)	272
Exit	181
Expression	125

-F-

Fairfield	29
Faith and Hope	462
Family Bible	165
Family Circle	333
Farewell Anthem	260
Farewell to All (second)	570
Farewell to All (first)	69
Fatherland	449
Federal Street	515
Fellowship	330
Few Happy Matches	96
Fight On	385
Fillmore	434
Fleeting Days	348
Florence	121
Florida	203
Fredericksburg	389
Friendship	458
Frozen Heart	93
Fulfillment	102
Funeral Anthem	320
Funeral Thought	158

-G-

Gainsville	70
Garden Hymn	284
Georgia	197
Golden Streets	425
Gospel Trumpet	99
Grantville	423
Granville	547
Green Field	127
Green Street	198
Greenland	301
Greensborough	289
Greenwich	183

-H-

Hallelujah	146
Hampton	538
Happy Christian	399
Happy Home	343
Happy Land	354
Harmony	172
Harpeth Valley	573
Haynes Creek	466
Heaven's My Home	119
Heavenly Anthem	518
Heavenly Armor	129
Heavenly Dove	371
Heavenly Home	286
Heavenly Land	303
Heavenly Port	378
Heavenly Rest	403
Heavenly Union	484
Heavenly Vision	250
Hebrew Children	133
Hebron	566
Help Me To Sing	376
Highlands of Heaven	175
Holcombe	77
Holiness	76
Holly Springs	453
Holy City	101
Holy Manna	59
Home in Heaven	41
Home of the Blest	541
Homeward Bound	373
Horton	330
Humility	50
Huntington	193

-I-

I Want to Go to Heaven	568
I Would See Jesus	75
I'll Seek His Blessings	542
I'm Going Home	282
I'm on My Journey Home	345
Idumea	47
Imandra	45
Immensity	315
Infinite Day	446
Infinite Delight	562
Invitation	327
Invocation (first)	131
Invocation (second)	492
Irwinton	229

-J-

Jackson	317
Jacob's Vision	551
Jasper	426
Jefferson	148
Jerusalem	53
Jester	331
Jesus Is My Friend	345
Jesus Rose	156
Jewett	105
Jordan (first)	66
Jordan (second)	439
Journey Home	111
Joyful	513
Jubilee	144

-K-

Kedron	48
Kelley	426
King of Peace	74
Kingwood	266

-L-

Laban	147
Land of Rest	285
Lawrenceburg	380
Leander	71
Lebanon	354
Lena	210

Lenox	40
Let Us Sing	46
Liberty	137
Lisbon	467
Liverpool	37
Living Hope	500
Living Lamb	309
Living Streams	558
Lloyd	503
Logan	302
Long Sought Home	235
Look Out	90
Lord, We Adore Thee	477
Louisiana	207
Love Divine	30
Love Shall Never Die	278
Love the Lord	375
Lover of the Lord	124
Loving Jesus	361
Loving Kindness	275

-M-

Majesty	291
Man's Redemption	322
Manchester	392
Marlborough	228
Mars Hill	517
Martin	452
Mary's Grief and Joy	451
McGraw	353
McKay	433
Mear	49
Melancholy Day	419
Mercy's Free	337
Messiah	131
Milford	273
Millennium	130
Minister's Farewell	69
Mission	204
Monroe	370
Montgomery	189
Morality	136
Morgan	304
Morning	163
Morning Prayer	411
Morning Sun	436
Mortality	50
Mount Desert	474
Mount Pleasant	218
Mount Vernon	110
Mount Zion (first)	220
Mount Zion (second)	88
Mulberry Grove	482
Mullins	323
Murillo's Lesson	358
Mutual Love	410
My Brightest Days	546
My Home (first)	51
My Home (second)	560
My Life and Breath	527
My Rising Sun	478
My Shepherd Guides	490

-N-

Nashville	64
Natick	497
Nativity	350
Never Part	94
Never Turn Back	378
New Agatite	485
New Bethany	431
New Bethel	395
New Britain	45
New Georgia	534
New Harmony	406
New Hope	316
New Hosanna	412
New Jerusalem	299
New Jordan	442
New Lebanon	202
New Prospect	390
New Topia	215
Newburgh	182
Newnan	321
Nidrah	540
Ninety-fifth	36
Ninety-third Psalm	31
North Port	324
North Salem	440
Northfield	155
Norwich	362
Notes Almost Divine	396
Novakoski	481

-O-

O'Leary	501
O, Come Away	334
Ocean	222
Ode of Life's Journey	227
Ode on Science	242
Odem (first)	295
Odem (second)	340
Ogletree	138
Oh, Sing with Me	374
Oh, What Love	491
Old Hundred	49
Olney	135
Ortonville	68
Our Humble Faith	463
Oxford	306

-P-

Panting for Heaven	384
Parting Friend	414
Parting Friends (first)	267
Parting Friends (second)	308
Parting Friends (third)	521
Parting Hand	62
Passing Away	445
Peace and Joy	532
Penick	387
Penitence	571
Petersburg	174
Phillips Farewell	549
Phoebus	173
Pilgrim	201
Pilgrim's Farewell	185
Pisgah	58
Pittsford	351
Pleasant Hill	205

Plenary	162
Pleyel's Hymn (first)	143
Pleyel's Hymn (second)	523
Poland	86
Portland	556
Portuguese Hymn	223
Praise God	328
Praise Him	544
Pray, Brethren, Pray	167
Present Joys	318
Primrose	47
Primrose Hill	43
Promised Day	409
Prospect	30
Protection (first)	187
Protection (second)	402
Providence	298

-R-

Ragan	176
Rainbow	344
Raymond	441
Redemption	480
Reese	418
Religion Is a Fortune	319
Repentance	214
Rest for the Weary	154
Restoration (first)	312
Restoration (second)	271
Resurrected	153
Return Again	335
Reverential Anthem	234
Reynolds	225
Rockport	372
Rocky Road	294
Roll Jordan	274
Roll On	275
Rose of Sharon	254
Russia	107

-S-

Sabbath Morning	283
Sacred Mount	456
Sacred Rest	435
Sacred Throne	569
Saint's Delight	114
Saints Bound for Heaven	35
Salem	68
Samaria	26
Sardinia	296
Sardis	460
Save, Lord, or We Perish	224
Save, Mighty Lord	70
Sawyer's Exit	338
Schenectady	192
Send a Blessing	369
Sermon on the Mount	507
Service of the Lord	80
Sharon	212
Sharpsburg	39
Shawmut	535
Shepherds Rejoice	152
Sheppard	464
Sherburne	186
Shining Star	461
Shouting Song	80
Showers of Blessings	528
Sidney	437
Silver Street	311
Sing On	381
Sing to Me of Heaven	312
Sinner's Friend	132
Sister's Farewell	55
Soar Away	455
Soft Music	323
Soldier of the Cross	325
Soldier's Delight	487
Sons of Sorrow	332
Sounding Joy	391
Southwell	365
Span of Life	379
Spring	188
St. Thomas	34
Stafford	78
Still Better	166
Stockwood	118
Stony Point	368
Stratfield	142
Struggle On	400
Supplication	539
Swanton	352
Sweet Affliction	145
Sweet Canaan	87
Sweet Home	161
Sweet Majesty	536
Sweet Morning	421
Sweet Prospect	65
Sweet Rivers	61
Sweet Solitude	140
Sweet Union	424
Symphony	151

-T-

The American Star	346
The Ark	506
The Better Land	454
The Blessed Lamb	54
The Bower of Prayer	100
The Bride's Farewell	359
The Child of Grace	77
The Christian Warfare	179
The Christian's Flight	177
The Christian's Hope	134
The Christian's Nightly Song	416
The Church's Desolation	89
The Converted Thief	44
The Dying Boy	398
The Dying Californian	410
The Dying Christian	123
The Dying Friend	399
The Dying Minister	83
The Enquirer	74
The Fountain	397
The Golden Harp	274
The Good Old Way	213
The Gospel Pool	34
The Great Day	567
The Great Redeemer	511
The Grieved Soul	448

The Happy Sailor	388	
The Hill of Zion	565	
The Lamb of God	572	
The Last Words of Copernicus	112	
The Lone Pilgrim	341	
The Loved Ones	413	
The Lovely Story	104	
The Marcellas	405	
The Marriage in the Skies	438	
The Mercy Seat	470	
The Messiah's Praise	394	
The Midnight Cry	495	
The Morning Trumpet	85	
The Old Ship of Zion	79	
The Old-Fashioned Bible	342	
The Pilgrim's Way	545	
The Prodigal Son	113	
The Promised Land	128	
The Resurrection Day	498	
The Rock That Is Higher Than I	496	
The Royal Band	360	
The Savior's Call	489	
The Savior's Name	471	
The Shepherd's Flock	279	
The Spirit Shall Return	512	
The Throne of Grace	476	
The Traveler	108	
The Trumpet	149	
The Twenty-third Psalm	524	
The Weary Soul	72	
Thou Art God	543	
Thou Art Passing Away	231	
To Die No More	111	
Tolling Bell	459	
Traveling On	208	
Traveling Pilgrim	278	
Tribulation	29	
Turn, Sinner, Turn	160	

-U-

Union — 116

-V-

Vain World, Adieu	329
Vale of Sorrow	83
Vermont	180
Vernon	95
Victoria	290
Villulia	56
Virginia	191

-W-

War Department	160
Warning	213
Warrenton	145
Wayfaring Stranger	457
We'll Soon Be There	97
Weary Pilgrim	326
Webster	31
Weeping Mary	408
Weeping Pilgrim	417
Weeping Savior (first)	33
Weeping Savior (second)	310
Weeping Sinners	108
Wells	28
Westford	280
When I Am Gone	339
Where Ceaseless Ages Roll	505
Where There's No Trouble and Sorrow	465
White	288
Whitestown	211
Windham	38
Winter	38
Wondrous Cross	447
Wondrous Love	159
Wood Street	504
Wootten	548
Worcester	195
World Unknown	428

-Y-

Ye Heedless Ones	522
Youth Will Soon Be Gone	404

-Z-

Zion — 564